First World War
and Army of Occupation
War Diary
France, Belgium and Germany

24 DIVISION
Divisional Troops
107 Brigade Royal Field Artillery
21 August 1915 - 31 March 1919

WO95/2197/4

The Naval & Military Press Ltd
www.nmarchive.com
Published in association with The National Archives

Published by

The Naval & Military Press Ltd

Unit 10 Ridgewood Industrial Park,
Uckfield, East Sussex,
TN22 5QE England
Tel: +44 (0) 1825 749494

www.naval-military-press.com

www.nmarchive.com

This diary has been reprinted in facsimile from the original. Any imperfections are inevitably reproduced and the quality may fall short of modern type and cartographic standards.

© Crown Copyright
Images reproduced by permission of The National Archives, London, England, 2015.

Contents

Document type	Place/Title	Date From	Date To
Heading	WO95/2197/4		
Heading	107th Brigade R.F.A. Aug 1915-Mar 1919		
Heading	War Diary Headquarters, 107th Brigade, R.F.A. (24th Division) August And September (21.8.15 to 30.9.15) 1915		
War Diary	Deep Cut	21/08/1915	31/08/1915
War Diary	Marenla	01/09/1915	10/09/1915
War Diary	Annequin Nr Bethune	12/09/1915	12/09/1915
War Diary	Annequin	12/09/1915	25/09/1915
War Diary	Le Rutoire	25/09/1915	22/10/1915
Heading	24th Division Nov 15 107th Bde, R.F.A. Vol 2		
War Diary	Reninghelst	01/11/1915	01/11/1915
War Diary	Dickebusch	08/11/1915	30/11/1915
Heading	24th Div 107th Bde R.F.A. Vol 3		
War Diary	Acquin	01/12/1915	29/12/1915
War Diary	Ref St Omer Map	30/12/1915	31/12/1915
Heading	107th Bde, R.F.A. Vol 4		
War Diary	Ypres	01/01/1916	29/02/1916
War Diary	Poperinghe	01/03/1916	09/03/1916
War Diary	Ypres	10/03/1916	31/03/1916
War Diary	Neuve Eglise	01/04/1916	30/04/1916
Miscellaneous	Appendix 1 (To War Diary May 1916, Sheet XIX)	30/04/1916	30/04/1916
War Diary	Neuve Eglise	01/04/1916	31/05/1916
Operation(al) Order(s)	Operation Order No. 9 Schedule For D/106 (How)		
Heading	107 R.F.A. June Vol 9		
War Diary	Neuve Eglise.	01/06/1916	30/06/1916
Miscellaneous	A Battery. Report On Enemy's Gas Emission On Night Of 13th/17th June 1916		
Miscellaneous	B Battery.	17/06/1916	17/06/1916
Miscellaneous	C Battery.	17/06/1916	17/06/1916
Miscellaneous	B/109 Battery	17/06/1916	17/06/1916
Miscellaneous	D/106 How. Battery	17/06/1916	17/06/1916
Miscellaneous	B Battery.	17/06/1916	17/06/1916
Miscellaneous	C Battery	17/06/1916	17/06/1916
Miscellaneous	B/109 Battery	17/06/1916	17/06/1916
Miscellaneous	D/106 How. Battery.	17/06/1916	17/06/1916
Operation(al) Order(s)	Operation Orders No. 10 By Lt. Colonel D.R. Coates, Commanding 107 F.A.B. Group.	27/06/1916	27/06/1916
Miscellaneous	7th Australian Infantry Brigade Order No. 20	20/06/1916	20/06/1916
Miscellaneous	7th Australian Infantry Brigade Order No. 19		
Miscellaneous	7th Australian Infantry Brigade Order No. 19. Time Table "A"		
Miscellaneous	7th Australian Infantry Brigade. Amendments To Operation Order No. 19	27/06/1916	27/06/1916
Miscellaneous	Reference Sheet 28.S.W.	29/06/1916	29/06/1916
Operation(al) Order(s)	Operation Orders No. 9 By Lt. Colonel D.R. Coates, Commanding 107 F.A.B. Group.	26/06/1916	26/06/1916
Miscellaneous	Operation Order No. 9 Schedule For A/107		
Miscellaneous	Operation Order No. 9 Schedule For B/107		
Miscellaneous	Operation Order No. 9 Schedule For C/107		

Miscellaneous	Operation Order No. 9 Schedule For B/109		
Miscellaneous	Operation Order No. 9 Schedule For Section of Z/24 T.M. Batty.		
Miscellaneous	Appendix To Operation Order No. 9.		
Operation(al) Order(s)	Operation Order No. 13 by Lt. Colonel D.R. Coates, Commanding 107 F.A.B. Group.	29/06/1916	29/06/1916
Miscellaneous	Operation Order No. 12 by Lt. Colonel D.R. Coates, Commanding 107 F.A.B. Group.	29/06/1916	29/06/1916
Miscellaneous	106th F.A.B. Group.	29/06/1916	29/06/1916
Operation(al) Order(s)	Operation Orders No. 11 By Lt. Col. D.R. Coates.		
Miscellaneous	7th Australian Infantry Brigade.	22/06/1916	22/06/1916
Miscellaneous	Reference Trench Map Sheets 28. S.W. 2 & 4. S.19	24/06/1916	24/06/1916
Miscellaneous	Appendix 1. Operation "A" (With Gas And Smoke).		
Miscellaneous			
Miscellaneous	Appendix I Operations "B"		
Miscellaneous	Appendix 11. Table A.		
Miscellaneous	Number of Guns. Rates of Fire. Ammunition.		
War Diary	Neuve Eglise	01/07/1916	06/07/1916
War Diary	Boisseille	07/07/1916	07/07/1916
War Diary	Neuve Eglise	08/07/1916	31/07/1916
Miscellaneous	S. 40 (6)	21/07/1916	21/07/1916
Miscellaneous	All Batteries 107 F.A.B.	19/07/1916	19/07/1916
Operation(al) Order(s)	Operation Orders No. 24 By Lt. Colonel D.R. Coates, Commanding Centre Group.	21/07/1916	21/07/1916
Operation(al) Order(s)	Operation Order No. 23 By Lieut. Col. D.R. Coates, Commanding Centre Group.		
Miscellaneous	S. 40 (7)	21/07/1916	21/07/1916
Operation(al) Order(s)	Op. Order No. 24 by Lt Col D.R. Coates.		
Miscellaneous	Relief Orders by Lt. Colonel D.R. Coates, Commanding Centre Group.	22/07/1916	22/07/1916
Miscellaneous	S. 40 (3)		
Miscellaneous	Appendix 1. Relief Table.		
Miscellaneous	Appendix 11. March Table Of 24th D.A. To Rest Area.		
Miscellaneous	106th F.A.B.	07/07/1916	07/07/1916
Miscellaneous	Appendix 1 Brigades will march on July 8th to their old wagon lines		
Miscellaneous	Appendix II. Temporary Grouping		
Operation(al) Order(s)	Operation Order No. 18. By Lieut. Colonel D.R. Coates, Commanding 107th Field A.B. Group.		
Miscellaneous		08/07/1916	08/07/1916
Miscellaneous			
Miscellaneous	106th F.A.B.	01/07/1916	01/07/1916
Miscellaneous	Appendix 11 Reference Sheets 28 & 36.		
Miscellaneous			
Miscellaneous	S. 25	04/07/1916	04/07/1916
Miscellaneous	Appendix 1 On night July 4th/5th		
Miscellaneous	Appendix 1 On night 5th/6th		
Miscellaneous	Appendix II D.a. after relief of Right Group 50th D.A.		
Miscellaneous	Appendix III Reference Sheet 28.S.W.		
Miscellaneous	S. 24 (1)		
Miscellaneous	O.C. Ginger Sheet 1	16/06/1916	16/06/1916
Miscellaneous	106th F.A.B.	08/07/1916	08/07/1916
Miscellaneous	Reference Sheet 28. S.W.	08/07/1916	08/07/1916
Miscellaneous	106th F.A.B. Group.	14/07/1916	14/07/1916
Miscellaneous	106th F.A.B.	10/07/1916	10/07/1916
Miscellaneous	Reference Sheet 28. S.W.		

Miscellaneous	S. 29		
Miscellaneous	S. 26		
Operation(al) Order(s)	Operation Orders No. 14. By Lt. Colonel D.R. Coates Commanding 107/F.A.B. Group.	04/07/1916	04/07/1916
Miscellaneous	106th F.A.B.	08/07/1916	08/07/1916
Heading	107 R.F.A. Vol 6		
War Diary	Daours-Braquemont	01/08/1916	31/08/1916
Heading	107th Brigade Royal Field Artillery August 1916		
Operation(al) Order(s)	Operation Order No. 29 By Lieut. Colonel D.R. Coates, Commanding 107 F.A. Brigade.	09/08/1916	09/08/1916
Operation(al) Order(s)	Operation Order No. 30 By Lieut. Colonel D.R. Coates, Commanding 107 F.A. Brigade.	10/08/1916	10/08/1916
Miscellaneous	24th D.A. Order No. 3	10/08/1916	10/08/1916
Miscellaneous	Reference Sheet 62.c. N.W. & 62.d. N.E. Appendix. Relief Table.		
Operation(al) Order(s)	Operation Order No. 31 By Lieut Colonel D.R. Coates, Commanding 107/F.A./Brigade.	12/08/1916	12/08/1916
Operation(al) Order(s)	Operation Order No. 33 By Lieut Colonel D.R. Coates, Commanding 107/F.A./Brigade.	12/08/1916	12/08/1916
Operation(al) Order(s)	Operation Order No. 33 By Lieut Colonel D.R. Coates, Commanding 107/F.A./Brigade.	14/08/1916	14/08/1916
Operation(al) Order(s)	Operation Order No. 34 By Lieut Colonel D.R. Coates, Commanding 107/F.A./Brigade.	16/08/1916	16/08/1916
Miscellaneous	Programme-18-Pdrs. Phase 1		
Miscellaneous	Phase II. 18-Pdr Batteries.		
Miscellaneous	Programme-4.5 How. Phase. 1		
Operation(al) Order(s)	Operation Order No. 35. By Lieut. Colonel D.R. Coates. Commanding 107/F.A./Brigade.	16/08/1916	16/08/1916
Operation(al) Order(s)	Operation Order No. 36. By Lieut. Colonel D.R. Coates. Commanding 107/F.A./Brigade.	17/08/1916	17/08/1916
Operation(al) Order(s)	Operation Order No. 37. By Lieut. Colonel D.R. Coates. Commanding 107/F.A./Brigade.	17/08/1916	17/08/1916
Miscellaneous	Programme For 18-Pdr Batteries.		
Miscellaneous	24th D.A. Order No. 6	17/08/1916	17/08/1916
Miscellaneous	Appendix. Table "B"		
Miscellaneous	Appendix Table "E"		
Miscellaneous			
Miscellaneous	Operation Programme No. 38 A/107		
Miscellaneous	A/109/19th		
Miscellaneous	B/107		
Miscellaneous	C/107		
Miscellaneous	D/107		
Miscellaneous	Appendix. Table A.		
Miscellaneous	Appendix. Table "C"		
Miscellaneous	Appendix. Table "D"		
Operation(al) Order(s)	Operation Order No. 39 By Lieut. Colonel D.R. Coates Commanding 107/F.A Brigade	21/08/1916	21/08/1916
Operation(al) Order(s)	Operation Order No. 40 By Lieut. Colonel D.R. Coates Commanding 107/F.A Brigade	22/08/1916	22/08/1916
Operation(al) Order(s)	Operation Order No. 41 By Lieut. Colonel D.R. Coates Commanding 107/F.A Brigade	24/08/1916	24/08/1916
Miscellaneous	Programme-18-Pdr Batteries		
Operation(al) Order(s)	Operation Order No. 42. By Lieut Colonel D.R. Coates, Commanding 107/F.A./Brigade.	26/08/1916	26/08/1916
Operation(al) Order(s)	Operation Order No. 41. By Lieut Colonel D.R. Coates, Commanding 107/F.A./Brigade.		

Operation(al) Order(s)	Operation Order No. 43. By Lieut Colonel D.R. Coates, Commanding 107/F.A./Brigade.	26/08/1916	26/08/1916
Operation(al) Order(s)	Operation Order No. 44. By Lieut Colonel D.R. Coates, Commanding 107/F.A./Brigade.	27/08/1916	27/08/1916
Operation(al) Order(s)	Operation Order No. 45 By Lieut Colonel D.R. Coates, Commanding 107/F.A./Brigade.	28/08/1916	28/08/1916
Miscellaneous	Programme For 4.5 Howitzer Appendix 1		
Miscellaneous	Programme For 18-Pounders Appendix 1		
Miscellaneous	24th D.A. Order No. 11	28/08/1916	28/08/1916
Miscellaneous			
Miscellaneous	Artillery Programme, August 30th 1916		
Operation(al) Order(s)	Operation Order No. 46. By Lieut Colonel D.R. Coates, Commanding 107/F.A./Brigade.	29/08/1916	29/08/1916
Operation(al) Order(s)	Operation Order No. 47. By Lieut Colonel D.R. Coates, Commanding 107/F.A./Brigade.	29/08/1916	29/08/1916
Miscellaneous	All Batteries 107 F.A.B.		
Miscellaneous	All Batteries 107 F.A.B.	30/08/1916	30/08/1916
Heading	107th Brigade R.F.A. September 1916		
War Diary	Longueval	01/09/1916	06/09/1916
War Diary	Bois De Tailles	06/09/1916	12/09/1916
War Diary	Longueval	13/09/1916	15/09/1916
War Diary	Sheet 62 C	16/09/1916	17/09/1916
War Diary	Longueval	18/09/1916	30/09/1916
Miscellaneous	XIII Corps. Fourth Army No. GX.3/1/2. P. XIII Corps No. 25/5/(G)	01/08/1916	01/08/1916
Operation(al) Order(s)	Operation Order No. 49. By Lieut Colonel D.R. Coates, Commanding 107/F.A./Brigade.	02/09/1916	02/09/1916
Miscellaneous	Appendix III, 18-Pounder Batteries For September 3rd		
Miscellaneous	Appendix III. 4.5. Howitzer Battery For September 3rd		
Miscellaneous	All Batteries, 107/F.A./Brigade.		
Miscellaneous	Reference Sheets 57c S.W.	04/09/1916	04/09/1916
Operation(al) Order(s)	Operation Order No. 52. By Lieut Colonel D.R. Coates, Commanding 107/F.A. Brigade.	04/09/1916	04/09/1916
Miscellaneous	106th F.A.B.	04/09/1916	04/09/1916
Miscellaneous	24th D.A. Order No. 12	03/09/1916	03/09/1916
Miscellaneous			
Miscellaneous	6th Division G.15/73	10/09/1916	10/09/1916
Miscellaneous		11/09/1916	11/09/1916
Miscellaneous	106 F.A.B.	12/09/1916	12/09/1916
Miscellaneous	16th Infantry Brigade. 18th Infantry Brigade. 71st Infantry Brigade. C.R.E. Signals. A.D.M.S.	13/09/1916	13/09/1916
Miscellaneous	6th Div. No. G/18/13/1	13/09/1916	13/09/1916
Miscellaneous	Amendment to 6th Div. G/18/13/1 "Special Instructions Regarding Action Of Tanks"	14/09/1916	14/09/1916
Miscellaneous	107 F.A. Brigade.	13/09/1916	13/09/1916
Operation(al) Order(s)	Operation Order No. 1. by O.C., Left Group, Centre Divnl Artilleries.	14/09/1916	14/09/1916
Miscellaneous	Left Group Centre Divisional Artilleries.		
Miscellaneous	Reference Left Group Operation Order No. 1	14/09/1916	14/09/1916
Miscellaneous	Left Group Centre Divisional Artilleries.		
Miscellaneous	A Form. Messages And Signals.	14/09/1916	14/09/1916
Miscellaneous	C Form (Duplicate). Messages And Signals.	14/09/1916	14/09/1916
Miscellaneous	Right Group. Left Group.	14/09/1916	14/09/1916
Operation(al) Order(s)	Operation Order No. 1. by O.C., Left Group, Centre Divnl Artilleries.	14/09/1916	14/09/1916
Operation(al) Order(s)	Operation Order No. 1		

Category	Description	Date	Date
Miscellaneous	Guards Divisional Artillery Order No. 50	15/09/1916	15/09/1916
Miscellaneous	Table Of Tasks.		
Miscellaneous	Messages And Signals.	15/09/1916	15/09/1916
Miscellaneous		15/09/1916	15/09/1916
Miscellaneous		15/09/1915	15/09/1915
Miscellaneous	A Form. Messages And Signals.	15/09/1916	15/09/1916
Miscellaneous		15/09/1916	15/09/1916
Miscellaneous	A Form. Messages And Signals.	15/09/1916	15/09/1916
Miscellaneous	Messages And Signals.	15/09/1916	15/09/1916
Miscellaneous	C Form (Duplicate). Messages And Signals.	15/09/1916	15/09/1916
Operation(al) Order(s)	Operation Order No. 2 by Left Group Centre Divisional Artilleries.		
Miscellaneous	107 F.A.B. For D. Batty Only.	16/09/1916	16/09/1916
Miscellaneous	107 F.A.B.	16/09/1916	16/09/1916
Miscellaneous	A Form. Messages And Signals.	16/09/1916	16/09/1916
Miscellaneous	Messages And Signals.	16/09/1916	16/09/1916
Miscellaneous		16/09/1916	16/09/1916
Miscellaneous	A Form. Messages And Signals.	16/09/1916	16/09/1916
Miscellaneous	Centre Divisional Artilleries. XIV Corps, Operation Order No. 5	16/09/1916	16/09/1916
Miscellaneous	No. 9 Squadron, Royal Flying Corps.	17/09/1916	17/09/1916
Miscellaneous	List of Targets to be registered by Aeroplane.	17/09/1916	17/09/1916
Miscellaneous	C Form (Duplicate). Messages And Signals.	17/09/1916	17/09/1916
Miscellaneous	Centre Divisional Artilleries XIV Corps, Operation Order No. 6	17/09/1916	17/09/1916
Miscellaneous	Standing Barrage 18-Pounders. Table A		
Miscellaneous	Creeping Barrage. 18-Pounders. Table "B"		
Miscellaneous	Table "C" 4.5" Howitzer Batteries.		
Miscellaneous		17/09/1916	17/09/1916
Miscellaneous		18/09/1916	18/09/1916
Miscellaneous			
Miscellaneous		18/09/1916	18/09/1916
Miscellaneous	C Form (Duplicate). Messages And Signals.	18/09/1916	18/09/1916
Miscellaneous	Table "A"		
Miscellaneous	106th F.A.B.	18/09/1916	18/09/1916
Miscellaneous	C Form (Original). Messages And Signals.	18/09/1916	18/09/1916
Miscellaneous	A Form. Messages And Signals.	18/09/1916	18/09/1916
Miscellaneous	C Form (Duplicate). Messages And Signals.		
Miscellaneous	C Form (Duplicate). Messages And Signals.	18/09/1916	18/09/1916
Miscellaneous	C Form (Original). Messages And Signals.	18/09/1916	18/09/1916
Miscellaneous			
Miscellaneous	106th F.A.B.	18/09/1916	18/09/1916
Miscellaneous	C Form (Duplicate). Messages And Signals.	18/09/1916	18/09/1916
Miscellaneous	Centre Divisional Artilleries XIV Corps. Operation Order No. 7	19/09/1916	19/09/1916
Miscellaneous	C Form (Original). Messages And Signals.	19/09/1916	19/09/1916
Miscellaneous		19/09/1916	19/09/1916
Miscellaneous		20/09/1916	20/09/1916
Miscellaneous	C Form (Duplicate). Messages And Signals.	20/09/1916	20/09/1916
Miscellaneous	106th F.A.B.	20/09/1916	20/09/1916
Miscellaneous	Operation Order No. 1 by Brigadier General H.C. Sheppard Commanding Left Centre Divisional Artillery XIV Corps.	21/09/1916	21/09/1916
Miscellaneous	A Form. Messages And Signals.	22/09/1916	22/09/1916
Miscellaneous		22/09/1916	22/09/1916
Miscellaneous	C Form (Duplicate). Messages And Signals.	22/09/1916	22/09/1916

Miscellaneous	Left Centre Divisional Artillery.	23/09/1916	23/09/1916
Miscellaneous		23/09/1916	23/09/1916
Operation(al) Order(s)	Left Centre Divisional Artillery XIV Corps Operation Order No. 2	24/09/1916	24/09/1916
Miscellaneous	Reference Operation Order No. 2	24/09/1916	24/09/1916
Miscellaneous		24/09/1916	24/09/1916
Miscellaneous			
Miscellaneous		24/09/1916	24/09/1916
Miscellaneous			
Miscellaneous		24/09/1916	24/09/1916
Miscellaneous	A Form. Messages And Signals.	24/09/1916	24/09/1916
Miscellaneous	107th F.A.B.	24/09/1916	24/09/1916
Miscellaneous	C Form (Duplicate). Messages And Signals.	25/09/1916	25/09/1916
Miscellaneous	C Form (Original). Messages And Signals.	25/09/1916	25/09/1916
Miscellaneous		25/09/1916	25/09/1916
Miscellaneous			
Miscellaneous	A Form. Messages And Signals.	25/09/1916	25/09/1916
Miscellaneous	A Form. Messages And Signals.	26/09/1916	26/09/1916
Miscellaneous	A Form. Messages And Signals.		
Miscellaneous		26/09/1916	26/09/1916
Miscellaneous	A Form. Messages And Signals.	26/09/1916	26/09/1916
Miscellaneous	Left Centre Divisional Artillery.	27/09/1916	27/09/1916
Miscellaneous		27/09/1916	27/09/1916
Miscellaneous	A Form. Messages And Signals.	27/09/1916	27/09/1916
Miscellaneous	Messages And Signals.	27/09/1916	27/09/1916
Miscellaneous	A Form. Messages And Signals.	27/09/1916	27/09/1916
Miscellaneous	24th Div. Arty March Table.	29/09/1916	29/09/1916
Miscellaneous	24th Divisional Artillery March Table.	30/09/1916	30/09/1916
Miscellaneous			
War Diary		01/10/1916	04/10/1916
War Diary	Bois de Bouvigny	05/10/1916	31/10/1916
Miscellaneous	O.C. "Ginger"	11/10/1916	11/10/1916
Operation(al) Order(s)	Operation Order No. 7. By Lieut. Colonel D.W.L. Spiller., Commanding 107/F.A./Brigade.	11/10/1916	11/10/1916
Operation(al) Order(s)	Operation Order No. 9. By Major G.L. Popham D.S.O., Commanding 107/F.A./Brigade.	14/10/1916	14/10/1916
Miscellaneous	Operation Order No. 10. By Major G.L. Popham D.S.O., Commanding 107/F.A./Brigade	14/10/1916	14/10/1916
Operation(al) Order(s)	Operation Order No. 11. By Major G.L. Popham D.S.O., Commanding 107/F.A. Brigade	19/10/1916	19/10/1916
Miscellaneous	Operation No. 8 by Lt Col D.W.L. Spiller Comdg 107 F.A.B.		
Miscellaneous	Artillery Programme. for the Morning of the 14th List		
Miscellaneous	24th Divisional Artillery.	02/10/1916	02/10/1916
War Diary		01/11/1916	30/11/1916
War Diary	Vimy	01/12/1916	04/12/1916
War Diary	Fosse VII & Maroc	05/12/1916	31/12/1916
Operation(al) Order(s)	Operation Order No. R. 30 by Brigadier General H.C. Sheppard, D.S.O. Commanding 24th Divisional Artillery.	30/11/1916	30/11/1916
Miscellaneous	Addenda To O.O. No. R.30	30/11/1916	30/11/1916
Operation(al) Order(s)	Operation Order No. 5 by Lt. Col. Walthall D.S.O. Commanding 24th Divisional Artillery.	25/12/1916	25/12/1916
Map			
War Diary	Fosse VII and Maroc	01/01/1917	31/01/1917
Miscellaneous	One Battery 106.6 18-prs. (Left Group).	12/01/1917	12/01/1917

Miscellaneous	One Battery Right Group.	12/01/1917	12/01/1917
Miscellaneous	Left Group (B/106) Co-operation in Enterprise on Centre Group Front.	12/01/1917	12/01/1917
Miscellaneous	B/107. Minor Enterprise on Centre Group Front. Case I	12/01/1917	12/01/1917
Miscellaneous	C/107. Minor Enterprise on Centre Group Front	12/01/1917	12/01/1917
Miscellaneous	D/107. Minor Enterprise on Centre Group Front.	12/01/1917	12/01/1917
Miscellaneous	Artillery Arrangements.		
Miscellaneous	Minor Enterprise on Centre Group Front.	23/01/1917	23/01/1917
Miscellaneous	Officer Commanding.	25/01/1917	25/01/1917
Miscellaneous	All Batteries. 107th F.A. Bde.	23/01/1917	23/01/1917
Miscellaneous	Head Quarters, 24th D.A.	10/01/1917	10/01/1917
War Diary	Fosse VII & Maroc	01/02/1917	13/02/1917
War Diary	Annezin & Vaudricourt	14/02/1917	06/03/1917
War Diary	Souchez	07/03/1917	31/03/1917
Heading	107th Brigade R.F.A. 24th Division April 1917		
War Diary	Souchez	01/04/1917	13/04/1917
War Diary	Angres	14/04/1917	16/04/1917
War Diary	Lievin	17/04/1917	24/04/1917
War Diary	Lievin & Hesdigneul	25/04/1917	25/04/1917
War Diary	Quernes	26/04/1917	26/04/1917
War Diary	Verchin	27/04/1917	30/04/1917
War Diary	Souchez	01/05/1916	11/05/1916
War Diary	Angres	16/05/1917	16/05/1917
War Diary	Lievin	18/05/1917	25/05/1917
War Diary	Souchez	01/05/1917	13/05/1917
War Diary	Angres	15/05/1917	16/05/1917
War Diary	Lievin	18/05/1917	18/05/1917
War Diary	Verchin	29/05/1917	29/05/1917
War Diary	Verchin	01/05/1917	11/05/1917
War Diary	Hardifort	12/05/1917	16/05/1917
War Diary	Ypres	17/05/1917	04/07/1917
War Diary	Pradelles	05/07/1917	05/07/1917
War Diary	Racquinghem	06/07/1917	12/07/1917
War Diary	Pradelles	13/07/1917	13/07/1917
War Diary	Dickebusch	14/07/1917	16/07/1917
War Diary	Ypres	17/07/1917	31/08/1917
Heading	107 Bde RFA Vol 24		
War Diary	Ypres	01/09/1917	12/09/1917
War Diary	Pradelles	13/09/1917	14/09/1917
War Diary	Eecke	15/09/1917	16/09/1917
War Diary	Baupaume	17/09/1917	25/09/1917
War Diary	Peronne	26/09/1917	30/09/1917
Heading	War Diary For October 1917 Of 107 Bde R.F.A. Vol 25		
War Diary	Hervilly	01/10/1917	31/10/1917
Heading	War Diary 107th Bde R.F.A. From Nov 1st To Nov 30th 1917		
War Diary	Hervilly	01/11/1917	31/01/1918
Miscellaneous	Code Wards For Minor Enterprise	24/01/1917	24/01/1917
War Diary	Hervilly	01/02/1918	17/03/1918
War Diary	Vermand	18/03/1918	22/03/1918
War Diary	Bouvincourt	22/03/1918	31/03/1918
Heading	Headquarters, 107th Brigade, R.F.A. April 1918		
War Diary		01/04/1918	30/04/1918
Heading	107th Bde RFA Vol 5		
War Diary	Lievin	01/05/1918	31/05/1918

Heading	War Diary Of 107th Bde Royal Field Artillery From 1st June 1918 To 30th June 1918 Vol 33		
War Diary	Lievin	01/06/1918	30/06/1918
Heading	War Diary Of 107th Brigade. R.F.A. From 1st July 1918 To 31st July 1918 Vol 34		
War Diary	Lievin	01/07/1918	31/07/1918
Heading	War Diary Of 107th Brigade Royal Field Artillery From 1st August 1918 To 30th August 1918 Vol 35		
War Diary	Lievin	01/08/1918	16/10/1918
War Diary	Cambrai Area	17/10/1918	31/10/1918
War Diary	Vendegies	01/11/1918	01/11/1918
War Diary	Artres	02/11/1918	02/11/1918
War Diary	Sepmeries	03/11/1918	04/11/1918
War Diary	Jenlain	05/11/1918	05/11/1918
War Diary	La Bois Crette	06/11/1918	06/11/1918
War Diary	Bavay	07/11/1916	08/11/1916
War Diary	Feignies	09/11/1918	16/11/1918
War Diary	Bry	17/11/1918	17/11/1918
War Diary	Escaudain	18/11/1918	18/11/1918
War Diary	Lewarde	19/11/1918	26/11/1918
War Diary	Landas	27/11/1918	16/12/1918
War Diary	Tournai	17/12/1918	31/12/1918
War Diary	Vaulx Lez Tournai	01/01/1919	31/01/1919
War Diary	Vaulx Lez Tournai	01/02/1919	28/02/1919
War Diary	Vaulx-Lez Tournai	01/03/1919	31/03/1919

Woods 12/17/14

24TH DIVISION
DIVL ARTILLERY

107TH BRIGADE R.F.A.
AUG 1915 - MAR 1919

Box 2197

Brigade disembarked
Havre from England
31.8.15.

WAR DIARY

Headquarters,

107th BRIGADE, R.F.A.

(24th Division)
AUGUST AND SEPTEMBER

(21.8.15 to 30.9.15)

1 9 1 5

Army Form C. 2118

WAR DIARY
or
INTELLIGENCE SUMMARY.
(Erase heading not required.)

107/Bde/R.F.A.
H.Q.S.
Sheet I

Instructions regarding War Diaries and Intelligence Summaries are contained in F.S. Regs., Part II. and the Staff Manual respectively. Title pages will be prepared in manuscript.

Place	Date	Hour	Summary of Events and Information	Remarks and references to Appendices
Deepcut	24/8/15	11 am	Mobilization orders received. Centre to close at midnight 31/8/15 - Mobilization continued to end of week.	
	26/8/15	5 pm	Ammunition SAA & QF - 2in HE. complete.	
	28/8/15		Orders for entrainment received - immediate orders re. 2/Lt. SPENCER falls from his horse. Too ill to proceed with unit (B Battery) - no further officers available to replace.	
	29/8/15	8.30pm	1st unit (BAC) entrains from FARNBORO' L.S.W.Ry. for SOUTHAMPTON DOCKS.	
	30/8/15	9.20 am	Last unit (HQS) finishes entraining. All units left exactly to time without hitch or casualty.	
	31/8/15	7 am	HQS (Less 20 men & 3 officers stopped on MONA QUEEN dissembark from SS NORTH WEST MINER AT HAVRE.	
		12 mid	HQS & 'A' Battery reach Camp 5 - C & D Batteries also at Camp 5.	
		2 pm	OC BAC reports by telephone illness of T 2/Lt T.B.DARNEY. Left at SOUTHAMPTON.	
MARENLA	1/9/15	4 pm	First unit 'B' Battery arrives at MARENLA, FRANCE	Ref. Off. Map 6. MONTREUIL
	2/9/15	7 am	Last " " " "	
			Attn. Concentration of Brigade completed.	
			" " " D " Owing to interpreter not joining till evening of 2/9/15. Some difficulties experienced in billeting by names unit where officers could not speak French.	
	3/9/15 - 9/9/15		Training continued in billeting areas. B 24th Division.	
	10/9/15		Thanksgiving & by pres day under orders of Maj-Gen HAKING (OC 11No Corps) or ANCIEN MOULIN DE SEMPY-	Ref Off Map 6. MONTREUIL
			Brigade marches q/s Ant. to LAIRES- Res SAA to LAIRES - 'A' Battery of BAC - await LAIRES 6 p.m.	Ref 7 ARRAS.
	11/9/15		C & D Batteries & ½ AC with Pickt HOWARD-SMITH join 109/FA/Bde at FRECHIN - remain there	
	10/9/15		Column march thro INKSTREHEM - HINERS - CHOCQUES to first Corps area & billet for night at AMUERIE. Ry. "n" "n"	
ANNEQUIN	12/9/15	8.30pm	Battery occupy prepared pits at G 1. a. 4.8 (Ref Map 36 a N.W Sheet 3.4 pt of 1) - began firing at F 22 a 2.1 (Ref Sheer 36 B. NE) - BAC under 1st Riley at E 26 centre (same map).	
			Refs. 107/FA/Bde less 'C','D' + part BAC now under 7th Div. arty & grouped under OC 2/N/Bde/	
BETHUNE				

Army Form C. 2118

107/FA/BA

Sheet II

WAR DIARY
or
INTELLIGENCE SUMMARY.
(Erase heading not required.)

Place	Date	Hour	Summary of Events and Information	Remarks and references to Appendices
ANNEQUIN	19/9/15		Alloy 135/107 + HQ Bty under 7 DA for tactical purposes, orders spent on magnetoharm.	
	21/9/15	6 p.m.	Batteries commenced night firing on outer-work in front of Lacks Muller, & fired 48 rds per hour till 6 AM following day."	
	22/9/15	7.55 am 8.8 am	Batteries bdr part in front attack on BRESLAU TRENCH. (Map 36C NW - Sheet 3 Pot of I)	
		6 p.m.	" resumed night firing till 6 am 23/9/15	
	23/9/15 noon	" " bombarded la tria German trenches near POPES NOSE.	
		6 p.m.	Light firing afterwards.	
	24/9/15 noon	Bombardment of German front line trenches continued.	
		6 p.m.	Light firing resumed.	
	25/9/15	5.45 am	Batteries took part in intense bombardment German front.	

BATTLE OF LOOS.

		7 am	" opened to shew lifts on CITÉ ST ÉLIE to hamper counterattacks.	
		6 p.m.	OC Brigade ordered to report to 24 D.A. at VERMELLES; there he received instructions to report to GOC 71/Inf/Brs at LE RUTOIRE to support attack of that Brigade on the following morning; has been also informed that C + D 107/FA/Bde has been withdrawn from 1st DN. + on rejoining 107/FA/Bde, at LE RUTOIRE. OC Bde returned to ANNEQUIN & issued orders for A + B to cease firing & advance to LE RUTOIRE; & set out himself at once for that place, accompanied by his Adjt, arriving there at 9 p.m.	
		9 p.m.	There was no trace of GOC/71/Inf/Brs at LE RUTOIRE; he had left no officer & no orderly there; nor of it to ascertained Adjutkay Mun has had been there there. OC Bty met OC Batts about 9.30 p.m. & informed him that No two had had instructions to report to GOC 71/Inf/Bde at LE RUTOIRE. He failed to find him & sent word written word to that effect to B.M. 24 D.A.	

Army Form C. 2118

Sheet III

107/FA/BA

WAR DIARY
or
INTELLIGENCE SUMMARY.
(Erase heading not required.)

Place	Date	Hour	Summary of Events and Information	Remarks and references to Appendices
LE RUTOIRE	25-9-15	9.30pm	OC D/107 had been at LE RUTOIRE since 8 pm. Adjt & OC D/107 were instructed to go forward and endeavour to find GOC 21 D/Arty/Bde; OC Brigade also went forward in a different direction.	Ref. map 36 c N.W. 3 ypart. sh. I 1 inch. map 10,000 map
	26-9-15	1 AM.	OC Res. Arty, OC D/107 returned to cross roads at G15c leaving found no trace of Brigadier, and were sent back to Brigade (which had been halted in VERMELLES) for Bde to come up. The night was pitch dark, heavy rain was falling. No water & feeds charmed with cavalry, infantry corps, limbers & men. OC Bde asked officers to find Brigade into action near the cross roads (G15c), positions were found, the guns brought up, & the digging of gun pits commenced.	
		3 AM	Orders were received from RM 24 DA that the Brigade was to enhance East of LE RUTOIRE. Owing to prevailing conditions it was impossible to reconnoitre fresh positions before dawn. OC Brigade decided to remain where he was till daylight. Position of batteries approximately on a line G 21 a 9 6 - 7 55.	
		4.20 am.	Orders received from RM 24 DA that 107/FA/Bde would be under orders of GOC 21 DA; that OC Brigade would report to him at LE RUTOIRE at 5 am.	
		5 am	OC Brigade reported to GOC 21 DA, shewed him position of batteries, & explained it had not been possible to move further forward before dawn. GOC 21 DA approved position of batteries.	
		6.30am	Orders received to bombard enemy trenches at H 20 to 37 until 11 am. This was carried out.	
		11.15am	Verbal order received to reconnoitre forward position in view of infantry advance. Adjt & Orderly officer proceeded to reconnoitre towards LONE TREE (H17c). No definite information as to progress of our attack having been received Adjt went forward to LONE TREE itself, where found one of our FOO's Lt No. STUART C/107, who informed him that our infantry had not made further progress.	

Army Form C. 2118
Sheet IV

WAR DIARY
or
INTELLIGENCE SUMMARY.   107/FA/BA

(Erase heading not required.)

Instructions regarding War Diaries and Intelligence Summaries are contained in F. S. Regs., Part II and the Staff Manual respectively. Title pages will be prepared in manuscript.

Place	Date	Hour	Summary of Events and Information	Remarks and references to Appendices
LE RUTOIRE	26.9.15	Midday	Shearn was telephoned to O.C. Brigade. No orders were hitherto subsequent to the reconnaissance until 1 AM 27.9.15. Orders re opening fire had stated that fire was to cease at 11 am. Bn Fd's reports of the situation however decided O.C. Brigade to open fire in the afternoon. The 2nd's Counter-attack Bde. Fd's reported that our fire had checked German counter attacks forcing them to take cover. Afternoon was quiet. Night Guns were laid out on German trenches.	
	27.9.15	1 AM	O this line O.C. Brigade received orders from Arty. Gp Cdr. IV Corps that he was to command Regt Group Artillery under orders of G.O.C. Guards Div. Arty.	
		3 AM	A.D.C. G.O.C. G.D.A. arrived + his a.	
		9 AM	LT. COL. D.R. COATES + LT. + ADJT. G. FRANKAU arrived + various preliminary verbal instructions re near G.O.C. G.D.A. at cross roads - the General was not there - they therefore proceeded to Le Rutoire + reported to G.O.C. 1st Guards Brigade. Regt Group Artillery consists of 107/FA/Bde C + D/106/FA/Bde (position G 21 a - 7) 108/FA/Bde (position 100x NE of LE RUTOIRE) 109/FA/Bde (position A/109 G.14.a. B/109 G 21.a 7.2 C/109 G 19 & centre D/109 G 21 & 22). Communication was improvised by HQ Staff 107/FA/Bde. 9 wires throughout the 4 days of operations. Sergt Arthur James BARRACLOUGH was largely responsible for keeping these lines working frequently repairing them under shell fire.	
		2:15 pm	Personal orders received from B.G.C./G.D.A. to arrange covering fire for attack by 2nd Guards Brigade on CHALK PIT, PUITS 14 bis, + BOIS HUGO. Orders issued; zones of fire allotted, + all instructions as to rates + times of fire carried out.	

WAR DIARY or INTELLIGENCE SUMMARY

Army Form C. 2118

107/FA/BM Sheet V.

Place	Date	Hour	Summary of Events and Information	Remarks and references to Appendices
LE RUTOIRE	27.9.15	6 p.m.	Attack having been particularly successful orders were issued to lay out lights, guns & be prepared to cover 1/GB and they be attacked. Night passed off quietly.	
	28.9.15		Early on this day the enemy appeared to have recaptured RIDGE 8 at ST ELIE, then gaining an observing station for their artillery. Shelling of our guns & approaches of LE RUTOIRE FARM which had been spasmodic during the previous days, now became violent & continued to about 11a.30 a.m.	
		11 a.m.	A further attack by 1/GB on CHALK PIT & HILL 70. This attack was supported by fire of all guns. Posts & telephonist of our Batteries received good service of information. The following call for special mention in 107/FA/Bdw — Lt FRANK LUDLAM & Lt WM STUART — both of these officers were observing & reporting under shell & rifle fire; following telephonists Br GARDINER B/107 Br BUTTERS C/107 — Br ROSS D/107, Sergeants Capt. that trenches to repair wires under heavy shell & rifle fire.	
		2.5 p.m.	Various batteries both places and enemy guns 108/FA/Bdw heavily shelled by GAS + HE. Later guns inaction.	
		6 p.m.	Night passed quietly. During this night 108/FA/Bdw withdrew to new position at G 21 c, with exception of D Battery which had not been shelled. C & D/108 were not then withdrawn.	
	29.9.15		Firing in retaliation was continued during the whole day but no further attack was undertaken by our infantry.	
		3 p.m.	107/FA/Bdw reported 8 guns out of action owing to faulty springs. Spring crews.	
		3.30 p.m.	107/FA/Bdw heavily shelled by 4.9 + 6" howitzer – men ordered into communication trenches.	

Army Form C. 2118
Sheet VI

107/FA/BA

WAR DIARY
or
INTELLIGENCE SUMMARY.
(Erase heading not required.)

Place	Date	Hour	Summary of Events and Information	Remarks and references to Appendices
LE PREÜRE	29/9/15	4pm	Orders received for relief of 107/FA/Bde by Guards Div. Arty; also for relay of Sections of 107/FA/Bde. Relief carried out during night.	
		1 PM	At this hour Lt Col D.R. COATES was honoured by personal visit from HRH The Prince of Wales.	
	30/9/15	6 pm	Relief having been completed, Lt Col D.R. COATES handed over command to Lt Col CARTWRIGHT as OC Right Group Guards Div. Arty; & proceeded with his Adjt to SAILLY-LA-BOURSE arriving at 10 pm; where he reported to GOC 24 DA, rejoining 107/FA/Bde at 5 am 1/10/15.	
			Note. Total casualties of 107/FA/Bde during battles of LOOS:— OC 9/07 CAPT H.H. BAXTER - wounded in forward trenches on morning of 25/9/15 — B/10 T/2/Lt W.E. RUSSELL - " on morning of 26/9/15 Three other ranks wounded. CO's chargor & some other horses killed.	

2353 W. W2544/1454 700,000 5/15 D. D. & L. A.D.S.S./Forms/C. 2118.

WAR DIARY

INTELLIGENCE SUMMARY. H.Q.S.

107/FA/BA
October 1915.
Army Form C. 2118
Sheet VII

Place	Date	Hour	Summary of Events and Information	Remarks and references to Appendices
	1/10/15	5.30 a.m.	Brigade marches from NOEUX-LES-MINES to BOURECQ & billets for night. March continued to SERCUS.	
	2/10/15			
	3/10/15		Arrival at billeting area near WATOU – Belgium.	
	4/10/15		Examination of guns shows 15 requiring repair by I.O.M. One gun only (A/107) sound. This was a new gun replacing one burst by HE shell at HARLEQUIN. One gun sent to I.O.M. 5th CORPS at PROVEN.	
	9/10/15		Brigade marches to new billeting area near REXINGHERST. From this date to end of month guns being repaired & by end of month all save one of	
	11/10/15 to 20/10/15		C/107 repaired. A/107 invaded hostile officers, attached by OC Brigades having own telephone area by OC Brigades, & in pursuance of instructions from GOC 24 DA batteries ordered to dig gun positions for zones of fire as under:- A/107 Position – N.4.I.42. Zones – 07.b.65 to O.2.c.9.½.6 B/107 " N.5.a.28 – 02.c.9½.6 to O3.d.38 C/107 " H.35.a.63 – 03.d.38 to O4.a.5.7 D/107 " H.29.c.88 – 04.a.5.7 to I.34.d.30 Remainder of month spent in digging above & drawing of Brigades.	WORMEZEELE – HOLLEBEKE – French lines.

107th Bde, R.F.A.
Vol: 2

121/7754

34th Divison

Nov 15

Army Form C. 2118.

WAR DIARY
or
INTELLIGENCE SUMMARY.
(Erase heading not required.)

107/FA/13th HQ. SHEET VIII

Instructions regarding War Diaries and Intelligence Summaries are contained in F. S. Regs., Part II. and the Staff Manual respectively. Title pages will be prepared in manuscript.

Place	Date	Hour	Summary of Events and Information	Remarks and references to Appendices
RENINGHELST	1/11/15 7/11/15 to 8/11/15		Sgt A.R. Barraclough (HQS) & Corpl H.C. Gardiner (B/107) awarded DCM for gallant conduct at LOOS. Training continued. D/107 occupies position 1 26 d 11 (under command of Left Group - OC Col DUCHESNES 7 Belgian Artillery.	VOORMEZEELE & HOLLEBEKE trenches maps 1/10,000
DICKEBUSCH	9/11/15		One bombardier D/107 wounded by shell-splinter	"
	10/11/15		CO reconnoitring.	"
	15/11/15		Arty occupies position HQ at H 29 c 08 - communications by CENTRE GROUP Commdrs.	
	16/11/15	5.30 pm	Lt Col COATES takes over command of CENTRE GROUP 2A Div Arty - Jones 0 2 d 28 to Canal - consisting of:- D/107 at I 26 d 11 - D/109 (3 guns only - Hows) H 35 a 77 - 2/7 Belges H 30 a 18 - RX/A/107 - N4 a 19 - LX/A/107 - H 36 b 57 and D/108 (for night only) at I 26 b 44. (In support of 7/1/17 Bde)	
		9 pm	A/107 occupies above positions having relieved B/106	
	14/11/15		Capt. H.G. Chetwynd-Stapylton Rifles whilst reconnoitring by German 8" Shell.	
	15/11/15		Capt WURTELE takes over command C/107 vice Capt Stapylton.	
	16/11/15		2/Lt R.R. Baylor D/107 seriously wounded by rifle bullet while observing from fork trench from our lines.	
	17/11/15		Situation normal. - Battery's magazine. Adjutants groom wounded by shell. Communications allowance war rewising 24/11/15 150 rds per field battery 50 per How battery.	
	18/11/15		Adjutants groom died in hospital. (No 39063 Dr JEFFS JR) Situation normal. At 5:45 pm 7/127/13 Bde mads demonstration with machine guns - group ordered to avoid if enemy artillery replies - they did not give us opportunity.	
	19/11/15		Situation normal. Battery's firing occasionally	
	20/11/15	5.30 am to 8.30 am	On information received from deserter that rolled military be effected along ST ELOI-OSTAVERNE road D/109 & D/108 searched road from T 15 a 32 to T 84 a 6 during night hours.	

2353 Wt. W2514/1454 700,000 5/15 D.D.& L. A.D.S.S./Forms/C. 2118.

Army Form C.2118.

WAR DIARY
or
INTELLIGENCE SUMMARY. HQS / 107/FA/Bde Sheet IX

(Erase heading not required.)

Instructions regarding War Diaries and Intelligence Summaries are contained in F. S. Regs., Part II. and the Staff Manual respectively. Title pages will be prepared in manuscript.

Place	Date	Hour	Summary of Events and Information	Remarks and references to Appendices
HAZEBROUCK	21.		Situation normal - D/107 fired 29 rounds in retaliation on demand of Infantry - expends Rounds 28 - H.M. 820 and orders for relay of 2H DA by 2 DA received.	
	22.		Situation normal. At about 9 p.m. GOC 9/III/FA/Bde takes over command of Infantry Wimbles Vice GOC 17/IA/Bde whose unit is relieved. Capt. reports to him about 9.30 p.m. Foggy weather.	
	23.		Situation normal. Foggy weather.	
	24.	8 p.m.	Front sections A/107 relieved by 2 q/107 Battery - one section D/107 by one section A/64 Battery - relieving sections taking over guns.	Reference Sheet 27 1/40,000
		9 p.m.	Two sections relieved march to new billets near STEENVOORDE } A/107 P.16 d 38 C/107 P.24 a 75	
		4 p.m.	" " " " " " " " " } B/107 P.17 d 28 D/107 P.23 a 09½	
			Resting batteries (B + C) " " " " " " to STEENVOORDE - arriving M.N.	
	25.	1 p.m.	Rear of 107/FA/Bde by HQ/FA/Bde - HQS & remaining section of A/107 & D/107 march to STEENVOORDE - arriving M.N.	Ref. HAZEBROUCK Sts. too, and
			Resting - filling up with ammunition.	
	26.		Resting.	
	27.	9.45 a.m.	Brigade march via BAVINGHOVE - OCHTEZEELE to RUBROUCK arriving 2:30 p.m. and billets for night.	
	28.	8:45 a.m.	" " via WATTEN - LES BAS-SERQUES - MONTES to ACQUIN. Head Quart. Batteries arrive 4:30 p.m.	
			BAC delayed by passing of troops at LE BAS & changing of teams had to hand horse at WATTEN & proceed via ST. OMER. - QUIÉLMES - arriving 8:30 p.m. NO SUPPLIES till 11 a.m. on 29th.	
	29.		Resting. Billets of units - HQS at CHATEAU - TO n.s. ACQUIN - A ½ mile SE of ACQUIN - D at LE POOKRE - C at VAL D'ACQUIN - B.A.C. at ACQUIN.	
	30.		Resting - weather clearing up.	

J R Coulter Major
RFA
16 Bde RFA
OC 107 Bde RFA

107 c Bde: R.72.
Vol: 3

12/7931

24/4/5?

Army Form C. 2118.

WAR DIARY
or
INTELLIGENCE SUMMARY.
(Erase heading not required.) 107/FA Bde/HQ Sheet 1

Instructions regarding War Diaries and Intelligence Summaries are contained in F. S. Regs., Part II. and the Staff Manual respectively. Title pages will be prepared in manuscript.

Place	Date	Hour	Summary of Events and Information	Remarks and references to Appendices
ACQUIN Rly St OMER map	1/11/15 29/11/15 1/11/15		Brigade resting.	
	30/11/15	8.45am	Brigade - under orders to take place in 17 Div Arty moves to NOORDPEENE (arriving 5 pm) & billets for night.	
	31/11/15	9.30am	Brigade marches to STEENVOORDE and billets for the night.	

JR Coates Lt Col
OC 107th FA Bde

2353 Wt. W2541/1454 700,000 5/15 D. D. & L. A.D.S.S./Forms/C. 2118.

107th Bde. RFA.
Vol: 4

Army Form C. 2118.

WAR DIARY
or
INTELLIGENCE SUMMARY.
(Erase heading not required.)

107/(FA)/Bde/HQ   Sheet XI

Place	Date	Hour	Summary of Events and Information	Remarks and references to Appendices
YPRES	1/11/16	8 pm	Sections of 107/FA/Bde relieves Sections of 78/FA/Bde and took over their guns. Position of batteries A/107 I 2 d 10 B/107 I 19.55 C/107 I 2 d 39 D/107 I 1 d 84 HQ I 7.36	Ref. YPRES 1/10,000
			" Wagn Lines. # HQ - G 24 & 88 A/107 G 24 & 99 B/107 G 24 & 88 C/107 G 24 & 10.8	Ref. YPRES Sheet 28.
			D/107. G 24 d 19 107/BAC G 19 & 88	
	2/11/16	8 pm	Remaining Sections of 107/FA/Bde relieve remaining Sections 78/FA/Bde. Lt Col D.R. Coates takes over command of Left Group Artillery - consisting of:	HOOGE Trench map
			A/107 C/107 D/107 - B/79 C/79 D/79 - covering front line trenches H.11 - A.1	
	3/11/16	9 pm	First section C/106 relieving Section C/79.	
	4/11/16	8 pm	Second " " " " C/79 - Positions of C/106 at I 3 c 34	
	5/11/16		Situation normal	
	6/11/16		" "	
	7/11/16		" "	
	8/11/16		First Sections B/106 & D/106 relieve B/79 & D/79	
	9/11/16		Relief by B/106 & D/106 relief completed - positions B/106 I 8 & 24 D/106 I 2 d 15½. Enemy fire direct hit on one gun C/107. Battentos heavily shelled during afternoon. One Bombardier B/106 killed by shell.	

Army Form C. 2118.

WAR DIARY
or
INTELLIGENCE SUMMARY.
(Erase heading not required.)

109/FA/BG/HQ Sheet XII

Place	Date	Hour	Summary of Events and Information	Remarks and references to Appendices
YPRES	10/1/16		Situation normal.	
	11/1/16		Situation normal. C/106 having fired 40 rounds in the morning was heavily shelled by H.E. in afternoon. German Slow burst on gun-position C/107 - rendering 13 rds ammunition useless. No casualties.	
	12/1/16		A/116 fired 18 rounds registration and reassigned So. H.E. at 6 p.m.	
	13/1/16		Situation normal.	
	14/1/16		do do	
	15/1/16		do do	
	16/1/16		do do	
	17/1/16		Left Group reorganized. C/106 withdrawn. A/109 (Hows) came under command of Left Group. Position I.1.d.87. Left Group has care of 6 Stgs.	
	18/1/16		Situation normal.	
	19/1/16	8.30 am	Our Infantry being heavily shelled B/106 D/106 and A/107 retaliate with 740 rounds. Suggestion from Infantry Battalion Commander is case for immediate retaliation only sent to steretype replies on preavranged lines by 18 pr Batteries as much wastes of ammunition.	
	20/1/16		Situation normal. Capt W.S.M. CURLE takes over command of B/107 vice Capt V.B. TAYLOR to England.	
	21/1/16		Situation normal. 7M Ing/Bars relieving 17 Ing/Bars.	
	22/1/16		Situation normal. B/107 into new Gun Posn Right Group.	
	23/1/16		B/107 relieves D/107 in Left Group.	
	24/1/16		Situation normal.	
	25/1/16			

Army Form C. 2118.

WAR DIARY
or
INTELLIGENCE SUMMARY.
(Erase heading not required.)

104/SA/BdeHQ Sheet XIII

Instructions regarding War Diaries and Intelligence Summaries are contained in F.S. Regs., Part II. and the Staff Manual respectively. Title pages will be prepared in manuscript.

Place	Date	Hour	Summary of Events and Information	Remarks and references to Appendices
DICKEBUSCH YPRES	26/1/16		Situation normal	
	27/1/16		Further discussion re "Retaliation" — decided to adopt new Scheme of CounterStrafes — concentrating fire of 3 18/pr Batteries and one H.E. and one 6 inch onto front lines by Cartrain Zones of enemy — Front div Bde with 4 Zones. G.O.C. Inf. Bdes only to call for Counterstrafes. Battalion Comds for retaliation abolished except in case of S.O.S. call. Sergt W. DEAN shrapnel splinter. Situation normal.	
	29/1/16			
	29/1/16	2:30pm	Counterstrafes A (Right Sector) of Bdge (Group) fired. 60 rds HE from 18 prs; 20 rds H.E.; 16 rds 6". Enemy apparently surprised. Reply feeble. D/106 and B/106 suffered enemy trench mortars N of BEKKEWAARDE LAKE in support of Rifle Group.	1935
	30/1/16		GAS ALERT — wind having changed to E. Foggy. Skies or GAS ALERT.	
	31/1/16		Situation normal.	

George Houghton
Adjutant
107 Bde RFA

D.R Coates
Lt. Col RFA
OC 107"Bde RFA

F.A.B control area in January

Army Form C. 2118.

WAR DIARY
or
INTELLIGENCE SUMMARY.
(Erase heading not required.)

108 FA Bde HQ Sheet XIV

Place	Date	Hour	Summary of Events and Information	Remarks and references to Appendices
YPRES	1/2/16	11 am	Counterbatteries 3 fired. Enemy's reply feeble. Batteries shelled enemy posts.	as for January.
	2/2/16	3 am	Enemy fired 26 rds on trestles support trenches.	
	3/2/16	11 a.m.	Situation normal. Batteries registering. Alloq relieved by D/109	
	4/2/16		Lieut F.S. POTTER (RAC, attached C/109) slightly wounded by shrapnel. 2 OR wounded. D/109 demolition work at I 12. 3.58½	
	5/2/16	3.5 pm	Counterbatteries 2 fired. Situation generally normal. 1 OR wounded.	
	6/2/16	2.15 pm	Counterbatteries 2 fired. Situation normal.	
	7/2/16	3 pm	In conjunction with HAR batteries right groups carried out a bombardment of enemy's front & support lines — 40 rounds per battery were fired. On request of GOC ½ 7th IB Counterbatteries T was fired at 4 p.m.	
	8/2/16	11.35 am	Counterbatteries 2 fired. Hostile Shelling (aided by aeroplanes) fairly heavy all day. 73 IB taken over from 7th IB.	
	9/2/16		Situation normal. 1 OR killed, 2 OR wounded – 3 horses killed. Whilst bringing up D/109 ammunition.	
	10/2/16		Situation normal.	
	11/2/16		" but enemy snatter more active	
	12/2/16		Enemy activity increasing. Counterbatteries 4 fires at 4 p.m.	
	13/2/16		1 OR wounded. Enemy still very active. Counterbatteries 1, 2 & 3 fired during day. Group HQ moved to Ramparts and billeted with 73 IB HQ.	
	14/2/16		2 OR wounded. Counterbatteries 1 at 4 p.m. Enemy shite active. C/106 relieves D/106	
	15/2/16	3 pm	Large new HOOGE trenches being heavily shelled, we supported Rifle Group by harassing front line. 3 OR wounded.	

Army Form C. 2118.

WAR DIARY
or
INTELLIGENCE SUMMARY.
(Erase heading not required.)

107 FA Bde HQ   XV

Place	Date	Hour	Summary of Events and Information	Remarks and references to Appendices
YPRES	16/7/16		Friday. Everything very quiet. Bombardment 2 Guns at 3.40 pm. Station quiet.	
	17/7/16		Situation normal. Bombardment A at 4 pm.	
	18/7/16		Situation normal. C/107 relieved out same area.	
	19/7/16		" " Some salvoes at Wiewp M.G.'s during night. Bombardment A at 5.45 pm.	
	20/7/16		" "	
	21/7/16		2 OR wounded. moving to going for a water infront orders. Bombardment 2 at 11.20 am. Wire cutting continued.	
	22/7/16	1.40pm	Situation normal. Wire cutting continued. Ord Section 53rd Bty relieves 1 section B/106 a/107 " " " " "	
	23/7/16		Situation normal.	
		9.30pm	Ord section S3 relieves 1 section B/106 51 " " " " a/107 53 " " " " c/106 21 " " " " D/107 84 " " " " D/109	
	24/7/16	noon	OC 2 FAB takes over command of Left Group. HQ offices to 36 Rue des Postes POPERINGHE	
		10pm	Relief of C/107, D/107, B/107, D/109 completed. B/107 becomes new forward guns with detachment of officer under command of OC Rt. Group. All other 107 batteries withdrawn to wagon lines	
	25/7/16		C/107 lent to 17 DA for special purpose.	

Army Form C. 2118.

WAR DIARY
or
INTELLIGENCE SUMMARY.

(Erase heading not required.)

HQ 107 FAB

XVI

Instructions regarding War Diaries and Intelligence Summaries are contained in F. S. Regs., Part II. and the Staff Manual respectively. Title pages will be prepared in manuscript.

Place	Date	Hour	Summary of Events and Information	Remarks and references to Appendices
25/7/16 to 29/7/16			Brigades with the Exception of C/107 q forward guns of B/107 resting.	

J Rhodes Lieut Col RA
OC 107 FA Bde

Army Form C. 2118.

WAR DIARY
or
INTELLIGENCE SUMMARY.
(Erase heading not required.)

HQ 107 FAB   XVI

Place	Date	Hour	Summary of Events and Information	Remarks and references to Appendices
PIPERINGHE	1/3/16 to 8/3/16		Batteries (less C) and HQ resting.	
	9/3/16		Sections of 107 FAB relieve Sections 50 DA as under:— D/107 2nd Northumberland Bty B/107 2nd Durham Battery A/Col DR Coates Praules leaves to England. A/107 3rd Durham Battery.	
YPRES	10/3/16	10.20am	107 Brigade HQ - under temporary command Lt Col SR BURNIE DSO. assumes command of RA Group 2nd DA - consisting of A/107 (I 27 a 47) B/107 (I 27 b-7) (SL) D/107 (I 26 b-59) C/106 (I 26 c-57) D/106 Hows (I 15 b 89) HQ at H22 L59	YPRES map Sheet 28. 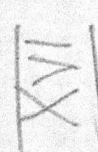
	11/3/16	9am	All reliefs completed. Situation normal.	
	12/3/16	"	"	
	13/3/16	"	"	
	14/3/16	12.30pm to 2.50pm	Enemy shelled our infantry (7th W IR) at B2 B3 B4. We retaliated. All batteries firing except D/107. HQ were shelled with 5.9 (about 60) in the morning. A fine clear day. After very quiet. C/107 returns from 17 DA to Ink. Situation normal.	HOOGE French map
	15/3/16		C/106 heavily shelled with 5.9 - 2 OR Killed, 2 wounded.	
	16/3/16		Gun Section A.R. D/107 & 1 & 2 Section 107 BAC march to new posn Wilts road BECKE	
	17/3/16	9am		map 27.40.000

2353 Wt. W2344/1134 700,000 5/15 D. D. & L. A.D.S.S./Forms/C. 2118.

WAR DIARY
or
INTELLIGENCE SUMMARY

Army Form C. 2118.

HQ 107 FAB

XVII

Place: YPRES

Date	Hour	Summary of Events and Information	Remarks and references to Appendices
17/3/16	10 pm	Section of Lahore DA relieves Section Rt Group 2/4 DA as under: Our Section comprises "Battery relieves I Section C/106. 94 " " " " A/107 8H " " " " B/107 83 " " " " D/107 A/124 " " " " D/109 (New)	
18/3/16 7.45am		107 FAB (less Section) marching 17/3/16 & detachments at (guns) marches to new gun billets at EECKE.	
	6.30pm	Rt Group HQ leaving Clossen into 59.	
	10 pm	Detachments at gun position relieved – convoy to EECKE by motor lorry. HQ II FAB (Col Trefusers) takes over from Rt Group 2/4 DA.	
19/3/16 to 30/3/16		Resting near W2933	
31/3/16	8 am	Section 107 FAB marches from Heut a relieve Section 2 CFAB as under: A/107 – 4th Canadians – B/107 6th Canadians – C/107 5th Canadians – D/107 8th Canadians 107 BAC – 2 C BAC (For map references, new guns see April.) A/107 Q13C11 – C/107 Q20C48 – D/107 Q19C48 B/107 Q22C52 107 BAC P24A43 HQ Q20C42	

J R Crate
LIEUT COL., R.F.A.
COMMANDING 107TH BRIGADE, R.F.A.

Army Form C. 2118.

107th Bde R/FA
Vol 3

WAR DIARY
or
INTELLIGENCE SUMMARY.
(Erase heading not required.)

HQ 107/FAB

Instructions regarding War Diaries and Intelligence Summaries are contained in F. S. Regs., Part II. and the Staff Manual respectively. Title pages will be prepared in manuscript.

Place	Date	Hour	Summary of Events and Information	Remarks and references to Appendices
NEUVE EGLISE	1/4/16	7.30a	Remaining Sections 107 FAB return rejoining Sections 2 C.F.A.B.	Pagan moor — 28,500 to 12,000
			HQ 107 FAB takes over command from 2 C.F.A.B.	Wytschaete 13,000
			107 FAB in support of 73 FAB – holding trenches 136 to C2 inclusive (U 2 C 11 to T 6 C 55)	28,500 to 20,000
			Cashric HQ T15.d.15 A/107 T17.a.15 B/107 T17.a.41.2 C/107 T16.d.65 D/107 T17.8.18 107 BAC B17.2.5	
	2/4/16		Situation normal, batteries registering	
	3/4/16		"	
	4/4/16		"	
	5/4/16	4pm	Capt WL Lucas assumes command of 107 FAB vice Col DR Coates in temporary command at Div Arty.	
	6/4/16		Batteries shelled ONTARIO FARM.	
	7/4/16		New retaliation schemes arranged with G.O.C. 73 IB. Situation normal.	
	8/4/16	2 pm	Infantry Majors Brigade retaliation – shelled BIRTHDAY & ONTARIO Farms.	
	9/4/16		Situation normal.	
	10/4/16		"	
	11/4/16	11am	Enemy shelled front line – was retaliated on BIRTHDAY FARM.	
		6 pm	4 trans T.M. bombs from U.2.d.15. was retaliated. Infantry lay very often.	
	12/4/16		Situation normal	
	13/4/16		"	
	14/4/16	4 pm	Retaliated when we trafficed in ONTARIO FARM.	
	15/4/16		Situation normal	

Army Form C. 2118.

WAR DIARY
or
INTELLIGENCE SUMMARY.
(Erase heading not required.)

HQ 107 FA6 XIX

Place	Date	Hour	Summary of Events and Information	Remarks and references to Appendices
N. FLOEGESTE	16/4/16	12 noon	Lt. Col. DR COATES assumed command. Situation normal	
	17/4/16		Situation normal	
	18/4/16		"	
	19/4/16	9 pm	In cooperation with 106 FA6 fired on enemy's transport routes in MESSINES	
	20/4/16		Situation normal.	
	21/4/16	5:30pm	Retaliated on ONTARIO FARM with all batteries	
	22/4/16		Situation normal.	
	23/4/16		" Synst.	
	24/4/16		" "	
	25/4/16	2 pm	Retaliated on ONTARIO Fm with all batteries	
	26/4/16		Situation normal.	
	27/4/16		" "	
	28/4/16		" "	
	29/4/16	11pm	GAS ATTACK - See appendix T attached. 2 OR wounded.	
	30/4/16	9:50pm	Renewed Gas attack on our Right - A107 & C107 fired a few rounds till tactical situation was cleared up.	

D Rl. M Col
30/4/16

APPENDIX 1 (To War Diary May 1916, Sheet XIX)

Report of events during Gas Attack on the night 29th/30th April 1916
by 107th Brigade R.F.A.

....

Generally.
        About 11.p.m. received warning of probable Gas Attack. Warned all Batteries and B.A.C.
12.50.a.m. report "Gas" from 73rd I.B. also heard horns and gongs. Warned all batteries, who immediately opened a slow rate of fire on night lines.
Shortly afterwards/73rd I.B. reported S.O.S. sent by Leinsters The Leinsters also buzzed "S.O.S" to A/107 battery.
No S.O.S. rockets were seen by Officers on duty at the O.Ps. Rate of fire was then increased, but gradually reduced. About 1.a.m. enemy opened a heavy bombardment on our trenches. Enemy bombardment gradually died away and finished about 2.30, when all firing practically stopped.
About 2.a.m. "O.K" was buzzed through from the Leinsters to A/107. 3.20.a.m. 73rd I.B. reported C2 heavily shelled with 77 mm. and 4.2's, at their request A/107 battery fired 32 rounds retaliation on front line and communication trenches. Enemy fire then ceased.

....

GAS.
Direction.   GAS passed over all 4 batteries in a south westerly direction.

Speed.   The gas arrived very quickly after the horns were sounded.

Kind.   It appeared to be a mixed gas, not pure Chlorine.

Affect on men.   It did not seem to affect the eyes. After affects were a feeling of Nausea and coughing.

Horses.   Many horses in Headquarters Staff and "D" Battery have been coughing today.

Cows.   Several cows were killed in rear of C/107 battery.

Herbage.   Grass behind batteries was turned a much darker green. The low country from enemy's front line trench, for about ½ mile west is coloured yellow - Brown except a strip opposite trenches from ONTARIO TO BIRTHDAY FARMS where gas apparently did not flow.

Material.   Report attached.

Communications.   Communication was broken with 108th F.A.B. about 2.a.m. A/107 kept in communication with their O.P. allthrough and although their line was broken they could still hear buzzing faintly.
All Headquarters wires (with exception to that going to 108th F.A.B.) were kept in working order all the time.

Report of events during Gas Attack continued.

Hostile fire.

A heavy barrage was put on behind HILL 63, A/107, B/107 and D/107 were shelled slightly.

Two men of C/107 Battery were slightly gassed. One was returning from the O.P. after having delivered a message. He saw gas and started to run to the battery. He became out of breath and took off his helmet but replaced it.
The other was in the gun pits and appears not to have put on his helmet quickly enough.

Tower Respirators.

Tower Respirators were proved to be very much more serviceable than the gas helmets.

Vermoral Sprayers.

Vermoral sprayers were used to clear gas away from dug-outs and gun-pits.

....

30/4/16.

Lieut.Colonel, R.F.A.
Commanding 107/F.A/Brigade.

24/ April & May
107 R.F.A.
Vols. 7 & 8

WAR DIARY
INTELLIGENCE SUMMARY

H.Q. 104 F.A.B.

Place	Date	Hour	Summary of Events and Information	Remarks and references to Appendices
NEUVE EGLISE	1/4	7.30 p	Forming section 104 F.A.B relieve remaining section 2 C.F.A.B. H.Q. 104 F.A.B. take over command from 2 R.F.A.B. 104 F.A.B in support of Y3 I.B. – Holding trenches 136 to C2 inclusive (11.2.c.1.1 to T6.b.5.5). Positions N.9.T.5.d.1.5, A/107 T17.a.1.5, B/107 T17.a.1.2, 8/107 T6.d.6.5, D/107 T17.b.1.8 R.16.b.6.25	References 28 SW to 4700 W7 chart to C2 28 SW 50 700
	2/5		Situation normal, batteries registering	
	3/5			
	4/5			
	5/5	4 pm	Capt W. Thomas assumes command of 104 F.A.B vice Col DeCoates in temporary command of 24th Divl: Arty. Batteries shelled ONTARIO FARM.	
	6/5	4 pm	NEW retaliation scheme arranged with Col Y3 I.B. Enemy shelled A/107 & B/107. No casualties. Situation normal.	
	7/5	2 pm	Infantry request barrage retaliation – shelled BIRTHDAY and ONTARIO FARMS. Situation normal.	
	8/5		ditto	
	9/5	11 a.m & p.m	Enemy shelled front line - We retaliated on BIRTHDAY FARM.	
	10/5	8 p.m	" shoot T.M bombs from N.2.d.15. We retaliated. Infantry say very effective.	
	11/5		Situation normal.	
	12/5		ditto	
	13/5		Retaliated with all batteries on ONTARIO FARM.	
	14/5		Situation normal.	

Army Form C. 2118.

WAR DIARY
or
INTELLIGENCE SUMMARY.

(Erase heading not required.)

H.Q. 107 F.A.B.   XIX

Instructions regarding War Diaries and Intelligence Summaries are contained in F. S. Regs., Part II and the Staff Manual respectively. Title pages will be prepared in manuscript.

Place	Date	Hour	Summary of Events and Information	Remarks and references to Appendices
N-U-VE FRAUSE	16-17/4/16	10 am	17 Cox D.R. COATES reconnes to and. Situation normal.	
	18/4/16		Situation normal.	
	19/4/16	9 pm	In co-operation with 106 F.A.B. fired on Enemy's transport routes in MESSINES.	
	20/4/16		Situation normal	
	21/4/16	5.30 pm	Retaliated on ONTARIO FARM with all batteries.	
	22/4/16		Situation normal.	
	23/4/16		Situation quiet	
	24/4/16		ditto	
	25/4/16	2 pm	Retaliated on ONTARIO FARM south with all batteries	
	26/4/16		Situation normal.	
	27/4/16		ditto	
	28/4/16		ditto	
	29/4/16	4 am	GAS ATTACK. 2 O.R. wounded.	
	30/4/16	3 am	Enemy GAS ATTACK on our left — M/107 & B/107 fired a few rounds till tactical situation was cleared up.	

(Certified true copy)

DKWales LIEUT COL., R.F.A.
COMMANDING 107TH BRIGADE, R.F.A.

Army Form C. 2118.

WAR DIARY
or
INTELLIGENCE SUMMARY.
(Erase heading not required.)

H.Q. 107 F.A.B.   XI

Instructions regarding War Diaries and Intelligence
Summaries are contained in F. S. Regs., Part II.
and the Staff Manual respectively. Title pages
will be prepared in manuscript.

Place	Date	Hour	Summary of Events and Information	Remarks and references to Appendices
N.N.V.F. T&158A	1-5-16		Situation normal, very quiet.	a- April
	2-5-16		" " " "	
	3-5-16		" " " "	
	4-5-16		" " " " Capt. Wh. Lucas (D/107) to BASE - sick - and subsequently to	
	5-5-16		" " " "	ENGLAND
	6-5-16		" " " "	
	7-5-16		" " " "	
	8-5-16		" " " "	
	9-5-16		" " " "	
	10-5-16	2.30pm	NBE Batteries shelled BIRTHDAY FARM - in retaliation.	
	11-5-16		Situation normal, very quiet. Two lucky shells on A/107 wounding 5 O.R.s. One dead subsequently.	
	12-5-16		Situation normal, very quiet.	
	13-14May 1916		107 F.A.B. reorganized B/107 becomes D/107 - 107 C.M.L. becomes H.Q.2 Section R.F.A. pro. under administration.	
			B/107 H. W. MAJOR JANES & BUTTS (CWAN Comdg, becomes D/107 for tactical purpose F.A.B. H.Q., assumes command of 107 F.A.B. Group consisting of four original 18-pdr Btys (i.e., A.B.C./107 & D/109) and B/116 How Capt GARDNER.	
			Situation normal.	
	16-5-16		" "	
	17-5-16		" "	
	18-5-16		" " B.S.M. 3/06 killed by shell at Batty.	
	19-5-16		" " GAS ALERT (false alarm during night) No firing - June 12.30pm.	

Army Form C. 2118.

WAR DIARY
or
INTELLIGENCE SUMMARY.

(Erase heading not required.)

Instructions regarding War Diaries and Intelligence Summaries are contained in F. S. Regs., Part II. and the Staff Manual respectively. Title pages will be prepared in manuscript.

107th F.A.B.

Place	Date	Hour	Summary of Events and Information	Remarks and references to Appendices
N. AVE FOUSE	20-5-16		Situation normal	
	21-5-16		do	
	22-5-16		do	
	23-5-16		do	
	24-5-16		do	
	25-5-16		do	
	26-5-16		do	
	27-5-16		do	
	28-5-16		do	
	29-5-16		do	
	30-5-16		do	
	31-5-16		do	

(Certified true copy)

H.R. Lake
LIEUT. COL., R.F.A.
COMMANDING 107TH BRIGADE, R.F.A.

OPERATION ORDERS No.9.   SCHEDULE FOR D/106(How)

TIME.	No. OF GUNS.	OBJECTIVE	RATE.	"B" or "BX"	REMARKS.	
.04 to Zero		NO FIRING				
Zero to .06	Three	Front line U 1 a 2.7 to U 1 a 4.7	XF 10"	BX	Sweep	PHASE 1.
Zero to .04	One	Point U 1 a 4½ 6½	XF 10"	BX		PHASE 1.
.04 to .31 (about)	One	Point U 1 a ½ 8	XF 20"	BX	Search & sweep.	
.06 to .31 (about)	Three	O 31 c 1½ ½ U 1 a 4½ 9½ U 1 a 7½ 9½	XF 20"	BX	Search and sweep	PHASE 2.

Fire of PHASE 2 will be <u>continued until the signal "AC" is telephoned from Brigade H.Q., when it will be brought back to PHASE 3 continue 5 minutes, and stop.</u>

TIME.	No. OF GUNS.	OBJECTIVE	RATE.	"B" or "BX"	REMARKS.	
.31 to .36 (about)	All	Front line U 1 a 2.7 to U 1 a 6½ 6	XF 20"	BX	Sweep	PHASE 3.
1.52 to 2.2	All	Search and sweep on Night lines with 50 rounds BX at irregular intervals.				PHASE 4.
3.17 to 3.27	All	Search and sweep on Night Lines with 50 rounds BX at irregular intervals.				PHASE 5.

XXIV 107 R.C.F.A.
of June
vol 9

Army Form C. 2118.

WAR DIARY
or
INTELLIGENCE SUMMARY.
(Erase heading not required.)

107 FMB
Mee.

XXII

Instructions regarding War Diaries and Intelligence Summaries are contained in F. S. Regs., Part II. and the Staff Manual respectively. Title pages will be prepared in manuscript.

Place	Date	Hour	Summary of Events and Information	Remarks and references to Appendices
Nave Eglise	1/6/16	—	Situation normal.	Same map as may.
	2/6/16	—	" (a R.D. balloon behind Ra Ha broke loose and drifted over enemy lines. Observers escaped by parachute)	
	3/6/16	12.30pm 5.1am	Batteries demonstrated to cover raids by Bryars on own left. (tr 113) Situation normal.	
	4/6/16			
	5/6/16			
	6/6/16			
	7/6/16			
	8/6/16		Batteries retaliated on ONTARIO Fm for shelling of our trenches. (5.30pm)	
	9/6/16			
	10/6/16			
	11/6/16			
	12/6/16			
	13/6/16		Batteries retaliated on ONTARIO Fm (11am)	
	14/6/16			
	15/6/16	6.30pm	Situation abnormal. Germans finished gas torpedos our front - batteries kept hee 1.5 aus. Germans did not leave their trenches. Repair of own battery attacked.	
	16/6/16		Situation normal.	
	17/6/16		Situation normal.	
	18/6/16		" " 4 Ouestions 1 R (Congoca) relieves 1/3 1B.	
	19/6/16		" " 4 pers B/107 Cut Russell & 6 to men U.2.a.17½	
	20/6/16		" " 3.50pm Allery " " " " U.1 a 56	
	21/6/16			
	22/6/16	8.30pm	Enemy shelled our trenches in South of ONTARIO FARM comb around GABION Fm heavily with guns, howers & Minenwerfer (contd)	

Army Form C. 2118.

WAR DIARY
or
INTELLIGENCE SUMMARY.

(Erase heading not required.)

XXIII   /04 FAB AEQ

Place	Date	Hour	Summary of Events and Information	Remarks and references to Appendices
NEAR EGLISE	2/11/16	Continued	The fire of guns & howitzers continued till about 8:30 am. At 9 pm an enemy S.O.S. was sent from Left Battn Hd., A/107 & C/107 opened as SOS line - the stopped at 9.8 pm. Brigade retaliated for Trench Strafing firing on MIDDLE Fm, & RUINS Fm, MESSINES, RONA batteries. At 0.27 a.m. an Enemy Trench Tramway along Front Line observed on ONTARIO Fm. Batteries cut wire as follows – A/107 – U12 47-56 B/107 U12 25-23 C/107 U12 17½-21½ B/107 could not complete with faulty telephone & had to abandon Corridor situation normal. D/109 Cut wire at U1c 6.9.	
	23/11/16		"	
	24/11/16		"	
	25/11/16		"	
	26/11/16	7am to 9am	Batteries continued cutting wire & enlarging existing lanes.	
		11.15 pm	All Group batteries bombarded Enemy front to cover raid by Anzacs in accordance with orders attached where was carried out as far as end of Phase 2. She refused to come back to Phase 2 were not reached and fire was stopped at 12.6 am by message of G.O.C. H.C. Anzac Brigade. The raid was completely successful – heavy MG resistance about support trenches – reported enemy wire chiefly cut. Communication trenches throughout Trenches from front line trenches and elsewhere.	
	27/11/16	7.10 pm 10.5 pm	Occurrence SOS signal received from TR – hon left battalion Fired for 5 mins. Bombarded ONTARIO Fm for 108 FAB (O) 106 A/107 C/107	
		11.31 pm	TMB in support of 106 FAB on our right – fire stopped.	
		9.3 am	Fired all batteries for 20 mins on rigourigues while our infantry emitted gas. North Kopjes Battery.	
	28/11/16	all day	Batteries cutting wire - A/107 U12 a 34 B/107 U12 a 18 B/109 U12 c 658 C/107 U12 a 21.9	
		7.6.16.30 12.3 & at (?)	Harassed enemy errs bomed in support of gas attack by 4th Divison on our right and in retaliation of TMK rd on our immediate right with fire of B/107 B/109 and D/106	

Suggested Gas Attack 8353 Wt.W3541/1454 700,000 5/15 D.D.&L. A.D.S.S./Forms/C. 2118.

Army Form C. 2118.

WAR DIARY
or
INTELLIGENCE SUMMARY.
(Erase heading not required.)

XXXIII   107 FAB HQ.

Place	Date	Hour	Summary of Events and Information	Remarks and references to Appendices
Near Pozieres	June 3rd		Major Boulday Honours list. Officers.	
			Mentioned in despatches Lt Col D.R. Coates.	
			NCO's and men.	
			D.C.M. No 23442 Corporal W. Ross. (for gallantry as Shelter) duty in D/107 (cus) hrs B/107	
			Military Medal No 23402 Sergeant R.G. Wright (" " " ") HQ 107 FAB.	
			do. 66344 Bomb. B. Divvan (" " " ") A/107	
			do. 38441 Gunner H. Buttery (" " " ") HQ 107 FAB	
			do. 411428 Driver Cope (" " " ") A/107.	

J R Coates
Lt Col
O.C. 107 F.A.B.
3/6/16

"A" Battery.

REPORT ON ENEMY'S GAS EMISSION ON NIGHT OF 16th/17th June 1916.

At 12.30.p.m Gas Horns were heard in the Junction of PLOEGSTREET Wood. Battery "Stood to" at once. The Infantry called up on phone reported that gas was coming.

Gas seemed to pass to East of line WULVERGHEM CHURCH — T.17.a.2.0 so that battery got very little. The farm T.16.b.9½.4 was practically clear. The gas arrived at about 12.40p.m and remained for about 1 hour 1V mins. There being apparently 2 clouds emitted. Casualties Nil.

Hostile shelling feeble, 5.9s 4.2s & 77s a few fell short of guns but were mostly over. Rate about one per minute. A large number of duds. The Communication trench leading from Battle H.Q. to fort EBULY was blown in. I know of know regular barrage being put up.

O.P. had a few 4.2s and 77s on their right and practically no gas.

The gas was very visible.

The battery opened fire at about 12.30 a.m. on the front line parapet.

Between U.1.a.0.8. — ;0.31.d.11 firing H.E. and Shrapnel.

Owing to a verbal error the guns were firing at fifteen secs. instead of 30 secs. This was not corrected for some ten or twelve minutes. When Sec. fire 30 secs. was ordered At 1.5 am, Sec. fire 1 minute at 1.25 to 1.50 am. Sec. fire 2 minutes. At 1.5.am the range was shortened to bring fire into Middle of "No mans Land".
Total No. fired 233 rds.

The infantry did not volunteered any information but were repeatedly asked and gave information required. S.O.S. was not sent on phone, nor were any rockets reported to me.

Communication. All air lines were cut. The line buried in Communication trench running N. from Battle H.Q. was cut, though B/107 wire are only about 3 inches apart on same side of Trench.

Otherwise communication very satisfactory.

(Sd)' Galloway. Capt.R.F.A.
Commanding A/107 R.F.A.

"A" Battery.

REPORT ON ENEMY'S GAS EMISSION ON NIGHT OF 16th/17th June 1916.

At 12.30.p.m Gas Horns were heard in the Junction of PLOEGSTREET Wood. Battery "Stood to" at once. The Infantry called up on phone reported that gas was coming.

Gas seemed to pass to East of line WULVERGHEM CHURCH - T.17.a.2.0 so that battery got very little. The farm T.16.b.9½.4 was practically clear. The gas arrived at about 12.40p.m and remained for about 1 hour 1V mins. There being apparently 2 clouds emitted. Casualties Nil.

Hostile shelling feeble, 5.9s 4.2s & 77s a few fell short of guns but were mostly over. Rate about one per minute. A large number of duds. The Communication trench leading from Battle H.Q. to fort EBULY was blown in. I know of know regular barrage being put up.

O.P. had a few 4.2s and 77s on their right and practically no gas.

The gas was very visible.

The battery opened fire at about 12.30 a.m. on the front line parapet.

Between U.1.a.0.8. - .0.31.d.11 firing H.E. and Shrapnel.

Owing to a verbal error the guns were firing at fifteen secs. instead of 30 secs. This was not corrected for some ten or twelve minutes. When Sec. fire 30 secs. was ordered. At 1.5 am, Sec. fire 1 minute. At 1.25 to 1.50 am. Sec. fire 2 minutes. At 1.5.am the range was shortened to bring fire into Middle of "No mans Land".

Total No. fired 233 rds.

The infantry did not volunteer any information but were repeatedly asked and gave information required. S.O.S. was not sent on phone, nor were any rockets reported to me.

Communication. All air lines were cut. The line buried in Communication trench running N. from Battle H.Q. was cut, though B/107 wire are only about 3 inches apart on same side of Trench.

Otherwise communication very satisfactory.

(Sd) Galloway. Capt.R.F.A.
Commanding A/107 R.F.A.

"B" Battery.

Gas alarm was heard by the Guard about 12.30.am and buzzed through from the trenches at the same time. Duration of emission is not known. Gas was felt slightly at the Battery & O.P. and more strongly at the Wagon Line. Where grass is killed and all the metal work on the harness quite discoloured. There were no casualties.

Barrages were put up on the roads about T.18.N & T.17.c The battery was not fired on, but 30 or 40 4.2s (many of which were blinds) fell about T.16.b N.

The gas was liberated from U.2.a.19, U.21a.36, U.2.a.34, U.2.a.05, O.32.c.45.

Section fire 30" was opened at once, and the interval was shortly increased to 1" which rate was maintained. Except at one time when the Infantry complained of heavy shelling when section fire 30" was used, for a few minutes. H.E. & Shrapnel were used along the German front line. All guns had orders to drop onto the STEENEBEEK Line in case of S.O.S. but this Signal was never received.

On Bde.Orders the right section was switched onto trenches in U.2.a. to support 106 Bde.Group and the left section was then opened out to the right of our own zone. Rates of fire - RX Sec. fire 30" - LX Sec. fire 1' till these intervals were doubled by Group H.Q. Last round 1 salvoe at 4 HUNS FARM was fired about 1.50.a.m

Uninterrupted communication was maintained throughout with Group H.Q. Infantry, O.P. and Wagon Line and special rocket look-out men were posted at battery and O.P.

Total expended 131 A. 87 AX. Guns were immediately cleaned and show no signs this morning. All ranks at O.P. and battery wore Tower Respirators. Goggles were worn for a short time. Several men complained that the sponge appears to close over the eyepieces and obscure vision.

17/6/16.

(Sd. W.S.N.CURLE. Capt.R.F.A.
Commanding B/107 R.F.A.

"C" Battery.

1. Gas, Chlorine.
   Time of emission 12.30.a.m.
   Duration of emission Not known.
   Casualties Nil.

2. Shelling In the vicinity of the O.P. a few 77mm shrapnel were fired. A few stray shells burst near the battery position. A barrage seems to have been formed on the road at T.11.c.3.0 (near KEEPAWAY Fm.)

3. Ammunition expended.

   H.E. 29   S.114.

   In under a minute from hearing the gas hooters, was fire was opened i.e. between 12.30 and 12.31 am Rate of fire 2 rounds a min. Objective, trenches O.31.d.2.2. to O.31.d.8.4 - 10.2 and U.2.a.19 xxx sweeping 10' with all guns. Rate of fire changed to one round a minute, but time of alteration unknown.

   On an order from Bde.H.Q.at 12.50 (approx) fire was opened on S.O.S. line O&31.d.4.2. - U.1.b.5.5. at 2 rounds a minute after which rate was cut down down to 1 round per minute.

   At 1.15 am 5 salvoes were fired 2 at trenches O.31.d.2.2. - 8.4 - 10.2 and U.2.a.1.9, and 3 at Communication trenches O.31.d.2.2. - 8.4. O.31.d.8.4. - 10.6½ O.32.c.0.2.- 2.3 and O.32.c.1.1 - 3.2 after which fire was kept up on S.O.S. Lines until "cease firing" was ordered by Bde. H.Q. (time not noted.)

4. Hooters were heard on 17th Infantry Bde.front and almost immediately they were heard on 73rd Inf.Bde.front.
   Infantry kept us informed of the situation, arrival of gas etc. They stated that the Germans were not attacking. A green rocket was seen on 17th Inf.Bde.front.

5. Gas was visible. Cloud at battery was not very strong.

6. Communications, with exception of the lines to O.P., were satisfactory O.P. lines were broken about 1.15 am by SERPENTINE trench being blown in. Air lines were broken as well.

7. A soon as firing was over all steel work on guns were rubbed over, with oil so no corrosion was noticed as in the last attack.

(Sd) H.S.WURTELE. Capt.R.F.A.
Commanding C/107 R.F.A.

17/6/16.

B/109 Battery.

Report of F.O.O. at I.13.a.4.7.

1st Gas Cloud was emitted about 12.25 a.m. at which time Gas horns were heard to sound from direction of BIRTHDAY FARM.
The cloud took about 5 minutes to reach O.P. - Gas cloud hung round O.P. from 2 to 3 minutes.

During the whole of this time visual communication with front line trench was impossible -

2nd Gas Cloud reached O.P. at about 1.30 am and lasted about 20 minutes In the morning light the gas track was clearly visible and extends from a line joining O.31.d.8½.2¾ and U.1.d.4.8. to a line joining U.2.c.8¼.7½ and U.8.a. 4¼.7¾ -

This corresponds with direction the cloud was observed to travel during attack.
During the attack the "Cellars" and vicinity were regularly shelled with 77 mm. There were no casualties, nor was any damage donw to the O.P.
From direction of shelling both previously to and during the attack it was evident that the zone covered by 73rd I.B. was not the objective.

S.O.S.

Representative of R.Fusiliers on observation duty at the CELLARS sent up the S.O.S. signal - 1 green rocket, at about 12.45 am.
I did not observe any rockets go up from our trenches but Capt. Hill 2nd in command R.Fusiliers who was at the CELLARS, stated that he had seen a rocket go up and that he placed it about trench 135 or 136 Lt.Dallas R.F.A. (106 Bde) who came over to the CELLARS confirmed this. but did not appear to argue as regards the place.

The left of the Bde.Zone was shelled for about 2 hours previous to gas emission with 4.2s & 5.9s This appeared to continue during gas emission. The 17th I.B. were heavily shelled at the same time.

Report from Battery.

At about 12.30 am on the report of the first gas emission a slow rate of fire was opened with H.E. on enemy front line trenches at about 12.50 am S.O.S. was received from O.P. and fire was opened with shrapnel about 100" short of enemy's front line trench except on the left of our zone (about 1½ L. of S. bend) where no 4 gun dropped 250" to get into the dead ground of the STEENBEEK A rapid rate of fire was maintained for 2 or 3 minutes and then a slow rate of fire resumed on failure to obtain information of S.O.S. from our Infantry with whom we were in constant communication. About 1.a.m. one gun was turned on to assist 106 Bde at request of 107 Bde.H.Q. this gun fired at 1 minute interval on U.8.d.1½.½ to U.8.a.9½.8 - until cease firing was ordered by 107 Bde at about 2.p.m. The remainig three guns were spread to cover our own zone on the withdrawal of this gun, but kept on their S.O.S. lines - communication was good throughout.

Remarks.   I would draw attention to F.O.O's remark about - impossibil impossiblity of visual communication with front line during gas attack.

Shelling.   The battery was shelled with 4.2s & 5.9s during gas attack.

No casualties - No damage - The gas hung round the battery about 20 minutes during 1st emission, but 2nd emission passed S.E. of the battery.

Expenditure of ammunition

A - 95
AX - 36

17/6/16.
(Sd) 'J.GRIEVE Capt.R.F.A.
Commandg. B/109 R.F.A.

D/106 How. Battery.

First gas alarm heard on our right at 12.20.a.m.; on our front at 12.30.a.m.: gas reached the battery at 12.50.a.m. and helmets were kept on till 2.a.m. There were no casualties from the gas.

Shrapnel was fired at O.P. in the hedge on HILL 63; our trenches was shelled, but not heavily with H.E. and shrapnel till about 1.15 am and afterwards accassionally H.E. was fired at them.

The battery was shelled with about 30 H.E.Shrapnel. The base of 5.9 cm shell was found this morning. A barrage was put up over HILL 63 on the road by ORCHARD DUMP.

The battery fired 140 rounds, commencing at 12.35 a.m. on night lines till 1.45 am: one gun on PETITE DOUVE Fm. from 1.30.am till 2.am

Rate 2 rounds a minute.

No news was received from the Infantry and no S.O.S. Signal was seen.

The gas was visible, like an ordinary ground mist in appearance.

Communication was maintained with all stations without a hitch.

No gas appears to have been smelt East of RED LODGE; there was no gas at my detached gun at HYDE PARK CORNER.

The buzzer of the telephone at my O.P. had to be kept working to keep the contacts clean.

17/6/16.

(Sd) H.GARDINER. Capt.R.F.A.
O.C. D/106 R.F.A.

"B" Battery.

Gas alarm was heard by the Guard about 12.30.am and buzzed through from the trenches at the same time. Duration of emission is not known. Gas was felt slightly at the Battery & O.P. and more strongly at the Wagon-Line. Where grass is killed and all the metal work on the harness quite discoloured. There were no casualties.

Barrages were put up on the roads about T.18.a & T.17.c The battery was not fired on, but 30 or 40 4.2s (many of which were blinds) fell about T.16.b W.

The gas was liberated from U.2.a.19, U.21a.36, U.2.a.34, U.2.a.05, O.32.c.45.

Section fire 30" was opened at once, and the interval was shortly increased to 1" which rate was maintained. Except at one time when the Infantry complained of heavy shelling when section fire 30" was used, for a few minutes. H.E. & Shrapnel were used along the German front line. All guns had orders to drop onto the STEENEBEEK Line in case of S.O.S. but this Signal was never received.

On Bde.Orders the right section was switched onto trenches in U.2.d. to support 106 Bde.Group and the left section was then opened out to the right of our own zone. Rates of fire - RX Sec. fire 30" - LX Sec. fire 1' till these intervals were doubled by Group H.Q. Last round less 1 salvoe at 4 HUNS FARM was fired about 1.50.a.m

Uninterrupted communication was maintained throughout with Group H.Q. Infantry, O.P. and Wagon Line and special rocket look-out men were posted at battery and O.P.

Total expended 131 A. 87 AX. Guns were immediately cleaned and show no signs this morning. All ranks at O.P. and battery wore Tower Respirators. Goggles were worn for a short time. Several men complained that the sponge appears to close over the eyepieces and obscure vision.

17/6/16.
         (Sd. W.S.N.CURLE. Capt.R.F.A.
         Commanding B/107 R.F.A.

"C" Battery.

1. Gas, Chlorine.
   Time of emission 12.30.a.m.
   Duration of emission Not known.
   Casualties Nil.

2. Shelling In the vicinity of the O.P. a few 77mm shrapnel were fired. A few stray shells burst near the battery position. A barrage seems to have been formed on the road at T.11.c.3.0 (near KEEPAWAY Fm.)

3. Ammunition expended.

    H.E. 29   S.115.

   In under a minute from hearing the gas hooters, was fire was opened i.e. between 12.30 and 12.31 am Rate of fire 2 rounds a min. Objective, trenches O.31.d.2.2. to O.31.d.8.4 - 10.2 and U.2.a.19 xxx sweeping 10' with all guns. Rate of fire changed to one round a minute, but time of alteration unknown.

   On an order from Bde.H.Q. at 12.50 (approx) fire was opened on S.O.S. line O&31.d.4.2. - U.1.b.5.5. at 2 rounds a minute after which rate was cut down down to 1 round per minute.

   At 1.15 am 5 salvoes were fired 2 at trenches O.31.d.2.2. - 8.4 -10.2 and U.2.a.1.9. and 3 at Communication trenches O.31.d.2.2. - 8.4. O.31.d.8.4. - 10.6½   O.32.c.0.2.- 2.3 and O.32.c.1.1 - 3.2 after which fire was kept up on S.O.S. Lines until "cease firing" was ordered by Bde. H.Q. (time not noted.)

4. Hooters were heard on 17th Infantry Bde.front and almost immediately they were heard on 73rd Inf.Bde.front.
   Infantry kept us informed of the situation, arrival of gas etc. They stated that the Germans were not attacking. A green rocket was seen on 17th Inf.Bde.front.

5. Gas was visible. Cloud at battery was not very strong.

6. Communications, with exception of the lines to O.P., were satisfactory O.P. lines were broken about 1.15 am by SERPENTINE trench being blown in. Air lines were broken as well.

7. A soon as firing was over all steel work on guns were rubbed over, with oil so no corrosion was noticed as in the last attack.

                                            (Sd) H.S.WURTELE. Capt.R.F.A.
17/6/16.   Commanding C/107 R.F.A.

B/109 Battery.

Report of F.O.O. at I.13.a.4.7.

1st Gas Cloud was emitted about 12.25 a.m. at which time Gas horns were heard to sound from direction of BIRTHDAY FARM.
The cloud took about 5 minutes to reach O.P. - Gas cloud hung round O.P. from 2 to 3 minutes.

During the whole of this time visual communication with front line trench was impossible -

2nd Gas Cloud reached O.P. at about 1.30 am and lasted about 20 minutes In the morning light the gas track wad clearly visible and extends from a line joining O.31.d.8½.2¾ and U.1.d.4.8. to a line joining U.2.c.8¼.7½ and U.8.a. 4¼.7¾ -
This corresponds with direction the cloud was observed to travel during attack.
During the attack the "Cellars" and vicinity were regularly shelled with 77 mm. There were no casualties, nor was any damage donw to the O.P.
From direction of shelling both previously to and during the attack it was evident that the zone covered by 73rd I.B. was not the objective.

S.O.S.

Representative of R.Fusiliers on observation duty at the CELLARS sent up the S.O.S. signal -: 1 green rocket, at about 12.45 am.
I did not observe any rockets go up from our trenches but Capt. Hill 2nd in command R.Fusiliers who was at the CELLARS, stated that he had seen a rocket go up and that he placed it about trench 135 or 136 Lt.Dallas R.F.A. (106 Bde) who came over to the CELLARS confirmed this. but did not appear to argue as regards the place.

The left of the Bde.Zone was shelled for about 2 hours previous to gas emission with 4.2s & 5.9s This appeared to continue during gas emission. The 17th I.B. were heavily shelled at the same time.

Report from Battery.

At about 12.30 am on the report of the first gas emission a slow rate of fire was opened with H.E. on enemy front line trenches at about 12.50 am S.O.S. was received from O.P. and fire was opened with shrapnel about 100" short of enemy's front line trench except on the left of our zone (about 1½ L. of S. bend) where no 4 gun dropped 250" to get into the dead ground of the STEENBEEK A rapid rate of fire was maintained for 2 or 3 minutes and then a slow rate of fire resumed on failure to obtain information of S.O.S. from our Infantry with whom we were in constant communication. About 1.a.m. one gun was turned on to assist 106 Bde at request of 107 Bde.H.Q. this gun fired at 1 minute interval on U.8.d.1½.½ to U.8.a.9½.8 - until cease firing was ordered by 107 Bde at about 2.p.m. The remainig three guns were spread to cover our own zone on the withdrawal of this gun, but kept on their S.O.S. lines - communication was good throughout.

Remarks.   I would draw attention to F.O.O's remark about - impossibility of visual communication with front line during gas attack.

Shelling.   The battery was shelled with 4.2s & 5.9s during gas attack.

No casualties – No damage – The gas hung round the battery about 20 minutes during 1st emission, but 2nd emission passed S.E. of the battery.

Expenditure of ammunition

                A – 95
              AX – 36

17/6/16.

                                        (Sd) J. GRIEVE Capt. R.F.A.
                                          Commandg. B/109 R.F.A.

D/106 How. Battery.

First gas alarm heard on our right at 12.20.a.m.; on our front at 12.30.a.m.: gas reached the battery at 12.50.a.m. and helmets were kept on till 2.a.m. There were no casualties from the gas.

Shrapnel was fired at O.P. in the hedge on HILL 63; our trenches was shelled, but not heavily with H.E. and shrapnel till about 1.15 am and afterwards accassionally H.E. was fired at them.

The battery was shelled with about 30 H.E.Shrapnel. The base of 5.9 cm shell was found this morning. A barrage was put up over HILL 63 on the road by ORCHARD DUMP.

The battery fired 140 rounds, commencing at 12.36 a.m. on night lines till 1.45 am: one gun on PETITE DOUVE Fm. from 1.30.am till 2.am

Rate 2 rounds a minute.

No news was received from the Infantry and no S.O.S. Signal was seen.

The gas was visible, like an ordinary ground mist in appearance.

Communication was maintained with all stations without a hitch.

No gas appears to have been smelt East of RED LODGE; there was no gas at my detached gun at HYDE PARK CORNER.

The buzzer of the telephone at my O.P. had to be kept working to keep the contacts clean.

(Sd) H.GARDINER. Capt.R.F.A.
O.C. D/106 R.F.A.

17/6/16.

OPERATION ORDERS No. 10

BY

LT. COLONEL D.R. COATES,   COMMANDING 107 F.A.B. GROUP.

Copy No. 1.   SECRET.   27th June 1916.

1. Wire will be cut to-morrow between 9.a.m. and 12 noon.

2. B/107, C/107, and B/109 will enlarge the lanes already made; A/107 will concentrate on U 1 a 4½.6½ to ensure that a lane is cut at this point.

3. Ammunition allowance - B/107, C/107, B/109, 150 rounds per Battery - A/107 200 rounds (up to 300 if necessary).

4. Times of firing

        9.am   - 10.30.am   A/107   B/107.
        10.30. - 12 noon   C/107   B/109.

5. Z/24 T.M., will register U 1 a 4.7 at 9.45.am under cover of A/107s fire.

6. D/106 will be ready to retaliate if necessary.

Copy No. 1 War Diary.
      2 A/107.
      3 B/107.
      4 C/107.
      5 B/109.
      6 D/106.
      7 B.M. 7 Anzacs.
      8 B.M. 24 D.A.

Lieut. R.F.A.
Adjutant, 107/F.A/Brigade.

7TH AUSTRALIAN INFANTRY BRIGADE ORDER NO. 20.

30th June 1916.   No. 31/71

SECRET

1. Gas will be discharged from those trenches in which it is installed on the 7th Australian Infantry Brigade front, on the first occasion during hours of darkness tonight or on subsequent nights when the wind is favourable.

2. Smoke will also be discharged at the same time from Trenches 136 to 140 inclusive. If necessary discharges from trenches 139, 140 and The DIAGONAL will take place independently.

3. If possible two successive discharges of gas (the first of 5 minutes duration and the second to last until the cylinders are empty) will take place from each trench, with an interval of not less than 1½ hours between such successive discharges. It will be decided at the time of the first discharge whether it is likely that a favourable wind and darkness will last sufficiently long to admit of a second discharge taking place that night, if not cylinders will be emptied at the first discharge.

4. The cylinders installed in the various trenches concerned may be discharged simultaneously or at different times as may be most favourable in view of the wind condition. Whatever gas is discharged from any trench on the Brigade front smoke should be discharged along all the Brigade front for 20 minutes, commencing 5 minutes after the gas.

5. Brigade Bomb Officer will be responsible that the necessary smoke bombs and smoke candles are discharged under instructions that have already been issued to him.

6. O.C. 107th Brigade R.F.A. will receive special orders from C.R.A. regarding artillery co-operation.

7. Half an hour before the time selected for the gas discharge Capt. Blacket with 27th Battalion will, after consultation with special officer "E" Company R.E., send the following message to Brigade Headquarters - "Blacket will report at -- p.m." Time mentioned in the message will be the hour gas is discharged.

8. Three minutes after gas discharge has commenced Artillery will be asked to open fire.

9. Capt. Blacket will ensure that gas is not let off from any of the trenches if the wind would cause the gas to travel in a more Northerly direction than 58 degrees. *true bearing*

10. Watches will be synchronised from Brigade Signal Office at 9 p.m. every night.

11. All instructions and precautions in 7th Australian Infantry Brigade Order No.19 will be carried out.

12. Great care must be taken to avoid using the telephone in such a way as to indicate to the enemy, if overheard, that any operation and the use of gas is contemplated.

13. Should the discharge take place tonight it will not be before 12 midnight.

14. Transport in the trench areas will be reduced to a minimum tonight and until further notice, and carts should be clear if possible by midnight.

15. 7th Bde Machine Gun Coy. will co-operate during bombardment as ordered in Operation Order No.19.

16. Acknowledge.

Copy No.1 War Diary
2 Capt. Blacket
3 Special Off. "E" Coy.
4 27th Bn.
5 28th Bn.
6 B/M/Officer
7 O.C. 107th Bde R.F.A.
8 7th Bde M/Gun Coy.

G. Rowan-Hamilton
Capt.
Brigade Major,
7th Aust. Infantry Bde.

Issued at 6.30 p.m.

COPY NO. 14

SECRET.

7TH AUSTRALIAN INFANTRY BRIGADE ORDER NO. 19.

Reference Sheet 28 S.W. 4. 1/10,000.

1. Minor enterprises to inflict losses on the enemy, to obtain identifications or to capture prisoners, to capture a gas cylinder and generally do as much damage as possible to the enemy will be carried out by the Brigades named below:
    17th Infantry Brigade.
    7th Australian Infantry Brigade.
    72nd Infantry Brigade.
The date on which these enterprises are to take place will be notified later by the 24th Division as also the Zero hour.
These enterprises will be carried out with the assistance of gas and smoke if the weather is favourable, otherwise gas and smoke will not be used.

2. A party composed of Officers and Other Ranks drawn from the 25th & 27th Bns. 7th Australian Infantry Brigade will leave our trenches from about U 1 a 3¼ 2 and enter enemy's trenches about U 1 a 4½ 6½.

3. Information concerning hostile trenches and the portion of NO MAN'S LAND to be traversed has already been communicated to all concerned.

4. ARTILLERY.   The following artillery is available to support attack :-
Centre Group of 24th Divisional Artillery, consisting of 4 18 pdr. batteries, 1 4.5 howitzer battery, 2 2" trench mortars and 1 6" howitzer gun.
During the preceding days wire-cutting will have been carried out in different places on the enemy's front, and a path cut in enemy's wire at proposed point of entry.
On the night selected for the attack supporting artillery commencing at Zero time will bombard enemy's front line trenches - actual tasks shown on artillery orders attached.
At 0.4 Zero time 4.5 howitzer and 2" trench mortars lift on to targets in rear.
At 0.9 Zero time a barrage is formed round the objective.
On receipt of information that our party is clear (about 0.31) artillery will again drop on to front line trenches, and at 0.36 artillery will cease fire.
The artillery Liaison Officer will be situated in our front trenches in telephonic communication with Brigade Headquarters and take up a position in Company Signal Office at U 1 a 5 1.
Time table attached shows times artillery bombardments commence and barrages are placed.

5. COMPOSITION OF PARTIES:-

O.C. Attack	Capt. Page 25th Bn.
Scouts	Lt. Southon 27th Bn. & 6 O/R's
Right Bombing Party	Lt. Julge 27th Bn. & 7 O/R's
Left Bombing Party	Lt. Stuart 25th Bn. & 7 O/R's.
Right Blocking Party	5 O/R's.
Left Blocking Party	5 O/R's.
Covering Party	14 O/R's.
Stretcher Bearers	4 O/R's. with 4 stretchers.
Telephonist & Linesman	2 O/R's.
Engineers	2 O/R's. with explosives.
Runners	2 O/R's.
Intelligence men	2 O/R's.
Carriers for Gas Cylinders if found	2 O/R's.

6. Instructions have already been issued regarding the preparation of trenches and the installation of the gas cylinders.

The Officer Commanding the Special Company R.E. will be responsible for the inspection of the cylinders in the trenches, for the attachment of pipes to cylinders, and for the discharge of the gas and smoke on the night selected.

Additional men will be required to assist in the discharge of smoke, and will be detailed for this purpose by Brigade Headquarters.

Arrangements will also be made for the gas helmets of parties taking part in the enterprise and of garrison in the fire trenches to be inspected by Div. Gas personnel prior to the night of the enterprise.

Whilst "White Star" gas cylinders are being discharged all ranks in front and support trenches will wear gas helmets or box respirators.

A time table is attached showing time of artillery bombardment and release of gas.

No smoke will be released from the Diagonal.

While gas is being released garrison of Trenches 139 & 140 will be withdrawn except one man per bay.

Trenches will not be manned till ½ hour after gas has been discharged.

Personnel for discharging gas will not enter DIAGONAL till 1 hour Zero time and this party will remain in FORT OSBORNE Barracks until required for the DIAGONAL.

7. DUTIES. Raiding Party will leave our trenches as per time-table.

Scouts will leave our trenches first, followed by one telephonist and one linesman laying wire as they go.

Remainder of party will follow as arranged by O.C. Attack and will lie down under cover and wait for the artillery to commence, and after 4 minutes bombardment they will move forward again.

As soon as artillery lift scouts will move forward and report where wire is well out.

The Assault Party will enter enemy's trenches and will act as ordered by the O.C. They will not go more than 50 yds to either flank and more than 25 yds down the hostile communication trenches.

Signallers will open communication from a point just outside the enemy's parapet.

The covering party will leave our trenches immediately behind the Assault Party and will cover the flanks while halted in NO MAN's LAND, moving forward and doing the same work while the Assault Party are in the enemy's trenches. They will be available to help in bringing back prisoners and wounded and will cover the Assault Party with smoke bombs when it withdraws if required. The men for escorts for prisoners should be detailed beforehand.

Engineers with explosives will accompany scouts either to complete destruction of enemy's wire, or destroy machine gun emplacements or trench mortars found in the enemy's trenches.

Two men detailed to carry gas cylinders will search enemy's trenches for a full or empty specimen and return with it at once. They will be provided with a pole for carrying the cylinder.

O.C. Attack will remain at point of entry and will direct operations by means of his two runners.

Intelligence men will search trenches and enemy dead collecting identifications, correspondence etc., and will take a sack with them for this purpose.

While party is in enemy's trenches, scouts will break down enemy's parapet to improve means of egress, and will lay back luminous tape (white) from this point in the direction of our own trenches.

8. The Raiders will proceed to PLUS DOUCE in small parties arriving at 9 p.m. Transport as far as the SHRINE will be provided.

Raiding Party will be examined at PLUS DOUCE to make sure that there are no means whereby the enemy might discover to which unit or formation they belong.

The Raiding Party proceed to Trench 142 via MEDICINE HAT TRAIL - KING EDWARD'S TRENCH - BOYLES FARM. Returning after operation the same way.

O.C. "B" Bn. will detail two guides to report to O.C. Attack at

9.30 p.m. at PLUS DOUCE. These men should be thoroughly conversant with the trenches and communications between PLUS DOUCE and the DIAGONAL.

9. Raiding Party will have their faces and hands blackened, and will wear gas helmets rolled up on their heads, and white bands on each arm; this band will be covered by some dark material tacked lightly on and which will be removed before entering the enemy's trenches.

All men taking part in the raid will be warned that if captured they should give no information to the enemy other than their rank and name.

The men of each bombing and blocking party will be numbered in order to facilitate identification. The Right Bombing Party will be numbered 1 to 7, Left Bombing Party 8 to 14 and so on. By this means if they wish to identify each other they need only quote their numbers. Officers will know that they are responsible for numbers 1 to 7 or 8 to 14 as the case may be when collecting their men when withdrawing. Otherwise dress and equipment will be as ordered by O.C. Attack.

10. The code signal notifying when the raid will take place will be as follows, and will be sent to all concerned on the day fixed :-

"Mail leaves at - - - p.m. tonight AAA Acknowledge.

Zero time will be the time given on the above message.

As soon as possible after reaching and entering enemy's trenches telephonist will send the following signal message - "ETD", as sokn as the raiders have left the hostile trenches - "AC".

The above messages will be checked back and reported to Brigade Headquarters immediately.

The signal for the Raiders to leave the enemy's trenches will be green very lights fired obliquely by O.C. Attack or his representative. In addition to this runners will be available to warn parties to withdraw. In default of any signals the parties will leave the hostile trenches 10 minutes after entering. The Officer on duty in trenches should report to Brigade Headquarters if he sees the green very light signals.

11. 7th Brigade Trench Mortar Battery will co-operate and will fire from the DIAGONAL on to enemy's front line trench from U 1 a 2 7 to U 1 a 3½ 7, commencing at 0.9 Zero till 0.28. Rate of fire 20 rounds per Battery per minute.

12. O.C. "B" Bn. will arrange for two good signallers to be put in charge of the Company telephone in dugout which is being used by O.C. Attack.

The telephone line that is taken out with Raiding Party will be connected up with nearest Company Signal Office in the front line U 1 a 5 1. A line will also be laid from 2" Trench Mortar Battery position to the same Company Signal Office and the F.O.O. will be in direct communication with Centre Group Commander.

13. MACHINE GUNS   O.C. 7th Brigade Machine Gun Company will arrange to enfilade enemy's front line from U 1 a 2½ 6¾ to U 1 a 4 7½ from a position in rear of our front line selected by him. He will also enfilade enemy's communication trench with indirect fire from O 31 c 9 1 to O 31 d 7½ 4½. He will also sweep WULVERGHEM-MESSINES ROAD from O 32 c 3½ 0 to O 32 d 5 3.

Other machine guns will stand by ready to engage with direct fire hostile machine guns if they come into action.

They will not fire across the area within the following points until the raiders have returned :-
U 1 a 7 1½ - U 1 a 6½ 6¾ - U 1 a 2½ 7 6¾ - U 1 a 0 2.

14. Any prisoners captured should be hurried back to our lines as soon as possible via MEDICINE HAT TRAIL to PLUS DOUCE FARM. They will not be interrogated or allowed to talk among themselves. If necessary they will be kept separate.

O.C. "B" Bn. will detail a guard to take charge of prisoners to be at PLUS DOUCE FARM at 10.30 p.m.

Prisoners will be brought back with Raiding Party in transport from the SHRINE to Brigade Headquarters.

15. From the 24th inst. watches will be synchronised at 9 a.m. and 6 p.m., Divisional time being given by Brigade Headquarters Signal Section.

16. All units in the 7th Brigade Area will be warned that these operations are likely to provoke retaliation. They will be so disposed as to be as little vulnerable as possible to hostile shell fire.

   No working parties will be employed on the night on which the operation takes place, and the transport other than that for the raiders will be taken down to dumps.

17. O.C. "B" Bn. will arrange for 6 stretchers to be placed in the front line near BOYLES FARM and will arrange for Medical Officer to be in readiness to deal with any casualties.

   O.C. "D" Bn. will send his Medical Officer to "B" Bn. Headquarters to report by 11 p.m. to give additional assistance and will put 4 of his stretchers at the disposal of O.C. Raid to be used by his stretcher bearers.

18. The result of the operation will be reported by "priority" wire to Brigade Headquarters and O.C. Raid and intelligence men will report to Brigade Headquarters on their way back to billets.

19. Machine Gunners will take advantage of hostile working parties repairing damage caused by our artillery fire after operations have ceased.

20. Reports to Brigade Headquarters.

21. Acknowledge.

[signature]
Capt.
Brigade Major,
7th Australian Infantry Brigade.

```
Copy No.  1      G.O.C.
          2      War Diary
          3      File
       4 & 5     O.C. Attack
          6      25th Bn.
          7      26th Bn.
          8      27th Bn.
          9      28th Bn.
         10      7th Bde M/G/Coy.
         11      7th Bde T/M/Batt.
         12      6th Field Co. Aus Engrs.
         13      Bde T/Officer
         14      O.C. 107th Bde R.F.A.
         15      2nd Aus. Infy. Bde.
         16      17th Infy. Bde.
         17      72nd Infy. Bde.
      25&18      24th Division.
         19      D.T.M.O.
         20      O.C. "K" Co. R.E.
         21      2nd Aust. Div.
    22, 23, 24   Spare.
```

SECRET

7TH AUSTRALIAN INFANTRY BRIGADE ORDER NO.19.

TIME TABLE "A" (With Gas and Smoke)

TIME	OPERATION	REMARKS
Minus 4	Raiding Parties leave our trenches and advance to selected positions in NO MAN's LAND.	Establishing communication from here by telephone.
0.0. Zero	Artillery Bombardment commences. Gas released from 139 and 140 Trenches.	
0.3.	Smoke commences along Trenches 139 & 140 and remainder of front except DIAGONAL.	
0.4.	4.2. Howitzers and 2" Mortars lift on to other targets.	
0.9	Gas ceases. Smoke continues from 139 and 140 Trenches. Artillery Lift.	
0.11	Raiding Parties advance on enemy's trenches.	Withdrawal covered by smoke bombs thrown, if required, by covering party. O.C. will use his discretion as regards returning immediately to our trenches or not.
0.31 (about)	Artillery bring back fire on to enemy's front trenches if message from Raiding Party "AC" is received.	
0.35 (about)	Artillery cease fire.	
1.50 to 1.55.	Second gas discharge from Trenches 139 & 140. First Gas discharge from DIAGONAL	
1.52	Bombardment by Divisional Artillery on Front Line.	
3.15 to 3.20	3rd Gas discharge if any gas remaining.	
3.17	Bombardment by Divisional Artillery on enemy front line.	NOTE. - If weather is not suitable for use of gas or smoke, operations will be carried out at the same times but without smoke.

SECRET.   COPY No. 14

           7th AUSTRALIAN INFANTRY BRIGADE.

        Amendments to OPERATION ORDER NO. 19.   27/6/16.

                    ※※※※※※※※※※※※

Reference Sheet 28 & S.W. 4 1/10,000

Para 4, line 12.   Omit "4.5 Howitzer and"
                   Add after "in rear" line 13 "at 0f zero time 4.5
                   Howitzers lift on to other targets".

Para 6.   Add at end of paragraph.-
                   "Captain J.W. Blacket, 27th Battalion, O.C. Company
                   garrisoning trench 141 to 142 and Diagonal will be
                   responsible for saying whether or not gas will be
                   discharged from our trenches either at zero or at
                   the later times. He will be assisted by the officer
                   of the Special Company R.E. (Lt Stuart) who will
                   advise him. His decision should be made after
                   taking into consideration.-
                        (a) The direction of the wind with reference
                            to the trenches, when the gas is to be
                            discharged and also of adjoining trenches.
                        (b) Whether any of our wounded are still in
                            front of our parapets.
                       Capt. Blacket will also supervise the work
                   in the Company Signal Office, keep in touch
                   with the Liaison officer. He will assist
                   O.C. Attack as much as possible.
                       All instructions regarding the throwing of
                   smoke bombs and smoke candles have been issued
                   to all concerned".

Line 7.   Time Table. Erase "4.2 Howitzers and"
                   Add a new line after line 7.-
                   "0.6 4.2 Howitzers lift on to targets in rear".

                                                 [signature]
                                                      Capt.
                                                 Brigade Major,
                                                 7th Aust Inf Brigade.

SECRET.

Reference Sheet 28.S.W.   S.22.

106th F.A.B.Group.
107th   "   "   "
108th   "   "   "
151st   "   "   "   (For information.)
41st DIV. ARTY. ("   "   )
Heavy Arty. V.Corps. (For information.)

1. Gas and smoke will be discharged from the 2nd Aust.I.B. and 7th Aust.I.B. fronts. This will take place on first favourable night, from to-night inclusive. The G.O.C., Inf. Bde. concerned will decide when this is to take place.

2. The gas may be discharged at one period, or in two periods with an interval of at least 1½ hours between them. Smoke will last for 20 minutes commencing 5 minutes after gas discharge begins.

3. Half an hour before the time selected for a gas discharge, the G.O.C., Inf. Bde. will send a pre-arranged signal to the Artillery Group Commander as a warning. Batteries will then be ready to open fire at the hour selected. Three minutes after actual discharge has commenced, a message will be sent to the Group Commander asking for the immediate opening of fire.

    The Group will then bombard enemy's trenches for 20 minutes.

    There is no ammunition limit for this.

4. (i) During discharge on 106th F.A.B. zone, the 107th F.A.B. will fire with the batteries told off for the arranged overlap.

    The 41st Div.Arty. will also be asked to fire their overlap in support of 106th F.A.B.

    (ii) During discharge on 107th F.A.B. zone, the 106th & 108th F.A.B's will fire on their overlap on 107th F.A.B. zone.

    (iii) The Group Commanders, 106th & 107th Bdes. will notify flank brigades of the time for "overlap" batteries to open.

5. The Heavy Artillery, V.Corps will be asked to undertake counter-battery work, upon reports being received from Groups of the hostile batteries that have opened.

6. Transport in the trench area affected will be reduced to a minimum till further notice.

7. Special care should be taken in using the telephone, not to give any indication of the proposed operation, in case of over-hearing by the enemy.

8. Acknowledge.

29/6/16.   Captain.R.A.

                                    Brigade Major, 24th Divisional Artillery.

OPERATION ORDERS No.9

by

LT. COLONEL D.R. COATES,   COMMANDING 107 F.A.B. GROUP.

Copy No. I..   S E C R E T.   26th June 1916.

1. A raid on the enemy's trenches will be carried out by our Infantry on a date and at a zero time to be notified later.

2. The firing schedule of each Battery is attached. Fire is divided into 5 PHASES; of these PHASES 1, 2, 4 and 5 are fired by Schedule time. Phase 3 is fired on receipt of the Signal "AC" — from Brigade H.Q. *for guns – from LIAISON Officer at Company H.Q. for T.M's.*

3. Batteries will be prepared to fire the programmes herewith at any time after receipt of these orders.

4. Zero time will be telephoned personally by the Adjutant to B.C's about an hour before firing is to commence. Watches to be checked at the same time.

5. Special orders will be issued to the LIAISON OFFICER on duty.

6. The telephonist on duty at the Battery is to be made acquainted with the fact, that, he is to expect the signal "AC" in order to avoid unnecessary repetitions.

Copy No. 1 War Diary.
        2 A/107.
        3 B/107.
        4 C/107.
        5 B/109.
        6 D/106.
        7 O.C 24 T.Ms.
        8 B.M 24 D.A.
        9 B.M 7 Anzacs.

                                        Lieut. R.F.A.
                                Adjutant, 107/F.A/Brigade.

OPERATION ORDERS No. 9.　　　　　　SCHEDULE FOR A/107.

TIME	No. OF GUNS.	OBJECTIVE.	RATE.	"A" or "AX"	REMARKS.	
.04 to Zero		——— NO FIRING ———				
Zero to .05	All	Wire on Front line U 1 a 4.7 to U 1 a 5.6	XF 10"	"AX"	Sweep	))) PHASE 1.)
.05 to .09	All	FRONT LINE. " " " "	XF 5"	"AX"	"	)))
.09 to .31 (about)	All	Area U 1 a 1½ 7½ U 1 a 3.8 O 31 c 4½ 0	XF 10"	"A"	Search and sweep. Barrage	PHASE 2.
Fire of PHASE 2 will be continued until the signal "AC" is telephoned from Brigade H.Q., when it will be brought back to continue 5 minutes, and stop.						PHASE 3,
.31 to .36 (about)	All	Front line U 1 a 4.7 to U 1 a 5.6	XF 15"	50% AX 50% A	Sweep.	PHASE 3.
1.52 to 2.2		Search and sweep on Night lines with 60 rounds - half "A" and half "AX" at irregular intervals.				PHASE 4.
3.17 to 3.27		Search and sweep on Night lines with 60 rounds - half "A" and half "AX" at irregular intervals.				PHASE 5.

OPERATION ORDERS No.9.   SCHEDULE FOR B/107.

TIME.	No. OF GUNS.	OBJECTIVE.	RATE.	"A" or "AX"	REMARKS.	
.04 to Zero		NO FIRING				
Zero to .05	One	M.G. U 1 a 5½ 6	XF 10"	"AX"		)
	One	M.G. U 1 a 6½ 6	XF 10"	"AX"		)
	One	U 1 a 6½ 6 to U 1 a 7½ 9½	XF 10"	50% AX 50% A	Search	)))
	One	O 31 d 8.5 to U 2 a 1.9	XF 10"	50% AX 50% A	Search & sweep Front line & CME trenches.	)))) PHASE) 1.
.05 to .09	One	M.G. U 1 a 5½ 6	XF 5"	"AX"		)
	One	M.G. U 1 a 6½ 6	XF 5"	"AX"		)
	One	U 1 a 6½ 6 to U 1 a 7½ 9½	XF 5"	50% AX 50% A	Search	)))
	One	O 31 d 8.5 to U 2 a 1.9	XF 10"	50% AX 50% A	Search & sweep Front line, support & CME trenches	))))
.09 to .31 (about)	All	O 31 c 9.1 to U 2 a 1.9	XF 15"	50% AX 50% A	Search and sweep.	PHASE 2.
	Fire of PHASE 2 will be continued until the signal "AC" is telephoned from Brigade H.Q., when it will be brought back to PHASE 3, continue 5 minutes, and stop.					
.31 to .36 (about)	~~One~~ Two.	U 1 a 5½ 6 to U 1 a 6½ 6	XF 15"	50% AX 50% A	Sweep.	)) PHASE
	One	U 1 a 6½ 6 to U 1 a 7½ 9½	XF 15"	"	~~Sweep.~~ SEARCH.	) 3)
	~~Two~~ ONE.	O 31 d 8.5 to U 2 a 1.9	XF 15"	"	Search & sweep	)
1.52 to 2.2	Search and sweep on Night lines with 60 rounds – half "A" and half "AX" at irregular intervals.					PHASE 4
3.17 to 3.27	Search and sweep on Night lines with 60 rounds – half "A" and half "AX" at irregular intervals.					PHASE 5.

OPERATION ORDERS No.9.   SCHEDULE FOR C/107.

TIME.	No. OF GUNS.	OBJECTIVE.	RATE.	"A" or "AX"	REMARKS.	
.04 to Zero	------NO FIRING------					
Zero to .05	All	Front line U 1 a 4.7 to U 1 a 1.7	XF 10"	"AX"	Sweep)	PHASE 1.
.05 to .09	All	" " " " "	XF 5"	"AX"	Sweep)	
.09 to .31 (about)	All	O 31 c 4½ 0 to U 1 a 7.8	XF 10" barrage	"A"	Search & sweep	PHASE 2.
Fire of PHASE 2 will be <u>continued until the signal "AC"</u> is telephoned from Brigade H.Q., when it will be brought back to PHASE 3, continue 5 minutes, and stop.						
.31 to .36 (about)	All	Front line U 1 a 4.7 to U 1 a 1.7	XF 15"	50% AX 50% A	Search & sweep.	PHASE 3.
1.52 to 2.2	Search and sweep on Night lines with 60 rounds - half "A" and half "AX" at irregular intervals.					PHASE 4.
3.17 to 3.27	Search and sweep on Night lines with 60 rounds - half "A" and half "AX" at irregular intervals.					PHASE 5.

OPERATION ORDERS No.9.   SCHEDULE FOR B/109.

TIME	No. OF GUNS.	OBJECTIVE.	RATE.	"A" or "AX"	REMARKS.	
.04 to Zero		——————— NO FIRING ———————				
Zero to .09	All	Front line U 2 a 1.9 to U 2 d 1.5	XF 10"	50% AX 50% A	Front line CME & support trenches.	PHASE 1.
.09 to .31 (about)	All	" " " "	XF 15"	50% AX 50% A	" " "	PHASE 2.

Fire of PHASE 2 will be <u>continued until the signal "AC" is</u> telephoned from Brigade H.Q., when it will be brought back to PHASE 3, continue 5 minutes, and stop.

.31 to .36 (about)	All	Front line U 2 a 1.9 to U 2 d 1.5	XF 15"	50% AX 50% A	Front line CME and support trenches	PHASE 3.
1.52 to 2.2		Search and sweep on night lines with 60 rounds - half "A" and half "AX" at irregular intervals.				PHASE 4.
3.17 to 3.27		Search and sweep on Night lines with 60 rounds - half "A" and half "AX" at irregular intervals.				PHASE 5.

OPERATION ORDERS No.9.   SCHEDULE FOR SECTION OF Z/24 T.M.BATTY.

TIME.	No. OF GUNS.	OBJECTIVE.	RATE.	REMARKS.	
.04 to Zero		——————— NO FIRING ———————			
Zero to .04	Two	Wire on Front line U 1 a 5.6 to U 1 a 4½ 6½	XF 30"		)))) PHASE 1.
.04 to .05	Two	M.G. U 1 a 4.7	XF 30"	Two rounds only.	)
.05 to .31 (about)	One One	U 1 a 4½ 8½ U 1 a 5½ 8½	XF 1" XF 1"		))) PHASE 2.)

Fire of PHASE 2 will be continued until raiders return to our trenches when fire will be brought back to PHASE 3, continue for 5 minutes and stop.

.31 to .36 (about.)	Two	Front line U 1 a 3.6 to U 1 a 4.6½	XF 1"		PHASE 3
1.52 to 2.2	Two guns exactly as in PHASE 3.				PHASE 4.
3.17 to 3.27	" " " " " " 4.				PHASE 5.

The signal to commence PHASE 3 ("AC") will be telephoned by the LIAISON OFFICER at Company H.Q. to B.C. "Z"/24 T.M.Battery.

APPENDIX TO OPERATION ORDERS No.9.

Orders for 2/Lieut. T.G. Jefferies, C/107.

1. You will be LIAISON OFFICER on Duty with the Infantry on the night

2. Your post will be at Right Company H.Q. of Left Battalion at BOYLES FARM (U 1 a 5.1)

3. Your pricipal duties are :-

   (a) To communicate Zero time to O.C. Z/24 T.M's who will report to you at BOYLE'S FARM.

   (b) To send the signal "AC" to 107 F.A.B. H.Q. and O.C. Z/24 T.M.Battery, who will be with his guns, as soon as the raiding party has returned to the trenches.

   (c) To keep 107 F.A.B.,H.Q. informed of the progress of the fight and of any unusual occurrence.

4. You will proceed (accompanied by 2/Lt. F.J.Taylor) to Left Battn. H.Q. reporting there by 6.30.pm; you will disconnect the metallic telephone line of C/107 from the Battalion Switchboard in such a way that the Battalion Signallers are unable to use it, making a through connection from Company H.Q. at BOYLE'S Fm. direct to 107 F.A.B.,H.Q. You will take a signaller with you and post him at Left Battalion H.Q. to see the wires are not interfered with.

5. You will then proceed to Company H.Q. and get into touch with O.C. Z/24 T.M. Battery, test your wires to his guns and to Brigade H.Q. You will see that both these wires are tested half-hourly.

6. Zero time will be telephoned you personally by the Adjutant who will say "I shall see you at (zero time)" You will answer "I shall be here".

7. Immediately the raiders return you will give the signal "AC" by voice to the Adjutant and O.C. Z/24 T.M's.

8. You will avoid any unnecessary talking on the wires.

9. You will not leave your post at BOYLE'S Fm. until the Adjutant telephones you may do so.

10. On relief you will re-establish the metallic circuit of C/107 to Battn.H.Q.

Copy No.1 War Diary.
     2 Liaison Officer.
     3 O.C. C/107.
     4 B.M. 7 Anzacs.
     5 B.M. 24 D.A.

, Lieut.R.F.A.
Adjutant, 107/F.A/Brigade.

OPERATION ORDERS No. 13.

by

LT. COLONEL D.R. COATES,   COMMANDING 107 F.A.B.GROUP.

Copy No. 1.   SECRET.   29th June 1916.

1. To be read in conjunction with Operation Orders No. 12.

2. Gas will be emitted on the 106th Bde. front also on favourable night.

3. B/107 and B/109 must be ready to give Retaliation as in Appendix 3, Operation Order No. 1, searching Communication and Support trenches.

4. Orders will be :-

   Right Retaliation   ...p.m. or ...a.m.

5. D/106 will fire on LA PETITE DOUVE FARM, front line, communication and support trenches in rear.

6. Rate of fire etc for 18 prs. as in Operation Order No. 12.
   Howitzers will fire H.E. Section fire 20 secs. for 20 minutes.

7. Transport in trench area affected is to be reduced to a minimum until further notice.

8. Special care should be taken not to mention these operations on the telephone.

9. Acknowledge.

Copy No. 1 War Diary.
        2 A/107.
        3 B/107.
        4 C/107.
        5 B/109.
        6 D/106.
        7 B.M. 7 Anzacs.
        8 B.M. 24 D.A.

D R Coates Lieut.Colonel.R.F.A
Commanding 107/F.A/Brigade.

OPERATION ORDERS No. 12

by

LT. COLONEL D. R. COATES,   COMMANDING 107 F.A.B. GROUP.

Copy No. 1.   VERY SECRET.   29th June 1916.

1. Gas may be emitted from our Front Line at any suitable moment — most probably to-night.

2. On its emission, batteries will bombard on their Night Lines, searching and sweeping the enemies Front line, Communication and Support Trenches.

3. Time of emission.

   Time of emission will be notified as follows :—

   JOLLY ROGER   ....p.m.   2 am

   If there are to be two emissions :—

   JOLLY ROGER   ....p.m. and ....p.m.

   Fire will be opened at each time mentioned.

4. Rate and duration of fire.

   Section fire 15 sec. on each occasssion for 20 minutes.

5. Projectiles.

   50% H.E.   50% Shrapnel.

6. Minenwerfer.

   If a Minenwerfer should at any time open fire on our Front Line, the fact and if possible its map locality is to be reported to these Hd.Qrs. at once.

   Acknowledge

Copy No. 1 War Diary.
     2 A/107.
     3 B/107.
     4 C/107.
     5 B/109.
     6 D/106.
     7 B.M. 7 Anzacs.
     8 B.M. 24 D.A.

D R Coates   Lieut. Colonel, R.F.A.
Commanding 107/F.A/Brigade.

SECRET.   B.M.367.

106th F.A.B.Group.
107th "   "   "   "
108th "   "   "   "
251st "   "   "   "

===================

   Wire cutting will be carried out continuously all day on the 24th Division front, on June 30th.

   Group Commanders will arrange that wire-cutting is taking place on some part of their front during the whole day. The programme arranged, showing the places at which wire is to be cut, should be forwarded to this Office by last D.R. to-night.

   There is no limit of ammunition for this operation.

   When forwarding the 4-30.p.m. telegraphic report on 30th inst., a short report should be included of the wire cutting carried out during the day, saying how much wire has been cut and giving map references.

29/6/16.
                                                    Captain.R.A.
                              Brigade Major, 24th Divisional Artillery.

Operation Orders No 11 ~~for Lt Col~~ DR Coates

1. All 18 pr batteries will cut wire to northward inc 30.

2. Places at which wire is cut
   A/107 U.1.a.3½   B/107 U.2.a.18
   B/109 U.2.c.6½.8 C/107. U.2.a.½.9

3. Ammunition expended need not be limited to be considered 400 rounds per battery will be used. 200 in the morning & 200 in afternoon at different times. Officer to observe each battery place

4. A/107 and B/109 up to 1 pm   8am 1pm
   B/109 and C/107 from 1 pm   Times   1pm 6pm
   BC's will arrange times making so that wire is being cut continuously all day.

5. Reports by wire to Bde Hdqrs by 4 pm as soon as task is completed re amount of wire cut in morning; & that in afternoon as soon as possible

6. D/106 will be ready to retaliate.

A B C/107
B/109
D/106
BM 7 Anzac
BM 24 Div

7th AUSTRALIAN INFANTRY BRIGADE.

SECRET.

Headquarters,
   24th Division.
   O. C. Centre Group R.F.A.
   O. C. Attack
   Filed (1 copy)
   War Diary (1 copy)

22nd June 1916.

Reference Map Sheet 28 MESSINES 1/10,000, corrected 9.4.16.

1. On a night to be notified later a party of officers and other ranks drawn from the 25th and 27th Battalions of the 7th Australian Infantry Brigade, will leave our trenches from about U 1 a 5 2¼, and enter the enemy's trenches at about U 1 a 4½ 6½.

2. **ACTION BY ARTILLERY.** At 0000 zero time gas will be released on flanks of 7th Brigade. At 0003 smoke will be discharged all along the 24th Divisional front. At 0004 Artillery will open on the flanks, and Centre Group will commence to bombard the front line trenches in the vicinity of ONTARIO FARM, U 1 a, and also between BIRTHDAY FARM, O 31d and SNIPERS' HOUSE, U 2 a. At 0013 Artillery will commence lifting and will form a barrage by 0015, and smoke will stop. At 0035 Artillery will drop on to front line. At 0040 Artillery will cease fire.
   TRENCH MORTARS. Two trench mortars at 0004 will commence wire cutting and at 0013 will lift on to the machine gun positions on the flanks of point of entry.

3. **COMPOSITION OF PARTY.**
   O. C.,) Captain H. H. Page, 25th Battalion.
   Attack)

Scouts	1 officer,	6 other ranks
Right Bombing Party	1 "	7 "
Left " "	1 "	7 "
Right Blocking Party	5 other ranks	
Left " "	5 "	
Covering Party	14 "	
Stretcher Bearers	4 "	(with 4 stretchers)
Telephonist & Linesman	2 "	
Engineers	2 "	(with explosives)
Runners	2 "	
Intelligence Men	2 "	
Carriers for gas cylinders, if found.	2 "	

4. **ACTION OF ASSAULT PARTY.** A party preceded by Scouts will leave our trenches before the bombardment commences, and will take up a position in NO MAN'S LAND. As soon as the Artillery bombardment starts they will move in as close as possible with safety. On the Artillery fire lifting party will enter and clear the enemy's trenches in both directions, right and left, for about 50 yards to either flank. Covering Party and Stretcher Bearers will remain outside. The withdrawal will be covered by smoke bombs thrown by the Covering Party and will take place not later than 0031.

5. **GAS.** More gas will be released after attacking party has returned to our trenches, at a time to be decided by Divisional Commander. Gas in trenches 139 - 140 will be released at commencement of operations, and gas in Diagonal will only be released after the party returns.

Detailed Orders will be prepared and forwarded later if proposals are approved.

Brigadier General,
7th Aust Inf Brigade.

Copy No. 2

Reference Trench Map Sheets 28.S.W. 2 & 4.   S.19.

S E C R E T.

~~106th F.A.B.Group.~~
107th F.A.B.Group.
~~108th F.A.B.Group.~~
~~109th F.A.B. (For information.)~~
~~Trench Mortars, 24th D.A. (For information.)~~
~~251st F.A.B.~~
~~24th D.A. (For information.)~~
~~H.A. V. CORPS (" ")~~

1. Minor enterprises will be carried out by the 17th I.B., 2nd AUS. Bde. and 72nd I.B. on a date and from a zero hour to be notified later.

2. Gas and smoke will be used if the wind is favourable. The G.O.C. each Inf. Bde. Sector will decide whether they are to be used or not. Appendix 1. Table "A" (with gas and smoke) Table "B" (without gas and smoke) gives the Divisional Programme.

3. Group Commanders will arrange with their Infantry Brigadiers, the details of artillery support (including Medium Trench Mortars) for the actual raids. Appendix 11 gives the programme for the Heavy Artillery also the programme for the Divisional Artillery during the subsequent discharges of gas.

4. The 251st F.A.B. will fire with one 18-pr battery along the road KRUISSTRAAT CABT to O.31.a.4.2 from zero time till stopped by O.C. 108th F.A.B. Group. The remainder 251 F.A.B. will demonstrate on BLACK REDOUBT (N.30.a.4.2½) from zero time to zero 40.

5. On the nights on which gas cylinders are being transported to the trenches and on the night of the enterprises, transport in the trench area will be reduced to a minimum. The dates on which cylinders are to be transported will be notified to Groups. Ammunition should as far as possible be taken up on the 24th inst.

6. From the time at which the first gas cylinders are brought into Infy. Bde. Areas, and during the whole time that the cylinders remain full in the trenches the "Gas Alert" will be ordered in all Infantry Brigade Areas.
Should a cylinder be burst in our trenches, the usual warnings for gas which are given by Strombos Horns, etc. will <u>not</u> be given.

7. From the 24th inst. watches will be synchronised at 9.a.m. & 6.p.m. daily, Divisional Time being given by R.A. Signals.

8. No working parties will be employed on the night on which the operation takes place.

9. On completion of wire cutting on 24th inst. Groups will maintain at least 500 rounds per 18-pr and 300 rounds per 4.5 How. in gun positions, until the raids take place. After the night of the raids the present amount of 203 rounds per 18-pr. and 156 rounds per 4.5 How. will be kept.

10. Please acknowledge.

24/6/16.

R. W. Griffin
Captain. R.A.
Brigade Major, 24th Divisional Artillery.

APPENDIX 1.

OPERATION "A" (WITH GAS AND SMOKE).

TIME.	72nd INF. BDE.	2nd AUS. BDE.	17th INF. BDE.
-10.			Raiding parties leave our trenches and advance towards ASH ROAD BARRIER (U.15.a.2.8.)
-4		Raiding parties leave our trenches and advance towards objective U.1.a.4½.6½	
00 Zero.	Artillery bombardment commences. Gas discharged from trenches D 1, D 2, D 3. Smoke discharged on remainder of Brigade front.	Artillery bombardment commences. Gas released from 139 & 140 trenches and smoke on the remainder of front.	Artillery bombardment commences.
0 9	Gas ceases. Smoke continues.	Gas ceases. Smoke continues from 139 & 140 trenches. Artillery lift. Raiding parties enter enemy trenches.	
0 19	Artillery lifts. Raiding parties leave our trenches and advance rapidly towards objective N.36.d.2½.7½. Smoke ceases opposite point to be raided at a time to be determined by Officer i/c Smoke Discharge.		Artillery lift.
0 20 (about)	Raiding parties enter enemy trenches.		Raiding Parties enter trenches.

TIME.	72nd INF. BDE.	2nd AUS. BDE.	17th INF. BDE.
0.30 (About)	Raiding parties return to our trenches. Withdrawal covered by smoke bombs, thrown by covering party. Artillery bring fire back on to enemy trenches on pre-arranged signal to do so.	Raiding parties return to our trenches. Withdrawal covered by smoke bombs thrown by covering party. Artillery bring fire back on to enemy front trenches on a pre-arranged signal to do so.	Raiding parties return to our trenches. Artillery bring fire back on to enemy front trenches on a pre-arranged signal to do so.
0.35 (About)	Second gas discharge from flanks of 72nd Bde., smoke continuing on remainder of front.		
0.40 (About)	Second gas discharge. Smoke ceases.		
0.50 (About)	ARTILLERY CEASES WHEN DIRECTED TO DO SO BY B.Gs.C. INFANTRY BRIGADES.		
1.50 -		Second Gas discharge 1st Gas discharge accompanied by smoke.	
1.55.			
1.52.	BOMBARDMENT BY DIVISIONAL ARTILLERY ON ENEMY FRONT LINE.		
1.55.	COUNTER - BATTERY WORK BY HEAVY ARTILLERY.		
3.15 -		Third gas discharge. Second gas discharge.	
3.20.		(if any gas remaining)	
3.17.	BOMBARDMENT BY DIVISIONAL ARTILLERY OF ENEMY FRONT LINE.		
3.20.	COUNTER BATTERY WORK BY HEAVY ARTILLERY.		

APPENDIX E.I

OPERATIONS "B" (WITHOUT GAS AND SMOKE)

TIME.	72nd INFANTRY BRIGADE.	2nd AUSTRALIAN BRIGADE and 17th INFANTRY BRIGADE.
00 Zero.	Artillery bombardment commences.	Programme as for Operation "A", finishing at 0 30 minutes.
02	Artillery lift. Raiding parties start from our trenches and advance rapidly towards point to be raided.	
012	Raiding parties withdraw from enemy trenches. Artillery fire brought back on to the enemy front trenches on pre-arranged signal to do so.	

ARTILLERY CEASES WHEN DIRECTED TO DO SO BY B.Gs.G. INFANTRY BRIGADES.

Trench Mor. Shoot 28.S.W. 2 & 4.

APPENDIX 11.

TABLE A.

TIME.	No. of Guns.	NATURE.	OBJECTIVE.	REMARKS.
Zero to Zero 40.	1	6 inch How.	ASH ROAD BARRIER.	Detailed task given to Btty. Commander by O.C. 106th F.A.B. Group
	1	" "	BIRTHDAY FARM.	"
	2	" "	Road 0.31.a.4.2 to 0.31.a.0.4 to KRUISTRAAT CABT.	"
1-55 till 2-5 or until hostile Artillery stop.			Counter Battery work from zero time on selected battery positions.	
3-20 till 3-30 or until hostile Artillery stop.		60 pdr.	Counter Battery work on selected Battery positions	
		"	"	"

TABLE B.

TIME.	GROUP.	OBJECTIVE.	REMARKS.
1-52 to 2-2.	106th F.A.B. 107th F.A.B.	German front line and communication trenches opposite which gas is being discharged.	Allowance per Group for each 10 minutes 18-pr 250 rounds. 4.5 How. 50 rounds.
3-17 to 3-27.	108th F.A.B.	Selected places on German trenches opposite 72nd I.B. front.	

NUMBER OF GUNS.
RATES OF FIRE.
AMMUNITION.

Assuming Raiding Party are 30 minutes in enemy's lines and bombardment 34 mins.

Piece.	Number.		
(1) 18-pdrs.	30	at 3 rounds per minute.	3060 (1836 Shrapnel / 1224 H.E.
(2) 4.5 Hows.	16	at 2 rounds per minute	1088 All H.E.
(3) 2" T.Ms	4	at 1 round per minute	136 H.E.
(4) H.A. 60-pdrs.	10	at 2 rounds per minute	680 (510 Shrapnel / 170 (75% " / 25% H.E.)
6 in.	6	at 1 round per minute	204 H.E.
9.2"	2	at ¾ round per minute	51 all H.E.

(1) Centre Group	18	(2) Centre Group	4
Right Group	—	Right Group	8
Left Group	12	Left Group	4
	30		16.

AMMUNITION FOR WIRECUTTING.

3 lanes to be cut, 10 yards wide each, and wire to be damaged at other places.

	18-pdrs.
Rounds required —	500.

Army Form C-2118

24th July
107 RFA
Vol 10

107 FAB HQ.
XXIV

WAR DIARY
or
INTELLIGENCE SUMMARY.
(Erase heading not required.)

Instructions regarding War Diaries and Intelligence Summaries are contained in F. S. Regs., Part II and the Staff Manual respectively. Title pages will be prepared in manuscript.

Place	Date	Hour	Summary of Events and Information	Remarks and references to Appendices
Kruiv. Eglise	1/7/16		Situation normal.	
	2/7/16		" "	
	3/7/16		" "	
	4/7/16	10:30pm	Group batteries relieved (one section) as follows ABC/107 D/106 by batteries 6th Australian FAB. R/107 by Battery 5th FAB. Engr	
	5/7/16	10am	Composite batteries Brig Group Shoot and ONTARIO Fm	
	6/7/16	2am	Relief of Group Complete - Col Cohen (etw A. F.A.12) takes over from Col Coates.	
		10am	107 FAB move situated as follows. A B and C Batteries as follows. AB and C Batteries resting at S8a93, S8a66, S4c56 respectively. } Sheet 28	
			HQ at S8d79. D/107 in above unit. OC 107 FAB at N 26 c 87 - wagon lines M34 d 16.	
Millencourt	7/7/16		107 FAB No. were responsible for work and new position to be carried out by various batteries	
	8/7/16		Above orders cancelled. Batteries again ordered into FABs in old positions.	
Mailly Maillet		10:30pm	A Col Coates takes over from Lt Col Cohen - Remaining batteries with command of 107 FAB HQ, covering 42 IB - A/107 (at its old position) B/107 & C/107 with D/106 ditto B+C/107 detailed to cover Left Battn. A/107 Right Battn.	
	9/7/16		Situation normal.	
	10/7/16			
	11/7/16	10pm	73 IB relieves 42 IB. (New zone of 43 IB trenches 141 to D4 inclusive)	
	13/7/16	4pm	24 DA regrouped. 107 FAB HQ now commands A + C/107 (positions unaltered) C/108 (N33 a 8) C/109 T31r55 and D'nng Mor T 18 C79 - Two commands known as "Centre Group." - covering front as above, less (say 43 IB.	

WAR DIARY or INTELLIGENCE SUMMARY

Army Form C. 2118.

XXV

Place	Date	Hour	Summary of Events and Information	Remarks and references to Appendices
MONT KEMMEL	13/7/16		Situation normal. (1 OR Killed by stray shell on patrol)	
	14/7/16		" "	
	15/7/16	18 prs at work	See Op Orders No 21. Capt Winterscale 2/Lt C/107 proc'd to Command 39th Anti-aircraft Bty.	
	16/7/16	do do		
	17/7/16	do do		
	18/7/16	4 am morning	Transport heard on WYTSCHAETE-MESSINES road — one 18pr has a shot.	
	19/7/16	18prs at work		
	20/7/16		Situation normal.	
	21/7/16		Rations 2/Lt Waddell DT from C/107 to 172 F.A.B. (36th Div Arty)	
	22/7/16	10 am	All Centre Group Batteries relieved by 172 F.A.B. Q19 & 88 HQ Q20 c 95 Sheet 27	
			Lt Col Wand DSO hands over command from Lt Col DR Gates.	
	23/7/16		A/107 and 107 HQ arrive at billets in EECKE. A/107 Q19 a 48 C/107 Q19 & 88 HQ Q20 c 95 Sheet 27	
			B/107 and D/107 arrive (after relief by French) Lieut & Frankau from adjutant 107 to Brigade to B/107.	
	24/7/16		B/107 (Q28 c 59) D/107 Q114 d 45.	Ry AMIENS 14 —
			Batteries marching. Lieut J.H. Cumlay 51/107 appt'd	
	25/7/16		Batteries and HQ entraining for new area (rendezvous marked)	
	26/7/16	am	adjutant 107 F.A.B. proc'd to HQ in Staff	
		pm 3:30am	107 FAB arrives at new billeting areas in HANGEST. Major GL Popham Lancs proc'd the 107 H.Q.B. proc'd to CORBIE-DAOURS area.	
	27/7/16		Resting.	
	28/7/16		do	
	29/7/16		do	
	30/7/16		do	
	31/7/16		107 F.A.B moved to CORBIE-DAOURS area.	

31/7/16   D Rooke Lt Col RFA
OC 107 FAB

SECRET.   S.40(6)

Copy No 2

1. The relief of the 24th Divisional Artillery is to be accelerated.

2 (a) On the night 21st/22nd July, the whole of the centre Group, 24th D.A. will be relieved. On completion of relief, the centre Group will march direct to rest area under orders of O.C.,107th F.A.B.

(b) On night 22nd/23rd July, the whole of the Right and Left Groups, 24th D.A. will be relieved. On completion of the relief the Right and Left Groups will march direct to rest area under orders of Right and Left Group Commanders.

3. An experienced subaltern, one batman and two signallers per battery, also one signaller per Group H.Q. will be left behind.
The above will leave the present area on July 24th to rejoin their units, under orders to be issued by 36th D.A.

4 (i) All guns will be handed over to incoming batteries. They will not be stripped, but will be handed over complete in action with all component parts. Batteries will obtain a receipt for everything handed over.

(ii) On relief, batteries will take over guns from 36th D.A. in the present wagon lines.
Some of these are deficient of sights and other stores. Batteries will obtain a signed list of everything taken over from Batteries, 36th D.A.

5 (i) The two southern 2" Trench Mortars will be withdrawn from the line to-night.

(ii) The T.M.Batteries, 36th D.A. will arrive at 24th D.A.,T.M. Camp to-day by lorry.
The personnel of the 7 northern trench mortars will be relieved by personnel of 36th D.A. to-night. Guns and ammunition will be handed over. O.C.,T.M. 24th D.A. will report to this Office what is handed over.

O.C.,T.M.24th D.A. will take over 7 guns complete in exchange from T.M.,36 D.A.

One Officer and one N.C.O. will remain behind with mortars in action. They will leave the area on evening July 22nd and will march with 108.F.A.B. Group that night. Arrangements to be made between O.C.,T.M.24.D.A. and O.C.,108.F.A.B.

(iii) On July 22nd the medium T.M.Batteries (12 guns) will move to rest area. Transport arrangements will be notified by Staff Captain.

6. Command will now pass from C.R.A., 24th Div. to C.R.A. 36.Div. at 6.p.m. on July 22nd.
H.Q.,24.D.A. will close at BAILLEUL at 6.p.m. on July 22nd and re-open at EECKE on the night of July 22nd.

7. Please acknowledge.

21/7/16.   Captain, R.A.
                        Brigade Major, 24th Divisional Artillery.

P.T.O.

COPIES TO

	No.
106th F.A.B.Group.	1.
107th F.A.B.Group.	2.
108th F.A.B.Group.	3.
109th F.A.B.Group.	4.
T.M., 24th D.A.	5.
24th D.A.C.	6.
24th Div.G.	7,8.
" " Q.	9.
" " Train.	10.
" " Signals.	11.
A.D.M.S. 24th Div.	12.
A.P.M. " "	13.
36th D.A.	14, 15.
153 F.A.B.	16.
154 " " "	17.
172 " " "	18.
173 " " "	19.
36th D.A.C.	20.
41st D.A.	21.
50th D.A.	22.
H.A.V.Corps.	23.
20th Div.	24.
11th H.A.G.	25.
No.1 Squadron, R.F.C.	26.
WAR DIARY.	27,28.
File.	29.
SPARE.	30, 31 & 32.

S E C R E T.

All Batteries,
107 F.A.B.

107th BRIGADE,
R.F.A.
No. BM/253.
Date 19/7/16.

Reference move :-

1. All stores in good condition not required, are to be returned to Divn. Ordnance Stores by 5.p.m. tomorrow.

2. All stores not in good condition which are not required are to be returned to Divl. Salvage Dump at S 4 c 8.5 by 5.p.m. tomorrow.

3. If, after the above has been done, batteries still wish to "dump", Brigade Dump will be at C/107 Wagon Line for "A", "B" & "C" Btys. Batteries dumping there must each leave one man as a Guard. This man will be rationed for three days.

4. If after complying with 1 & 2, D/107 wishes to carry out the operations mentioned in 3, O.C. that battery will make arrangements with O.C.,108 F.A.B. to use one of his dumps.

5. No unauthorized equipment will be tolerated on the march.

Lieut. R.F.A.
19/7/16. Adjutant,107/F.A/Brigade.

OPERATION ORDERS No.24

by

LT.COLONEL D.R. COATES, COMMANDING CENTRE GROUP.

Ref. Map 27.

Copy No. 1.   SECRET.   21st July 1916.

1.   CENTRE GROUP will be relieved on night 21st/22nd and 22nd/23rd, one section nightly.

2.   Relieving Batteries.

      A/107   A/172.   C/107   B/172.   C/108   C/172.
                   C/109   A/154.   D/108   D/172.

3.   (a) No relief before 10.p.m.
      (b) B.C's hand over on completion.
      (c) Reliefs to report by wire using the code word "JACK-POT".

4.   Batteries will march out with ammunition complete – all dumped ammunition will be handed over – amount handed over to be reported to Group H.Q., by wire when announcing completion of relief.

5.   <u>All maps in possession</u> except Sheet 27 and HAZEBROUCK 5a to be handed over, and accurate receipts obtained.

      Trench Stores, Airplane photos etc. as usual.

6.   Batteries (less Sections sent off 21/7/16) will march independently to rest areas given in OPERATION ORDERS No.23 on completion of reliefs on night 22nd/23rd, on arrival in rest area batteries come under their Brigade Commanders.

7.   Rest area of H.Q. 107 F.A.B., will be at Q 20 c 4.2.

Copy No. 1   War Diary.
         2   B.M. 24 D.A.
         3   A/107.
         4   C/107.
         5   C/108.
         6   D/108.
         7   C/109.

                                                  Lieut. R.F.A.
                                     Adjutant, 107/F.A/Brigade.

OPERATION ORDER No. 23.

BY

LIEUT. COL. D.E.COATES COMMANDING CENTRE GROUP.

Copy No. 1...   SECRET.   Reference Map 27.

1. Detailed relief orders will be issued to-morrow.

2. To-morrow morning (21st) batteries will send one section (less teams to take away guns, which will be removed to-morrow night) to rest area as below.

	STARTING POINT.	HOUR TO PASS.	DESTINATION.
A/107.)	cross road	10 a.m.	Q 19 a 4.8.
C/107.)	B 1 centre	10.5 a.m.	Q 19 b 8.6.
D/108.)		10.30 a.m.	Q 14 a 9.9.
C/108.	Own W.L.	9.45 a.m.	Q 15 b 3.5.
C/109.	Own W.L.	10 a.m.	P 24 a 6.3.

Route for all units - via BAILLEUL - CAESTRE.

3. Incoming units arrive at Wagon Line sometime to-morrow.

Copy No 1 War Diary.
       2 A/107.
       3 C/107.
       4 C/108.
       5 C/109.
       6 D/108.
       7 B.M. 24 D.A.

Adjutant 107th Brigade, R.F.A.

Lieut. R.F.A.

Copy No. 2

S.40(7)

1. It has been decided that the 24th Divisional Artillery are to move out complete with their own guns. Para 4 of S.40(6) dated 21/7/16 is accordingly cancelled.

2. In order to complete equipment to relieve the 24th D.A., Batteries 36th D.A. will do as follows:-

C/154 to hand over 4 guns and sights to B/172.

B/154 to hand over two guns to C/172.

C/108 to hand over the two guns collected from the Station to C/172.

3. The reliefs each night will take place by sections at one hours interval commencing at 10.p.m.

Not more than 2 guns per Battery will be out of action at the same time.

21/7/16.

H W Crippin
Captain. R.A.
Brigade Major, 24th Divisional Artillery.

Copies to

	No.
106th F.A.B. Group.	1
107th " " " "	2
108th " " " "	3
109th " " " "	4
24th Div. G.	5, 6.
36th D.A.	7. 8.
153rd F.A.B.	9
154th " " "	10
172nd " " "	11
173rd " " "	12
50th D.A.	13
File.	14

Op Orders No 24
by Lt Col DR Coates.

1. Centre Group will be relieved on nights 21/22 and 22/3, one section nightly.

2. Relieving batteries
A/107 A/172 B/107 B/172 C/108 C/172 C/109 A/154
D/108 D/172.

3. (a) No relief before 10 pm ✓
   (b) BC's hand over on completion ✓
   (c) Reliefs to reported by wire using the codeword JACK-POT. ✓

4. Batteries will march out with ammunition complete — all dumped ammunition will be handed over — amount handed over to be reported to Group HQ by wire when announcing completion of relief.

5. ~~All trench maps, airplane photos &c and~~ All maps in possession except Sheet 24 and HAZEBROUCK 5a to be handed over, & accurate receipts obtained. Trench Stores, airplane photos &c as usual.

6. Batteries (less sections shut off 21/7) will march independently to rest areas given in Op Orders 23 on completion of relief, on arrival in rest area batteries come under their Brigade Commanders.

HQ 104 FAB will march to at Q20c42.

RELIEF ORDERS

by

Lt. COLONEL D.P. COATES,   COMMANDING CENTRE GROUP.

Copy No...   SECRET.   22nd July 1916.

1. All CENTRE GROUP Batteries will be relieved as soon as ever possible. Incoming Battery Commanders will take over responsibility at 7.p.m. tonight.

2. An experienced Subaltern, one batman and two signallers per battery will be left behind.
    The above will leave the present area on July 24th to rejoin their units, under orders to be issued by 36th D.A.

3. (1) All guns will be handed over to incoming batteries. They will not be stripped, but will be handed over complete in action with all component parts. Batteries will obtain a receipt for everything handed over.
    (2) On relief, batteries will take over guns from 36th D.A. in the present Wagon Lines.
    Some of these are deficient of sights and other stores. Batteries will obtain a signed list of everything taken over from batteries 36th D.A.

4. Batteries will march to Rest Area independently.

Copy No.1 War Diary.
     2   A/107.
     3   C/107.
     4   C/108.
     5   D/108.
     6   C/109.

Lieut. R.F.A.
Adjutant, 107/F.A/Brigade.

SECRET.   S.40(3).

Copy No. 2

1   The 36th Divisional Artillery will relieve the 24th Divisional Artillery on the nights 21st/22nd, 22nd/23rd & 23rd/24th July.

2   The reliefs at gun positions and wagon lines, also the march table of the 24th D.A. to the rest area, are shown in the Appendices 1 & 11, attached. On arrival in the rest area, Batteries 24th D.A. leave their Groups and come under the orders of their Brigade Commander.

3   (i) No relief to take place before 10.p.m. each night.
(ii) Battery and Group Commanders will hand over command on completion of relief of their units.
(iii) Completion of reliefs to be reported to this H.Q. by wire each night.

4   (i) All echelons, 24th D.A. will march out with their full establishment of ammunition. All dumped ammunition in excess of this will be handed over to incoming units.
(ii) Groups and the 24th D.A.C. will report by 4.p.m. on 24th inst. what ammunition they have handed over.

5   All trench maps, aeroplane photographs, panoramas, etc. will be handed over.

6   Separate orders will be issued about relief of trench mortars.

7   All other details of the relief will be arranged between Group Commanders.

8   Command will pass from C.R.A. 24th Div. to C.R.A. 36th Div. at 6.p.m. on July 23rd.
H.Q.,24th D.A. will close at BAILLEUL at 6.p.m. on July 23RD and re-open at EECKE on the night of 23RD July.

9   Please acknowledge.

20/7/16.
Captain. R.A.
Brigade Major, 24th Divisional Artillery.

Copies to   No:

106th F.A.B.Group.	1	172 F.A.B.	18
107th " " " "	2	173 " " "	19
108th " " " "	3	36th D.A.C.	20
109th " " " "	4	41st D.A.	21
T.M., 24th D.A.	5	50th D.A.	22
24th D.A.C.	6	H.A.V.Corps.	23
24th Div.G.	7 - 8	20th Div.	24
" " Q.	9	11th H.A.G.	25
" " Train.	10	No.1 Squadron.R.F.C.	26
" " Signals.	11	WAR DIARY.	27 - 28
A.D.M.S. 24th Div.	12	File.	29
A.P.M. " "	13	SPARE.	30 - 31 - 32.
36th D.A.	14 - 15.		
153 F.A.B.	16		
154 " " "	17		

APPENDIX 1.

RELIEF TABLE.

1. Units 36th D.A. relieve units 24th D.A. as under:-

	Unit 36 D.A.	Unit 24 D.A.	Location of Wagon Line 24th D.A.
Right Group.	153 F.A.B.H.Q.	106 F.A.B.H.Q.	T.27.c.7.1½.
	A/153.	A/106.	T.28.b.4.9.
	B/153.	B/106.	T.28.d.8.7.
	C/153.	B/107.	T.28.c.0.9.
	D/153.	D/106.	B.3.d.2.9.
Resting Group.	154 F.A.B.H.Q.	109 F.A.B.H.Q.	M.24.a.5.4.
	B/154(less 1 sec)	A/109(less 1 sec)	M.24.a.3.3.
	C/154.	C/106.	M.28.d.1.5.
Centre Group.	172 F.A.B.H.Q.	107th F.A.B.H.Q.	T.21.b.2.3.
	A/172.	A/107.	T.21.c.2.2.
	B/172.	C/107.	T.20.c.9.9.
	C/172.	C/108.	M.35.d.8.3.
	D/172.	D/108.	T.27.c.5.1.
	A/154.	C/109.	M.35.d.5.3.
Left Group.	173 F.A.B.H.Q.	108 F.A.B.H.Q.	M.35.d.6.3.
	A/173.	A/108.	S.4.c.8.6.
	B/173.	B/108.	M.35.c.9.3.
	C/173.	B/109.	M.35.c.5.3.
	D/173.	D/107.	M.34.d.2.8.
	1 Sec.B/154.	1 Sec.A/109.	M.24.a.3.3.
	36 D.A.C.H.Q.	24th D.A.C.H.Q.	S.15.d.1.3.
	No.1 Section.	No.1 Section.	T.20.c.8.9.
	No.2 "	No.2 "	B.1.b.2.5.
	No.3 "	No.3 "	S.5.b.9.5.
	No.4 "	No.4 "	S.22.a.2.3.
	Medium T.M.Btties.	Medium T.M.Btties.	
	36th D.A.	24th D.A.	T.19.b.8.4.
	V/36 T.M.Batty.	V/24 T.M.Batty.	N.19.c.0.5.

2. On July 21st the 154th & 173rd Brigades will march into Wagon Lines 24th D.A. as per para 1.
On July 22nd the 153rd & 173rd Brigades, also 36th D.A.C. will march into wagon lines 24th D.A. as per para 1.

3. Relieving units at gun positions will correspond with relieving units at wagon lines.
On night 21st/22nd 1 Sec. A/109 Batty. will be relieved in gun positions.
On night 21st/22nd and 22nd/23rd the Centre Group, 24th D.A. will be relieved. (1 Section each night)
On night 22nd/23rd and 23rd/24th the Right and Left Groups (less 1 sec. A/109 relieved on 21st/22nd) 24th D.A. will be relieved (1 sec each night)
The resting Group, 24th D.A. and 24th D.A.C. will move off as shown in march table.

Reference sheets
27, 28 & 36.

APPENDIX 11.

MARCH TABLE OF 24th D.A. TO REST AREA.

July 21st.	Unit.	Starting Point.	Hour of passing starting point.	ROUTE.	DESTINATION.
	1 Sec.A/107.	Cross roads.		)	Q.19.a.4.8.
	1 Sec.C/107	B.1.centre.	10.a.m.	) via	Q.19.b.8.8.
	1 Sec.D/108.	"	10-30"	)	Q.14.a.9.9.
	1 Sec.C/108.	Present W.L.	9-45"	) BAILLEUL	Q.15.b.3.5.
	1 Sec.C/109.	"	10" a.m.	)	P.24.a.6.3.
	C/106 Batty.	"	9.a.m.	) - CAESTRE.	Q.24.d.1.8.
	A/109	)		)	Q.32.b.5.6.
	109.F.A.B.H.Q.	"	9.a.m.	)	Q.32.b.7.8.

(i) Sections 107th F.A.B.Group and A/109 Batty. to leave gun teams for removal of guns from action on night 21st/22nd July. On relief the guns and detachment 107 F.A.B.Group are withdrawn to present wagon lines. The Section A/109 marches direct to Rest Area.

(ii) 109 F.A.B.H.Q. and C/106 Batty. to leave an Officer behind till arrival of 154 F.A.B.H.Q. and C/154 Batty. to hand over camp.

22nd.	1 Sec.A/106.	Cross roads			Q.31.b.2.8.
	1 Sec.B/106.	B.1.centre.	10.a.m.	) Q.30.d.5.7.	Q.30.b.3.7.
	1 Sec.D/106.	)		)	Q.21.d.8.2.
	1 Sec.B/107.	"	9-45"	)	Q.28.b.5.9.
	1 Sec.A/108.	)		) via	Q.15.c.4.9.
	1 Sec.B/108.	S.9.a.7.7.	9-30"	)	Q.15.d.5.1.
	1 Sec.B/109.	"	10.a.m.	) BAILLEUL	P.24.a.6.3.
	1 Sec.D/107.	"	10-15"	)	Q.14.d.4.5.
	24th D.A.C.H.Q.			) - CAESTRE.	GODEWAERSVELDE
	No.1 Sec.			)	Q.22.b.0.9.
	No.2 Sec.			)	Q.16.b.3.8.
	No.3 Sec.			)	Q.32.a.9.2.
	No.4 Sec.			)	Q.17.b.6.9.

24th D.A.C.H.Q. and Sections to march out on arrival of corresponding formations, 36 D.A.C. which should arrive between 2 & 3 p.m.

(i) Sections 106 F.A.B. 108th F.A.B.Groups to leave gun teams for removal of guns from action on night 22nd/23rd July. On relief the guns and detachments will withdraw to wagon lines.

night 22/23. Remainder of 107 F.A.B.Group on completion of relief will march direct to Rest Area under orders to be issued by O.C. 107 F.A.B.

night 23/24 Remainder 106 & 108 F.A.B.Groups on completion of relief will march direct to Rest Area under orders to be issued by 106th & 108th F.A.B. Group Commanders.

106th F.A.B.H.Q. will be at Q.20.d.2.4.
107th F.A.B.H.Q. " " " Q.20.c.4.2.
108th F.A.B.H.Q. " " " Q.20.d.4.4.

S E C R E T.

106th F.A.B.
107th F.A.B.
108th F.A.B.
109th F.A.B.
Trench Mortars, 24th D.A.
251st F.A.B.
50th D.A.
24th DIV.

S.31

1. That part of S.28 dated 4/7/18 which refers to reliefs night 7th/8th July is cancelled.
    The following will take place instead :-

    1 Sec. B/251 will relieve 1 Sec. A/106.
    1 "   A/250   "   "   1 "   C/106.
    1 "   D/107   "   "   1 "   D/251.
    1 "   B/108   "   "   1 "   A/253.
    1 "   B/109   "   "   1 "   C/251.

    Sections A/106 & B/106 to wagon lines.

2. At 4.p.m July 8th the following re-grouping will take place:-

    LEFT GROUP.   Zone N.29.b.9½.6½ to N.24.a.5.7.

        Lt.Col.MOSS BLUNDELL & 251 F.A.B.,H.Q.
        A/250 Battery.
        A/251   "
        B/251   "

    O.C. 251 F.A.B. will have a call on D/107(How) Battery, and should also call on the How.Battery 50th D.A. which covers from the North to N.1.a (exclusive).

    LEFT CENTRE GROUP.   Zone N.24.a.7.1 to N.29.b.9½.6½.

        Lt.Col.WALTHALL & 108.F.A.B.,H.Q.

        A/108 Battery.
        B/108   "
        B/109   "
        D/107(How)"

    (i) Alterations in communications will be arranged by 4.p.m.

    (ii) Any necessary registration on change of zones will be carried out on the morning of the 7th.

    (iii) Group Commanders will report when they have assumed command of their new Groups.

4. On night 8th/9th complete batteries will go into action as follows:-

    To come under orders of Left Centre Group on completion of relief, when zone of this Group will be extended to former right of 108.F.A.B.

        C/108 Battery in present position.
        C/109   "   " former   "
        D/108

    Right Centre Group. Zone. Former 107.F.A.B. zone.

= 2 =

Lt.-Col. COATES and 107.F.A.B., H.Q.

A/107 Battery in former position.
B/107   "   "   "   "
C/107   "   "   "   "
D/106(How) "   "   "   "

Right Group. Zone former 106th F.A.B. zone.

Lt.-Col. BURNE and 106th F.A.B. H.Q.
A/106 Battery in former position.
B/106   "   "   "   "
C/106   "   "   "   "

A 106 F.A.B. will have call on D/106(How) Bty.

5 (i) Medium Trench Mortar Batteries now in Trench Mortar Camp, will march back to their former T.M. Camp on July 7th.

(ii) Arrangements for transport will be notified later by Staff Captain.

(iii) The relief of 50th D.A. Trench Mortars is cancelled.

(iv) Trench Mortars, 24th D.A. will return to their former positions in the line on night 8th/9th.

6 Arrangements will probably be made to move 24th D.A.C. back to old line.

7 Orders for march on 8th inst and details of relief will be notified later.

8 All working parties for night 7th/8th are cancelled. All 24th D.A.C. wagons, less those permanently lent to units, are to return to the D.A.C. to-night.

7/7/16.

Captain. R.A.
Brigade Major, 24th Divisional Artillery.

APPENDIX 1.

A.   Brigades will march on July 8th to their old wagon lines as follows:-

   (i)   107.F.A.B. - Head of column to reach SQUARE, BAILLEUL at 11.a.m.

   (ii) 106.F.A.B. - Head of column to reach SQUARE, BAILLEUL at 12 noon.

   (iii) A/109 Battery - Head of column to reach SQUARE, BAILLEUL at 12-45.p.m.

   (iv) 24th D.A.C., less No.3.Sec. will move off from their present wagon lines at 12 noon, at which hour 50th D.A.C. take over responsibility of ammunition supply, and will march to their old lines.

   Units AUS.D.A. will move out of wagon lines on arrival of units, 24th D.A., leaving gun teams and limbers to remove guns at night.

B. (i)   The 106th F.A.B. will relieve the 21st F.A.Bde.

   106th F.A.B. will take over their old position in relief of 21st F.A.B., H.Q.

   A/106 Batty. will take over their old position in relief of 22nd Batty.
   B/106   "   "   "   "   "   "   "   "   "   "   " 23rd   "
   C/106   "   "   "   "   "   "   "   "   "   "   " 24th   "

   (ii) The 107.F.A.B.,H.Q. will take over their old position in relief of 6th.F.A.B.,H.Q.

   A/107 Batty. will take over their old position in relief of 1.Batty. 6th F.A.B.
   B/107 Batty. "   "   "   "   "   "   "   "   "   " 1 " 6th F.A.B.
   C/107 Batty. "   "   "   "   "   "   "   "   "   " 1 " 6th F.A.B.
   D/106(How) "   "   "   "   "   "   "   "   "   "   " " 6th F.A.B.

   (iii) A/109 Batty. will take over their old position in relief of 1 Batty. 5th F.A.B.
   D/108(How) "   "   "   "   "   "   "   "   "   "   " 1 Batty. 5th F.A.B.
   C/109 Batty. "   "   "   "   "   "   "   "   "   "   " 1 Batty 4th F.A.B.

   (iv) O.C., 108th F.A.B. will take over tactical Command of C/109 Batty. & D/108 Battery in action from O.C., 4th F.A.B. on completion of relief.

Reference Sheet 28.S.W.

APPENDIX 11.
TEMPORARY GROUPING.

Right Group.   Cover trenches 128 to 135 (both inclusive).

        Lt.Col.BURNE & 106.F.A.B.,H.Q.
           A/106 Batty.
           B/106 "
           C/106 "
           A/109 "
        Has a call on D/106 (How) Battery.

Centre Group.   Covers trenches 135(inclusive) to junction of C.2 with SURREY LANE.

        Lt.Col.COATES & 107.F.A.B.,H.Q.
           A/107 Batty.
           B/107 "
           C/107 "
           D/106(How)"
        Has a call on D/108(How) Battery.

Left Group.   Covers from junction of C2 with SURREY LANE to KEMMEL WYTSCHAETE road (inclusive).

        Lt.Col.WALTHALL & 108th.F.A.B.,H.Q.
           A/108 Batty.
           B/108 "
           C/108 "
           D/108(How)"
           B/109. Batty.
           C/109. "
           D/107(How)"

251.F.A.B.Group.   Covers from KEMMEL - WYTSCHAETE road (exclusive) to N.24.a.4.7.

        Lt.Col.MOSS BLUNDELL & 251 F.A.B.,H.Q.
           A/251 Batty.
           B/251 "
           A/250 "
        Has a call on D/107(How) Battery.
         " " " " How.Battery. 50th D.A. of the group on the left of 251st F.A.B.

SECRET.   Copy No. ......

OPERATION ORDER NO. 19.

By
Lieut.Colonel D. R. Coates,
Commanding, 107th Field A.B. Group.
----

1. The 107th F.A.Brigade Group will relieve 6th Australian F.A.M. to-night.

2. | 16th Battery | by | A/107 |
    | 17th   " | " | B/107 |
    | 18th   " | " | C/107 |
    | 106th   " | " | D/106 |

3. No reliefs will commence before 10.30 p.m. and will be carried out by sections at one hour intervals. No more than two guns to be out of action at any one time.

4. Ammunition. All ammunition in pits will be taken over, receipts given, and amount telephoned to Headquarters before 11 p.m. to-night.

5. (a) Until further orders are issued A/107 will cover Left Battalion and will be on duty, providing Liaison Officer and O.P. Officer. *and Recces Guards for to-night.*
   (b) Night lines of A/107 :-
       3 guns from U.1.a.0.7½. to U.1.a.6.8.
       1 gun on O.31.d.8.4. -

7. (a) B/107 and C/107 will cover Right Battalion.
   (b) Night lines of C/107, from O.31.d.8.4. to U.2.a.2½.2½.
   (c) Night lines of B/107, from U.2.a.2½.2½. to U.2.d.1.6.

8. Arrangements for Night lines, S.O.S. lines, Liaison Officer, and O.P. Officer will be the same as those previously laid down for these positions.

9. Battery Commanders will get into touch with Battalions and Companies they are supporting, tonight. These will be the 72nd Brigade when tonights Infantry relief is completed.

10. It is understood that the old B/106 positions are not being occupied. If this is so, O.C. A/107 will take over the ammunition in these positions and place a guard on same. He will find out the situation with regard to this battery and report same to Headquarters.

11. O.P. Officers are to be sent up at once on receipt of this order as the Australians are short of Subaltern Officers.

12. D/106 will hold their left section at disposal of 107th F.A.B. Group, and will lay out night lines of 1 howitzer on ONTARIO FARM, and 1 howitzer on Trench Tramway, SNIPERS HOUSE. The remaining section of D/106 will be at disposal of 106th F.A.B. Group.

                                              [signature]
                                              Lieut. R.F.A.
                                    Adjutant, 107th F.A.B. Group.

Copy No. 1. A/107
         2. B/107
         3. C/107
         4. D/106
         5. Brigade Major, 72nd I.B.
         6. Brigade Major, 24th D.A.

1. The 24th Divisional Artillery will relieve the 2nd Aus.Div.Arty. and the 21st F.A.Bde., 1st Div.Arty. on the night 8th/9th July.

2. The reliefs at gun positions and instructions for the march are shown in appendix 1, attached.
   Appendix 11 shows the temporary grouping.

3. The reliefs will be carried out by sections (including the guns) at about one hours interval, not more than two guns are to be out of action at any one time.
   No relief to commence before 10-30.p.m.
   Battery and Group Commanders will take over command on completion of relief on night: 8th/9th July.
   Completion of reliefs to be reported by wire to 2nd AUS.D.A.

4. (i) Brigades will take over all dumped ammunition in gun positions.
   Brigade Commanders will arrange, as under, for ammunition to be taken over at 10-30.p.m. at following former battery positions, 24th D.A., which are not at present being re-occupied.

   O.C. 106.F.A.B. - Ammunition in former D/107 position.
   O.C. 107 F.A.B. -   "   "   "   B/109   "
   O.C. 108.F.A.B. -   "   "   "   B/108   "
     "   "   "   -   "   "   " extra position adjoining
                                             B/109.

   (ii) Nos.1 & 2 Sections, 24th D.A.C. will march full. All ammunition in excess of establishment will be handed over to 50th D.A.C., under arrangements to be made between D.A.C. Commanders.
   The 24th D.A.C. will take over all ammunition dumped in AUS. D.A.C. wagon lines.
   (iii) Brigades and the 24th D.A.C. will report by 12 noon 9th inst. what ammunition they have taken over.

5. All maps, aeroplane photographs, panoramas etc. will be taken over.
   All existing communications will be taken over.

6. (i) 2" Trench Mortars, 24th D.A., will relieve 2" Trench Mortars, AUS.D.A. on the night 8th/9th under arrangements to be made direct between T.M. Commanders.

   (ii) All ammunition will be taken over, and a report is to be rendered by 12 noon 9th inst., of the amount taken over.

   (iii) V/24 T.M. Battery will not move.

7. All other details of the relief will be arranged between Group Commanders.
   As far as possible the teams which take guns into action, should bring back AUS.D.A. guns to wagon lines, and so reduce traffic to a minimum.

8. Command will pass from C.R.A. 2nd AUS.D.A. to C.R.A., 24th D.A. at 9.a.m. on July 9th.

9. Please acknowledge.

8/7/16.

Captain.R.A.

Brigade Major, 24th Divisional Artillery.

P.T.O.

Issued at 2.a.m.

Copies to

106th F.A.B.	No.1
107th F.A.B.	2
108th F.A.B.	3
109th F.A.B.	4
251st F.A.B.	5
Trench Mortars, 24th D.A.	6
24th D.A.G.	7
24th Div.G. two copies	8 & 9
" " Q	10
" " Train.	11
" " Signals.	12
A.D.M.S.,24th Div.	13
A.P.M. " "	14
41st D.A.	15
50th D.A.	16
2nd AUS.D.A.	17
H.A.,V.Corps.	18
11th.H.A.G.	19
No.1 Squadron.R.F.C.	20
WAR DIARY. two copies	21 & 22.
File	23
Spare Three copies	24, 25, 26.

S E C R E T.   S.23.

106th F.A.B.
107th F.A.B.
108th F.A.B
251st F.A.B.
T.M.24th D.A.
24th D.A.C.
==========

1 (a) The 41st Division will take over on the night 4th/5th July, the front south of the River DOUVE, but excluding the WINTER TRENCH.

   (b) The 2nd AUS. BDE. will on night 5th/6th July extend its front as far north as WULVERGHEM - MESSINES road (trench 140 inclusive.)

2   The front will continue to be covered vby the 24th Divisional Artillery as at present.

3   At 10.p.m. on July 3rd the 24th Division will come under the orders of the lX.Corps.

   At the same hour the command of troops in 1st. A. & N.Z.A.C. area (i.e. 2nd & 7th AUS I. BDES. and other details.) will pass from G.O.C., 24th DIVISION to G.O.C. 1st. A. & N.Z.A.C.

1/7/16.

Captain.R.A.

Brigade Major, 24th Divisional Artillery.

Reference Sheets 28 & 36.

APPENDIX 11.

Date.	Unit 24th D.A.	Unit vacating Wagon line to be taken over.	Destination wagon line at	Head of Column to pass road junction B.l.centre at	ROUTE.
July 4.	No.1.Sec.1.A.C.	No.2 Sec.50th.D.A.C.	M.34.b.3.9.	To move off on arrival of "A" Echelon, 2nd AUS.D.A.C. One Section 2nd NBS D.A.C. will billet at one farm at present occupied by No.4 Section. (S.21.b.6.3.)	B.l.centre - BAILLEUL - road-junction S.3.d.2.7.
" 2 Sec. "	" 3 "	" "	M.21.c.5.7.		

Nos. 1 & 2 Sections, 24th D.A.C. will leave guides to show incoming Sections places to which ammunition is supplied. "A" Echelon, 2nd AUS. D.A.C. will be responsible for the ammunition supply on completion of relief.

No.1 Section, 24th D.A.C., on relieving No.2 Section, 50th D.A.C. will be responsible for the ammunition supply, at present done by letter. Guides will be left by the 50th D.A.C.

July 5.	No.4.Sec.D.A.C.	No.4.Sec.50th D.A.C.	M.28.c.2.8½.	To move off from present wagon line at 9.a.m.	BAILLEUL - road junction S.3.d.2.7.
	H.Q.	H.Q.50th.D.A.C.	M.20.d.5.5.	To move off on arrival of H.Q. 50th D.A.C. 2nd AUS.D.A.C. about 1.p.m.	Ditto.
July 5.	1.Sec.A/106.	B/251 Batty.	M.28.d.5.6.	10.a.m.	B.l.centre - BAILLEUL - road junction.S.3.d.2.7
	1.Sec.C/106.	A/251 "	M.29.a.8.3.	10-20.a.m.	
	1.Sec.D/107.	D/251 "	M.54.d.1.6.	10-40.a.m.	
	1.Sec.B/108.	C/251 "	M.55.c.8.4.	To leave Wagon Line on morning 5th. 11-20.a.m.	via DRANOUTRE. B.l.centre- BAILLEUL - road junction S.3.d.2.7.
	1.Sec.B/109.	A/255. "	M.21.b.6.2.		

These Sections will relieve sections in action of the batteries, 50th D.A., named on night 5th/6th except C/106 Battery which relieves A/250 Battery, but takes over the wagon line of A/251 Battery.

Date.	Unit 24th D.A.	Unit vacating Wagon line to be taken over.	Destination Wagon Line at	Head of column to pass road junction B.1.centre at X	ROUTE.
July 5.	106th.F.A.B.,H.Q.	New Lines.	S.7.d.7.9	}	
	Remainder A/106 Batty.	B/251 Batty.	M.28.d.3.6.	} 3.p.m. and to be	
	B/106 "	New Lines.	M.33.a.2.9.	} clear of it by	
	Remainder C/106 "	A/251 Batty.	M.29.c.8.3.	} 5-30.p.m.	
	D/106. "	New Lines.	M.33.a.6.9.	}	ALL EXCEPT
	107th.F.A.B.,H.Q.	New Lines.	To be selected	}	B/108 via B.l.
	A/107 Batty.	" "	S.8.a.9.3	} 4.p.m. and to be	centre -
	B/107 "	" "	S.8.a.6.5	} clear of it by	BAILLEUL.
	C/107 "	" "	S.4.c.5.6	} 4-50.p.m.	
	Remainder D/107 "	D/251 Batty.	M.34.d.1.6	}	
	Remainder B/108 Batty.	C/251 Batty.	M.35.c.8.4.	To leave wagon line on afternoon 5TH and. 5-p.m.	
	D/108 "	New Lines.	M.35.d.5.3.		
	A/109 Batty.	New Lines.	M.24.a.5.3.	5-20.p.m. & to be clear by 5-45.p.m.	
	Remainder B/109 "	A/253 Batty.	M.21.b.5.2.		

H.Q. and Batteries will completely vacate old wagon lines, only leaving teams, etc. necessary for relief on night 5th/6th July. The latter will march direct to new wagon lines on effecting relief.

S E C R E T.   Copy No. 2

S.25.

1. The Right Group, 50th D.A. will be relieved by Col. BURNE's GROUP on night 5th/6th & 6th/7th July.
A list of Battery positions, etc. will be sent to Col. Burne.
Table of reliefs is shown in attached Appendices.

2. Reliefs at gun positions will be carried out by sections (including the guns) no relief to take place before 10-30.p.m. each evening.
Col Burne and relieving Battery Commanders will take over command on completion of reliefs on night 6th/7th July.
Completion of reliefs each night to be reported by wire to 24th D.A., H.Q.

3. (i) Outgoing batteries will march with their full establishment of ammunition, and will hand over all dumped ammunition to incoming batteries.

(ii) 251 F.A.B. will report by 12 noon on 7th July how much ammunition they have handed over, and 106 F.A.B. how much they have taken over.

4. All trench maps and aeroplane photos will be taken over.

5. All existing communications will be taken over.

7. All other details of the relief will be arranged between Group Commanders.

8. Please acknowledge.

4/7/16.

Captain. R.A.
Brigade Major, 24th Divisional Artillery.

Copies to

106th F.A.B.	No.1
107th F.A.B.	" 2
108th F.A.B.	" 3
109th F.A.B.	" 4
251st F.A.B.	" 5
Trench Mortars	
24th D.A.	" 6
24th D.A.C.	" 7
17th Inf.Bde.	" 8
73rd Inf.Bde.	" 9
24th Div.G.	" 10
" " "	" 11
24th Div.Q.	" 12
A.D.M.S.24th.D.	" 13
24th Div.Train.	" 14
24th Signals.	15.
50th D.A.	" 16
H.A.,V.Corps.	" 17
2nd AUS&D.A.	" 18.
WAR DIARY.	" 19 & 20.
File.	" 21
Spare.	" 22. 23 & 24.

APPENDIX 1.

On night July 4th/5th.

1 Section Batty, F.A.Bde, 1st AUS.DIV. relieve 1 Section A/106.
1   "   "   "   "   "   "   "   "   1   "   B/106.
1   "   "   "   "   "   "   "   "   1   "   C/106.
1   "   "   "   "   "   "   "   "   1   "   D/107.

1 Section Batty, 6th F.A.Bde, 2nd AUS.DIV. relieve 1 Sec. A/107. ✓
1   "   "   "   "   "   "   "   "   1   " B/107. ✓
1   "   "   "   "   "   "   "   "   1   " C/107. ✓
1   "   "   "   "   "   "   "   "   1   " D/106.

1 Section Batty., 4th or 5th F.A.Bde. 2nd AUS.DIV. relieve 1 Sec. B/108.
1   "   "   "   "   "   "   "   "   "   1   " D/108.
1   "   "   "   "   "   "   "   "   "   1   " A/109.
1   "   "   "   "   "   "   "   "   "   1   " B/109.

On being relieved on 4th/5th, Sections will go to their Wagon Lines.

On night 5th/6th.

H.Q., F.A.Bde. 1st.AUS.DIV. relieve H.Q. 106th F.A.B.
1 Section Batty.   "   "   "   1 Section A/106.
1   "   "   "   "   "   1   "   B/106.
1   "   "   "   "   "   1   "   C/106.
1   "   "   "   "   "   1   "   D/107.

H.Q. 6th F.A.Bde. 2nd AUS. DIV. relieve H.Q., 107th F.A.B.
1 Section Batty.   "   "   "   "   1 Section A/107.
1   "   "   "   "   "   "   1   "   B/107.
1.   "   "   "   "   "   "   1   "   C/107.
1   "   "   "   "   "   "   1   "   D/106.

1 Section Batty. 4th or 5th F.A.Bde. 2nd AUS.DIV. relieve 1 Sec. B/108.
1   "   "   "   "   "   "   "   "   "   1   " D/108.
1   "   "   "   "   "   "   "   "   "   1   " A/109.
1   "   "   "   "   "   "   "   "   "   1   " B/109.

On completion of relief 5th/6th, Bde.H.Q. and sections march to new wagon lines.

APPENDIX 1.

On night 5th/6th.

1 Section A/106 Batty relieve 1 Section B/251 Battery.

1	"	C/106	"	"	1	"	A/250	"
1	"	D/107	"	"	1	"	D/251	"
1	"	B/108	"	"	1	"	C/251	"
1	"	B/109	"	"	1	"	A/253	"

     On 6th inst. 106th F.A.B.,H.Q. Staff relieve 251 F.A.B.,H.Q. Staff at Wagon Line N.19.c.8.4½.

On night 6th/7th.

H.Q. 106th F.A.B. relieve H.Q. 251 F.A.B.

1 Section A/106 relieve 1 Section B/251 Battery.

1	"	C/106	"	1	"	A/250	"
1	"	D/107	"	1	"	D/251	"
1	"	B/108	"	1	"	C/251	"
1	"	B/109	"	1	"	A/253	"

(1) 1 Officer from each relieving battery 24th D.A. will be sent over on July 5th to see new battery position.

(2) Incoming Battery Commanders should go to new positions on morning on July 6th.

APPENDIX 11.

Dispositions of 24th D.A. after relief of Right Group, 50th D.A.

RIGHT GROUP.

Lt.Col.WALTHALL & 108th.F.A.B.,H.Q.
A/108 Battery.
Battery relieving B/108.
C/108 Battery.
Battery relieving D/108.
C/109 Battery.

LEFT GROUP.

Lt.Col.BURNE & 106th F.A.B.,H.Q.
A/106 Battery.
C/106   "
D/107   "
B/108   "
B/109   "
A/251   "

IN REST.

B/106.
D/106.
107th F.A.B.,H.Q.
A/107.
B/107.
C/107.
D/108.
109th F.A.B.,H.Q.
A/109

Reference Sheet 28.S.W.

APPENDIX 111.
****

Batty. 24th D.A.	Battery 50th D.A. relieved.	Battery Position.	O.P.	ZONE.
A/106.	B/251.	N.15.d.2.2.	N.26.b.4.8½.	opposite E1, E2, E3, F2.
C/106.	A/250.	N.14.c.8.9.	N.20.d.4.3.	opposite H2. J3.
D/107.	D/251	N.26.c.8.7 (3 guns) T.5.c.3.8 (1 gun)	N.23.c.3.7.	" E1 to H1 a.
B/108.	C/251	N.34.a.7.2.	N.26.b.3.9.	" F4, F5, G1.
B/109	A/253	N.27.c.8¾.¾.	N.26.c.2½.3.	" F2, F3, F4.
	A/251 (Not relieved)	N.16.a.3.3½.	N.20.d.4.7.	" G2, G3, G4, H1 c.

H.Q. 108th F.A.B. relieve H.Q. 251 F.A.B. at N.20.a.4.2½

Issued only to 106th F.A.B.
     107th " "
     108th " "
     109th " "
     251st " "

Copy No. 2

S E C R E T. S.24(1)

1. Artillery of the 1st A. & N.Z.A.C. will relieve the 106 F.A.B. and 107 F.A.B. Groups, also B/108 & D/108 Batteries, on the nights 4th/5th & 5th/6th July.
    The batteries which relieve B/108 & D/108 batteries will be under the tactical control of the 108th F.A.B. Group.
    The 24th D.A.C. will be relieved on the 4th & 5th July.

2. The reliefs at gun positions and the march tables to new wagon lines are shown in appendices attached.

3. Reliefs at gun positions will be carried out by sections (including the guns), no relief to take place before 10-30.p.m each evening.
    Battery & Group Commanders will hand over command on completion of relief on night 5th/6th July.
    Completion of reliefs each night to be reported by wire to 24th D.A., H.Q.

4. (i) Batteries and "A" Echelon D.A.C. will march with their full establishment of ammunition.
   (ii) "B" Echelon will march empty.
   (iii) All remaining ammunition will be left in the present dumps at gun positions and at the D.A.C.. Groups and the D.A.C. to report by 12 noon July 6th what ammunition has been handed over.
   The D.A.C. will also report what dumped ammunition is taken over from 50th D.A.C.

5. All trench maps and aeroplane photos will be handed over.

6. All existing communications will be handed over.

7. All other details of the relief will be arranged between Group Commanders.

8. C.R.A., 2nd AUS. DIV. will take over command from C.R.A., 24th DIV. at 10.a.m. on July 6th.

9. Please acknowledge.

[signature]
Captain. R.A.

Brigade Major, 24th Divisional Artillery.

Copy No. 1 106th F.A.B.
"   " 2   107th F.A.B.
"   " 3   108th F.A.B.
"   " 4   109th F.A.B.
"   " 5   251st F.A.B.
"   " 6   Trench Mortars. 24th D.A.
"   " 7   D.A.C. 24TH DIV.
"   " 8   2nd AUS INF BDE.
"   " 9   7th   "   "   "
"   " 10 17th "   "   "
"   " 11 24th Div.G.
"   " 12   "   "   "

Copy No. 13 24th Div.Q.
"   " 14 24th Div.Train.
"   " 15 24th Div.Signals.
"   " 16 A.D.M.S. 24th Div.
"   " 17 A.P.M. 24th Div.
"   " 18 41st D.A.
"   " 19 50th D.A.
"   " 20 H.A., V. CORPS.
"   " 21 2nd AUS D.A.
"   " 22 & 23 WAR DIARY.
"   " 24 File.
"   " 25, 26 & 27. Spare.

O.C. GINGER   Secret. 1

1. A minor enterprise will be carried out by
   73rd Infy. Bde. on the evening of 7th inst at a
   Zero hour to be notified later.

2. Point of attack. S.15.a 2.8½.

3. On return of raiding party probably about +80'
   the Left Group may be required to barrage
   the Support & Communication trenches.
   The time to commence will be sent from this
   office by the words "go on".

4. The barrage will last for 5', stop for 10',
   start again for 5'.
   Rate 2 rds. per gun & howr. per minute

5. Your barrage will be —
     1 Battery   S.9.c.5.2 — 5.4 — 8.4
       (1½ way between pts 65 & 71 enfilade 71 to 73)

     1 Battery. S.9.c 9½ to 7½ . 5
       (pts. 67 to 79)

     Howrs.   pts. 73 & 67.

                                   F.C. Walthall
   acknowledge.   Lt. Col. R.F.A
   6 /1b/16   Comdg. 108 Bde. R.F.A

SECRET.   S.33.

106th F.A.B.
107th F.A.B.
108th F.A.B.
109th F.A.B.
251st F.A.B.
Trench Mortars, 24th D.A.
24th D.A.C.
50th D.A.
================

1   On the night 8th/9th July :-

(a) 41st DIV. continue to hold the line as far north as R.DOUVE.

(b) 72nd I.B. relieve 2nd AUSTRALIAN DIV. on front R.DOUVE to C 3 trench inclusive.

(c) 17th I.B. extend their southern flank, and will hold front from C 4 trench to F 5 trench, both inclusive.

(d) A Brigade, 50th DIV. relieve 73rd I.B. in the trenches G 1 to J 3 R, both inclusive.

2   The 251.F.A.B.Group come under the command of the C.R.A. 50th DIV. on completion of relief in para 1 (d)
    O.C., 251.F.A.B. will report by wire to this H.Q. when Infantry relief is completed.

3   The 50th D.A. are leaving 3 2" trench mortars on the front between E 1 & F 5 trenches. These come under the tactical command of O.C., 108.F.A.B.

8/7/16.
                                            Captain.R.A.
              Brigade Major, 24th Divisional Artillery.

Reference Sheet 28.S.W.　　　　　　　　　　　　　　Copy No. 2

SECRET.　　　　　　　　　　　　　　　　　　　　　S.35.

1. On completion of Artillery relief on night 11th/12th July, the 41st D.A. will take over the Artillery support of the line as far north as the R.DOUVE.

2. Reliefs will take place as follows. No relief to take place before 10.p.m. Guns to be removed.

　(i) On each night 9th/10th and 11th/12th July.

　　　1 Sec. A/109 Batty. is relieved by 1 Sec. C/183 Batty. 41st D.A. (each night)
　　　On relief the Sec. A/109 Batty. will occupy former B/108 Batty. position (T.34.a.2.9) and will be under tactical command of O.C.,108th F.A.B.

　(b) In addition on night 11th/12th July.
　　　B/106 Batty. will withdraw from its present position, and come under tactical command of O.C.,107th F.A.B. It will go into action again the same night in former B/109 Batty. position (T.11.a.5.5)
　　　B/106 & A/109 batteries will keep their present wagon lines.

3. A/109 & B/106 Batteries will march out with their full establishment of ammunition.
　　A/109 & B/106 Batteries will hand over all dumped ammunition to C/183 Battery. A report of the amount handed over will be rendered to this Office by 12 noon, 12th July.
　　A/109 Battery will take over all dumped ammunition in former B/108 Battery position.
　　B/106 Battery will take over all dumped ammunition in former B/109 position.
　　A/109 & B/106 batteries will hand over trench maps, aeroplane photographs, panoramas, etc. to C/183 Battery.

4. A/109 & B/106 Batteries will hand over all existing communications to C/183 Battery.

5. (i) The 3 2" trench mortars, 24th D.A. in vicinity of ANTON'S FARM will be withdrawn on the night 9th-10th and will be replaced by two 2" mortars, 41st D.A.

　(ii) The 3 2" trench Mortars, 50th D.A., between E.1 and F 5 trenches will be relieved by 3 2" trench mortars, 24th D.A. on the night 11th/12th July.

　(iii) All arrangements for (i) and (ii) will be made between Trench Mortar Commanders concerned.
　　All dumped ammunition will be taken over by incoming T.M. Battery. O.C. Trench Mortars, 24th D.A. will report by 12 noon on 10th inst., how much ammunition he has handed over on night 9th/10th. and will report by 12 noon on 12th inst., how much ammunition he has taken over on night 11th/12th July.

6. All other details of the relief will be arranged Left Group Commander, 41st D.A. and Right Group Commander, 24th D.A.

7. Please acknowledge.

8/7/16.　　　　　　　　　　　　　　　　　　　　　Captain. R.A.
　　　　　　　　　　　　　　　　Brigade Major, 24th Divisional Artillery.

Copies to
106th F.A.B.	No.1	T.M.24th D.A.	No.5	50th D.A.		No.9
107th " " "	2	24th D.A.C.	6	R.A.IX.Corps.		10
108th " " "	3	24th Div.	7	War Diary		11 & 12
109th " " "	4	41st D.A.	8	File		13
				Spare		14. 15. 16.

SECRET.   B.M.446.

106th F.A.B.Group.
107th "   " "   "
108th "   " "   "
================================

    Wire cutting will be carried out along the whole 24th Divisional Front on July 15th. 16th & 17th.

    As a rough guide about 600 rounds per Group should be expended each day on wire cutting, but this may be exceeded, if required.

    Groups will consult with Infantry Brigadiers as to the places at which wire is to be cut. Support line as well as front line wire should be cut. A report is required by the 1st D.R. on 15th inst., of the places at which wire is to be cut each day.

    The 4-30.p.m. telegraphic report should give briefly the results obtained. The daily operation report should contain further details.

14/7/16.

Captain.R.A.
Brigade Major, 24th Divisional Artillery.

Reference Sheet 28.S.W.

S E C R E T.

106th F.A.B.
107th F.A.B.
108th F.A.B.
109th F.A.B.
T.M. 24th D.A.
24th D.A.C.
24th DIV.

S.37.

1. On completion of infantry relief on night 11th/12th July, the 24th Division front will be held as follows:-

   (a) RIGHT SECTOR.   72nd I.B.

      Front.   R. DOUVE to trench 140 (inclusive)

   (b) CENTRE SECTOR.   73rd I.B.

      Front.   Trench 141 to Trench D 4 (both inclusive)

   (c) LEFT SECTOR.   17th I.B.

      Front.   Trench D 5 to Trench F 5 (both inclusive)

2. The 24th Divisional Artillery will be re-grouped at 4.p.m. on July 12th as follows:-

   (a) RIGHT GROUP.   To cover RIGHT SECTOR.

          Lt.Col.BURNE & 106.F.A.B.,H.Q.
             A/106 Batty.
             B/106 "
             C/106 "
             D/106(How)"
             B/107 "

   (b) CENTRE GROUP.   To cover CENTRE SECTOR.

          Lt.Col.COATES & 107 F.A.B.,H.Q.
             A/107 Batty.
             C/107 "
             C/108 "
             C/109 "
             D/108(How)"

   (c) LEFT GROUP.   To cover LEFT SECTOR.

          Lt.Col.WALTHALL & 108 F.A.B.,H.Q.
             A/108 Batty.
             B/108 "
             A/109 "
             B/109 "
             D/107(How)"

3. The single gun B/106 Battery at U.12.d.8.1 will be put back in the main battery position on the night 12th/13th July.

4. Arrangements for new communications should be made forthwith.

All details of the re-grouping will be arranged between Group Commanders concerned.
Group Commanders will report by wire, when they assume command of their new Groups.

5   Please acknowledge.

10/7/16.

Captain. R.A.
Brigade Major, 24th Divisional Artillery.

Reference Sheet. 28.S.W.   Copy No. 2

SECRET.   S.28.

1   At 4.p.m. on July 7th the batteries 24th D.A., in action will be re-grouped as follows:-

RIGHT GROUP. To cover 17th I.B. front, N.36.a.7.1 to N.29.b.8½.6½.

    Lt.Col.WALTHALL & 108.F.A.B.,H.Q.
    A/108 Battery. R.F.A.
    B/108   "   " " "
    B/10.9   "   " " "
    D/107(How) "   " " "

LEFT GROUP. To cover 73rd I.B. front N.28.b.9½.6½ to N.24.a.5.7.

    Lt.Col.BURNE and 106th F.A.B.H.Q.
    A/106 Battery.R.F.A.
    C/106   "   " " "
    A/251   "   " " "

2   (i) Alterations in communications will be arranged by 4.p.m. on July 7th.
    (ii) Any necessary registration on change of zones will be carried out on the morning of the 7th.
    (iii) Group Commanders will report when they have assumed command of their new Groups.

3   (i) D/106(How) Battery will commence on 7th inst. to construct a battery position at N.21.b.9.2½ and will occupy it as soon as ready. When in action D/106 Battery will be grouped with Left Group.
    Until D/106 Battery is in action both groups will have a call on D/107 Battery.

4   From 4.p.m. July 7th No.3 Sec. 24th D.A.C. will be responsible for the ammunition supply of Right Group 24th D.A. and No.1.Sec. 24th D.A.C. for that of Left Group 24th D.A.

5   Please acknowledge.

Copies to

106th F.A.B.	No.1
107th " " " "	2
108th " " " "	3
109th " " " "	4
Trench Mortars 24th D.A.	5
24th D.A.C.	6
17th I.B.	7
73rd I.B.	8
24th Div.	9
11th H.A.G.	10

[signature]
Captain.R.A.
Brigade Major, 24th Divisional Artillery.

Reference Sheet 28.S.W.

S E C R E T.   S.27.

1   (i) On July 5th, the Heavy Trench Mortar Battery, and the three Medium Trench Mortar Batteries of the 2nd AUS. DIV. will arrive at 24th D.A., T.M. CAMP.

       (ii) V/24 Heavy T.M. Battery will move to camp at N.19.c.0.5 on July 5th.

2   On night July 6th/7th two Medium Trench Mortar Batteries, 2nd AUS.D.A., will relieve the right and centre Trench Mortar Batteries 24th D.A.

3   On July 7th, the three Medium Trench Mortar Batteries, 24th D.A., less equipment and personnel in action now on 17th I.B. front, will move to Camp at N.19.c.0.5.

4   On night July 8th/9th two Medium Trench Mortar Batteries, 24th D.A. less 2 guns, will relieve the six guns 50th D.A. in the line between E1 & N.24.a.5.7.

5   For both reliefs

       (i) Guns will be removed, but all ammunition in each sector will be taken over.

       (ii) Trench Mortar Commander, 24th D.A., will report amount of

           (a) Ammunition handed over to 2nd AUS.D.A.
           (b)   "   taken   "   from 50th D.A.

       (iii) All other details of relief to be arranged by Trench Mortar Commanders concerned.

6   Arrangements for transport will be notified by the Staff Captain.

7   Completion of reliefs to be notified by wire to H.Q., 24th D.A.

                                                       [signature]
                                                       Captain.R.A.

                           Brigade Major, 24th Divisional Artillery.

Copies to

106th F.A.B.
107th   "   "   "
108th   "   "   "
109th   "   "   "
251st   "   "   "
Trench Mortars, 24th D.A.
V/24 Heavy T.M. Batty.
24th D.A.C.
2nd AUS I.B.
7th   "   "   "
17th I.B.
73rd I.B.
24th Div. G.
24th Div. Q.
24th Div. Train.
50th D.A.
2nd AUS.D.A.

SECRET.   S.29.

24th DIVISIONAL ARTILLERY Headquarters will close at BAILLEUL at 11.a.m. on July 6th, and re-open at LOCRE at the same hour.

[signature]
Captain. R.A.
Brigade Major, 24th Divisional Artillery.

Copies to

106th F.A.B.
✓107th   "   "   "
108th   "   "   "
109th   "   "   "
251st   "   "   "
Trench Mortars. 24th D.A.
24th D.A.C.
17th I.B.
73rd I.B.
24th Div. G.
24th   "   Q.
24th   "   Train.
24th   "   Signals.
A.D.M.S. 24th DIV.
A.P.M.   "   "
A.D.O.S.   "   "
A.D.V.S.
2nd AUS.D.A.
50th D.A.
H.A., V. CORPS.
11th. H.A.G.
No.1 Squadron, R.F.C.

SECRET S.26.

1. (i) C/109 Battery will be relieved by a battery of the 2nd AUS.DIV. on nights 5th/6th & 6th/7th July.
Command to pass to incoming battery commander on completion of relief on night 6th/7th July.

   (ii) One section of an "extra battery" will also come into action in the additional gun pits on the left of C/109 Battery on night 5th/6th July. The remaining section of this battery will come into action when two more pits are completed.

   (iii) No section to move up to battery position before 10-30.p.m.

2. On relief, C/109 Battery will withdraw to rest in their present wagon line. The incoming batteries, 2nd AUS. DIV., will occupy new wagon lines.

3. All communications will be handed over, also maps and aeroplane photographs.

4. (i) On the night 6th/7th July, on completion of relief of C/109 Battery, a Group Commander, 2nd AUS.DIV.ARTY., will take over command of batteries of Col WALTHALL'S GROUP, less A/108 Battery.

   (ii) The Left Group Commander, 2nd AUS.DIV.ARTY, will be responsible for the Artillery support of the line as far north as WULVERGHEM - WYTSCHAETE road inclusive.

   (iii) (a) When the "extra battery" 2nd AUS.D.A. is in action and registered, the Left Group Commander, 2nd AUS.D.A. will at once inform H.Q.108.F.A.B. C/108 Battery will then come under the orders of the 108.F.A.B. and will be withdrawn the same night to rest in wagon line.
   (Note - When one section "extra battery" is registered, if Group Commanders concerned agree, one section C/108 may be withdrawn to wagon line.)

   (b) Completion of withdrawal to be reported by wire to this Office.

   (c) C/108 will withdraw to wagon with its full establishment of ammunition. All ammunition surplus to this will be left dumped in evacuated gun position and a guard left on it. The amount of ammunition left dumped, will be reported to this office on the day following withdrawal of C/108.

   (iv) The Left Group Commander, 2nd AUS.DIV.ARTY. will take over the present 108th.F.A.B.Battle.H.Q. as his Group H.Q.

5. From 4.p.m. on July 7th., the 2nd AUS. D.A. will be responsible for the ammunition supply of the Left Group, 2nd AUS.D.A.

6. All other details of the relief will be arranged between Group Commanders.

[signature]
Captain.R.A.
Brigade Major, 24th Divisional Artillery.

Copies to
106th F.A.B.
107th " " "
108th " " "
109th " " "
251st " " "
24th D.A.C.
7th AUS.I.B.
17th I.B.
24th DIV.
2nd AUS.D.A.
File.

OPERATION ORDERS No. 14.   Ref. Sheet 28.

BY

LT. COLONEL D. R. COATES,   COMMANDING 107/F.A.B. GROUP.

Copy No. 1.   SECRET.   4th July 1916.

1. Batteries of 107 F.A.B. Group will be relieved and march as stated below.

2. Guns will be removed, relief will be by sections. No relief before 10.30.p.m.
    B.C's hand over command on completion.

3. Ammunition. Batteries will march out with complete establishment. Surplus will be handed over, receipts obtained, and forwarded to 107 F.A.B. Hd.Qrs. by 10.am 6/7/16.

4. Trench maps, airplane photos and communications will be handed over.

5. Location of new Hd.Qrs. will be communicated as soon as known.

6. Baggage wagons re-join this afternoon.

6(a) A/107, B/107, C/107 relieved by Batteries F.A.B., 2nd Anzac Division.

   First Section night 4th/5th :-   Second Section night 5th/6th.
   Sections relieved first night go to their present Wagon Lines.
   First Sections march to New Wagon Lines on afternoon of July 5th.
   Second Sections follow on completion of reliefs.

(b) Location of New Lines for above units.
     A/107 S 8 a 9.3.   B/107 S 8 a 6.6.   C/107 S 4 c 5.6.

(c) March table of first Sections of above units.(2nd Sections march by same route at their own time)

     Starting point   Road junction B 1 central.

     Route   Via BAILLEUL.

     Time to pass S.P. C/107 4.p.m.   A/107 4.5.p.m.   B/107 4.10.p.m.
     HQ will pass B1 central at 4.15 pm
     Batteries march independently.

OPERATION ORDERS No. 14 continued.

7(a) B/109 relieved by 13th Battery 5th F.A.B. 2nd Anzac Division.

First Section night 4th/5th :- Second Section night 5th/6th.

Section relieved first night goes to its present Wagon Lines; and marches to New Wagon Lines of A/253 on morning July 5th; relieving section of A/253 battery in action on the night 5th/6th.

Second Section follows to wagon lines of A/253 on completion of relief.

(b) Location of Wagon Lines A/253 - M 21 b 6.2.
    "   " Battery Position A/253 - (not known)

(c) March Table of above unit:-
    Starting Point.   Road junction B.1 central.
    Route.   BAILLEUL - road junction S 3 d 2.7.
    Time to pass S.P.   11.20.a.m.

Above time for first section only; second section marches by same route on completion of relief.

8(a) D/106 relieved by Battery 6 F.A.B. 2nd Anzac Division.

First Section night 4th/5th. Second Section night 5th/6th.
Section relieved first night goes to present Wagon Lines.
First Section marches to New Wagon Lines on afternoon July 5th.
Second Section follows on completion of relief.

(b) Location of New Wagon Lines of above unit M 33 a 6.9.

(c) March Table of First Section (Second Section follows by same route at its own time)

    Starting Point.   Road Junction B.1 central.
    Route.   Via BAILLEUL.
    Time to pass S.P.   3.15.p.m.

9. Wagon Lines are to be cleared of everything, except the necessary teams etc. for Second Sections, when First Sections march out.

Copy No. 1 War Diary.   No. 5 B/109.
        2 A/107.   6 D/106.
        3 B/107.   7 B.M. 7 Anzacs.
        4 C/107.   8 B.M. 24 D.A.

                                        Lieut.R.F.A.
                              Adjutant, 107/F.A/Brigade.

SC/2685

106th F.A.B.
107th F.A.B.
108th F.A.B.
109th F.A.B.
24th D.A.C.
==========

Tentage may be taken from present wagon lines in cases where no incoming units are taking over Camps at present occupied by Batteries or Sections of D.A.C.

Note

The 50th D.A.C. will not re-occupy the present Camps of Nos 1. 2 & 4 Sections, 24th D.A.C.

8/7/16.

Captain. R.A.

Staff Captain, 24th Divisional Artillery.

24th

107 Elward
R F A
Vol 6

Vol II
Army Form C. 2118.
107 R.F.A

WAR DIARY
INTELLIGENCE SUMMARY
107 F.A. Bde — XXVI

August 1916

Place	Date	Hour	Summary of Events and Information	Remarks and references to Appendices
Daours-Fréquent	1st		Resting	Ref Orders
	2nd		"	
	3rd		"	
	4th	2.30.AM	107th F.A.B. marched to BOIS DES TAILLES NORTH. C.K.12.a.7.b. arrived	France sheet 62d. March orders attached
	5th		Resting	
	6th		"	
	7th		"	
	8th		"	
	9th		"	
	10th		Brigade less section relieved 163 F.A.B. 35th D.A. 12 noon	
	11th		Brigade on return to HQ	
	12th		A/Bty relieved A/163 position a.3.a.40 — ship completed by 11 noon 2nd Oct	Reference sheets 62.c.N.W.
			B/ " " B/163 " a.3.a.8.2	62.d.n.s.
			C/ " " C/163 " a.3.c.6.5	
			D/ " " D/163 " a.3.c.5.3	163 relief orders attached
			107 F.A.B. HQ " a.3.c.5.3	
	13th		Reported fired at night on area allotted by G.O.C. R.A. 300 Rds 18pr 150 Rds 4.5 Hrs	Counterfire attacked
	14th		"	No 32 Ops I Operation
			One 18pr cut wire and repaired. 4.5 How fired on taught in Conversation with a heavy	orders 33 Opsn I
			Bty as Ref. 1.O.R. at their daily allowance of Rd. 1.O.R. omitted night Rds ½ 19/8/16	attached
	15th		Wire cutting all 18pr batteries. 4.5 Hrs. Reported.	Operation orders
	16th		107 F.A.B. supported the 42nd & 9/B in their attack CS30t7 2 K.S.30 67.4 ½ also with parallel to French hand	No 34 Opsn I sheets 57.c.S.W.
			the SUNKEN Rd. just E of H in Conjunction with the FRENCH and 3rd Division on our right.	62.c.N.W.I. and
			107/C.N.W. B/107 stoutly knocked @ July.	Guadecourt attached

Army Form C. 2118.

WAR DIARY
or
INTELLIGENCE SUMMARY.
(Erase heading not required.)

10½/F MIBde   XXVII

August 1916.

Place	Date	Hour	Summary of Events and Information	Remarks and references to Appendices
	16/8	From 7 pm to 6.30 pm	NEW S.O.S lines for 18th. A/104. T.25.a.2.3.4. T.25.a.4.4. B/104. T.25.a.4.4.6. S.30.6.9.2.6. C/104. S.30.6.9.2.6. & S.30.6.9.4.7.	Maps Ref: LONGUEVAL 57C.SW.3. Operation order No 35. attached.
		4.5 Hrs. Stry Hrs. T.25.a.3.1.6. S.30.6.9.9.	
		night firing 18 pm	A/104. T.25.a.2.3. b. S.30.6.9.7.7. b.T.25.6.0.5. b. T.25.b.0.9. B/104. T.25.b.0.5. – T.25.b.0.9. – T.26.a.2.2.6. – T.26.a.2.2.9. C/104. T.26.a.2.2.9. – T.26.a.2.2.g – T.20.a.9.0. – T.27.b.0.10. T.25.a.5.8. – T.25.a.10.3. – T.25.f.1.8.2. – T.25.a.7.8. – T.26.6.8.8.2. – T.27.a.8.0. – T.20.d.9.0.	ditto. Operation order no 36. attached.
		4.5 Hrs. D/104.	
	17.	4.7 pm	104th F.a.B. Carried out Bombardment I & Repulsed. night firing. Searched the area as per Operation order no 32. of the kings completed. Searched also as per operation order no 36. S.O.S. lines for Bde. as per operation order N°36.	Operation order no 37 attached.
	18/8		20 the Rants killed 104 Rants wounded.	Ref Map. 1/10000 Trench/O.S.W.3. 57 C. CM &. Map 1/5000. family out Guillemont. operation order no 38. attached.
	18/8		104th F.a.B. took part in the attack by the Scott Pivision. Y3 – 9.B. ø 1/4th 9.B. 1st objective. Z09.Y3 r 9.B. The enemy defences from S.30.b.6.2. clear of the Sunken road and including trench from S.30.b.6.2. which runs East of The Sunken road" b.T.25.a.2.0.9. Thence to The street b. S.24.d.8.6.2	
	19/8		14 th 9.B. Enemy defences from S.24.d.8.6. – Sept.d.4.2. – M.G. House inclusive) T.19.a.1.6. b. S.28.W.5.2.4. 2nd objective. Z09.2.4 hrs. Y3 9.B. The line T.25.a.3.3 – T.25.a.2.8 – T.25.a.3.9. – T19.c.3.v. Thence	
			the Eastern & northern edges of The Quarry (T.19.C.) S.24.d.6.8. – T.19.d.19.5 – S.24.b.7.4. Toast The Station and defences round it from 9. B. The Station and defences round it Rt. Austin F. wounded 10 Others. Rant wounded Rt. Stinich. W. Gray R. Austin F wounded 16 Others Rant wounded	

WAR DIARY or INTELLIGENCE SUMMARY

Army Form C. 2118.

10th/F.A./1 Bde   **August 1916**   **XXVIII**

Place	Date	Hour	Summary of Events and Information	Remarks and references to Appendices
	19th		Night firing. Searched back from the S.O.S. lines as far East as a North and South line through T.19.d.4.0. Registering all 18 pdrs and 4.5" How and usual routine firing with allotted rounds. S.O.S. lines 18 hrs. A/107. T.25.b.0.4. — T.19.d.2.4. B/107. T.19.d.3.3. — T.19.c.9½.4. C/107. T.19.c.9½.4½. — T.19.a.9.1. (along road).	Map Ref. LONGUEVAL 57c. S.W.3. 2 pdrs lost (attached Army N°1)
	20th			
	21st	4.30 pm	18 pdr Hows as before. Attd by the 2nd Div. survivors reserved 107th supported same. Active area north of Mount Street from T.19.c.3.2. — Road junction T.19.c.4.6 bn. Road junction T.24.d.8 and to form a defensive flank on the railway MOUNT STREET and 2nd Corps trench 14th & 9/13 Bn. Rifle Bgt. 2 Other ranks wounded.	Map Ref. V. 10000. LONGUEVAL 57c. S.W.3. Operation order N°39 attached. Copy N°1.
	22nd		18 pdrs moved up into new positions which were originally selected as part of 22nd & morning 23rd. A/107 & B/107 moved up into new position. A4a.5.9.4. & 28.C.4.2. 1 8 pdr & 1 O.R. wounded. Steady fire on S.O.S. lines by day. New S.O.S. lines his operation order N° 40 para 3. Night firing from 7.30 pm as per operation order N° 40 para 4. All batteries.	Map Ref. LONGUEVAL I MARICOURT. Operation order N°40 attached copy N°1
	23rd		Registering by all batteries and checking lines, also ranged alarm S.O.S. line S.O.S. and night firing as laid down in operation order N° 40 of 22-8-16. Enemy moved up new position. Night firing.	Map Ref. 1/20000 Ginchy & Guillemont Operation order N°41 attached copy N°1
	24th	3.45 pm to 8.6 pm	Morning: Registered all batteries. 107 Bde and checked lines. Afternoon: Carried out programme as laid down in operation order N°41. 2 O.R. wounded.	

Army Form C. 2118.

WAR DIARY
or
INTELLIGENCE SUMMARY.
(Erase heading not required.)

161 1/FA/16/26   August 1916.   XXIX

Place	Date	Hour	Summary of Events and Information	Remarks and references to Appendices
	25th	8 AM	18 pdrs fired their allotment of rounds, reported and checked lines. 2/Lt: D.T. WEDDELL seriously wounded.	LONGUEVAL. 57cS.W.3.
		8 pm	4.5 Hows R/PoY. ditto	
		8 pm	18 pdrs and 4.5 Hows fired allotment of rounds Search areas and down operation order 40.	
	26th	8 AM	18 pdrs all fired allotment of rounds reported and checked lines, three officers joined 147 Bde 2/Lts L. CHOY, 4.5 How.	4.16. operation order no 40 attached
		8 pm		
		8 pm	ALL Batteries fired in their areas in accordance with operation order no 40. 3 Lieuts SGS king	
	27th	8 AM	2nd Lt S.A.SHARLAND. 2/Lt W.E.EVANS. 2/Lt A.O.FOSTER the two former L.C."M" the latter to D/147.	4.16 operation order no 40 attached
		8 pm	All batteries reporting rounds on New Zones per operation order no 43 SGSwell Wired R/147. ditto	
		8 pm	4.5 Hows in Lime zones in operation order no 48.	Jona Zone order no 43 attached
	28th	8 AM	18 pdr & Hows fired their allotment of Rds on day areas	
		8 pm	ditto " " " " night "	
		8 pm 1.M no 1/16		
	29th		ditto & carried out harassing & preparative operations 17-28th in operation order no 45. operations performed. 1 other Rank wounded 10 other Rank missing.	operation order no 45 attached
	30th		ditto 18 pdrs & 4.5 Hows fired their allotted rounds on day areas night	operation order no 45 performed
	31st		" " " " " " " " " " " " " " night " 3 other Ranks wounded, all 10 pdr batteries	
			Shelled by hostile 4.2 and howitzers for 18 hours. 3 18 pdr enemy Howitzer fired 8 rds. Reference Map.	LONGUEVAL. 57c S.W.3.

O.C. 161 F.A. Bde D R Cook LtCol RFA

24th Divisional Artillery

107th BRIGADE

ROYAL FIELD ARTILLERY

AUGUST 1 9 1 6

OPERATION ORDERS 29

BY

LIEUT. COLONEL D.R. COATES, COMMANDING 107 F.A. BRIGADE.

Copy No.... S E C R E T. 9th August 1916.

1. The 17th Infantry Brigade on the night 9th/10th August will take over the present 2nd Division front from about the Railway Line to DELVILLE WOOD (exclusive)

2. The 72nd Infantry Brigade on the night 10/11th August will take over part of the 55th Division front and will hold from just South of ARROW HEAD COPSE to the Railway Line.

3. The 73rd Infantry Brigade will relieve the 5th Infantry Brigade, in Squares A.8.a, A.8.b, A.2.d, (Headquarters A.3.c.0.5) Head of 73rd Infantry Brigade to reach A.8.a by 10.a.m on August 10th.

4. It is understood that the 24th Division will be supported by two Divisional Artilleries.
   The 107th F.A.Brigade will relieve the 163rd F.A.Brigade as under :-

   107th H.Q. in relief of 163rd F.A.B.,H.Q.   A.3.c.5.3.
   "A", "B" & "C"   "   A.B & C Battys.   A.3.a.4.0 to A.3.a.8.2.
   D/107   " "   D/163   A.3.c.6.5.

5. Batteries will be prepared to move so as to reach these positions at 8.a.m. and will march independantly.

6. All batteries must register at once, en the zone from WEDGE WOOD to DELVILLE WOOD.

7. All ammunition is to be taken over in dumps and a return sent in to Bde.H.Q. as early as possible.

8. More definite orders will be issued later.

Copy No. 1 War Diary.
       2 A/107.
       3 B/107.
       4 C/107.
       5 D/107.

Lieut. R.F.A.
Adjutant, 107/F.A/Brigade.

OPERATION ORDER 30

by

LIEUT. COLONEL D.R. COATES,   **COMMANDING 107 F.A. BRIGADE.**

Copy No. 1   SECRET.   10th August 1916.

Reference Sheets 62.c.N.W. & 62.d.N.E.

1. The 24th Divisional Artillery will go into action in support of the 24th (Left) Division on August 11th & 12th.

2. (1) Seperate orders will be issued regarding move of Wagon Lines.

   (2) All trench maps, aeroplane photos, etc will be taken over.
All existing communications will be taken over.

   (3) All ammunition is to be taken over in Gun Positions and a return sent in to Bde.H.Q. as early as possible. 800 rounds per gun 18-pr. and 500 rounds per gun 4.5 How. will be kept at battery positions, 25% of this to be H.E.

3. Brigade and Battery Commanders will take over Command on completion of relief on Augt.12th.

4. At 3.p.m. on Augt. 12th the C.R.A. 24th Division will take over control of 2nd Divisional Artillery in support of 24th Division. H.Q., 24th D.A., will be at MINDEN POST (F.18.c.3.4)

5. Positions to be taken up by 107th F.A.B.

107 F.A.B.,H.Q.	163 F.A.B.,H.Q.	A.3.c.5.3.
A/107	A/163	(A.3.a.4.0.
B/107	B/163	(to
C/107	C/163	(A.3.a.6.2.
D/107	D/163	A.3.c.6.5.

NOTES. (1) Reliefs of one section each day will take place as under during the 11th & 12th August, at (three-quarter) ¾ hour intervals, providing hostile shelling permits.

         A/107 - 8.a.m.   C/107 - 9.30.a.m.
         B/107 - 8.45.a.m.   D/107 - 10.15.a.m.

   (2) Bde.H.Q., will close at 7.30.a.m. on the 12th and re-open at New Position at 10.a.m. on the 12th.

Copy No. 1 War Diary.
         2 A/107.
         3 B/107.
         4 C/107.
         5 D/107.
         6 163 F.A.B.
         7. 24 D.A.

D R Coates
Lieut.Colonel,R.F.A.
Commanding 107/F.A/Brigade.

S E C R E T.   Copy No. 2

24th D.A. Order No. 3.

Reference Sheets 62.c.N.W. & 62.d.N.E.   10th August 1916.

1. The 24th Divisional Artillery will go into action in support of the 24th (Left) Division on August 11th & 12th.

2. Attached Appendix shows positions to be taken up.

3. (1) Separate orders will be issued regarding move of wagon lines.

   (ii) All dumped ammunition will be taken over in gun positions.

4. All trench maps, aeroplane photos, etc. will be taken over. All existing communications will be taken over.

5. (1) Brigade and Battery Commanders will take over Command on completion of relief on August 12th.

   (ii) All other details of the relief will be arranged between Brigade Commanders.

6. The Medium T.M.Batteries, 24th D.A. and V/24 T.M.Battery will take over the 2nd D.A. Trench Mortar Camp at CARNOY at 4.p.m. on August 11th.
   Details of relief to be arranged between T.M.Commanders concerned. Arrangements for transport will be notified by the Staff Captain, R.A.

7. At 3.p.m. on August 12th, the C.R.A. 24th Division will take over control of all Field Artillery supporting the 24th Division. The 2nd Divisional Artillery remain in action in support of the 24th Division. Tactical orders for the C.R.A. 2nd Division, will come through the C.R.A.,24th Division.
   H.Q.,24th D.A. will close at THE CITADEL at 3.p.m. on August 12th and re-open at MINDEN POST (F.18.c.3.4) at the same hour. The Staff Captain, R.A. will move at that hour to "Q" Branch camp at THE CITADEL.

8. Please acknowledge.

Issued at 4.p.m.

Captain.R.A.
Brigade Major, 24th Divisional Artillery.

Copies to	No.		No.
106th F.A.B.	1	A.P.M. 24th Div.	13
107th " " "	2	A.D.O.S. "	14
108th " " "	3	A.D.V.S. "	15
109th " " "	4	2nd D.A.	16
T.M.24 D.A.	5	35th D.A.	17
V/24 T.M.Batty.	6	55th D.A.	18
24th D.A.C.	7	17th D.A.	19
24th Div.G.	8	H.A. XIII Corps.	20
" " Q.	9	No.9 Squadron.R.F.C.	21
" " Train.	10	FILE.	22.
" " Signals.	11	WAR DIARY.	23, 24.
A.D.M.S.24 Div.	12.	SPARE.	25, 26, 27.

P.T.O.

Reference Sheets 62.c.N.W. & 62.d.N.E.

APPENDIX
RELIEF TABLE.

Unit 24 D.A.	Unit 35 D.A.	Location of H.Q. or Gun Position.
106 F.A.B., H.Q.		A.4.c.7.3.
A/106.		A.4.c.7.7½.
B/106.	NEW	A.4.c.4.7.
C/106.		A.4.c.7.5.
D/106.	POSITIONS.	A.4.c.8.5.
107 F.A.B., H.Q.	163 F.A.B., H.Q.	A.3.c.5.3.
A/107.	A/163.	(A.3.a.4.0
B/107.	B/163.	to
C/107.	C/163.	(A.3.a.8.2.
D/107.	D/163.	A.3.c.6.5.
108 F.A.B., H.Q.	157 F.A.B., H.Q.	A.2.d.7½.6½.
A/108.	A/157.	(A.3.d.6.5.
B/108.	B/157.	to
C/108.	C/157.	(A.3.d.6.7.
D/108.	D/157.	A.10.a.6.4.
109 F.A.B., H.Q.	158 F.A.B., H.Q.	A.15.c.40.50.
A/109.	A/158.	A.10.d.6.5½.
B/109.	B/158.	A.10.d.5½.7.
C/109.	C/158.	A.10.d.5.9.
T.M. 24 D.A. }		
V/24 T.M.Batty. }	T.M. 2nd D.A.	CARNOY.

Notes.

(1)   Reliefs of a Section each day will take place during day time of August 11th & 12th.
Reliefs to commence at 8.a.m. each day. The whole of the 106 F.A.B. will come into action on August 11th.

(2)   Brigade Commanders to report by wire to H.Q., 2nd D.A. on taking over command.

OPERATION ORDER NO.31.

BY

LIEUT COLONEL D.R.COATES,   COMMANDING 107/F.A/BRIGADE.

Copy No....   SECRET.   12th August 1916.

(S.O.S)

The S.O.S lines of the Brigade from 6 pm tonight will be as follows:-

    A/107.   T 25 a 0.0.   - T 25 a 0.2.

    B/107.   T 25 a 0.2.   - T 25 a 0.5.

    C/107.   T 25 a 0.5.   - S 30 b 9½.7.

18 Pdr Batteries to overlap 25 yards.

    D/107.   Road T 25 c 3.9.   - T 25 a 2.7.

Copy No 1 War Diary.
     2   A/107.
     3   B/107.
     4   C/107.
     5   D/107.
     6   B.M. 24 D.A.

D R Coates   Lieut Colonel, R.F.A.
Commanding 107/F.A/Brigade.

OPERATION ORDER NO. 32.
BY
LIEUT COLONEL D.R.COATES.   COMMANDING 107/F.A/BRIGADE.

Copy No .1..   SECRET   12th August 1916.

1. Operation Order No. 31 is cancelled.

2. The S.O.S. lines for the Brigade from 6 pm tonight will be as follows:-

    A/107.   S 30 b 6½.1½ to S 30 b 7½.4.

    B/107.   S 30 b 7½.4 to S 30 b 8½.7.

    C/107.   S 30 b 8½.7. to S 30 b 9½.8½.

18 Pdr Batteries to overlap 25 yards.

    D/107 (How) S 30 b 6½.1½.

A/107 Battery will provide a Guard of One Sergeant and 3 men to watch for S.O.S. signal and also to report GAS SHELL? he will report to his O.C. Battery who will at once report to Head Quarters. The S.O.S. signal Five Parachute Red Rockets will be sent from S 30 b 4.0.

NIGHT FIRING. will be carried out as follows,

A/107 on the area S 30 b 8.5. S 30 b 9½.0, T 25 c 3.9. T 25 a 3.2½.

B/107.   ditto S 30 b 8.5 - S 30 b 9.7 - T 25 a 3.2½ - T 25 a 2½.7½

C/107.   ditto S 30 b 9.7 - T 25 a 3.8½ - T 19 c 0.0. - T 25 a 2½.7½

Number of rounds to be fired from dark to dawn 300 rounds per each 18-Pdr Battery.

Rate of fire about one round every 1½ minutes.

D/107 (How) Communication Trenches S 30 b 9½.0 to T 25 c 3½.8½
           ditto   S 30 b 8.5. to T 25 a 3.6.
           Road   T 25 c 3.9 to T 25 a 2.7.

Firing from dark to dawn, rate of fire one round every three minutes, number of rounds to be fired 150.

Copy No 1 War Diary
     2 A/107.
     3 B/107.
     4 C/107.
     5 D/107.
     6 B.M.24 D.A.
     7 B.M.72 I.B.

D R Coates
Lieut Col. R.F.A.
Commanding 107/F.A/ Brigade.

Operation Order No. 33.
by
Lieut. Col. D.R. Coates. Comdg 107 F.A.B.
Copy No. 1.   Secret.   14-8-16.

1. 18-Pdr Batteries will cut wire, where it exists daily, until further order.
   A/107. T.25.a.4.0 to S.30.b.9.1½.
   B/107. S.30.b.9.1½ to S.30.b.7½.4.
   C/107. S.30.b.7½.4 to S.30.b.9½.7.

2. Every endeavour should be made to ensure that this wire is cut.

3. There is no limit to the amount of Ammunition to be expended, but, this should not be wasted.

4. B.C's will make mutual arrangements as to the use of the Brigade wire for the above. The end nearest the enemy will require repair.

5. After the wire has been cut, batteries should spray their allotted fronts with shrapnel, to prevent its repair.

Copy No 1 War diary
  "   2 A/107
  "   3 B "
  "   4 C "
  "   5 D "
  "   6 BM 24 D.A.

D R Coates
..............LIEUT COL., R.F.A.
COMMANDING 107TH BRIGADE, R.F.A.

OPERATION ORDER NO. 34.
BY
LIEUT. COLONEL D.R.COATES.   COMMANDING 107/F.A/BRIGADE.

Copy No. 1.   SECRET.   16th AUGUST 1916.

Ref. Map 1/10000. Sheets 57 c S.W. & 62 c N.W.1. and Map 1/5,000,
GINCHY and GUILLEMONT.

1. GUILLEMONT and the Enemy's line North and South of the village is to be attacked. A preliminary operation will take place on August 16th at a "ZERO" hour to be notified later, to you by the Adjutant.

2. In conjunction with the French and the 3rd Division on our right, the 72nd I.B. will attack and consolidate the enemy trench along the SUNKEN ROAD from the strong point (inclusive) at S 30 b 7.2. to S 30 b 7½.4½ ; also the trench parallel to the SUNKEN ROAD and East of it.

3. The 107 F.A.B. will support the attack vide the attached programme.

4. After the attack on AUGUST 16th the trench from T 25 c 4.9. to S 30 b 8.2½, will be taken over by the 24th Division.

5. The 73rd I.B. will relieve the 72nd I.B. on the night 16th/17th August.

6. Please acknowledge.

Copy No 1 War diary.
     2 A/107.
     3 B/107.
     4 C/107.
     5 D/107.
     6 B.M. 24 D.A.
     7 B.M. I.B.

Lieut, R.F.A.
Adjutant 107/F.A/Brigade.

PROGRAMME - 18-Pdrs.   PHASE 1.

107 F.A.B. for August 16th 1916.

TIME	UNIT	OBJECTIVE	RATE OF FIRE	PROJECTILE	PHASE
0 hr 30 mins to 0 hr 15 mins.	"A" "B" "C"	Trench S 30 b 7.2 to S 30 b 7½.5. Trench S 30 b 7½.5 to S 30 b 9.7. Trench S 30 b 9.7 to T 25 a 0.9.	Ordinary one round per gun per min.	H.E.	
-15 mins to -3 mins.	"A" "B" "C"	--- ditto --- --- ditto --- --- ditto ---	Medium 2 rounds per gun per min.	H.E.	
-3 mins to Zero.	"A" "B" "C"	--- ditto --- --- ditto --- --- ditto ---	Intense 3 rounds per gun per min.	S.S.	
Zero to +3 mins.	"A") "B") "C"	Barrage S 30 b 7.2. to S 30 b 5.4. Trench S 30 b 7.2 to T 25 a 0.9.	Intense 3 rounds per gun per min.	S.S.	

With reference change of objective between Zero and +3 fuzes should be set carefully beforehand; and thorough supervision that the correct shell are used at this period.

Reference period — 0h 30mins to −3 mins. Batteries will overlap 25 yards. If machine gun is reported at S 30 b 8½ 7½ B & C batteries will concentrate their left & right guns on this point

PHASE 11. 18-Pdr Batteries.

TIME.	UNIT.	OBJECTIVE.	RATE OF FIRE.	PROJECTILE.	REMARKS.
+0 hr 3 to +0 hr 4.	"A" & "B"	S 30 b 8.3 to S 30 b 6.5.	Intense.	S.S.	At +0 4 lift 50 yards and continue to lift 50 yards every minute until line T 25 a 3.3½ to T 25 a 0.9. is reached, where a barrage will be formed.

Fuzes must be carefully set beforehand and great care be taken that these shell are used at this period.

+0 hr 3 to +0 hr 4.	"C"	S 30 b 7½.4½ to T 25 a 0.9.	Intense.	S.S.	At +0 4 lift as for "A" and "B" Batteries above.

Fuzes must be carefully set beforehand and great care be taken that these shell are used at this period.

+0 4 to +30	"A" "B" "C"	T 25 a 3.3½ to T 25 a 2½.5. T 25 a 2½.5 to T 25 a 1½.7. T 25 a 1½.7 to T 25 a 0.9.	Intense.	S.S.	Continue to lift as above until you reach line T 25 a 3.3½ to T 25 a 0.9, forming a barrage on this line. It is most important that no fire be directed South of a line joining S 30 b 8.3 to T 25 a 3.3½.
+0 30 to +1 hr.	"A" "B" "C"	T 25 a 3.3½ to T 25 a 2½.5. T 25 a 2½.5 to T25 a 1½.7. T 25 a 1½.7 to T 25 a 0.9.	Medium two rounds per gun a minute.	S.S.	BARRAGE line T 25 a 3.3½ to T 25a 0.9. It is most important that no fire be directed South of line joining S 30 b 8.3 to T 25 a 3.3½.
+1 hr to +2 hr.	"A" "B" "C"	as above.	Ordinary one round a gun per min.	S.S.	Barrage as above.
+2 hrs until stopped.	"A" "B" "C"	as above.	One round a battery per min.	S.S.	Barrage as above.

During the barrage batteries will overlap 25×

PROGRAMME – 4.5 How.   PHASE 1.

107 F.A.B., for August 16th 1916.

TIME.	UNIT.	OBJECTIVE.	RATE OF FIRE.	PROJECTILE.
-0 hr 30 mins to -0 hr 15 mins.	"D"	Trench S 30 b 7.4½ to T 25 a 3.4½.	Ordinary one round per gun per min.	H.E.
-0 hr 15 mins to 0 hr 3 mins.	"D"	---ditto---	Medium 2 rounds per gun per min.	H.E.

PHASE 11. 4.5 How.

TIME.	UNIT.	OBJECTIVE.	RATE OF FIRE.	PROJECTILE.	REMARKS.
+ 03 to + 1 hr.	"D"	T 25 a ½.4½, to T 25 a 3.4½.	Medium two rounds a gun a min.	H.E.	) It is important) that there should) be no fire South of) the line going) S 30 b 8.3 to) T 25 a 3.3½.))))))
+ 1 hr to + 2 hr.	"D"	---ditto---	Ordinary one round a gun a min.		
+ 2 hr till stop.	"D"	---ditto---	One round a battery a min.	H.E.	

OPERATION ORDER NO. 35.
BY
LIEUT. COLONEL D.R. COATES.   COMMANDING 107/F.A/BRIGADE.

Copy No. 1   SECRET.   16th August 1916.

1. With reference to Operation Order No. 32 d/- 12/8/16.
   The new S.O.S. lines for the Brigade from 6.30 pm., tonight will be as follows:-
   A/107   T 25 a 2.3 to T 25 a $\frac{3}{4}$.4½
   B/107   T 25 a $\frac{3}{4}$.4½ to S 30 b 9¾.6
   C/107   S 30 b 9¾.6 to S 30 b 9½.7

   18-Pdr Batteries to overlap 25 yards.

   D/107 How.   T 25 a 3.3½ to S 30 b 9.9.

   A/107 Battery will provide a guard of one Sergeant and 3 men to watch for S.O.S.Signal and also report GAS SHELL; he will report to his O.C.Battery who will at once report to Head Quarters. The S.O.S Signal Five Parachute Red Rockets sent up from S 30 b 4.0.

2. NIGHT FIRING will be carried out as follows:-
   A/107 on the area T 25 a 2.3; - S 30 b 9½.7 - T 25 b 0.5; -
                       T 25 b 0.9.
   B/107   ditto   T 25 b 0.5; - T 25 b 0.9 - T 26 a 2½.6; -
                       T 26 a 2½.9.
   C/107   ditto   T 26 a 2½.7; - T 26 a 2½.9; - T 20 d 9.0 -
                       T 27 b 0.10.

   Number of rounds to be fired from dark to 8.30.am., 300 rounds per each 18-Pdr Battery. D/107 How., on the area T 25 a 5.8 - T 25 a 10.5;
                       T 25 b 1.8½ - T 25 a 7.8, T 26 b 8.8½ -
                       T 27 a 8.0 - T 20 d 9.0.

   Firing from dark to 8.30.am., 150 rounds.

Copy No. 1 War diary.
         2 A/107.
         3 B/107.
         4 C/107.
         5 D/107.
         6 B.M. 24 D.A.
         7 B.M. 73 I.B.

                                            - Lieut R.F.A.
                                    Adjutant 107/F.A/ Brigade.

OPERATION ORDER NO. 36.
BY
LIEUT. COLONEL D.R.COATES.   COMMANDING 107/F.A/BRIGADE.
Copy No. 1.   SECRET.   17th August 1916.

BOMBARDMENT 1.

TIME.	UNIT.	OBJECTIVE.	RATE OF FIRE.	PROJ-ECTILE.	DATE.	REMARKS.
ZERO to +3 mins.	"A" "B" "C"	Trench S 30 b 7.2 to S 30 b 7½.5. Trench S 30 b 7½.5 to S 30 b 9.7. Trench S 30 b 9.7 to T 25 a 0.9.	Intense 3 rounds per gun per min.	S.S.	17/8/16.	
+3 mins to +4 mins.	"A" "B" "C"	Lift 100 yards from above.	ditto.	S.S.	ditto.	
+4 mins to +5 mins.	"A" "B" "C"	Drop 100 yards, i.e., same as from Zero to +3.	ditto.	S.S.	ditto.	
+5 mins.		STOP FIRING.				

4.5 Howitzer Battery.

TIME	UNIT	OBJECTIVE	RATE OF FIRE	PROJECTILE	DATE	REMARKS
ZERO to +3 mins.	"D"	Trench S 30 b 7.4½ to T 25 a 3.4½.	Medium 2 rounds a gun per minute.	H.E.	17/8/16.	
+3 mins to +4 mins.	"D"	Lift 100 yards from above.	ditto.	H.E.	ditto.	
+4 mins to +5 mins.	"D"	Drop 100 yards, i.e., same as from Zero to +3 mins.	ditto.	H.E.	ditto.	
+5 mins.		STOP FIRING.				

Zero time to-day will be 4.7. pm., watches will be checked by the Adjutant. There will be two similar bombardments to-morrow at 9.17.am and 12.37.pm. All batteries will arrange to Register Targets when necessary, between the hours of 9.30.am and 10.am, 2.30. pm and 3 pm., daily until further orders, these being the only hours allotted 24th Divi:Arty: for registration.

Copy No. 1 War Diary.
     2 A/107.
     3 B/107.
     4 C/107.
     5 D/107.
     6 B.M.24 D.A.

Lieut, R.F.A.
Adjutant 107/F.A/Brigade.

OPERATION ORDER NO. 37.
BY
LIEUT. COLONEL D.R. COATES.   COMMANDING 107/F.A/BRIGADE.

Copy No.   SECRET.   17th August 1916.
                        17th/18th
1. At some period during the night/the Brigade will be called upon to fire a BARRAGE as per attached programme.

2. NIGHT FIRING. Until you are requested to fire this BARRAGE you will search the old areas, as detailed in my Operation Order No. 32. After you have completed the BARRAGE as per attached programme you will search the New Areas as detailed in my Operation Order No. 35.

3. S.O.S. Lines. The S.O.S. lines of the Brigade will be those as detailed in Operation Order No. 35.

4. B/107 will provide the Rocket and Gas guard of One Sergeant and 3 men. The S.O.S. Signal of Five PARACHUTE RED Rockets will be sent up from S 30 b 4.0.

5. Watches ~~ZERO Time~~ will be Synchronised ~~communicated to you~~ by the Adjutant or Orderly Officer. at 9.15 pm.

6. Zero time is 10 pm

Copy No. 1 War Diary.
       2 A/107.
       3 B/107.
       4 C/107.
       5 D/107.
       6 B.M. 24 D.A.

                              D R Coates Lieut. Colonel, R.F.A.
                                Commanding 107/F.A/Brigade.

PROGRAMME FOR 16-Pdr Batteries.   Night 17th/18th.

TIME.	UNIT.	OBJECTIVE.	RATE OF FIRE.	PROJECTILE.	REMARKS.
ZERO to +10.	"A" "B" "C"	S 30 b 7½.4½ to S 30 b 8.5½. S 30 b 8.5½ to S 30 b 9.7. S 30 b 9.7 to T 25 a 0.8.	Intense 3 rounds a gun a min.	S.S.	A BARRAGE is to be formed on this trench. No lift is required. Batteries will overlap 20 yards, but, A/107 must not fire further South than S 30 b 7½.4½
+10 to +20.	"A" "B" "C"	ditto.	Medium 2 rounds a gun a min.	S.S.	
+20 to +1 hr.	"A" "B" "C"	ditto.	Ordinary one round a gun a min.	S.S.	
+1 hr till stopped.	"A" "B" "C"	ditto.	One round a battery per min.	S.S.	

D/107. HOWITZER.

TIME.	UNIT.	OBJECTIVE.	RATE OF FIRE.	PROJECTILE.	REMARKS.
ZERO to +20.	"D"	S 30 b 7½.4½ to T 25 a 3.4½.	Medium 2 rounds a gun a min.	H.E.	SEARCH UP AND DOWN THIS TRENCH.
+20 to +1 hr.	"D"	ditto.	Ordinary one round a gun a min.	H.E.	
+1 hr till stopped.	"D"	ditto.	One round a battery a min.	H.E.	

SECRET.   Copy No. 2

24th D.A. ORDER No. 6.

Reference
Map 1/10,000.
Sheet 57.c.S.W.3.
      62.c.N.W.1.   17th August 1916.
Map 1/5,000.
GINCHY & GUILLEMONT.

1. The XIV Corps will attack GUILLEMONT on August 18th & 19th. Attacks will be made at the same time on the right and left of the Corps.

2. The attack by the 24th Division will be carried out as follows:-

18th August.

1st Objective.
Zero.
    73rd Inf Bde. The enemy defences from S.30.b.6.2 along the sunken road and including the trench which runs east of the sunken road to T.25.a.0.9., thence the trench to S.24.d.8.5.

    17th Inf Bde. The enemy defences from S.24.d.8.5 – S.24.b.4.2 – M.G. House (inclusive) – T.19.a.1.6 – S.18.d.5½.4.

2nd Objective.
Zero + 2 hours.
    73rd Inf.Bde. The line T.25.a.3.3 – T.25.a.2.8 – T.25.a.3½.9 – T.19.c.3.2 thence round the Eastern and Northern edges of the QUARRY (T.19.c).

    17th Inf.Bde. The STATION and defences round it from S.24.d.6.8 – T.19.c.1.9½ – S.24.b.7.4.

19th August.

Zero.
    73rd Inf.Bde. The line T.25.a.9½.4½ – cross-roads T.19.c.6.3½ thence along the GUILLEMONT – LONGUEVAL road as far North as the cross-roads at T.19.c.2.8½ (exclusive).

    17th Inf.Bde. The enemy defences West of the cross-roads at T.19.c.2.8½ and North of BROMPTON ROAD.

Zero + 1½ hours.
    73rd Inf.Bde.
    (a) To advance to the Eastern edge of the village from T.25.b.1.4½ – T.19.a.8.2 and establish a defensive line on the outskirts of the village.

    (b) To push forward a line of outposts on the line T.25.b.1.4½ – CEMETERY – T.19.b.0.2½.

    17th Inf.Bde.
    To capture and consolidate the portion of the ZZ trench between the village and T.19.a.1.6, and the German trench on the BROMPTON Road between T.19.c.2.8½ and T.19.a.5.0.

                                                                               P. T. O.

3   'Zero' hour on the 18th & 19th August will be notified separately.

4   The objectives to be gained by the left of the 3rd Division on the right of the 24th Division are as follows :-

18th August.

            1st Objective : trench from T.25.c.4.9 - S.30;b.8.2½.

            2nd Objective : road from T.25.c.4.9 - T.25.a.3.3.

19th August.

            1st Objective : From cross-roads T.25.c.5.4 - road junction T.25.a.9.0 - T.25.a.8.4.

            2nd Objective : From T.25.a.9.0 - T.25.b.1.4½.

5   The Artillery Programme and Barrages are given in Attached Appendix.

6   In addition to the present liason with Battalions, the O.C., 107 F.A.B. with his Orderly Officer will be at 73rd I.B. Battle H.Q. and will be in communication from there with his Adjutant at 107 F.A.B.,H.Q.

      The C.R.A.,2nd Division will arrange liason with 17th I.B.

7   Watches will continue to be synchronised at 12 noon and 6.p.m. daily, until further orders.

8   Please acknowledge.

                                                Captain.R.A.
                Brigade Major, 24th Divisional Artillery.

Issued at

Copies to	No.		No.
106 F.A.B.	1	72nd I.B.	12
107 " " "	2	73rd I.B.	13
108 " " "	3	24th Div.	14
109 " " "	4	3rd D.A.	15
158 " " "	5	5th D.A.	16
2nd D.A.	6	R.A.,XlV.Corps.	17
T.M.,24 D.A.	7	No.9 Squadron.R.F.C.	18
V/24 T.M.Batty.	8	No.12 Kite Balloon Sec.	19
24 D.A.C.	9	FILEa	20
Staff Captain.R.A.	10	WAR DIARY.	21, 22
17th I.B.	11	SPARE.	23, 24, 25.

APPENDIX.

TABLE "B".

Formation.	Time. From.	Time. To.	18-pr.	4.5 How.	Remarks.
	August 18th.				
107 F.A.B. Nos.1,2 & 3(18-pr) Batteries.	-	Zero.	S.30.b.$7\frac{1}{2}$.$4\frac{1}{2}$ to S.30.b.$9\frac{1}{2}$.$7\frac{1}{2}$.		At zero 2 18-pr Btties. drop 100 yds. to line in next para.
D/107 How.Bty.	-	+1½ min.		S.30.b.$7\frac{1}{2}$.$4\frac{1}{2}$ to S.30.b.$9\frac{1}{2}$.$7\frac{1}{2}$.	At +1½ min. lift to next objective.
Nos. 1 & 2 Batteries.	Zero	+1 min.	S.30.b.6.4 to S.30.b.$6\frac{1}{2}$.$7\frac{1}{2}$.		At +1 min. lift 50 yds. & lift 50 yds a min till on next barrage.
Nos 1 & 2 Batteries.	+4 min	+5 min	S.30.b.$8\frac{1}{2}$.$4\frac{1}{2}$ to T.25.a.2.8.		At +5 min lift 50 yds & lift 50 yds a min till on next barrage.
No.3 Batty.	Zero	+3 min.	S.30.b.$7\frac{1}{2}$.$4\frac{1}{2}$ to S.30.b.$9\frac{1}{2}$.$7\frac{1}{2}$		At +3 min lift to next Barrage.
No.3 Batty.	+4 min	+5 min	S.30.b.$8\frac{1}{2}$.$4\frac{1}{2}$ to T.25.a.2.8.		At +5 min. lift 50 yds & lift 50 yds a min. till on next barrage.
Nos.1, 2 & 3 Batteries.	+7 min.	+2 hrs.	T.25.a.$1\frac{1}{2}$.2 to T.25.a.$2\frac{1}{2}$.$7\frac{1}{2}$ to T.25.b.$2\frac{1}{2}$.$3\frac{1}{2}$ to T.19.c.0.7.		At +2hrs. lift 50 yds. & continue to lift 50 yds a min till on next barrage.
Nos. 1,2 & 3 Batteries.	+2hrs.3min.	Zero Aug.19th.	T.25.a.5.$2\frac{1}{2}$ to T.25.a.$5\frac{1}{2}$.$8\frac{1}{2}$ to T.19.c.5.4 to T.19.c.$2\frac{1}{2}$.8.		At zero Aug.19th. lift 50 yards & continue to lift 50 yds. a min till on next barrage.
D/107 How.Bty.	+1½ min.	+2 hr.		T.25.a.$3\frac{1}{2}$.3 to T.25.a.$2\frac{1}{2}$.4.	At 2 hr. lift to next objective.
D/107 How.Bty.	+2 hr.	Zero Aug.19th.		T.25.a.9.4 to T.25.a.$6\frac{1}{2}$.$8\frac{1}{2}$.	At zero Aug.19th. lift to next objective.

T A B L E "B" contd.

August 19th.

Formation.	Time. From.	To.	18-pr.	4.5 How.	Remarks.
Nos.1,2 & 3 (18-pr) Btties.	+ 5 min	+1½hrs.	T.25.b.3.4½ to T.25.b.0.10 to T.19.c.8½.6 to T.19.c.5½.9½.		*Lift & line* At +1½hrs. lift 50 yds. & continue to lift 50 yds. & min. till on next barrage.
D/107 How.Bty.	Zero	+1½ hrs.		T.25.b.3.8.	At +1½hrs. lift to next objective.
Nos.1,2 & 3 (18-pr) Batteries.	+1hr.40. Stopped.	Till nine.	T.25.b.6.4½ to T.19.d.0.4 to T.19.d.7.9½ to T.19.h.2.5.		
D/107 How.Bty.	+1½hrs.	Till stpd.		Road T.26.a.1.5 T.20.c.1½.4.	

APPENDIX.
TABLE "E".

Notes.-1 Rates of fire 18-prs. August 18th. Zero to +5 min. Very Intense (3 rounds a gun a minute.)
                                        +5 to 15   "   Intense.
                                       +15 to 1hr.   Medium.
                                        + 1hr.   "   Ordinary.
                                        + 2hr.   "   2.hr.5.Very Intense.
                                        + 2hr.5   "   2hr.15.Intense.
                                        + 2hr.15"   3hr. Medium.
                                        + 3hr.   "   5hr. Ordinary.
                                        + 5hr till Zero. Slow.

          "   "   "   August 19th. Zero to +5min. Very Intense.
                                        + 5min   " 10 " Intense.
                                        +10   " 30 " Medium.
                                        +30   " 1hr.15. Ordinary.
                                        + 1hr.15" 1hr.20. Intense.
                                        + 1hr.20" 1hr.30. Medium.
                                        + 1hr.30" 5hr.15. Ordinary.
                                        + 5hr.15" at stop Slow.

Rates of Fire 4.5 How. As for 18-prs, except for "Very Intense" & "Intense" substitute "Medium".

2. After Zero, Augt. 18th. no gun is to fire South of line S.50.b.9½.2 to T.25.a.1½.2½.

3. "Zero" hour on the 18th Augt. will be 2-45.p.m.
         "   "   " " 19th   "   "   5-00.a.m.

4. The attacking troops of the 17th Infantry Brigade between S.24.b.5.6 & S.18.d.4.5 will not start till "Zero" & 2 minutes or 2-47.p.m.

5. Great care is to be taken that there is no increase in rate of Artillery fire prior to "Zero. At "Zero" except where other orders have been issued, the Infantry will leave their assembly trenches and advance to the assault, covered by the Field Artillery curtain.

6. (a) Troops will show their flares and mirrors at the following times:-
   (1) On reaching each objective.
   (2) At 7-45.p.m. on August 18th.
   (3) At 6.a.m.   "   "   19th.
   (4) At 10.a.m.   "   "   19th.

(b) Wireless Stations will be established at:—

ARROW HEAD COPSE.
WATERLOT FARM.
S.22.d.9.1.
S.23.c.8.5.

7. Inf.Bde. H.Q. will at commencement of operations be at:—

17th Inf.Bde.: S.23.c.8.5.
73rd Inf.Bde.: BRIQUETERIE (A.4.b.)

A { S.30.b.8½.c.½ T.25.a.2.8
    S.30.b.8½.c.½ S.30.9½.6   A
    S.30.b.9½.6   T.25.a.½.6 B
                   T.25.a.0.7
  { T.25.a.0.7   —T.25.a.2.8

S.30.b.6.2 to S.30.b.7.4
S.30.b.7.4 to S.30.b.8½.6
S.30.b.8½.6 to 9½.7½

S.30.b.6.2 to S.30.b.6.6.5
S.30.b.6.4.5   6½.7½

"Operation Programme N° 38 A/107 & 18th August 1916." 1 map.
July August 18th 1916.

Time.	Unit.	Objective.	Rate of fire.	Projectile.	Remarks.
mph 3.0.0.	A V	S30b 6.2 & S30b 6 7.4	Intermittent	HE	at zero drop 25 × 100 to S 1.2 P.S.
Zn + 3 mins	V	S30b6.2 & S30b 6.5 30	very intense later very intense	SS	St +1 mins Lyft 50 mins +Shift 100 y range
Zn + 3		S30b 8½ a 3 to S30b 6 9½ 6	intense		At +5 Lyft 50 mins till end of range
+7 to 15	V	T25 a 0/½ 2.2 to T25 a 2½ 7½	intense		No fire in the walk of hun St br 30 9½ 2 6 T25 - a -½ 2 2
1h to 1h		do	ordinary	SS	
1h to 2h		do	ordinary		to T 2 3 a - ½ 2 6
+2h to 2h + 5		T25 a 5½ 2½ to T25 a 5½ P½	very intense intense		2 mins Lyft 50 y range over 52 Pt (No change)
+2½ to 2½ + 15		do	intense		
12.15 to 3h		do	ordinary	SS	T 25 a 2.0
+2h to 5h		do	ordinary		
+5h to 6 3000		do	slow		

A/109/19

Time.	Unit.	Objective.	Katastoffene	Projectile	Reports Remarks
Zero + 5min	M	T25 b 34 ± to 25 b 010			
zero + 3 min		do	very short		
0.5 to 0.10		do	very short entirer		at 12 hrs SSO increase before 50 % aimed fell or nast average
0.10 to 0.30		do	medium		
0.30 to 1.15		do	strong		
1.15 to 1.30		do	medium		
1.30 to 1.30		T25 b 64 ± to T 19 d 94	medium		
1.30 to 5.15			ordinary		
5.10 till stoppe			slow		

B/107

Time	Unit	Objective	Rate of fire	Projectile	Remarks
until zero	B/107	S 30 b 7 4 6 5 2 f 8 2 6	intermittent	H E	at zero drop 100ˣ then in mid range
zero h +1		S 30 b 6 5 b 5 3 0 6 6 5 7½	unregistered into barrage	S S	+at 1 min left 30ˣ tenderne + 30ˣ enters till next barrage
+4 h +15 min		S 30 b 9½ 6 h T 25 b 9½	do		at +5 left 30ˣ tenderne + left 30ˣ enters incl next barrage
+5 h +15 +15 h, 1 h +1 h 6 hrs		T 25 a 2½ 7½ E T 19 C 2½ 3½	intense medium ordinary		at +2 hrs left 50ˣ + continue left enters & next barrage
zero 19th		T 25 a 5 2 8½ B T 19 C 5 e 4	intense		at zero 19th drop same left 50ˣ + continue
+5 h +½ hr		T 26 b 0 10 & T 19 C 8 2 6			
+1½ hrs till +14 0 S½ hrs					

Coy 7

Time	Unit	Objective	Rate of fire	Projectile	Remarks
hrH 30m	Coy 7	S 30 b 8½ 6 h S 30 b 9½ 7½	intermittent	HE	at zero
+ 2	C	S 30 b 6 2 to S 30 b 9½ 7½	volume very	SS	at + 2 left barrage
+2½ +3	C	S 30 b 7¼ 4½ to S 30 b 9½ 7½	" "		lift at +3 to next barrage
+3 +5	C	S 30 b T2 S 2 07 to T2 S 2 28	do		at +5 lift to +10 +50 to next barrage
+16 K/7 hr		T 19 c 2½ 3½ to T 19 c 07			at + rate left 50' to next barrage
+2h 30m		T 19 c 54 to T 19 c 22½ 8			
2h 30m Sam gahr 19th barrage		do			at 2m 19th left 50' to next Lift next to next barrage
+5 +12 hr		T 19 c 8½ 6 to T 19 c 5½ 9½			at 12 hr left 50 to
4.40 till stopped		T 19 [c] 7.9 ½ to T 19 b 0.5 do			

Line	Unit	Objective	Rate of fire	Projectile	Remarks
Until Zero	7/167	S.30.b.62 to S.30.b.9½.7½	intermittent	HE	at zero left
Barrage		T.25.a.3.3 to T.25.a.2½.4			at 2 hrs left
2 hrs b zero		T.25.a.9.4 to T.25.a.6½.8½		HE	at 5 am zero 19 hr left
19 3rd W + 5th		T.25.b.3.8.			
+ 12 hr W. Upper		Road T.26.a. 1.5 to T.20.c.1½.4		HE	
		Attack 2 at objective has been gained Gun will fire m3 T.25.c.6.32 until further orders.			

APPENDIX.
TABLE A.

Formation.	Time. From.	Time. To.	18-pr.	4.5 How.	Remarks.
106 F…B. All 18-pr Batteries.	August 18th. —	Zero.	S.30.b.9¾.7 to S.24.d.7½.5.	—	At zero drop fire into NO MAN'S LAND to barrage given
D/106 How.Bty.	—	+2¾ min.		S.24.d.9.5½ to S.24.d.7½.5.	At+2¾ min.lift to next Objective.
All 18-pr Batteries.	Zero	+1 min.	S.30.b.6½.7½ to S.30.b.5.4.		At +1 min. left 50 yds and continue to lift 50 yards till on next barrage.
All 18-pr Batteries.	+7 min	+1 hr.	T.25.a.2½.7½ to T.19.c.0.7.		At +1hr re-adjust front.
All 18-pr Batteries.	+1hr.	+2 hr.	T.25.a.2½.3½ to T.19.c.0.7.		At +2hr. lift 50 yds. and continue to lift 50 yds. till on next barrage.
D/106 How.Bty.	+2hr.2½min.	+2 hr.		Dug-outs T.19.c.2½.8 to T.19.b.8.1.	At +2hr. lift to next Objective.
All 18-pr Batteries.	+2hr.3rmin. August 19th.	Zero Aug. 19th.	T.19.c.5.4 to T.19.c.2¾.8.		At zero Aug. 19th. lift 50 yds.& continue to lift 50 yds. till on next barrage.
D/106 How.Bty.	+5 min.	+1½ hr.		T.19.a.5.0 to T.19.a.5.1.	At +1½ hr. lift on to new objective.
All 18-pr Batteries.	+1hr.40.min	till stpd.	T.19.d.7.9½ to T.19.b.2.5.		
D/106 How.Bty.	+1½ hrs.	Till stpd.		T.20.a.8.1 to T.19.b.2¾.7.	

APPENDIX.
TABLE "G"

Action.	From.	Time. To.	18-pr.	4.5 How.	Remarks.
EOS F.A.B. all 18-pr. Batteries.	—	Zero.	S.30.b.9½.7½ to S.24.d.7½.5.		
B/108 How.Bty.	—	+14 min.		N. end QUARRY T.19.c.1½.3½.	At +14 min lift to next objective.
Nos.1 & 2 Batteries.	Zero	+5 min.	S.30.b.9½.7½ to S.24.d.9.3½.		At +5 mins.lift 50 yds a min. & continue to lift 50 yds. a min.till on next barrage.
No.3 Batty.	Zero	+4 mins.	S.24.d.9.3½ to S.24.d.7½.5.		At +4 mins.lift 50 yds a min. & continue to lift 50 yds.a min.till on next barrage.
All 18-pr Batteries.	+7 min.	+1 hr.	T.25.a.2½.7½ to T.19.c.0.7.		At +1hr. re-adjust front.
All 18-pr. Batteries.	+1 hr.	+2 hrs.	T.25.a.2½.7½ to T.19.c.2½.3½.		At +2 hrs. lift 50 yds & continue to lift 50 yds. a min. till on next barrage.
B/108 How. Bty.	+14 min.	+Zero Aug.19th.		Road T.25.c.6½.8½ to T.19.c.4½.6.	At Zero 18th.Aug.lift. to next objective.
All 18-pr. Batteries.	+2hr.3.min. Zero-Aug.19th.	till	T.25.a.5½.8½. to T.19.c.5.4.		At Zero,Aug.19th.lift 50 yds.& continue to lift 50 yds a min till on next barrage.
All 18-pr. Batteries.	+5 min.	+1½hrs.	T.25.b.0½.0 to T.19.c.8½.6.		At +1½ hrs. lift 50 yds & continue to lift 50 yds. a min.till on next barrage.

TABLE "C" contd.

Formation.	Time.		18-prs.	4.5 How.	Remarks.
	From.	To.			
D/108 How.Bty.	Zero	+1½hrs.		Gun pits T.19.d.3.5 to T.19.d.1.9.	At +1½ hrs. lift to next objective.
All 18-pr Batteries.	+1hr.40.min	till stopped.	T.19.d.9.4 to T.19.d.7.9½		
D/108 How.Bty.	+1½ hrs.	till stopped.		T.20.c.1½.4 to T.20.a.½.1.	

APPENDIX
TABLE "D"

18-prs.

Formation.	Time. From.	To.		Remarks.
109 F.A.B. No.1 Batty. No.2 & 3 "	Augt.18th. Zero. -	Zero. + 5 min.	S.30.b.9.2 to S.30.b.8½.4½. S.30.b.8½.4½ to T.25.a.2.3.	At +5 min lift 50 yds & continue to lift 50 yds a minute till on next barrage.
No.1 Batty. No.2 & 3 "	Zero +8 min.	+2 hrs. +2 hrs.	T.25.a.1½.2 to T.25.a.2.4½. T.25.a.2.4½ to T.25.a.3.7½.	At +2 hrs lift 50 yds & continue to lift 50 yds a minute till on next barrage.
All Batteries.	2.hr.5.min Zero Aug.19th.		T.25.a.5½.2½ to T.25.a.5½.8½.	At zero Aug.19th. lift 50 yds & continue to lift 50 yds a minute till on next barrage.
All Batteries.	+8.min +1½.hrs.	August 19th. +1½.hrs.	T.25.b.3.4½ to T.25.b.0.10.	At +1½.hrs.lift 50 yds & continue to lift 50 yds a min.till on next barrage.
All Batteries.	+1.hr.37.min. Stopped.	Till	T.25.b.6.4½ to T.19.d.8½.4.	

APPENDIX.

TABLE "D" (contd).

Formation.	From.	To.	18-pr.	4.5 How.	Remarks.
158 F.A.B. (less 2-18-pr Batteries)	Zero Aug.18th	Zero August 19th.		Search and sweep area T.19.c.6.5 - T.19.d.3.4 - T.19.a.8½.1½ - T.19.c.2½.8.	
	Zero Aug.19th	Till stopped.		Search and sweep area T.20.a.7.1 - T.14.c.0.2 - T.13.c.0.0.	

OPERATION ORDER NO. 39.
BY
LIEUT. COLONEL D.R.COATES.   COMMANDING 107/F.A/BRIGADE.

Copy No. 1. SECRET. 21st August 1916.

1. The 24th Division will renew the attack on GUILLEMONT on August 21st.

2. OBJECTIVE. The area North of MOUNT STREET from T 19 c 3.2 - Road junction T 19 c 4½.6 - Road junction S 24 d 8.5, and to form a defensive flank on the right along MOUNT STREET and to connect with 17th I.B. on the left.

3. The 107/F.A/Brigade will fire on former Barrage, as follows:-

18- Pounders.

B/107 T 19 c 6.0 Road junction to T 19 c 7.1.
A/107 T 19 c 7.1 to T 19 c 8.2¾.
C/107 T 19 c 8.2¾ to T 19 c 8½.4 Road junction.

Each Battery is allotted 50 yards per gun in action and will sweep along their line.
Time shrapnel only to be used.

4.5 Howitzer.

D/107 T 25 a 8.5 to T 25 a 5.7 Trench.

4. Rates of fire.

18- Pounders.

Zero to 5   Very intense.
5 to 10   Intense.
10 to 20   Medium.
20 to 1½ hrs Ordinary.
1½ hrs till stopped Slow.

4.5. Howitzer.

Zero to 20   Medium.
20 to 1½ hrs Ordinary.
1½ hrs till stopped. Slow.

5. Zero time is 4.30.pm., watches will be synchronised by the Adjutant at 4 pm.

Copy No 1 War diary.
2 A/107.
3 B/107.
4 C/107.
5 D/107.
6 B.M.24 D.A.

Lieut, R.F.A.
Adjutant 107/F.A/Brigade.

OPERATION ORDER NO. 40.

BY

LIEUT. COLONEL D.R.COATES.   COMMANDING 107/F.A/BRIGADE.

Copy No.   SECRET.   22nd August 1916.

1. The 18-Pdr: Batteries will move up into the new positions, which were originally selected for them, tonight and to-morrow morning; S.W., of BERNAFAY WOOD.

A and B Batteries will move tonight and C Battery at 10.a.m., to-morrow morning. A and B Batteries will register as early as possible to-morrow morning and C Battery on completion.

Batteries should register places on the North and N.E. of GUILLEMONT., and also points in GINCHY and its vicinity. It is possible that the Brigade may be called upon to fire a barrage on the line T 19 b 0.2½ - T 19 b 2.6 - T 13 c 9.5., or else form a creeping barrage in front of it, points on this line should be registered. Batteries will forward to this Office a list of points registered as early as possible.

All registrations must be completed by 4.p.m., to-morrow.

Map with our line marked on it is forwarded for your inspection, by hand.

2. The Map References of Battery Positions are to be forwarded to the Adjutant by 2.p.m., to-morrow.

3. From 7.30.p.m., tonight the S.O.S.Lines for the Brigade will be as follows:-

Eastern Edge of GUILLEMONT VILLAGE.
A/107   T 25 c 0.4 to T 19 d 4.0
B/107   T 19 d 4.0 to T 19 d 3½.4½.
C/107   T 19 d 3½.4½ to T 19 b 0.2½
18-Pdr Batteries to overlap 25 yards.
D/107   T 25 a 8½.5 to T 25 a 5.7.

Roads must be covered as a probable relief is suspected tonight.

4. NIGHT FIRING. Batteries will fire intermittently on their S.O.S. Lines.

A/107 will search Northern half of Square T 25 b, T 26 a & b.
B/107 will search Squares T 19 d, T 20 c & d.
C/107 will search half of Square T 19 b, and Squares T 21 c, T 27 a.
D/107 will search LEUZE WOOD and southern end of BOULEAUX WOOD in Square T 21 d., also QUARRY in T 20 d and track leading to main road also roads in T 20 c & d.

18-Pdrs will be careful to search all tracks especially those shown in Aeroplane Photos, as well as the roads.

Copy No. 1 War diary.
        2 A/107.
        3 B/107.
        4 C/107.
        5 D/107.
        6 B.M.24 D.A.

D R Coates
Lieut. Colonel, R.F.A.
Commanding 107/F.A/Brigade.

OPERATION ORDER NO. 41.
BY
LIEUT. COLONEL D.R. COATES.   COMMANDING 107/F.A/ BRIGADE.

Copy No. 1.   SECRET.   24th August 1916.

1. The 35th Division on the Right and the 14th Division on the Left will attack this afternoon.
   The Left of the attack of the 35th Division will be at T 25 c 3.8.

2. Zero hour will be 5.45 p.m.

3. The 6th and 24th Divisional Artilleries will carry out the programme attached.

4. There will be no infantry assault on the front of the 20th Division.

5. An Officer of each Battery will attend at the telephone to receive the correct Divisional time from the Adjutant at 5 p.m.

6. Please acknowledge.

Copy No. 1   War diary.
        2   A/107.
        3   B/107.
        4   C/107.
        5   D/107.
        6   B.M. 24 D.A.

                                      Lieut, R.F.A.
                            Adjutant 107/F.A/Brigade.

PROGRAMME :- 18-Pdr BATTERIES.

TIME.	UNIT.	OBJECTIVE.	RATE OF FIRE.	PROJ-ECTILE.	REMARKS.
Zero to +0 hr 3 mins.	"A"	T 19 c 2.9 to T 19 a 5.0.			Lift 50 yards every minute to +0 hrs 5 mins.
From +0 hrs 5 mins to +0 hrs 7 mins.	"A"	T 19 c 4½.6 to T 19 c 7.7½.			Search.
From +0 hr 7 mins to +0 hr 20 mins.	"A"	ditto.			ditto.
+0 hr +20 mins to ~~8 p.m.~~ 7.45 pm.	"A"	T 26 a ½.5 to T 20 c 2.2. (SUNKEN ROAD)			Search and sweep and also in its vicinity, especially tracks shown on Airplane Photos.
Zero to +0 hrs 3 mins.	"B"	T 19 a 5.0 to T 19 a 8.2.			Lift 50 yards every minute, to +0 hrs 5 mins.
+0 hrs 5 mins to +0 hrs 7 mins.	"B"	T 19 c 7.7½ to T 19 d 0.9.			Search.
+0 hr 7 mins to +0 hr 20 mins.	"B"	ditto.			ditto.
+0 hrs 20 mins to ~~8 p.m.~~ 7.45 pm.	"B"	T 20 c 2.2 to T 20 c 1½.9. (SUNKEN ROAD)			Remarks as for "A" Bty.
Zero to +0 hrs 3 mins.	"C"	T 19 a 7½.0 to T 19 a 7.2.			Lift at +0 hr 3 mins.
+0 hr 3 mins to +0 hr 5 mins.	"C"	T 19 a 8½.0 to T 19 a 8.2.			Lift at +0 hr 5 mins.
+0 hr 5 mins to +0 hr 7 mins.	"C"	T 19 b ½.0 to T 19 b 0.2.			Lift at +0 hr 7 mins.
+0 hr 7 mins to +0 hr 20 mins.	"C"	T 19 d 0.9 to T 19 b 3.½.			Search.
+0 hr 20 mins to ~~8 p.m.~~ 7.45 pm.	"C"	T 20 c 1½.9 to T 20 a 1.6. (SUNKEN ROAD)			Remarks as for "A" and "B".

Rates of fire 18-Pdrs Zero to +1 hr medium.   +1 hr to 7.45 p.m. ordinary.

SHRAPNEL to be fired.

OPERATION ORDER NO. 42.

BY

LIEUT. COLONEL D.R. COATES.   COMMANDING 107/F.A. BRIGADE.

Copy No. 1.   SECRET.   26th August 1916.

1. The 20th Division will take over some line from the 35th Division and attack GUILLEMONT.

2. The southern boundary of the 20th Division is readjusted as follows:-
   S 30 d 7.6½ - JACKSON TRENCH (inclusive) up to its junction with SWITCH TRENCH (S 30 c 9.1½) - SWITCH TRENCH - HOOGE ALLEY.

3. The Right (59th) Infantry Brigade H.Q. at the BRIQUETERIE will hold the line with two Battns.

   Right Battn. H.Q.   S 30 d 2½.9½ A6.a.2.6.
   Left Battn. H.Q.   S 30 b 1.9.

4. (1) The 106 F.A.B. will keep a Liason Officer permanently at the 59th Infantry Brigade H.Q. who will be in communication with 106 F.A.B. H.Q. This Officer should be an experienced subaltern.
   (2) The 107 and 109 F.A. Bdes. will be in communication with and will take it in turn to keep a Liason Officer permanently at Right Battn. H.Q.
       The 106 and 108 F.A. Bdes. will be in communication with and will take it in turn to keep a Liason Officer permanently at Left Battn. H.Q.
       When Brigades do not have a Liason Officer at Battn H.Q. an Information Officer will be kept continuously at the Brigade Information Centre.

5. The S.O.S. lines and areas for night firing given in Operation Order No. 40 remain the same.

Copy No. 1 War diary.
        2. A/107.
        3. B/107.
        4. C/107.
        5. D/107.

D R Coates Lieut. Colonel. R.F.A.
Commanding 107/F.A/Brigade.

OPERATION ORDER. 41.
BY
LIEUT. COLONEL D.R.COATES.   COMMANDING 107/F~~ER~~ F.A.BRIGADE.

Copy No.....   S E C R E T.   24th August 1916.

Programme for 107/F.A/Brigade for to-day 24th August 1916.

4.5. HOWITZER.

TIME.	UNIT.	OBJECTIVE.	RATE OF FIRE.	PROJECTILE.	REMARKS.
-2 hrs to +0 hrs 1½ mins.	"D"	T 19 c 2.9 to T 19 a 5½.½.	From -2 hrs to Zero, Ordinary.	H.E.	Lift to Second Target.
+0 hrs 1½ mins to 8.p.m.	"D"	T 19 c 9½.4.	Zero to 0 hrs 20 mins. Medium. 0 hrs 20 mins to 8 p.m., Ordinary.	H.E.	

18-Pdr. BATTERIES.

OPERATION ORDER NO. 43.
BY
<u>LIEUT. COLONEL D.R.COATES.</u>   COMMANDING 107/F.A/BRIGADE.

Copy No. 1.   S E C R E T.   26th August 1916.

1. The attack on GUILLEMONT will be shortly resumed, possibly on the 28th. The actual date will be notified later.

2. The 20th Division will attack GUILLEMONT in conjunction with other troops to the North and South.
   The final objective of the 20th Division will be WEDGE WOOD, GINCHY Road to T 20 a 1.5½.

3. (a) The following will be the forward boundary of the 20th Division:-

   Southern Boundary.   S 30 d 5.8½ - T 26 a 1.8.

   (b) The inter-Brigade boundary will run from S 24 d 7.1½ - T 19 c 0.1½, along the GUILLEMONT - LEUZE WOOD ROAD (inclusive to Right Brigade) to T 20 c 1½.4½.
   The 24th D.A. will support the attack of the Right Inf: Bde:
   All Batteries are to register at once all points within this area.

4. All Brigades 24th D.A. should register the zone to be attacked by the 59th Infantry Brigade. The 107 and 109 F.A.Bdes. will probably cover the Right Battn. and the 106 and 108 F.A.Bdes. the Left Battn. The 106 F.A.Bde. will be affiliated to the 59th Inf.Bde.

5. The 4.5.How Battery should carefully register that part of WEDGE WOOD - GINCHY Road in its area.

6. Reference Operation Order No. 42 Right Battn:H.Q. should read A 6 a 2.6. and not S 30 d 2½.9½.

Copy No 1 War diary.
   2. A/107.
   3 B/107.
   4. C/107.
   5. D/107.

Lieut. R.F.A.
Adjutant 107/F.A/Brigade.

OPERATION ORDER. NO.44.
BY
LIEUT. COLONEL B.R.COATES.   COMMANDING 107/F.A/ BRIGADE.

Copy No. 1.   S E C R E T.   27th August 1916.

1. The 24th D.A. will cover the front of the 59th (Right) Inf: Bde: and the 6th D.A. that of the 60th (Left) Inf: Bde: The change of the front will take effect from 7.p.m. to-day.

2. The forward boundaries are :-
Southern Divisional Boundary.

S 30 d 5.8½ to T 26 a 1.8.

Inter-Brigade Boundary.

S 24 d 7.1½ - T 19 c 0.1½ along the GUILLEMONT - LEUZE WOOD Road (inclusive to Right Brigade) to T 20 c 1½.4½.

Northern Divisional Boundary.

S 24 b 9.9 to T 20 a 1.5½.

3. From 7.p.m. the S.O.S. Lines for the brigade will be as follows:-
    A/107. T 25 a 3.3. to T 25 a 3.4½.
    B/107. T 25 a 3.4½ to T 25 a 2½.6½.
    C/107. T 25 a 2½.6½ to T 25 a 2.8.

Left gun of "C" Battery to be on road at T 25 a 2.8.
18-Pdr Batteries to overlap 25 yards.

    D/107. S 30 b 8½.4½ (one section) T 25 a 3.4.(one section)
These two trenches to be searched.

4. NIGHT FIRING. Batteries will fire intermittently on their S.O.S., Lines.
A/107 will search area T 25 a 3.3. - T 25 b 0.4 - T 25 a 3.4½ - T 25 b ½.6.
B/107   ditto   T 25 a 3.4½ - T 25 b ½.6 - T 25 a 2½.6½ - T 25 b 1¼.7½.
C/107   ditto.   T 25 a 2½.6½ - T 25 b 1¼.7½ - T 25 a 2.8 - T 25 b 2.9.

D/107 will ~~fire as laid down in Operation Order No.40 dated 22/8/16.~~
will search the area T25 a 3.3 - T25 b 0.4 - T25 a 2.8 - T25 b 2.9.

Copy No. 1 War diary.
     2 B/107.
     3 C/107.
     4 D/107.
     5 A/107.
     6 B.M.24 D.A.

for J.H. Curley. Lieut
Lieut. Colonel. R.F.A.
Commanding 107/F.A/Brigade.

OPERATION ORDER. NO. 45.

BY

LIEUT. COLONEL. D.R. COATES.   COMMANDING 107/F.A/BRIGADE.

Copy No. 1.   S E C R E T.   28th August 1916.

1. The 20th Division will attack on the afternoon of August 30th, at a zero hour to be notified later. Attacks will be made at the same time by the 5th Division on the Right, and by the 7th Division on the Left.

2. The final objective of the 20th Division is the WEDGE WOOD-GINCHY road from T 26 a1.8 to T 20 a 1.5½.

3. There will be a prelininary bombardment by the Heavy Artillery and 4.5 Howitzers.
The 18-pdrs and 4.5 Howitzer will fire as per attached appendices 1 & 2. Details of firing on the 30th inst from zero will be issued later in Appendix 3.

4. Details of the Infantry arrangements for the attack will be notified later.

5. Battery Commanders will ensure that all ranks are thoroughly aware of the great importance of this operation. It has got to succeed.

6. Zero time will be notified later. Watches will be synchronised at various hours during the day by the Adjutant.

7. Please acknowledge.

Copy No. 1. War diary.
       2. A/107.
       3. B/107.
       4. C/107.
       5. D/107.
       6. B.M.24 D.A.

D R Coates
                                    Lieut. Colonel. R.F.A.
                              Commanding 107/F.A/Brigade.

Reference Map 1/10,000. Sheet 57 c S.W.3.
                              62 c N.W.1.
        Map 1/5000. GINCHY & GUILLEMONT.

PROGRAMME FOR 4.5 HOWITZER.

APPENDIX 1. for 29/8/16.

TIME.	UNIT.	OBJECTIVE.	RATE OF FIRE.	REMARKS.
8 a.m. to 11 a.m.	"D"	General bombardment. All trenches in Brigade area. T 25 a & b, also area T 25 a 0.8 - T 25 a 3.8 - T 19 c 3.0 - T 19 c 0.0.	Slow deliberate fire to include registration. ~~30~~ rounds a gun per 8 hour.	
11.30 a.m. to 1 p.m.	"D"	ditto.	ditto.	
1 p.m. to 2.5 p.m.	"D"	Front line S 30 b 7.2. to S 30 b 7½.5.	1 p.m. to 2 p.m. half ordinary. 2 p.m. to 2.5 p.m. Medium. 2.5 p.m. Lift.	
2.5 p.m. to 2.9 p.m.	"D"	T 25 a 3.4 to T 25 a 2.8.	Medium.	
2.10 p.m. to 4.30 p.m.	"D"	General Bombardment.	~~30~~ rounds a gun per hour.	
5 p.m. to 5.2 p.m.	"D"	Front Line S 30 b 7.2 to S 30 b 7½.5.	2 rounds rapid fire.	
5.2 p.m. to 6.30 p.m.	"D"	General Bombardment.	~~30~~ rounds a gun per hour.	

APPENDIX 11. for 30/8/16.

TIME.	UNIT.	OBJECTIVE.	RATE OF FIRE.	REMARKS.
8 a.m. to 9 a.m.	"D"	General Bombardment.	~~30~~ rounds a gun per hour.	
9.15 a.m. to 10 a.m.	"D"	S 30 b 7.2 to S 30 b 7½.5.	Half ordinary.	
10 to 10.15 am.	"D"	ditto.	Ordinary.	
10.15 a.m. to 10.18 am	"D"	T 25 a 3.4 to T 25 a 2.8.	Medium.	
10.33 to 11.33 a.m.	"D"	T 19 a 5½.1½ to T 19 a 8½.1½.	10.33 to 11.30 General Bom	Poison Shell.
11.30 a.m. to 11.35 a.m.	"D"	T 19 d 6½.6½ to T 20 c 1.6½.	Medium.	
11.36 to - 1 hr 35'	"D"	General Bombardment.	Ordinary.	
- 1 hr 35' to - 40'	"D"	ditto.	ditto.	
- 40' to - Zero.	"D"	ditto.	Medium.	

During General Bombardments you will engage targets given in Appendix 1. 8 a.m. to 11 a.m.

PROGRAMME FOR 18-POUNDERS.

APPENDIX 1.   for 29/8/16.

TIME.	UNIT.	OBJECTIVE.	RATE OF FIRE.	REMARKS.
2.7 p.m. to 2.9 p.m.	"A" "B" "C"	Front Line. S 30 b 7.2 to S 30 b 3.7/24 S 30 b 3 to S 30 b 7½.4.8.6 S 30 b 8.6 to S 30 b 7½.5.9.7 Front, Support and Communication trenches as detailed for S.O.S. lines and areas to be searched in Operation Order No.44.	3 rounds rapid fire.	"A" & "C" batteries will fire H.E. "B" battery will fire S.S.
5.1 p.m. to 5.2 p.m.	"A" "B" "C"	ditto.	3 rounds rapid fire.	

APPENDIX 11.   for 30/8/16.

TIME	UNIT	OBJECTIVE	RATE OF FIRE / REMARKS
10.15 a.m.	"A" "B" "C"	Front Line and Communication Trenches as in Appendix 1.	3 rounds rapid fire.
11.30 a.m. to 11.35 a.m.	"A" "B" "C"	Search Area:— T 19 d 4.5 – T 20 c 1.6 – T 19 d 4.9.	Rate of fire Intense. All batteries will search this area. "A" will fire H.E. and "B" will fire S.S. commencing on line T-19 d 4.5 – T 19 d 4.9. "C" will fire 50% S.S. and 50% H.E. commencing on line T 19 d 7.6 – T 19 d 7.7½. march to T 20 c 1.6
-1 hr 35' to -40'.	"A" "B" "C"	Will search all ground in their areas likely to contain Machine Guns.	Fire occasional bursts of fire 50% H.E. and 50% S.S.

Note:— Reference Appendix 11, 11.30 to 11.35 a.m., the Communication Trench which has not been fired on for two days is a trap to catch the "unsuspicious" BOSCHE.

SECRET.   Copy No. 2

24th D.A. ORDER No. 11.

Reference Map
~~1/10,000. Sheet 57.c.S.W.3.~~
62.&.N.W.1.
Map 1/5,000. GINCHY & GUILLEMONT.   28th August. 1916.
============

In continuation of 24th D.A. Order No. 10.

1. The 59th Inf.Bde. will attack on the right, and the 60th Inf.Bde. on the left.

(i) Dividing line with 5th Division (on the right) S.30.d.5.8½ – T.25.a.3½.2 – Strong Point T.25.b.1.5 (inclusive to 20th Division) T.26.a.1.7.

(ii) Dividing line between 59th & 60th Infantry Brigades, S.34.d.7.1½ – Road junction T.19.c.½.1½ – GUILLEMONT – COMBLES road to T.20.c.1½.4½ (latter point inclusive to right Brigade.)

(iii) Dividing line with 7th Division (on the left) S.24.b.8½.8½ – T.19.b.2.6 – T.20.a.1.5.

2. The objectives allotted to the Brigades are as follows:-

(a) **59th Infantry Brigade.**

   1st Objective. – German trenches in Sunken Road from T.25.a.3½.5 to T.25.a.2.7½ thence North to Mount Street.

   2nd Objective. – Trench junction T.25.b.1.4½ (inclusive) thence SOUTH STREET as far as MOUNT STREET.

   3rd Objective. – WEDGE WOOD – GINCHY road from T.26.a.1.7 to Cross roads T.20.c.1½.4½ (inclusive) touch being established with 5th Division on the Right and 60th Infantry Brigade on the Left.

(b) **60th Infantry Brigade.**

   1st Objective. – MOUNT STREET at T.19.c.8.2 – Eastern end of QUARRIES – thence German trench to T.19.c.2½.9 – thence BROMPTON Road to T.19.a.8.2 – T.19.a.9.1.

   2nd Objective. – NORTH STREET – T.19.a.9.1 – GINCHY Road, including holding South of Road T.19.c.9.9, to T.19.b.2.6 where touch will be established with 7th Division.

   3rd Objective. – WEDGE WOOD – GINCHY ROAD from Cross roads T.20.c.1½.4½ (exclusive) to T.20.a.1.5, where touch will be established with 7th Division.

(c) The advance from the first to the second Objective will commence at 0 + 50.

   The advance from the second to the third Objective will commence at 0 + 2 hours.

3. The Appendix gives the Artillery Programme.   Separate instructions will be issued to T.M.Batteries and to 'A' Battery, R.O.H.A.

4. A "pusher" mine under the strong point at S.30.b.7.1 will be exploded at Zero minus 10 seconds, and the Flammenwerfer will open fire at the same hour if in position. The front trench will be cleared for 20 yards on either side of SCOTTISH LANE.

                                                              P.T.O.

- 2 -

5.(i) Flares will be lit by the Infantry as follows:-

(a) On attaining each objective.
(b) at 7.p.m. August 30th.
(c) At 6.a.m. on August 31st.

(ii) The assaulting troops of the 59th Inf.Bde. will carry RED flags, and those of the 60th Inf.Bde. YELLOW flags, to denote where the most forward infantry have reached.

6. Medical arrangements :-

   Bearer Posts.

   Left Brigade - BERNAFAY WOOD, S.22.d.9.1.
   Right   "   - BRIQUETERIE, A.4.b.5.5.

   Adv. Dressing Station. - CARNOY, A.13.d.3.8.

   Walking cases through MONTAUBAN or BRIQUETERIE to A.D.S.

7. In addition to the present liaison with Battns., The O.C., 106 F.A.B. with his Orderly Officer will be at 59th Inf.Bde.Battle H.Q., and will be in communication from there with his Adjutant at 106 F.A.B.,H.Q.

   The C.R.A., 6th Division will arrange liaison with the 60th Inf. Bde.

8. Watches will be synchronised at (7.a.m.) & 6.p.m. on August 29th.
   & at 9 am on Aug: 30th

9. Please acknowledge.

                                                    Captain.R.A.
                              Brigade Major, 24th Divisional Artillery.

Issued at

Copies to	No.		No.
106 F.A.B.	1	20th DIV.	16
107th " "	2	3rd D.A.	17
108 " "	3	7th D.A.	18
109 " "	4	H.A.,XIV.Corps.	19
6th D.A.	5,6,7,8.	R.A., " "	20
T.M.,24 D.A.	9	No.9 Squadron,R.F.C.	21
V/24 T.M.Batty.	10	No. 4, Kite Balloon Section.	22
24 D.A.C.	11	No.12, " " "	23
Staff Captain.R.A.	12	FILE.	24
59th I.B.	13	WAR DIARY.	25,26.
60th I.B.	14	SPARE.	27,28,29.
61st I.B.	15		

Formation.	Time.		Objective.	Remarks.
	From.	To.		
D/107 How.Bty.	-40.min.	Zero.	S.30.b.7.2 - S.30.b.7½.5.	Lift at zero.
"	Zero	+45.min.	T.25.b.3½.4½ - T.19.d.3.0.	Search the area to 100 yds West of this line. Lift at 45.mins.
"	+45.min.	+125.min.	Road T.26.c.1.7 to T.20.c.1½.4½. (Exact place to be notified.)	
"	+125.min.	Till.stpd.	T.20.c.1½.4½.	Lift at +125.mins.
108 F.A.B.				
All 18-pr Btties.	Zero	+2.min.	S.30.b.9.7 - T.19.c.0.2.	At +2.min. lift direct to next Barrage. X
"	+2.min.	+6.min.	T.25.a.6.8 - T.19.c.5.3.	At +6.min. lift direct to next Barrage. 0/
"	+6.min.	+57.min.	T.19.a.5.0 - T.19.d.3.4.	At +57.min. lift direct to next Barrage. 6/
"	+57.min.	+127.min.	T.20.a.2½.2½ to T.20.c.5.4½.	At +127.min. lift direct to next Barrage. 12/
"	+127.min.	Till Supd.	T.20.c.5.4½ - T.20.d.6.1.	
D/108(How)Bty.	-40.min.	Zero.	S.30.b.9.7. - T.19.c.0.2.	Lift at zero.
"	Zero	+45.min.	T.19.d.5.0 - T.19.c.9.4.	Search the area 100 yds West of this line. Lift at +45.mins.
"	+45.min.	+125.min.	Road T.26.a.1.7 to T.20.c.1½.4½. (Exact place to be notified.)	Lift at +125.min.
"	+125.min.	Till stpd.	T.20.d.6.6.	
109 F.A.B.	Zero	+2.min.	S.30.b.7.2. - S.30.b.3.7.	
All 18-pr Btties.	+7.min.	+10.min.	T.25.a.3½.3 - T.25.a.2.7.	Lift 50 yds at +2.min. and continue lifting 50 yds every min. till on next barrage.
"	+10.min.	+50.min.	T.25.a.7.4 - T.25.a.6.8.	Lift 50 yds at +10.min. & continue lifting 50 yds every min. till on next barrage.
"	+50.min.	+120.min.	T.19.d.5.0.	Lift 100 yds at +50.min. & continue lifting 100 yds every 4.min. till on next barrage.
"	+67.min.	+120.min.	T.19.d.5.0.	Lift 50 yds at +120.min. & continue lifting 50 yds every min. till on next barrage.
"	+150.min.	Till Stpd.	T.26.a.5.7½ - T.20.c.5.1.	

Rates of fire:-
 18-prs. Zero +15. Intense.
 +15. +50. Ordinary.   4.5 How. As for 18-prs., except for "Intense" read "Medium."
 +50. +65. Intense.
 +65. +120. Ordinary.
 +120. +145. Intense.
 +145. Till Stopped. Ordinary.

ARTILLERY PROGRAMME, August 30th 1916.

Formation.	From.	To.	Objective.	Remarks.
106 F.A.B. All 18-pr Bttios.	Zero	+2.mins.	S.30.b.8.7 — T.24.d.9.1½.	At +2.mins. lift 50 yds. & continue lifting 50 yds every min. till on next barrage.
"	+.9.mins.	+50.mins.	T.25.a.6.8 — T.19.c.5½.3.	At +50.mins. lift 100 yds. and continue lifting 100 yds every four mins till on next barrage.
"	+67.mins.	+120.min.	T.19.d.5.0 — T.19.d.3.4.	At +120.mins. lift 50 yds. and continue lifting 50 yds. every min. till on next Barrage.
"	+131.mins.	Till stopped.	T.20.c.5½.1 — T.20.c.5½.4½.	
D/106 How.Bty.	-40.mins.	Zero.	S.30.b.7½.5 to T.25.a.0.8	Lift at Zero.
"	Zero.	+45.mins.	T.25.a.9.4 – T.25.a.7.7.	Lift at +45.mins.
"	+45.mins.	+125.mins.	Road T.26.a.1.7 to T.20.c.1½.4½	Lift at +125"
			(Exact place to be notified.)	
"	+125.mins.	Till stopped.	T.23.b.C.9.	
107 F.A.B. All 18-pr Bttios.	Zero	+3.mins.	S.30.b.7.2 — S.30.b.9.7.	At 3.mins. lift direct to next barrage.
"	+3.mins.	+7.mins.	T.25.a.3½.3 — T.25.a.2.7.	At +7.mins. lift direct to next Barrage.
Nos.1 & 2 Bttios.	+7.mins.	+55.mins.	T.25.b.1.4½ — T.25.a.8.6½.	At +55.mins. lift direct to next Barrage.
No.3 Battery.	+7.mins.	+50.mins.	T.25.a.8.½ — T.25.a.6½.7.	At +50.mins. lift direct to next Barrage.
Nos.1 & 2 Bttios.	+55."	+67."	Southern 2/3rds. of T.25.b.5.5½ — T.19.d.5.0.	At +67.mins. lift direct to next barrage.
No.3 Battery.	+50."	+67."	Northern 1/3rd. of T.25.b.5.5½ — T.19.d.5.0.	
All Batteries.	+87."	+126."	T.25.a.1.7 to T.20.c.1½.4½.	At +126 mins lift direct to next Barrage.
All Batteries.	+126."	Till stopped.	T.26.a.5.7½ — T.20.c.5¼.1.	

P.T.O.

OPERATION ORDER. NO. 46.
BY

LIEUT. COLONEL. D.R.COATES.   COMMANDING 107/F.A/BRIGADE.

Copy. 1.   S E C R E T.   29th August 1916.

1. On receipt of the order BARRAGE SUNKEN ROAD, Batteries will fire as under :-

    A/107.   S 30 b 7.2 to S 30 b 7½.4.
    B/107.   S 30 b 7½.4 to S 30 b 8.6.
    C/107.   S 30 b 8.6 to S 30 b 9.7.
    D/107.How. T 25 a 3½.3½ to T 25 a 2½.8.

Battery Commanders must see that their guns are properly registered on this SUNKEN ROAD.

2. S.O.S. lines and areas for Night Firing will remain the same as in Operation Order No.44 dated 27/8/16.

Copy No 1. War diary.
    2. A/107.
    3. B/107.
    4. C/107.
    5. D/107.
    6. B.M.24 D.A.

Lieut. R.F.A.
Adjutant 107/F.A/Brigade.

OPERATION ORDER. NO. 46.
BY
LIEUT. COLONEL D.R.COATES.   COMMANDING 107/F.A/BRIGADE.

Copy No. 1.   S E C R E T.   29th August 1916.

In continuation of Operation Order No.45.

1. The 59th Infantry Brigade will attack on the Right, and the 60th Infantry Brigade on the Left.
(1) Dividing line with 5th Division (on the Right) S 30 d 5.8½ – T 25 a 3½.2 – Strong Point T 25 b 1.5. (inclusive to 20th Division) T 26 a 1.7.
(2) Dividing line between the 59th and 60th Infantry Brigades, S 24 d 7.1½ – Road Junction T 19 c ½.1½ – GUILLEMONT – COMBLES road to T 20 c 1½.4½. (latter point inclusive to Right Brigade)
(3) Dividing line with 7th Division (on the left) S 24 b 8½.8½ – T 19 b 2.6 – T 20 a 1.5.

2. The objectives allotted to the Brigades are as follows :–
(a) <u>59th Infantry Brigade.</u>
    1st objective.– German trenches in Sunken Road from T 25 a 3½.3 to T 25 a 2.7½ thence north to Mount Street.
    2nd objective.– Trench Junction T 25 b 1.4½ (inclusive) thence SOUTH STREET as far as MOUNT STREET.
    3rd objective.– WEDGE WOOD – GINCHY road from T 26 a 1.7 to cross roads T 20 c 1½.4½ (inclusive) touch being established with 5th Division on the Right and 60th Infantry Brigade on the Left.

(b) <u>60th Infanary Brigade.</u>
    1st objective.– MOUNT STREET at T 19 c 2.2 – Eastern end of QUARRIES – thence German Trench to T 19 c 2½.9 – thence BROMPTON Road to T 19 a 8.2 – T 19 a 9.1.
    2nd objective.– NORTH STREET – T 19 a 9.1 – GINCHY Road, including holding South of Road T 19 c 9.9, to T 19 b 2.6. where touch will be established with 7th Division.
    3rd objective.– WEDGE WOOD – GINCHY Road from Cross roads T 20 c 1½.4½ (inclusive) to T 20 a 1.5, where touch will be established with 7th Division.

(c) The advance from the first to the second Objective will commence at 0 50.
    The advance from the second to the third Objective will commence at 0 2 hours.

3. A "pusher" mine under the strong point at S 30 b 7.1 will be exploded at Zero minus 10 seconds, and the Flamsonwerfer will open fire at the same hour if in position. The front trench will be cleared for 20 yards on either side of SCOTTISH LANE.

4. (1) Flares will be lit by the Infantry as follows :–
(a) On attaining each objective.
(b) At 7 p.m. August 30th.
(c) At 6 a.m. on August 31st.

(2) The assaulting troops of the 59th Inf: Bde: will carry Red Flags and those of the 60th Inf: Bde: YELLOW Flags. to denote where the most forward Infantry have reached.

continued...............

5. Medical arrangements :-

   BEARER POSTS.
   Left Brigade - BERNAFAY WOOD, S 22 d 9.1.
   Right   "   - BRIQUETERIE , A 4 b 5.3.

6. In addition to the present liason with Battns: The O.C ., 106 F.A.B. with his Orderly Officer will be at 59th Inf: Bde: Battle H.Q., and will be in communication from there with his Adjutant at 106 F.A.B.,H.Q.

7. Watches will be synchronised by the Adjuant at 6.15 p.m. to-day and at 9.15a.m. on August 30th. An Officer of each Battery will be at the telephone at the above times to receiv e the correct Divisional time.

8. Please acknowledge.

Copy No 1. War diary.
        2. A/107.
        3. B/107.
        4. C/107.
        5. D/107.

                                            Lieut. Colonel. R.F.A.
                              Commanding 107/F.A/Brigade.

S E C R E T.   R.P.306.
31/8/16.

All Batteries,
  107. F.A.B.
  ─────────

In continuation of Operation Order No.47 issued herewith, the following are the 59th Inf: Bde: arrangements for the attack.

1.   There will be three Divisional Objectives:-

(1) From T 19 a 8.2 to T 19 c 2½.8½, thence to T 25 a 4.1.
(2) From T 19 a 8.2 to T 19 c 9½.14 to T 25 b 1.5½.
(3) The GINCHY - WEDGE WOOD Road from T 20 a 1½.5½ to T 26 a 2.8½.

The first two Divisional Objectives will be sub-divided into two Brigade Objectives :-
(a) The 1st Brigade Objective - From T 19 c 0.1½ to T 25 a 0.8 to S 30 b 7.1 trenches on either side of the SUNKEN ROAD to be included in this Objective.
(b) The 2nd Brigade Objective - (1st Divisional Objective) - From T 19 c 2.1½ to T 25 a 2½.8, and thence on the East side of the 2nd SUNKEN ROAD to T 25 a 4½.1.
(c) The 3rd Brigade Objective - From T 19 c 6½.3⅜ to T 25 a 7½.7½ to the S.E.end of the Village at T 25 a 10.4½.
(d) The 4th Brigade (2nd Divisional) Objective. - T 19 c 9½.4 to point of the village T 25 b 1.5½.
(e) The 5th Brigade (3rd Divisional) Objective - From Cross-roads T 20 c 2½.5 to T 26 a 2.8½.

The Brigade attack will be divided into Right attack and Left attack the boundary line between the two attacks being DOWN STREET exclusive to the Left attack.
The frontage of the Right attack will be 350 yards at the 1st Brigade Objective narrowing to 200 yards at the 5th Brigade Objective. That of the Left attack will be 200 yards at the 1st Brigade Objective narrowing to 100 yards at the 5th Brigade Objective.

2.   ALLOTMENT OF TROOPS.
     ───────────────────

The 10 R.B. will attack on the Right with either 3 or 4 companies in the Front Line.
The 10th K.R.R.C. will attack on the Left with Nos. 1 & 2 Companies in the Front Line and Nos.3 & 4 Companies in close support. 1 Company of the 11th K.R.R. will also be allotted to the Left Attack as a general reserve and under the command of Lt.Col.Blacklock commanding the Left Attack. The 11th R.B. will be in support of the Right Attack and the 11th K.R.R. (less 1 Coy) in Brigade Reserve.

3. FIRST DIVISIONAL OBJECTIVE.
   ──────────────────────────

(a) Right Attack. 10th R.B. will capture and consolidate the 1st Brigade Objective of the Right Attack. The 11th R.B. will at once pass through the 10th R.B. and capture and consolidate the 2nd Brigade Objective.
(b) Left Attack. The leading 2 Coys. of the 10th K.R.R.C. will capture the 1st Brigade Objective. They will be closely followed by the 2nd two Coys. who will pass through them and carry and consolidate the 2nd Brigade Objective.
The Brigade will now be established at the 1st Divisional Objective.

continued...... ....

No advance from this point will be made until 50 minutes after Zero thus giving time for thorough consolidation.

As soon as the leading Battn: of the Right Attack leaves our trenches they will be followed up at only 100 yards interval by the 11th R.B. The 11th K.R.R.(less 1 Coy) from the reserve moving up with the greatest possible rapidity to the Front jumping off trenches of the Right Attack.

2nd Divisional Objective.
(A) The 11th R.B. will advance 50 minutes after Zero with their left on DOWN STREET, and will capture and consolidate the enemy's trenches forming the 3rd Brigade Objective from T 19 c 6½.3½ to the S.E.point of the Village/running T 25 a 10.4½ the 10th R.B. advancing simultaneously from the 1st SUNKEN ROAD and passing over the 2nd SUNKEN ROAD, will closely follow the 11th R.B. passing through them at the 3rd Brigade Objective and capturing and consolidating the 4th Brigade Objective.

The 11th K.R.R. (less 1 Coy) will similarly advance, passing over 1st SUNKEN ROAD and occupying the 2nd SUNKEN ROAD.
(b) Left Attack. The 10th K.R.R.C. will capture the 3rd Brigade Objective and will immediately advance on the 4th Brigade Objective, leaving sufficient men to consolidate. No advance will be made from the 4th Brigade (2nd Divisional) Objective until 2 hours after Zero.

3rd Divisional Objective.
The Brigade will advance from the 2nd Divisional Objective to the 3rd Divisional Objective, the 10th K.R.R. with its left on the GUILLEMONT - COMBLES Road, the 11th R.B. in the centre and the 10th R.B. on the right. The 10th K.R.R.C. will direct the 11th K.R.R.C. will be in support behind.

The advance will be made as rapidly as possible until the GINCHY - WEDGE WOOD road has been captured, when consolidation will immediately begin.

4. Distinguishing Flag.
Distinguishing flags will be carried as follows :-
59th Bde. - RED.
60th Bde. - YELLOW.
61st Bde. - YELLOW.

5. The S.O.S. Signal will consist of five red rockets sent up all at once.

6. Distinguishing Marks.
All personnel taking part in the assault will wear tin discs on their backs.

7. 59th Inf. Bde. H.Q. will be at the BRIQUETERIE with an advanced Bde. H.Q. at ARROW HEAD COPSE. All reports should be sent to ARROW Hd COPSE. Specially important ones to be sent to LA BRIQUETERIE as well as to ARROW Hd COPSE.

8. The following will be the Liason Arrangements
107 & 109 F.A. Bdes. will each be in communication with and will each have one Officer at the Battn. H.Q of the Battn. doing the Rt.Attack.
In addition, each Brigade will have an Information Officer at the Advanced Brigade Information Centre.
When fresh Battalions continue the Right or Left Attack, the Liason Officers will be with the Battalion Commander actually commanding the attack.

Lieut. R.F.A.
Adjutant 107/F.A/Brigade.

SECRET.

[Stamp: 107th BRIGADE R.F.A. R.P.304. No. Date 30/8/16.]

All Batteries,
107 F.A.B.

1. With reference to Operation Order No. 45 (Operation Order No. 46 will be issued later) the attack will now take place on September 1st. Zero hour will probably be about 12.55 p.m.

2. The preliminary bombardment ordered for the 29th and 30th will take place on the 31st and 1st.

3. There will be no increase in the intensity of this bombardment up to zero hour, except for the Chinese attacks, the Trap Area attack and the Gas Shells attack.
A revised Appendix 11 for September 1st (embracing the various amendments) will be issued later. The bombardment on the 31st will be carried out in accordance with Appendix 1.

4. The rate of fire of 4.5 Howitzers during the "General Bombardment" will now be 8 rounds per gun per hour, unless otherwise stated in the Appendices.

5. In addition to the programme with the Special Tasks on Appendix 1, 18-pdr Batteries will search the ground in their areas vide Operation Order No.44.(allotted for Night Firing), by bursts of fire at irregular intervals between the hours of 8 a.m. and 6.30 p.m.
Rate of fire for this searching should average about 8 rounds per gun per hour, 50% Shrapnel and 50% H.E. to be fired.

6. Reference remarks Appendix 1, "Special tasks" "B" and "C" Batteries will fire H.E. "A" Battery Shrapnel. All fire on this Front Line is to be observed.

7. It is reported that this SUNKEN ROAD S 30 b 7.5 to S 30 b 8.6½., is strongly held and has a couple of Machine Guns in it.
A strong point is suspected at S 30 b 7.6½. This is in front of the German line.

8. For the success of the operations it is very essential that accurate and observed fire should be brought to bear on this SUNKEN ROAD.

Copies to :-
A/107.   B/107.
C/107.   D/107.

Lieut. Colonel. R.F.A.
Commanding 107/FxA/Brigade.

Royal Artillery

24th Division

107th BRIGADE R. F. A.

SEPTEMBER 1916

Army Form C. 2118.

WAR DIARY
or
INTELLIGENCE SUMMARY.   XXX
(Erase heading not required.)

104 F.A. Bde.

Place	Date	Hour	Summary of Events and Information	Remarks and references to Appendices
LONGUEVAL	1st Sept. 1916	8 AM	18 pdrs fired three allotment of rounds, registered and checked lines on target. Shrapnel shell & direct.	LONGUEVAL 57.C.S.& 3. 1/10000
		8 pm	"	
		9 pm	Searched night area "operation order" no. 48. Known fire.	
	2nd	8 am	18 pdrs "	"
		4.5 How	"	
		8 pm	18 pdrs 4.6 How fired allotment of rounds, checked lines on day area.	
		9 pm	Searched area & night fire per operation order no. 48.	
	3rd	6 AM	104 FAB took part in attack on GUILLEMONT and carried out programme as per operation order no. 49. The attack was very successful and GUILLEMONT was taken but	operation order no. 49 attached
		to 7pm	batteries being specially marked upon for their accuracy and effect	
		9 AM	all batteries fired on new SOS lines. 10R killed	
	4th	8 AM	All batteries fired by day on SOS lines.	
		8 pm	" " " night.	
		5 pm	" " "	
	5th	6 am	A.O.R. remainder	
		8 am	all batteries fired by day on SOS lines.	
		8 pm	" " " night	
		A/104	5/104 } Relieved by sections of the 75th Bde R.F.A. Guards Division	
BOIS de TAILLES	7th	6/104	Head Qrs 104 FAB remaining. Lockers 18 hrs & 0 Hows relieved by 75 FAB as per operation order n. 52 marched to new lines at BOIS des TAILLES	Maps Ref. 52 d & Huaco operation order n. 52 attached

Army Form C. 2118.

WAR DIARY
or
INTELLIGENCE SUMMARY.
(Erase heading not required.)

10th/F.A. Bde.   XXXI

Place	Date	Hour	Summary of Events and Information	Remarks and references to Appendices
BOIS des...	7th		Rested.	Map Ref. 62 d.a.1/40,000
TAILLES	8th		} "All guns refitted/overhauled. Brig. Gen. Phillpotts L.M. and Capt. Crippen C.R.A. B Hqrs by S.A. Killed whilst visiting B.Sgts. Col. Dr Coates assumed temporary command. 2nd 9 a.m. night 8/9 Sep G. Major Pottinger 16 L.D. assumed temporary command of 107 F.A.B.	
	9th			
	10th		At FRANKAU G. to England.	Map Ref. 62d.a. NE.
	11th	10 AM	Moved to new wagon lines and reconnoitred new positions. 2/Lt. A.B. Longmuir joined Colonel Dr Coates resumed command 11th Sep. 11.15. 2/Lt. A.B. Longmuir joined	A.B.
			2/Lt. Moir A.A. Training & proba 6 6/7/14. " 7 A/117.	
	12th		Rested? Reconnoitred positions. 5/14/14/17.	
LONGUEVAL	13th	3 p.m.	One Section per A/117. B/117. C/117 moved up into new position.	Map Ref. 57c SW. Edit. 31/10,000
		8 p.m.	Remainder Sections A/117. B/117. C/117 D/117 moved up into new position 18 pdr. 5.3.06. 4.5 Hrs. B.16. 2nd cut over / 10 O.R. Killed. 2 O.R. wounded.	Longueval operation order attached no 1.
	14th	6 a.m.	107 B.A.C. in attack on Operation no 1. Tanks operated for the first time 107 9 a/b bat'y in attack on QUADRILATERAL on b'd'y between order no 2	
	15th	7.30 a.m.	107 9 a/b bde. moved up 4 new wagon line at A.H.d.	Operation order attached.
			B/117. 6 by instructions B.M. 38. SOS buried later 3/H 9/ 3. OR. wounded. 2/Lt. MANSEL-REYDELL J.M. wounded dangerously 1.30 OR wounded.	B.M. 38 attached.
Sheet 57 6.	16th		All 18 pdr. Cut wire and chetren wire 4.5 Hrs. replied and chetren lines and saps, and fired on buses as per B.M. 50.	A.7. attached.
			Carried out bally firing on ker instructions.	B.M. attached 50
			1 O.R. wounded	
	17th		Repeated 18 pdr. with air plane and cut wire as per B.M. 62. 5/Hrs/117. replied on policed	Map Ref. LONGUEVAL
	14th		Toys carried out programme H 53. S/Hrs 117. Carried out programme in Longueval. 6/Lt. PROCTOR G. joined & probs & A/117.	57 C S.W. 1/10000 AN 62 d.1 53 SW. attached.
			A.D.S.S./Corps/C. A.13. 2/Lt. WILCOXSON F.J. D/117	

2353 Wt W2541/1454 700,000 5/15 D, D, & L.

Army Form C. 2118.

WAR DIARY
or
INTELLIGENCE SUMMARY. XXXI

(Erase heading not required.)

167/F.A./Bde.

Place	Date	Hour	Summary of Events and Information	Remarks and references to Appendices
Longueval	18th	5.30 A.m.	18prs took part in attack as per operation order J.H. 69. B/Hw/114 took part in attack as above. S.O.S Line as per J.H. 74. & night firing as per J.H. 76. 77.	Maps Ref. LONGUEVAL 57. c. S.W. J.H. 69. 70. attached 74. 76. 77.
	19th		All batteries replied and reconnoitred to new O.P's and forward gun positions. New S.O.S. line for 18prs as per J.H. 86. night firing as per J.H. 92. Night firing for B/How/114 as per J.H. 93. Before line shelled.	ditto J.H. 86. 92. 93 attached
	20th		18prs cut wire as per J.H. 104. New S.O.S. line for all batteries as per operation order J.H. 110. Night firing same as 19th	ditto J.H. 104. 110. attached
	21st		B/How/114 Reconnoitred new position and moved to position at 7.19.6. and replace.	ditto
	22nd		B/How/114 moved to forward position at 7.20. 0.0.8. and replaced. S.O.S. Line for 18prs forward firing as per J.H. 128. 18prs attached B/Hw/114 replacing to bey J.H. 133. 18prs night firing as per J.H. 134. 18prs day firing as per J.H. 138.	ditto J.H. 128. 133. 134. 138 attached

Army Form C. 2118.

WAR DIARY
or
INTELLIGENCE SUMMARY.

(Erase heading not required.)

10th F.A./26th XXXIII

Place	Date	Hour	Summary of Events and Information	Remarks and references to Appendices
LONGUEVAL	23rd	18 hr	nght firing as per J.H. 140. Carried out day firing & registered. Bde Head Qrs moved up to S.7.25.b.4.2.2. SO & rules as per S.A.H.8.	Maps Ref. S.Y.E. S.W. LONGUEVAL. SO & WD attached
	24th	9 hr	Hv/hy repeated such heavy artillery as per operation order N°1	ditto. S.A.H.169 attached. S.A.169
		18 hr	" " " " " " " N°2	
			Barrage night firing as previous days orders. SOS as 23rd. and J.H. 169.	
	25th		10th F.A.B. took part in the attack on MORVAL and LES BOEUFS as per operation order N°3.	ditto. S.H. 184. S.A.H. 185 attached
		5 hr 10 f	10th Bn took part in. The attack " " " " "	
			S.H. 166. 190. night firing and SOS lines as per S.H. 183.	
			2/Lieut Ping night firing as per S.H. 185. 1 O.R. killed 1 O.R. wounded.	
	26th		18 hr reached attack as per S.H. 193. Hv/hy engaged battery as per S.H. 195.	
			SOS and night firing as per S.H. 184, 208, 18 hrs.	
			" " " " " " " S.H. 209.	

Army Form C. 2118.

WAR DIARY
or
INTELLIGENCE SUMMARY.
(Erase heading not required.)

107/FA/Bde   XXXIV

Place	Date	Hour	Summary of Events and Information	Remarks and references to Appendices
Longueval	27th		All batteries check hours and reported in morning.	Map Ref 57 C S.W
		2.16pm	Got hot part in CHINESE ATTACK. opened 2.4 to 9A.4. Sos. hurr and night firing as previous night. to 18 hrs.	
			D/4n/114 on pts Sept. 114	Q4.b.6.19 attached
			3 Sections of Eg.th F.A.B. 4th D.A. relieved like sections of 107 F.A.B.	
	28th	10 Am	Remaining sections of 29th F.A.B. relieved the sections of 107 F.A.B. Relief completed by 11 Am. copies 13 & 13764	13,7164 attached
			107 F.A.B. stayed till night in Bivouac at Bisde TAILLES.	
	29th		117 F.A.B. marched to TALMAS and billeted for night.	Map Ref LENS 4 100,000
	30.		107 F.A.B. marched to AMPLIER and billeted for night.	

Bruler Hlt.
4/10/16.

S.M.
BM/491

Fourth Army No. GX.3/1/2. P.
Xlll Corps. No. 25/25/(G)

Xlll Corps.

  Every possible measure must be taken beforehand by Corps to ensure that after the capture of the Green line, communications between the Infantry holding that line and the Artillery who are responsible for placing the barrage in front of that line, in case of counter-attack, firm are as rapid and reliable as possible.
  As many alternative means as possible should be provided.

1 There must be several alternative visual signal stations marked down beforehand close behind the Green line from which lamp signalling can be carried out with visual stations in rear and with the Kite Balloons.

2 Full use should be made of the Trench Wireless Sets.

3. Communication by means of Brigade and Battn. ground stations and tunnels panels with aeroplanes will materially assist by day.
  This will, however, be a somewhat slow channel of communication.

4 S.O.S. signals by means of rockets.
  It has been found impossible to procure any special rockets and the G.S. rocket is the only one available.
  The S.O.S. signal of five rockets fired as rapidly as possible one after another should be retained in use, and arrangements made for these rockets to be brought up as early as possible to selected stations behind the Green line.

H.Q. Fourth Army.   (Sd) A.A. MONTGOMERY. MAJOR-GENERAL.
27/6/16.   G.S. Fourth Army.

C.R.A.,
 24th Div.
========

  For information. Although these instructions were issued prior to the commencement of the general attack, the general principles still hold good.

1/8/16.   (Sd) HERBERT MUSGRAVE. Major.
        G.S. 24th Div.

106th F.A.B.
107th F.A.B.
108th F.A.B.
109th F.A.B.
T.M., 24th D.A.
24th D.A.C.
========

  For information.

1/8/16.
           Captain. R.A.
   Brigade Major, 24th Divisional Artillery.

Secret

OPERATION ORDER NO.49.
BY

LIEUT. COLONEL D.R.COATES,   COMMANDING 107/F.A/BRIGADE.

Copy No.1.   S E C R E T.   2nd September 1916.

1. In consequence of the hour fixed for Zero, there will be a modification in Appendix 11 for September 3rd. This will be at once notified.

2. The following are the Battle Battalion H.Q. of the 59th (Right) Infantry Brigade :-
    10th R.B.   S 30 b 3.1.   (S.E. of ARROW HEAD COPSE.)
    11th R.B.   S 30 a 2.3.   (S.E. end of TEALE TRENCH.)
    10th K.R.R. S 24 d 0.0.   (BRIGHTON ALLEY.)
    11th K.R.R. S 30 c 1.3.   (LIDDEL TRENCH.)

3. "C" battery will provide the Rocket and Gas Guard of One Sergeant and Three Men for the night 3rd September, to watch for S.O.S. Signal and report Gas Shell. The place from where the S.O.S. Signal is likely to be sent will be notified later.

4. Zero hour is 12 noon on September 3rd.

5. At 9 a.m. on September 3rd, FALFEMONT FARM will be taken as a separate operation.

6. Please acknowledge.

7. Reference para 1 above, please note that Appendix 11 will commence at 6 a.m. instead of 8 a.m. The tasks remain the same with an alteration of two hours to be made in the times, this means that an extra General Bombardment will take place for a period of two hours before Zero.

Copy No.1. War diary.
     2. A/107.
     3. B/107.
     4. C/107.
     5. D/107.
     6. B.M. 24 D.A.
     7. B.M. Infantry.

                                    D.R.Coates.
                                    Lieut. Colonel. R.F.A.
                                    Commanding 107/F.A/Brigade.

APPENDIX 111. 18-POUNDER BATTERIES FOR SEPTEMBER 3rd.

TIME.	UNIT.	OBJECTIVE.	REMARKS.
Zero to +3 min.	"A" "B" "C"	S 30 b 7.2 to S 30 b 7¼.3½. S 30 b 7¼.3½ to S 30 b 8.5½. S 30 b 8.5½ to S 30 b 9.7.	At +3 lift direct to next Barrage.
+3 mins to +9 mins.	"A" "B" "C"	T 25 a 3½.3 to T 25 a 3.4½. T 25 a 3.4½ to T 25 a 2½.6. T 25 a 2½.6 to T 25 a 2.7.	Batteries to overlap 25 yards. At +9 lift direct to next Barrage.
+9 mins to +55 mins.	"A" "B"	T 25 b 1.4½ to T 25 a 9.5. T 25 a 9.5 to T 25 a 8.6½.	Lift at +55 direct to next Barrage.
+9 mins to +51 mins.	"C"	T 25 a 8.6½ to T 25 a 6½.7.	At +51 lift direct to next Barrage.
+55 mins to +68 mins.	"A" "B"	T 25 b 5.5½ to T 25 b 5.7. T 25 b 5.7 to T 25 b 5.8½.	At +68 mins lift direct to next Barrage.
+51 mins to +68 mins.	"C"	T 25 b 5.8½ to T 19 d 5.0.	
+68 mins to +135 mins.	"A" "B" "C"	T 26 a 1.7 to T 26 a 1.8. T 26 a 1.8 to T 26 a 1½.9½. T 26 a 1½.9½ to T 20 c 1½.½.	Batteries to overlap 25 yards. At +135 lift to next Barrage.
+135 mins to +138 mins.	"A" "B" "C"	T 26 a 5.7½ to T 26 a 5.8½. T 26 a 5.8½ to T 20 c 5¼.0. T 20 c 5¼.0 to T 20 c 5¼.1.	Batteries to overlap 25 yards. Lift at +138 to next Barrage.
+138 mins to +177 mins.	"A" "B" "C"	T 26 b 8.8½ to T 26 b 6½.9½. T 26 b 6½.9½ to T 20 d 6.¾. T 20 d 6.¾ to T 20 d 5¼.1¾.	Batteries to overlap 25 yards. At +177 lift to next Barrage.
+177 mins till stopped.	"A" "B" "C"	T 21 c 1½.0 to T 21 c ½.1½. T 21 c ½.1½ to T 20 d 9½.2½. T 20 d 9½.2½ to T 20 d 9.3½.	Batteries to overlap 25 yards. S.O.S. 107 F.A.B. night of 3rd unless otherwise ordered.

RATES OF FIRE.

Zero	15 Intense.	15	51 Ordinary
51	65 Intense.	65	121 Ordinary.
121	135 Intense.	135	165 Ordinary.
165	180 Intense.	180	Till stopped. Ordinary.

APPENDIX 111, 4.5. HOWITZER BATTERY FOR SEPTEMBER 3rd.

TIME.	UNIT.	OBJECTIVE.	REMARKS.
−40 mins to Zero.	"D"	S 30 b 7.2 to S 30 b 7½.5.	Lift at Zero.
Zero to +45 mins.	"D"	T 25 b 3½.4½ to T 19 d 3.0.	Search the area to 100 yds. West of this line. Lift at +45 mins.
+45 mins to +130 mins.	"D"	Road T 26 a 1.7 to T 20 c 1½.0.	Lift at +130 mins.
+130 mins to +165 mins.	"D"	T 20 d 1½.1.	Lift at +165 mins.
+165 mins till stopped.	"D"	Area:− T 21 c 3½.1 − T 21 c 7.6 − T 21 c 3½.7 − T 21 c 1½.3½.	This will probably be your S.O.S. Area.

RATES OF FIRE :−
- Zero — 15 mins. Medium.
- 15 — 51 mins. Ordinary.
- 51 — 65 mins. Medium.
- 65 — 121 mins. Ordinary.
- 121 — 135 mins. Medium.
- 135 — 165 mins. Ordinary.
- 165 — 180 mins. Medium.
- 180 till stopped. Ordinary.

S E C R E T.

All Batteries,
    107/F.A/Brigade.

   Reference Operation Order No. 52.
1.   The Liason Officer will be found by "A" Battery, 75th F.A.B.
to-morrow the 6th inst.

2.   The teams of the 75th Brigade are kindly taking our guns back
to our Wagon Lines direct.
     The 75th F.A.B. will arrive in our present Wagon Line about
2.30 p.m. on the 6th inst.
     On their arrival they will hand over ammunition to the 107 F.A.B.
     The 107 F.A.B. will be ready to march to their new Wagon Lines
at the BOIS-DE-TAILLES at 2.30.p.m., 6th inst: under Major
G.L. POPHAM.D.S.O., on completion of transfer of ammunition.

3.   ROUTE. Road Junction L 7 a 1.½. BOIS-DE-TAILLES. No unit is
to march along the main BRAY-CORBIE Road.

SECRET.   O 12/1

Reference Sheets 57c S.W.
    "   62c N.W.
    "   62d N.E.

With reference to 24 D.A. Order No.12 dated 3/9/16

1.   The 106, 107 & 108 F.A. Bdes will be relieved in their present positions in action by the 74, 75 & 76 F.A. Bdes respectively.

2.   (i) Reliefs will be carried out by sections on the mornings of September 5th & 6th.

     (ii) All dumped ammunition, communications, aeroplane photos, etc. will be handed over.

     (iii) Battery and Brigade Commanders will hand over command on completion of reliefs. Completion of reliefs to be reported by wire to this Office.

     (iv) All other details of the relief to be arranged between Brigade Commanders concerned.

3.   Separate instructions are being issued by the Staff Captain, 24th D.A., for the moves of the Brigade Wagon Lines, the 24 D.A.C., and T.M. Batteries.

4.   The G.O.C., R.A. Guards Division will take over command from the G.O.C., R.A. 24th Division at 6.p.m. on September 6th.
     At that hour H.Q., 24 D.A. will close at MINDEN POST and re-open at THE CITADEL.

5.   Please acknowledge.

                                                    [signature]
                                                    Captain, R.A.
4/9/16.   Brigade Major, 24th Divisional Artillery.

Distribution as for 24 D.A. Order No. 12.

OPERATION ORDER. NO. 52.
BY
LIEUT. COLONEL. D.R.COATES.   COMMANDING 107/F.A/BRIGADE.

Copy No.....   SECRET.   4th September 1916.

1. Head Quarters and Batteries 107 F.A.B., will be relieved in their present positions by the 75th F.A.B.

2. (1) Reliefs will be carried out by sections on the mornings of September 5th & 6th. Sections will withdraw to their present Wagon Lines, and will march complete from there on September 6th, to new Wagon Lines at the BOIS-DE-TAILLES, time will be notified later.

(11) All communications, aeroplane photos, etc., are to be handed over, and B.C's will make known all information possible, to B.C's of corresponding batteries.

(111) All dumped ammunition will be handed over. Batteries will however march out from present Wagon Lines with full ammunition Echelons. To do this Batteries will arrange to transfer ammunition from the Wagons of incoming units of 75th F.A.B.
Reports showing amounts handed over to and taken over from relieving batteries are to reach this Office by 10 a.m. on the 6th inst.

(1V) Battery Commanders will hand over command on completion of reliefs. Completion of reliefs to be reported by wire to this Office.

(V) All other details of the relief to be arranged between Battery Commanders concerned.

3. Billeting parties of 1 Officer and 1 N.C.O. from each battery will report to the Adjutant at the present H.Q.Wagon Line at 10 a.m. on the 6th inst.

4. The G.O.C., R.A. Guards Division will take over command from the G.O.C., R.A. 24th Division at 6 p.m. on September the 6th.

5. Please acknowledge.

6. B.C's will ensure that their present Wagon Lines are left in a thoroughly clean & sanitary condition. One N.C.O. & 8 men per battery mounted will be detailed to remain on their camping ground with spades & shovels, who will report to the orderly office for instructions

Copy No.1. War diary
2. A/107.
3. B/107.
4. C/107.
5. D/107.

Lieut. R.F.A.
Adjutant 107/F.A/Brigade.

SECRET

S.C. 24th D.A.
No. 3078

106th F.A.B.
107th F.A.B. ✓
108th F.A.B.
109th F.A.B.
24th D.A.C.
Medium T.M. Batteries
V/24 Heavy T.M. Batteries.
Brigade Major 24th Div. Arty.
<u>Guards Div. Arty.</u>

1. The 109th F.A. Brigade and 24th D.A.C., will march complete to the BOIS DES TAILLES on completion of relief by corresponding units of Guards Divisional Artillery on 5th inst.
   Billeting parties will report to Camp Commandant, BOIS DES TAILLES at 11 A.M. on 5th to be shewn the area allotted them.

2. The 106th, 107th and 108th F.A. Brigades will march complete to BOIS DES TAILLES on completion of relief on 6th inst. Billeting parties to report to Camp Commandant at 11 A.M. on that day.

3. 24th T.M. Batteries will be relieved by Guards Trench Mortar Batteries on the 5th inst. The lorries which transport the Guards T.M. Batteries will arrive at CARNOY at 12 NOON and will take 24th T.M. Batteries back to BOIS DES TAILLES. Billeting parties to report to Camp Commandant one hour before arrival.
   All other details of relief will be arranged by the D.T.M.O's concerned.

4. O.C., 24th D.A.C., will arrange direct with O.C, Guards D.A.C., for the relief of 30 G.S. wagons parked at F.18.c.5.5., for the purpose of carrying ammunition for Heavy Artillery.

5. All guns on loan from 16th D.A., will be withdrawn with first sections of Batteries coming out of action and will be at once handed over to 24th D.A.C., at E.18.d.5.5. O.C., 24th D.A.C., will arrange to leave an Officer behind to take over these guns in the event of the relief of the D.A.C. being complete before their arrival.

6. All units will march out with full ammunition Echelons. To do this units will arrange to transfer ammunition from the wagons of incoming units of Guards Divisional Artillery.
   Reports showing amounts handed over to and taken over from relieving units are to reach this office by 2 P.M., on the 6th inst.

7. In marching to BOIS DES TAILLES the main BRAY-CORBIE Road is not to be used.

8. Please acknowledge

K.J. Seton-Smith Captain
Staff Captain, 24th Divisional Artillery.

4/9/16.

SECRET   Copy No. 2.

24th D.A. ORDER No.12.

Reference Sheets 57c S.W.
                 62c N.W.
                 62d N.E.

3rd September 1916

1. The 24th Divisional Artillery will be relieved by the Guards Divisional Artillery between September 4th & 6th. *(on the 6th inst)*

2. (1) The 109th F.A.B. will be relieved by the 61st F.A.B. Relief to be by Sections on the mornings of September 4th & 5th. Relief to be completed by 10.a.m. each morning.
   (2) The 109th F.A.B. will take away their own guns, less one gun, which will be handed over to 61st F.A.B. A gun will be taken over in exchange.
   (3) All dumped ammunition, communications, aeroplane photos etc. to be handed over.
   (4) On relief the 109th F.A.B. will move to their present Wagon Line.
   On September 5th the 109th F.A.B. will march to new Wagon Lines at the BOIS DES TAILLES under arrangements to be made by the Staff Captain, R.A.
   (5) Battery Commanders and the O.C., 109th F.A.B. will hand over command on completion of relief.

3. (1) The three remaining Guards F.A.Bdes., will come into action in new positions. When these Brigades are ready to cover the line, the 106, 107 & 108 F.A.Bdes will be withdrawn. This will probably be on the night of the 5th, or on the 6th. Orders will be sent these Brigades when they may withdraw.
   (2) The 106, 107 & 108 F.A.Bdes. will withdraw to their present Wagon Lines.
   On September 6th these Brigades will move to new Wagon Lines at the BOIS DES TAILLES under arrangements to be made by the Staff Captain, R.A.
   (3) All ammunition left behind by these Brigades in gun positions will be taken over by the Guards Div. Arty. Brigades will report to the Staff Captain, R.A., what ammunition is left behind.

4. The Guards D.A.C., will relieve the 24th D.A.C. on September 5th the relief to be completed by 12 noon, at which hour the Guards D.A.C., will be responsible for the ammunition supply.

5. Seperate orders will be issued to T.M. Batteries.

6. The C.R.A., Guards Division will take over command from the C.R.A., 24th Division at 6.p.m. on September 5th.
   At that hour H.Q., 24th D.A., will close at MINDEN POST and re-open at THE CITADEL.

7. Please acknowledge.

Issued at 5.45.p.m.

Captain, R.A
Brigade Major, 24th Divisional Artillery.

(P.T.B)

Copies to	No.		No.
106 F.A.B.	1	Guards D.A.	15
107 F.A.B.	2	3rd D.A.	16
108 F.A.B.	3	7th D.A.	17
109 F.A.B.	4	H.A. XIV Corps	18
6th D.A.	5	R.A. XIV Corps	19
T.M. 24 D.A.	6	No.9 Squadron R.F.H.	20
V/24 T.M. Btty.	7	No.4 Kite Balloon Sect.	21
24 D.A.C.	8	No.12 " " "	22
Staff Captain R.A.	9	File.	23
47th I.B.	10	War Diary.	24, 25
59th I.B.	11	Spare.	26, 27, 28.
60th I.B.	12		
61st I.B.	13		
20th Div.	14		

HQ

6th Division G.15/73.

With reference to the trench maps 1/10,000 MARICOURT and LONGUEVAL, the following procedure for co-ordination will be adopted:-

The overlapping at the junction of the "S" & "A" squares, and also of the "T" & "B" squares, is $1\frac{1}{4}$. A parallel line will, therefore, be drawn $1\frac{1}{4}$ points N. of the junction line between the "A" & "B" squares and the "S" & "T" squares, thus making the total N. & S. co-ordinates in the "A" & "B" squares 10 points instead of $8\frac{3}{4}$ points.

Similarly a parallel line will be drawn $1\frac{1}{4}$ points S. of the junction line between the "S" & "T" squares and the "A" & "B" squares, making the total N. & S. co-ordinates of the "S" & "T" squares 10 points instead of $8\frac{3}{4}$ points.

10th September, 1916.

M.K.Wardle Captain,
General Staff....

3 Copies each Bty. 13/9/16.

Secret

1. On the night 11th/12th September the 24th Divisional Artillery with one F.A.Bde. from each of the 6th and 16th Divisional Artilleries will occupy positions to support the centre section of the Corps front (held by 6th Division.)

   Approximate boundaries

      Northern - Line from B.M. 148.7 to T.14.central.

      Southern - Trench junction T.21.a.60.25. (Excl.)

The Artillery of the sector will be under the Command of Brigadier General E.S.CLEVE, Commanding 6th Divnl.Arty - the 24th D.A. forming a Left Group.

2. Area allotted for positions is bounded as follows:-
On the North by a line ARROWHEAD COPSE - GUILLEMONT.

On the South by a line A.6.central - WEDGE WOOD - N.W. face of LEUZE WOOD.

3. The valley in T.25.d is reserved for the Right Group.

4. The front to be covered in forthcoming operations will be MORVAL to LES BOEUFS (Both inclusive.)

5. The Artillery of the Centre Sector is to be registered and ready to take over the defence of the line not later than noon 13th inst.

6. Hd.Qrs. Centre Division will be in the new dug-outs in A.3.c.
Hd.Qrs. Left Group (24th D.A.) will be as near this as possible.

7.(a) The R.A.Signal Officer, 24th Division will be responsible for communications of Left Group Headquarters with Left Infantry Brigade Headquarters, and with Bdes. R.F.A. of the Group, and also for a direct line between the Left Infantry Brigade and the Brigade R.F.A. whose Brigade Commander will be Liaison Officer with the Left Infantry Brigadier during forthcoming operations.

(b) If possible an Artillery line will be established between each Battn. H.Q. in front line and the Infantry Brigade for exclusive use of Artillery Liaison Officers. Artillery Brigades concerned will be responsible for these communications.

8. During active operations, the Left Group will supply a Senior Officer as Liaison Officer with the Left Infantry Brigade, and one Subaltern as Liaison Officer with each Infantry Battn. in front line. These will remain with Brigade or Battn. Headquarters, and will not be Observing Officers.

9. From the time of taking over defence of the line, the Left Group will always keep one Liaison Officer at Headquarters of the Left Infantry Brigade.

10. Position of Left Infantry Brigade H.Q. will be notified later.

                                      Major.R.A.

11/9/16.
               Brigade Major, 24th Divisional Artillery.

106 F.A.B.
107 " " "
108 " " "
109 " " "
24 D.A.C.

B.M.717/1.

Reference this Office No. B.M.717 of to-day, it has now been arranged that the 107th and 108th Brigades will not go into action until the situation ~~until the situation~~ in T.20 is cleared up.

The O.C., 108th Brigade will detail his Howitzer Battery to come into action to-night (12th/13th Sept.) in a position near the 109th Brigade. The Battery will be under the orders of the O.C., 109th Brigade for the forthcoming operations from time of coming into action until the 109th Brigade advances, when it will revert to its own Brigade.

As soon as Brigades are in action, they will report to this Office the position of Brigade Headquarters and Batteries.

The C.R.A. hopes to meet O's C. Brigades and D.A.C. at 107th Brigade.H.Q. in Wagon Line during the late afternoon. Hour will be notified later.

12/9/16.

R.H. Fm. Capt.
S.C.
Major.R.A.

Brigade Major, 24th Divisional Artillery.

6th Div. No. G/18/15/1.

16th Infantry Brigade.	6th Division "Q".
18th Infantry Brigade.	11th Leicestershire Regt.
71st Infantry Brigade.	Divisional Train.
C.R.E.	A.P.M.
Signals.	Centre Division Artilleries.
A.D.M.S.	

The G.O.C. wishes to impress the following points on all Commanders:-

(1). The necessity for CONTROL and DIRECTION.

As regards the former, troops must be warned NOT to push on regardless of our own barrage, but must be kept well in hand and the advance must conform to the objectives as laid down.

As regards direction, units must be warned not to lose direction by following the Tanks, to which special tasks have been allotted, and which may not therefore move in the correct direction in which the Infantry should advance.

The G.O.C. wishes to lay particular stress on the necessity of laying down compass bearings for the advance, and warning all ranks that the general line of the Division's advance will be N.E.

(2). The best formation for reserves during the advance is small columns, which are best for keeping control and direction: only the most forward lines need be extended during the advance.

(3). The scarcity of water in our present front area must be borne in mind. Well thought out arrangements must be made for getting food and water, S.A.A., &c., forward to the troops.

(4). The construction of roads and tracks through the shell crater area must be carried out with the greatest energy.

The Divisional Pioneer Battalion has been detailed to carry out this work, but all troops in reserve not otherwise employed should carry on the above work throughout the advance whenever the situation permits; otherwise the troops in front line may suffer hardships owing to the non-arrival of stores.

H.Q. 6th Division.
13th September, 1916.

L.F. Renny
Lt. Colonel,
General Staff.

SECRET

6th Div. No. G/18/13/1.

SPECIAL INSTRUCTIONS REGARDING ACTION OF TANKS IN CONJUNCTION WITH THE ATTACK OF THE 6th DIVISION (Reference 6th Div. Operation Order No. 84, dated 13th September, 1916).

---

1. 3 tanks, commanded by Captain A. HALFORD WALKER, work entirely in 6th Division area, and will be known as "A" section.

    3 tanks, commanded by Captain HISCOCKS, work partly in Guards Division area and partly in 6th Division area, and will be known as "B" section.

2. "A" section will assemble about A.5.d.2.6. in neighbourhood of CHIMPANZEE Trench on 'W/X' night, and will be in position at the point of departure, about T.15.c.1.1., one hour before Zero hour on 'Z' day.

    "B" section assembles and moves to First Objective under instructions of Guards Division.

3. "A" section will move from position of departure at Zero minus 20 to First Objective about T.15.central.

    1 tank of "A" section will then visit COPSE about T.15.a.9.9. and bank S.E. of it and Wood to East of it (vide aeroplane map) - thence to wire on 6th Division 2nd Objective.

    During the halt of 6th Division Infantry on the First Objective, 2 tanks of "A" section will remain halted in advance of the Infantry and will keep down enemy fire or make use of any available cover in accordance with the situation.

    At Zero plus 1 hour 10 minutes, 2 tanks of "A" section will advance under cover of creeping barrage by the road to the wire in enemy's line forming 6th Division 2nd Objective (BLUE line on map) in T.16.a. and T.10.c.

    Action of tanks is left to Section Commanders. The main object is to destroy the enemy's wire and prevent his use of machine guns.

    At Zero plus 1 hour 50 minutes, the artillery barrage will lift from 6th Division 2nd Objective 200 yards to enable tanks to move up and down the objective and destroy wire and obstacles.

    "B" section, during halt of troops on 1st Objective, halts under instructions of Guards Division.

    At Zero plus 1 hour 10 minutes, "B" section will move from area T.15.a.0.9. to T.9.d.8.9. under cover of a creeping barrage.

    The rôle of "B" section is the same as for "A" section.

    ATTACK ON MORVAL. (3rd Objective of 6th Division).

    "A" section will move to MORVAL (point T.16.b.5.8.) in front of the Infantry under cover of a creeping barrage at Zero plus 3 hours 45 minutes.

Role

Rôle to prevent Machine Gun fire and destroy wire.

"B" section will advance at Zero plus 3 hours 30 minutes from point T.9.d.7½.8½. to T.10.d.8.8.

Rôle of "B" section is the same as for "A" section.

Tanks will not advance through the village of MORVAL until Infantry are close up.

Barrage will lift 200 yards clear of 6th Division 3rd Objective at Zero plus 4 hours 20 minutes to enable tanks to move up and down and destroy wire and obstacles.

On capture of MORVAL, Tanks will proceed to following points:-

SUNKEN ROAD, T.11.a.6.6.
T.11.central.
T.17.a.8.3.

2 Tanks to each objective.

Rôle to assist pushing out of battle patrols by the Infantry, and to cover the reorganisation of the Infantry for consolidation of positions gained.

4. Tanks will be withdrawn after capture of final objective under instructions issued by the XIV Corps for replenishing ammunition and petrol in accordance with para. 13 of Fourth Army instructions.

Tank officers will understand that they are to act on their own initiative and assist the Infantry to the utmost of their power. They are not to consider themselves tied down by map references in this order, except in so far as they are designed to meet the requirements of barrages as in the case of the movement from the point of departure to the First Objective.

H.Q. 6th Divn.
13th Septr, 1916.

L P Evans Major
for Lt. Colonel,
General Staff.

Copies to:- Heavy Section M.G. Corps
16th Infantry Brigade.
18th Infantry Brigade.
71st Infantry Brigade.
Centre Division Artilleries.
C.R.E.
11th Leicestershire Regt (Pioneers).
Guards Division.
56th Division.
20th Division.
1st Cavalry Division.
XIV Corps.
No. 9 Squadron R.F.C.

SECRET 6th Div. No. G/18/13/3.

AMENDMENT to 6th Div. G/18/13/1 - "SPECIAL INSTRUCTIONS REGARDING
ACTION OF TANKS".

Para. 2. Delete lines 1 to 4, and substitute:-

"   "A" section will assemble about A.5.d.2.6. in the neighbourhood
"   of CHIMPANZEE Trench on 'W/X' night, and will be in position
"   at the point of departure at cross roads E. of GUILLEMONT
"   CEMETERY, T.20.c.2.3., two hours before Zero hour on 'Z' day."

Para. 3. Delete lines 1 and 2 and substitute:-

"   "A" section will move from position of departure at Zero minus
"   1½ hours, and move to First Objective, T.15.central, along the
"   railway. German strong point about T.15.c.0.4. to be dealt with
"   on route.".

Para. 3. Delete last three lines on page1 and substitute:-

"   "A" section will move to MORVAL (point T.16.b.5.8.) in front of
"   Infantry under cover of a creeping barrage at Zero plus 3 hours
"   30 minutes.".

Add new para. 5:-

"   5. The signals from Tanks to Infantry will be made known to all
"   ranks:-
"   RED flag - out of action.
"   GREEN flag - am on objective.
"   Other flags are inter-tank signals.
"   Lamp signals:-
"   Series of T's.....out of action.
"   Series of H's.....am on objective."

L.F. Renny.
Lt. Colonel,
General Staff.

H.Q. 6th Division.
14th September, 1916.

Copies to Heavy Section M.G.Corps.
    16th Infantry Brigade.
    18th Infantry Brigade.
    71st Infantry Brigade.
    Centre Division Artilleries.
    C.R.E.
    11th Leicestershire Regt (Pioneers).
    Guards Division.
    56th Division.
    20th Division.
    1st Cavalry Division.
    XIV Corps.
    No. 9 Squadron R.F.C.

~~106~~ Fit Issue   BM 6
~~107~~
~~108~~
~~109~~

SOS Signal for XIV Corps from
6 pm 14th Sept will be

3 BLUE ROCKETS in rapid succession —
repeated until acted on by the
artillery.

Adv 2⁄1. DA.
13.9.16

Brown
Maj RA
OM. 2⁄1. DA.

SECRET.   Copy No. 8.

OPERATION ORDER No.1.

by

O.C., LEFT GROUP, CENTRE DIVNL. ARTILLERIES.
==

14th September.

1. The attack will be on 15th September. Zero hour will probably be between 6-0 and 6-30.a.m.

2. The Infantry will assault the successive Objectives at the following times :-

From departure Trench.

    1st Objective (GREEN Line) at Zero.

From Left of GREEN Line.

    2nd Objective (BROWN Line) at Zero + 1 hour. This does not apply to 6th Division.

From GREEN Line.

    3rd Objective (BLUE Line) at Zero + 2 hours.

From BLUE Line.

    4th Objective (RED Line) at Zero + 4 hours 30 minutes.

3. Field Artillery barrages will be organized as follows:-

At Zero. The creeping barrage (consisting of 50% of the guns of each Group) will start 100 yards in front of the Infantry, and will creep forward at the rate of 50 yards a minute to 200 yards beyond THE GREEN Line when it will become stationary.

The stationary barrage (remaining 50% of 18-prs.) opens on GREEN Line at Zero, and lifts on to the BLUE Line as the various Batteries on the creeping barrage reach it. Owing to the starting line and 1st Objective not be parallel, the times of arrival of Batteries will vary.

At Zero + 1 Hour 10 minutes. Creeping barrage will creep forward again and join the Stationary Barrage on the BLUE Line. Stationary Barrage remains on the BLUE Line.

At Zero + 1 hour 50 minutes. Creeping barrage will lift and form a Stationary Barrage 200 yards beyond the BLUE Line. Stationary Barrage will lift on to the RED Line.

At Zero + 3 hour 30 minutes. Creeping Barrage will creep forward and join the Stationary Barrage on RED Line. Stationary Barrage remains on RED Line.

At Zero + 4 hours 20 minutes. Creeping and Stationary Barrages lift 200 yards beyond RED Line, and form a Stationary Barrage there.

All Barrages lift 200 yards clear of 3rd and 4th Objectives (BLUE and RED Lines respectively.) At Zero + 1 hour 50 minutes and Zero + 4 hours 20 minutes to enable the Tanks to move up and down the Objectives and destroy more obstacles covering them.

4. A gap of a good 50 yards on either side of GINCHY - MORVAL Road YT.15.c.0.4½ - T.15.b.1.½. will be left in the 1st Stationary and Creeping Barrage to leave room for the Tanks to advance along this road. This gap will be closed when the Creeping Barrage halts 200 yards in front of 1st Objective.

P.T.O.

Advancing from the 1st Objective to subsequent Objectives, the Tanks will follow the Barrage, and no gaps will be required.
The greatest care must be taken to avoid hitting the Tanks. They are not more than bullet proof.

5. The fire will become intense between the following times :-

    Zero   to Zero + 15 mins.
    Zero + 1 hour.   to Zero + 1 hour 15 mins.
    Zero + 2 hours.   to Zero + 2 hours 20 mins.
    Zero + 4 hours 30 mins to Zero + 5 hours.

At other times the Rate of Fire will be Ordinary.

6. **BOUNDARIES.**

The Boundaries of the 6th Division are as follows:-

RIGHT.   T.21.a.3.3 - T.15.d.5.0 - T.16.b.0.5 - T.17.b.0.9.

LEFT.   T.14.central - T.15.a.1.9 - T.9.b.6.2 - T.4.b.8.0.

The Boundary between Groups is T.15.c.3.1 - T.10.c.5.2 - T.11.b.7.5.

The Left Group Zone will be divided into two sectors by a line through
    T.14.d. 85.70. - T.10.c.00.65 - T.5.c.66.15 -

	STATIONARY BARRAGE by.	CREEPING BARRAGE by
Right Sector	107 F.A.B.	108 F.A.B.
Left Sector	106 " " "	109 " " "

When the 106 or 109 F.A.Brigades advance the 107 or 108 F.A.Brigades respectively will be responsible for covering the whole front of the Group Zone.

7. OBJECTIVES.
1st Objective.   The Line T.15.d.5.0 - Road T.15.central - T.15.a.1.9.
2nd Objective.   Does not affect the 6th Division.
3rd Objective.   Hostile Trench line T.16.b.0.5 to T.9.b.6.2.
4th Objective.   The line T.17.b.0.9 - MORVAL MILL (T.11.b.0.8). T.4.b.8.0

8. LIAISON.

O.C. 108 F.A.Brigade will act as Liaison Officer with 71st Infantry Brigade.
O.C. 107 F.A.Brigade will detail a Subaltern as Liaison Officer with Right Battn. in front line (9th Norfolks at S.30.c.5.2) and O.C. 106 F.A.Brigade a Subaltern with Left Battn. (1st Leicesters at A.3.c.1.1)
They should report at 5.p.m. to-night.

9. On 15th inst., as soon as the 3rd Objective (BLUE Line) has been gained 106 & 109 F.A.Brigades will push forward to the Ridge about GINCHY Telegraph between the GINCHY - LESBOEUFS road and the Railway. The movement of these Brigades into action must be made as quickly as possible, as these Brigades are required to assist in the taking of MORVAL and LESBOEUFS.
These Brigades should be ready for either of them to move forward after the capture of the 1st Objective, if required.

10. All Wagon Lines will be kept full of ammunition and ready to move on the morning of the 15th.

11. The 4.5" How. Programme will be issued later.

12. In the event of the Cavalry advancing their route will be notified and care must be taken to avoid shooting on to their route. They will avoid all villages which can therefore be kept under fire at all times till occupied by our Infantry.

13. No firing is to take place on 15th inst. outside the Group Boundaries. This must be carefully observed to avoid causing casualties to troops in neighbouring Divisions etc.

14. Arrangements for food and water must contemplate supplies being cut off from the gun line for some time.

15. Headquarters Centre Divisional Artilleries will be at A.3.c.1.6. Headquarters Left Group Artillery at A.2.d.7.5.

16. Watches will be synchronised from this Office at hours to be notified later

17. RATES OF FIRE.

    INTENSE for 18-prs.   = 3 to 4 rounds per gun per minute.
    INTENSE for 4.5 Hows.   = 2 rounds per gun per minute.
    ORDINARY for 18-prs)
        and 4.5 Hows)   = 1 round per gun per minute.
    SLOW, if ordered   = 1 round per Battery per minute.

18. Acknowledge.

                                           Major. R.A.

Brigade Major, 24th Divisional Artillery.

    Left Group, Centre Divisional Artilleries.

Copies to
106 F.A.B.
107 " " "
108 " " "
109 " " "
24 D.A.C.
S.C., 24 D.A.
6th D.A.
71st I.B.
DIARY.
FILE.

LEFT GROUP CENTRE DIVISIONAL ARTILLERIES.

XIV.Corps.

4.5" Howitzer Programme.

Zero to Zero + 10 mins.	D/106 (Left) D/107 (Right) Dividing line Sector Boundary.	Area T.9.c.7.3 - T.15.a.2.8 - T.15.b.9.4 - T.15.b.9.5.
Zero to Zero + 7 mins.	D/108.	Creep up trench T.14.d.8½.3 by 75 yards a min. to T.14.b.8½.7.
Zero + 7 min to) Zero + 20 mins.)	"	Among trees T.15.b.4.8 to T.9.c.6.1.

On completion of above tasks to Zero + 1 hour 45 mins.	D/106.	3rd Objective T.9. d.2.8½ - T.9.d.8.8½ (incl)
	D/108.	" " T.9.d.8.8½ (incl) - T.10.c.½.6.
	D/107.	" " T.10.c.½.6 - T.10.c.4½.1½.

Zero + 1 hour 45 mins to) Zero + 3 hours 30 mins.)	D/106.	Portion of LES BOEUFS in divisional zone.
	D/107.	MORVAL on either side of MORVAL-LES BOEUFS road and N. of GINCHY - MORVAL Road. One Section occasionally sweeping the MORVAL - LES BOEUFS road.
	D/108.	MORVAL S. Western portion but N. of GINCHY - MORVAL Road.

Zero + 3 hours 30 mins. to) Zero + 3 hours 40 mins.)	All Batteries.	As above, but no firing W. of MORVAL - LES BOEUFS road. D/108 Northern half and D/107 Southern half of MORVAL.

Zero + 3 hours 40 mins onwards.	All Batteries.	Search beyond Fourth Objective. Batteries are allotted three equal Divisions of Sector. D/106 the Left 1/3rd. D/108 the Centre 1/3rd. D/107 the Right 1/3rd.

SECRET.   B.M.727.

Reference Left Group Operation Order No.1.

(1) The 1st Objective of 6th Division will be as shown in the attached tracing (GREEN LINE) approximately T.15.d.5.0 to cutting T.15.d.6.8., along cutting to T.15.b.2.½ - T.15.a.3½.9., along North of Copse to T.15.a.2.9 - T.15.a.1.9.

The 1st Stationary Barrage will be placed on this line and the Creeping Barrage will creep to 200 yards beyond (N.E. of) this line.

(2) 4.5" Howitzer Programme herewith.

(3) The taking of the QUADRILATERAL will, it is hoped, be carried out by Tanks prior to Zero hour. The line for the Creeping Barrage to start on will therefore be 100 yards beyond the QUADRILATERAL and front trenches as marked in blue on the attached tracing.

(4) The left boundary of 6th Division runs from point 148.7 (T.20.a.1.8) to T.14.central, and thence as in para 6 Left Group Operation Order No.1.

(5) Intense fire will be quickened up to four rounds a gun a minute for 18-prs. for the last five minutes before each Objective is reached.

(6) Zero hour will be 6-20.a.m.

(7) Acknowledge.

14/9/16.
                                                            Major.R.A.
                          Brigade Major, 24th Divisional Artillery.

LEFT GROUP CENTRE DIVISIONAL ARTILLERIES.

XIV. Corps.

4.5" Howitzer Programme.

Zero to Zero + 10 mins.	D/106 (Left) D/107 (Right) Dividing line Sector Boundary.	Area T.9.c.7.3 - T.15.a.2.8 - T.15.b.9.4 - T.15.b.9.5.
Zero to Zero + 7 mins.	D/108.	Creep up trench T.14.d.8½.3 by 75 yards a min. to T.14.b.8½.7.
Zero + 7 min to) Zero + 20 mins.)	"	Among trees T.15.b.4.8 to T.9.c.6.1.
On completion of above tasks to Zero + 1 hour 45 mins.	D/106. D/108. D/107.	3rd Objective T.9. d.2.8½ - T.9.d.8.8½ (incl) " " T.9.d.8.8½ (incl) - T.10.c.½.6. " " T.10.c.½.6 - T.10.c.4½.1½.
Zero + 1 hour 45 mins to) Zero + 3 hours 30 mins.)	D/106. D/107. D/108.	Portion of LES BOEUFS in divisional zone. MORVAL on either side of MORVAL-LES BOEUFS road and N. of GINCHY - MORVAL Road. One Section occasionally sweeping the MORVAL - LES BOEUFS road. MORVAL S. Western portion but N. of GINCHY - MORVAL Road.
Zero + 3 hours 30 mins. to) Zero + 3 hours 40 mins.)	All Batteries.	As above, but no firing W. of MORVAL - LES BOEUFS road. D/108 Northern half and D/107 Southern half of MORVAL.
Zero + 3 hours 40 mins) onwards.)	All Batteries.	Search beyond Fourth Objective. Batteries are allotted three equal Divisions of Sector. D/106 the Left 1/3rd. D/108 the Centre 1/3rd. D/107 the Right 1/3rd.

"A" Form.   Army Form C. 2121

MESSAGES AND SIGNALS

TO: **BREAM SHRIMP** ~~PRAWN~~ **SHARK**

Sender's Number: SA 1   Day of Month: 14/9/16   AAA

SOS lines will be the same as laid down for initial ~~of~~ barrage which is being sent.

Salmon

"A" Form. Army Form C. 2121
MESSAGES AND SIGNALS No. of Message _____

Prefix ___ Code ___ m.	Words	Charge	This message is on a/c of:	Recd. at ___ m.
Office of Origin and Service Instructions.	Sent			Date ___
	At ___ m.		___ Service.	From ___
	To ___			
	By ___		(Signature of "Franking Officer.")	By ___

TO { BREAM SHRIMP ~~FISH~~
                        SHARK

Sender's Number | Day of Month | In reply to Number
 SA 1 | 14/9/16 | AAA

S O S lines will be the same as laid down for initial ~~of~~ barrage which is being sent.

Salmon

From
Place
Time

The above may be forwarded as now corrected. (Z)

Censor. Signature of Addressee or person authorised to telegraph in his name.
* This line should be erased if not required.

"C" Form (Duplicate).
MESSAGES AND SIGNALS.

Army Form C. 2123.
(In books of 50's in duplicate.)
No. of Message ....

Charges to Pay. £ s. d.

Office Stamp.

Service Instructions.

Handed in at .... Office .... m. Received .... m.

TO: BREAM SHARK SHRIMP

Sender's Number	Day of Month	In reply to Number	A A A
SA1	14/9/16		

Please detach 1 copy of
orders attached & also see
tracing enclosed

FROM
PLACE & TIME

Salmon
7pm

SECRET

No. B.M. 921/10.

Right Group.
Left Group.

The following extracts from 1st Cavalry Division Operation Order No. 17 dated 14th September, 1916, are forwarded for information:-

6. The task allotted to the Cavalry is as follows:-
As soon as the villages FLERS, GUEUDECOURT, LES BOEUFS and MORVAL have been captured by the Infantry, the Cavalry will advance and seize the high ground ROCQUIGNY, VILLERS AU FLOS, REINCOURT LES BAPAUME, BAPAUME.
It is of special importance that the hostile artillery shall be captured during the advance.
The XIV and XV Corps will be prepared to support the Cavalry with Infantry on the above line at the earliest possible moment.

7. In order to carry out the above task :-
(a). The 1st Cavalry Division will move by the "Cavalry Track" between MORVAL and LES BOEUFS and seize the line of ROCQUIGNY and BARASTRE, both inclusive.
(b). The 2nd Indian Cavalry Division will seize the line VILLERS AU FLOS (inclusive) - REINCOURT LES BAPAUME - BANCOURT (inclusive), getting into touch with the 1st Cavalry Division. towards BARASTRE and reconnoitring towards VELU and BEUGNATRE.
(c). The 2nd Cavalry Division will seize BAPAUME and the high ground North of it, keeping in touch with the left of the 2nd Indian Cavalry Division about BANCOURT.

8. The 1st Cavalry Brigade will move forward towards ROCQUIGNY, as soon as the Infantry have secured the villages of MORVAL, LES BOEUFS and FLERS. The 1st Cavalry Brigade will -
(i). Send forward officers' patrols to follow the Infantry attack on the Blue line.
(ii). Detail a detachment to occupy the spurs North-east of MORVAL to prevent any hostile counter-attack from the direction of SAILLY SAILLISEL.
(iii). Despatch preventative reconnaissances towards BUS, LECHELLE and LE MESNIL, and a reconnoitring detachment towards FINS with special reference to the destruction of the railway junction just North of ETRICOURT.

9. The 2nd Cavalry Brigade will move forward towards BARASTRE as soon as the 1st Cavalry Brigade is committed to the attack on ROCQUIGNY. The 2nd Cavalry Brigade will send protective reconnaissances towards HAPLINCOURT and BERTINCOURT and a reconnoitring detachment towards VELU.

11. The following Heavy Artillery is placed at the disposal of the Cavalry Corps:-
  8th Siege Battery.   (Four 6" Howitzers).
  115th Heavy Battery.   (Six 60-pounders).
  26th Heavy Battery.   (Four 60-pounders).
  1st Canadian Heavy Battery. (Four 60-pounders).

PTO

12. Artillery fire will be maintained during the day on LE TRANSLOY and BEAULENCOURT, but the guns firing on LE MESNIL, BARASTRE, and ROCQUIGNY will stop as soon as the Cavalry is reported East of the PERONNE - BARASTRE road.

CAVALRY TRACK.

1. The 1st Cavalry Division Track will be completed as follows by Zero, September 15th.

LAPREE WOOD (East of CARNOY) - E of CAMBRIDGE COPSE - D of MACHINE GUN WOOD - outside N. end of FAVIERE WOOD - Cross roads A.12.a.9.9. - A.1.c.0.8. - to road at A.1.a.5.8.

It is marked by

(a) posts on each side painted red and white.
(b) 1st Cav. Div. sign-boards.
(c) Boards painted with luminous paint for night work.

2. After Zero, September 15th 1st Cav. Div. working parties will endeavour to complete this track on the following line:-

A.1.a.5.8. - T.25.d.1.6. - M of GUILLEMONT - T.20.d.1.9. - T.15.c.1.3. - to road at T.16.a.1.4.

L. Wray Saville.
Major, R. A.

14/9/16. Brigade Major, Centre Divisional Artilleries,
XIV Corps.

SECRET.   Copy No. 9

OPERATION ORDER No. 1.

by

O.C., LEFT GROUP, CENTRE DIVNL. ARTILLERIES.

14th September.

1. The attack will be on 15th September. Zero hour will probably be between 6-0 and 6-30.a.m.

2. The Infantry will assault the successive Objectives at the following times :-

From departure Trench.

    1st Objective (GREEN Line) at Zero.

From Left of GREEN Line.

    2nd Objective (BROWN Line) at Zero + 1 hour. This does not apply to 6th Division.

From GREEN Line.

    3rd Objective (BLUE Line) at Zero + 2 hours.

From BLUE Line.

    4th Objective (RED Line) at Zero + 4 hours 30 minutes.

3. Field Artillery barrages will be organized as follows:-

At Zero. The creeping barrage (consisting of 50% of the guns of each Group) will start 100 yards in front of the Infantry, and will creep forward at the rate of 50 yards a minute to 200 yards beyond THE GREEN Line when it will become stationary.
    The stationary barrage (remaining 50% of 18-prs.) opens on GREEN Line at Zero, and lifts on to the BLUE Line as the various Batteries on the creeping barrage reach it. Owing to the starting line and 1st Objective not be parallel, the times of arrival of Batteries will vary.

At Zero + 1 Hour 10 minutes. Creeping barrage will creep forward again and join the Stationary Barrage on the BLUE Line. Stationary Barrage remains on the BLUE Line.

At Zero + 1 hour 50 minutes. Creeping barrage will lift and form a Stationary Barrage 200 yards beyond the BLUE Line. Stationary Barrage will lift on to the RED Line.

At Zero + 3 hour 30 minutes. Creeping Barrage will creep forward and join the Stationary Barrage on RED Line. Stationary Barrage remains on RED Line.

At Zero + 4 hours 20 minutes. Creeping and Stationary Barrages lift 200 yards beyond RED Line, and form a Stationary Barrage there.

    All Barrages lift 200 yards clear of 3rd and 4th Objectives (BLUE and RED Lines respectively.) At Zero + 1 hour 50 minutes and Zero + 4 hours 20 minutes to enable the Tanks to move up and down the Objectives and destroy more obstacles covering them.

4. A gap of a good 50 yards on either side of GINCHY - MORVAL Road (T.15.c.0.4 - T.15.b.1.9.) will be left in the 1st Stationary and Creeping Barrage to leave room for the Tanks to advance along this road. This gap will be closed when the Creeping Barrage halts 200 yards in front of 1st Objective.

P.T.O.

Advancing from the 1st Objective to subsequent Objectives, the Tanks will follow the Barrage, and no gaps will be required.
The greatest care must be taken to avoid hitting the Tanks. They are not more than bullet proof.

5. The fire will become intense between the following times :-

    Zero   to Zero + 15 mins.
    Zero + 1 hour.   to Zero + 1 hour 15 mins.
    Zero + 2 hours.   to Zero + 2 hours 20 mins.
    Zero + 4 hours 30 mins to Zero + 5 hours.

At other times the Rate of Fire will be Ordinary.

6. **BOUNDARIES.**

The Boundaries of the 6th Division are as follows:-

<u>RIGHT</u>. T.21.a.6.3 - T.15.d.5.0 - T.16.b.0.5 - T.17.b.0.9.

<u>LEFT</u>. T.14.central - T.15.a.1.9 - T.9.b.6.2 - T.4.b.8.0.

The Boundary between Groups is T.15.c.3.1 - T.10.c.5.2 - T.11.b.7.5.

The Left Group Zone will be divided into two sectors by a line through
    T.14.d. 85.70. - T.10.c.00.65 - T.5.c.66.15 -

	STATIONARY BARRAGE by.	CREEPING BARRAGE by
Right Sector	107 F.A.B.	108 F.A.B.
Left Sector	106 " " "	109 " " "

When the 106 or 109 F.A.Brigades advance the 107 or 108 F.A.Brigades respectively will be responsible for covering the whole front of the Group Zone.

7. OBJECTIVES.
<u>1st Objective</u>. The Line T.15.d.5.0 - Road T.15.central - T.15.a.1.9.
<u>2nd Objective</u>. Does not affect the 6th Division.
<u>3rd Objective</u>. Hostile Trench line T.16.b.0.5 to T.9.b.6.2.
<u>4th Objective</u>. The line T.17.b.0.9 - MORVAL MILL (T.11.b.0.8). T.4.b.8.0.

8. <u>LIAISON</u>.

O.C. 108 F.A.Brigade will act as Liaison Officer with 71st Infantry Brigade.
O.C. 107 F.A.Brigade will detail a Subaltern as Liaison Officer with Right Battn. in front line (9th Norfolks at S.30.c.5.2) and O.C. 106 F.A.Brigade a Subaltern with Left Battn. (1st Leicesters at A.3.c.1.1)
They should report at 5.p.m. to-night.

9. On 15th inst-, as soon as the 3rd Objective (BLUE Line) has been gained 106 & 109 F.A.Brigades will push forward to the Ridge about GINCHY Telegraph between the GINCHY - LESBOEUFS road and the Railway. The movement of these Brigades into action must be made as quickly as possible, as these Brigades are required to assist in the taking of MORVAL and LESBOEUFS.
These Brigades should be ready for either of them to move forward after the capture of the 1st Objective, if required.

10. All Wagon Lines will be kept full of ammunition and ready to move on the morning of the 15th.

11. The 4.5" How. Programme will be issued later.

12. In the event of the Cavalry advancing their route will be notified and care must be taken to avoid shooting on to their route. They will avoid all villages which can therefore be kept under fire at all times till occupied by our Infantry.

13. No firing is to take place on 15th inst. outside the Group Boundaries. This must be carefully observed to avoid causing casualties to troops in neighbouring Divisions etc.

14. Arrangements for food and water must contemplate supplies being cut off from the gun line for some time.

15. Headquarters Centre Divisional Artilleries will be at A.3.c.1.6. Headquarters Left Group Artillery at A.2.d.7.5.

16. Watches will be synchronised from this Office at hours to be notified later

17. RATES OF FIRE.

    INTENSE for 18-prs. = 3 to 4 rounds per gun per minute.
    INTENSE for 4.5 Hows. = 2 rounds per gun per minute.
    ORDINARY for 18-prs)
        and 4.5 Hows) = 1 round per gun per minute.
    SLOW, if ordered = 1 round per Battery per minute.

18. Acknowledge.

                                            Major. R.A.
            Brigade Major, 24th Divisional Artillery.
                Left Group, Centre Divisional Artilleries.

Copies to
106 F.A.B.
107 " " "
108 " " "
109 " " "
24 D.A.C.
S.C., 24 D.A.
6th D.A.
71st I.B.
DIARY.
FILE.

Operation order No 1

SECRET.   Copy No:.....

GUARDS DIVISIONAL ARTILLERY ORDER NO: 50.

Reference Sheet 57C S.W.   15th September 1916.

1. The attack of the XIVth Corps and XVth Corps will be continued tomorrow morning.

2. The objectives of the Guards Division will be as follows :-
   1st Objective.
      BLUE LINE between T.9.d.8.7. and N.33.c.2.0.
   2nd Objective.
      LES BOEUFS from T.10.a.8.4. - SUNKEN ROAD T.10.b.6.10. - thence to SUNKEN ROAD T.4.d.7.0. to T.4.b.5.3. - thence SUNKEN ROAD to Cross Roads at T.34.a.2.9.

3. The attack will be carried out by the 61st Infantry Brigade on the Right, and the 3rd Guards Brigade on the Left.
   Dividing line between Brigades will be :-
   Line T.8.b.5.0. - T.3.d.2.7. - N.34.a.8.2.
   Dividing Line between 3rd Guards Brigade and XVth Corps;-
   Line from T.8.a.2.6. to N.33.b.20. - N.34.a.2.9. There will be no troops attacking on Right of 61st Infantry Brigade.

4. (a) Infantry will advance to the attack of 1st Objective at such time as to be within 100 yards of the Creeping barrage at Zero plus 10 mins.

   (b) Infantry will advance to the attack of 2nd Objective at Zero plus 35 mins.

5. Troops of 1st and 2nd Guards Brigades in GREEN Line will be in Divisional Reserve and will not move forward with the attack.

6. 60th Infantry Brigade will be in Divnl: Reserve at WATERLOT FARM at 7 a.m. to-morrow.

7. Guards Divnl: Artillery will be assisted by a Group of Centre Divnl: Arty.

8. Details of Artillery tasks are shown on attached sheet.

9. Right Group will find Liaison Officers with 61st Inf: Bde. Left Group with 3rd Guards Brigade.

10. 61st Inf: Bde: will take over present H.Q. of 2nd Guards Brigade.

    3rd Guards Brigade will take over present H.Q. of 1st Guards Brigade.

11. Zero hour will be 9.25 am.

12. Watches will be sychronized to Groups from this Hd: Qrs: on morning of 16th.

    ACKNOWLEDGE.

                                                    Major R.A.
Issued at:-
   15th Sept: 1916.   Brigade Major, Guards Divnl: Arty.

   Copy No: 1 R.A. XIVth Corps.Corps.   Copy No: 27-32 75th Bde: RFA.
           2   Guards Division.   37-42 76th Bde: RFA.
           3   7th Divnl: Arty.   43-48 24th Bde R.F.A.
           4 -15 Centre Div: Arty.   49-54 38th Div: Arty.
          16 -20 61st Bde: R.F.A.   55 D.A.C.
          56-57 Office.

TABLE OF TASKS.

1. Centre Div: Arty: Group will barrage on the right, Right Group in the Centre and Left Group on the Left.

   Dividing Lines.

   Between Centre Div: Arty: Group and Right Group T.9.b.0.4. - T.4.b.5.0.
   Between Right Group & Left Group, T.3.c.5.0. - T.3.d.2.7. - N.34.a.8.2.

2. 50% of 18½-Pdrs: will be employed in Creeping, and
   50% on Standing Barrages.

3. Intense fire will be for 18-Pdrs: 3 rounds per gun per minute.

4. Wirecutting.

   Separate instructions have been issued.

5. Standing Barrages.

   (a) 1st Standing Barrage Line.

   1st Objective - except that Northern Boundary of Barrage will be T.3.a.5.5.

   (b) 2nd Standing Barrage Line.

   Road T.10.a.7.3½. - T.4.a.3.1. - Cross Roads T.4.a.0.9½. - T.33.cent.

   (c) 3rd Standing Barrage Line.

   2nd Objective from T.4.d.7.0. to the North.

   (d) Times of Lifts.

   Will open on 1st Line(a) at Zero.
   Will remain on 1st Line(a) from Zero to Zero plus 15 mins.
   Will lift to 2nd Line(b) at Zero plus 15 mins.
   Will remain on 2nd Line(b) from Zero plus 15 mins: to Zero plus 43 mins.
   Will lift to 3rd Line (c) at Zero plus 43 mins.
   Will remain on 3rd Line(c) from Zero plus 43 mins: to Zero plus 50 mins.
   Will lift to 200 yards beyond 3rd Line at Zero plus 50 mins.

   (e) In addition from Zero onward Right Group will keep up a stationary barrage 200 yards South of and praellel with line T.9.d.8.7. - T.10.a.8.4. - T.10.b.6.10. T.4.d.7.0.

   (f) Fire will be intense from Zero to Zero plus 15 mins.
   Zero plus 45mins to Zero plus 50 mins.

6. CREEPING Barrage.

   Creeping Barrage will commence 250 yards West of 1st Objective at Zero.
   It will remain stationary from Zero to Zero plus 10 mins.
   It will commence Creeping at the rate of 50 yards per minute at Zero plus 10 to 200 yards beyond First Objective.

   It will remain stationary 200 yards beyond first objective till Zero plus 35 mins when it will creep forward at the rate of 50 yards per minute to 200 yards beyond 2nd Objective.

   Fire will be intense from Zero to Zero plus 5 mins.
   Zero plus 10 mins to Zero plus 19 mins
   Zero plus 35 mins: to Zero plus 40 mins
   Zero plus 50 mins to Zero plus 54 mins

P.T.C

7. Howitzers.

   (a) <u>Zero to Zero plus 13 mins.</u>

Centre Div: Arty: Group	2 Batteries on SUNKEN ROAD T.10.a.8.4. - T.4.c.5.5.
Right Group.	1 Battery SUNKEN ROAD T.3.d.5.2. - T.4.c.4.7½.
	1 Battery " " T.3.d.5.2. - T.3.b.8.0.
	1 Battery Cross Roads T.3.b.8.7.
Left Group.	1 Battery Cross Roads T.3.b.5.5.
	1 Battery " " T.3.a.9.8.

   (b) <u>1st Lift.</u> - From Zero plus 13 mins to Zero plus 35 mins.

Centre Div: Arty: Groups.	Same Tasks.
Right Group 3 Batteries	Along road from CHURCH in LES BOEUFS - T.4.a.1.9.
Left Group 2 Batteries	SUNKEN ROAD N.33.d.9.0. - N.33.b.8.0.

   (c) At Zero plus 35 mins: How: Batteries will cease firing unless situation requires their fire.

      All fire will be at Normal rate.

MESSAGES AND SIGNALS.

TO: Bream Shark Shrimp

Sender's Number: S.A.3. | Day of Month: 15/9/16 | AAA

Please report if you are firing on your last barrage if so continue to do so and search and sweep about aaa rate of fire one round per battery every two minutes. aaa Use H.E. aaa

From Place: Salmon
Time: 12.28 p.m.

To: BREAM SHRIMP SHAR

Sender's Number: SA 4 | Day of Month: 15/9/16 | AAA

Fire on ~~~~~ your 2nd or BLUE barrage Intense for 8 men. Search 500 x following ___ to _____ ~~~~~ on information

From:
Place: Salmon
Time: 4.50 pm

TO: PRAWN

Sender's Number: SA 5   Day of Month: 13/9/15   AAA

Open fire at once on quadrilateral T 14 d 9 4 T 15 c 05.10 — T 15 c 20.05 T 15 c 1 4 Rate of fire ordinary You are now under my orders

Place / Time: 4:50 pm

From: Salmon

"A" Form.   Army Form C. 2121
MESSAGES AND SIGNALS.   No. of Message _____

Prefix ... Code ... m	Words	Charge	This message is on a/c of:	Recd. at ... m
Office of Origin and Service Instructions.	Sent			Date ...
	At ... m		... Service.	From ...
	To			By ...
	By		(Signature of "Franking Officer.")	

TO {   S   MP

Sender's Number	Day of Month	In reply to Number	AAA
SA 7	15/9/16		

fire on trench
T 14 d 85 80 - T 14 b 90 15
search up + down.
Rate of Fire ordinary
30 % HE

From / Place / Time: 5/18 pm   Selmon

TO: SHARK

Sender's Number: SA8　　Day of Month: 15/9/16　　AAA

Fire on trench
T.14.b.90.15 to T.14.b.90.65
scand up down
Rate of fire ordinary
50% HE

From Place Time: 5.20 pm

Signature: Salmon

"A" Form. Army Form C. 2121
MESSAGES AND SIGNALS No. of Message _____

Prefix ___ Code ___ m.	Words	Charge	This message is on a/c of:	Recd. at _____ m.
Office of Origin and Service Instructions.	Sent			Date _____
	At _____ m.		_____ Service.	From _____
	To _____			By _____
	By _____		(Signature of "Franking Officer.")	

TO { **PRAWN**

| Sender's Number | Day of Month | In reply to Number | AAA |
| SA 9 | 15/9/16 | | |

Fire on trench running

North from quadrilateral

T 14 d 87 87 to T 14 6 87 25

Search up + down

Rate of fire ordinary

From
Place 5.37 pm   Salmon
Time
The above may be forwarded as now corrected. (Z)
Censor. Signature of Addressee or person authorised to telegraph in his name.

"A" Form.
MESSAGES AND SIGNALS.
Army Form C. 2121

Prefix	Code	m.	Words	Charge	This message is on a/c of:	Recd. at ___ m
Office of Origin and Service Instructions.			Sent At ___ m. To ___ By ___		___ Service. (Signature of "Franking Officer.")	Date 15-8-1_ From ___ By ___

TO OC Bram Shmuts & Shark

Sender's Number.	Day of Month	In reply to Number	AAA
FA 14	15		

The following ranges have been allotted for:-

A/106 T.14.d.85.43 & T.14.d.85.62
B/106 T.14.d.85.62 & T.14.d.85.85
C/106 T.14.d.85.85 & T.14.d.87.06

aaa

You will fire on above ranges at a slow rate of fire until further orders aaa

From OC 106 FAB
Place
Time 1.55 AM

"A" Form.   Army Form C. 2121
MESSAGES AND SIGNALS.   No. of Message

Prefix...Code...m.	Words	Charge	This message is on a/c of:	Recd. at......n.
Office of Origin and Service Instructions.				Date 15/9/16
	Sent At 11.12 m.		...Service.	From STAR
	To AE SF AR		(Signature of "Franking Officer.")	By
	By			

TO — All 18 pr batteries

| Sender's Number. | Day of Month | In reply to Number | AAA |
| JH.24 | 15th | | |

The Brigade SOS lines for all 18 pr batteries is as follows:—

T.15.b.0.9 — T.9.d.1.1.

aaa

Fog night firing BREAM will fire at irregular intervals four salvos an hour on above line until further orders. aaa

From OC 107 FAB
Place
Time 11.10 AM

J H Cartwright

MESSAGES AND SIGNALS. No. of Message ....

SM   KG SPM

Service Instructions. ES

Office Stamp. SAR 15/9/16

Handed in at .... Office .... m. Received .... m.

TO: SALMON

Sender's Number: BM 37   Day of Month: 15th   In reply to Number: AAA

~~STOP~~ firing on present targets.
AAA S O S Line for to-night
T15B05 to T9D00 to T9D58
AAA ROACH T15B05 to T15B09
AAA SALMON thence to T9D11
AAA SEAL thence T9D30 55
AAA HAKE thence to T9D58
AAA Night firing follows.

FROM: FISH ADVANCE

PLACE & TIME: 10.35 pm

"C" Form (Duplicate).
MESSAGES AND SIGNALS.

Army Form C. 2123.
(In books of 50's in duplicate.)
No. of Message..................

	Charges to Pay.	Office Stamp.
DB	£ s. d.	SAR 15/9/16
Instructions. FS		

Handed in at................... Office............m. Received............m.

TO SALMON

Sender's Number	Day of Month	In reply to Number	AAA
BM 38	15th		

Night firing to-night till 5.30 am AAA Target Blue Line Wire and Trenches. SALMON T10C 50 25 to T10C 40 25 AAA SEAL thence to T9D 85 75 AAA HAKE thence to T9B 58 20 AAA Four guns and one howitzer in action at once AAA Average rate four salvoes per hour AAA ROACH will fire bursts at intervals on Sunken road from Quadrilateral to T 15 Central and on into Valley AAA H.E. only

FROM	FISH ADVANCE
PLACE & TIME	11 pm

OPERATION ORDER No. 2.
by
LEFT GROUP CENTRE DIVISIONAL ARTILLERIES.
===========

Reference LONGUEVAL 1/10,000.

1. 18th Infantry Brigade will attack the QUADRILATERAL and the trench running North from T.14.d.85.45 to T.14.b.90.65 at 7-30.p.m. to-day.

The attack will be carried out/from north and south simultaneously. The Northern attack from about the line T.8.d.8.5 to T.9.c.2.8; the Southern attack from about T.21.central.

2. Until 7-30.p.m.

18-prs will bombard as follows:-

    106 F.A.B. 1 Batty on Copse T.15.a.2.8 to 7.8.
                2. " on the QUADRILATERAL.

    107 " " " The trench T.14.d.85.45 to T.14.b.90.65.

    109 " " " The area 200 yards on either side of the road T.14.d.85.45 to T.15.central.

From 7-30.p.m. to 7-35.p.m.

Half the 109 F.A.B. will fire on the road itself only.

When guns complete their tasks as above they will immediately form a Barrage as under:-

    106 F.A.B. T.9.c.5.0 to T.15.a.6.8.

    109 " " " T.15.a.6.8 to T.15.a.75.55.

    107 " " " T.15.a.75.55 to T.15.a.87.30.

    108 " " " T.15.a.87.30 to T.15.central.

3. 4.5" Hows. will bombard the trench T.14.d.85.45 to T.14.b.90.65 (as already detailed.) till 7-30.p.m. when they lift to the line

    D/106. T.9.d.60.85. to T.9.d.95.70.
    D/108. T.9.d.95.70 to T.10.c.2.5.
    D/107. T.10.c.2.5 to T.10.c.50.25.

4. Rates of fire till 7-30.p.m. Ordinary.
                  7-30 to 7-50. Intense.
                  After 7-50. Ordinary.

5. 18-prs firing on trenches use H.E. only, on areas 50% H.E. Barrage Shrapnel only.

6. Acknowledge by wire.

                                      Major.R.A.
Brigade Major, 24th Divisional Artillery.

Issued at 5-50.p.m.

Copie to
106 F.A.B.
107 " " "
108 " " "
109 " " "

SECRET.   B.M.42.

~~106~~ F.A.B.
107 " " "   for D. Batty only.
~~109~~ " " "
==========

1. Reference Centre Divisional Artilleries Operation Order No.5 para 5 and Guards D.A. Operation Order No.50.

   106 F.A.B. will form the Stationary Barrage.

   109 " " "   "   "   " Creeping   "

   As regards Howitzer task in para 7 Guards D.A. Operation Order No.50

   D/107 is allotted T.10.a.8.4 to T.10.a.70.95.

   D/106 T.10.a.70.95 to T.4.c.5.5.

2. ACKNOWLEDGE BY WIRE.

                                            Brown
16/9/16.   Major.R.A.
                        Brigade Major, 24th Divisional Artillery.
Issued at 5-30.a.m.

SECRET.

107 F.A.B.
108 " " "

B.M.43.

1. Reference Centre Divisional Artilleries Operation Order No.5.

The tasks in para 6 are allotted as under:-

<u>9-25 to 10-20.a.m.</u>

108 F.A.B. on the QUADRILATERAL and trench.

107 F.A.B. Western end of high ground in MORVAL.

<u>10-20.a.m. onwards.</u>

Both Brigades will sweep the whole front.

2. ACKNOWLEDGE BY WIRE.

16/9/16.
Issued at 5-35.a.m.

Major.R.A.
Brigade Major, 24th Divisional Artillery.

Postponed to 18th

"A" Form. Army Form C. 2121
MESSAGES AND SIGNALS.

Prefix... Code... ... m.	Words	Charge	This message is on a/c of:	Recd. at............m.
Office of Origin and Service Instructions.				Date 16/9/16
	Sent		Service.	STA/R
	At 12 pm m.			From.......
	To			
	By		(Signature of "Franking Officer.")	By ....

TO All 18 pdr batteries

| Sender's Number. | Day of Month | In reply to Number | AAA |
| JH 28 | 16 | | |

The line allotted for night firing is as follows:—

T.10.C.5.2½ — T.10.C.4.2½

aaa rate four Salvos at irregular intervals per hour aaa

B gram from 12.30 Am to 2 Am.
Shrapnel from 2 Am to 3.30 Am.
Shark from 3.30 Am to 5.30 Am.

aaa

From OC 107 AB
Place
Time 12.20 AM

"A" Form.
Army Form C. 2121
MESSAGES AND SIGNALS.

Sent At 12.45 a.m.
To PK
By [signature]

Date 16/9/16

TO PRAWN

Sender's Number: AH 29
Day of Month: 16th

AAA

The line allotted to you for night firing is as follows :—

T.10.C.5.2½ / T.10.C.4.2½

aaa Rate of fire 4 Salvos at irregular intervals per hour until 5.30 am. aaa.

From OC 107/415
Time 12.20 am

[signature] J H Coulson Lt

MESSAGES AND SIGNALS.

Prefix .... Code I.D.S. Words ....
Received From F.S. By 7/8
Sent, or sent out At .... m. To .... By ....
Office Stamp.

Charges to collect £ s. d.
Service Instructions. F.S.

Handed in at .... Office .... m. Received 9.41 m.

TO SALMON

Sender's Number: BM52
Day of Month: 16
In reply to Number:
AAA

Night firing tonight to 5.30am aaa
HAKE trench and wire T10c50 to T10c0065 aaa
SEAL valley in T15B aaa
SALMON copse T15A78 to 28 and thence to NE aaa
ROACH Nil aaa
HAKE 50% HE
SEAL 50% HE
SALMON 75% HE aaa
four guns and one how per brigade four salvos per hour average aaa There is to be no firing inside barrage lines

FROM
PLACE & TIME: FISH 9.20

			Charges to Pay.	Office Stamp.
			£ s. d.	

Service Instructions.

Handed in at................ Office.......... m. Received 9 46 m.

TO: SALMON

Sender's Number	Day of Month	In reply to Number	AAA
BM52	16		

Night firing tonight to 5.30am aaa

HAKE trench and wire T10C50 to T10C065 aaa
SEAL valley in T15B aaa
SALMON copse T15A78 to 28 and trees north east aaa
ROACH nil aaa
HAKE 50% HE
SEAL 50% HE
SALMON 75% HE
Four guns and one howitzer per brigade four salvos per hour average aaa There is to be no firing inside barrage lines

FROM: FISH AD
PLACE & TIME: 9.20pm

Code	Words		Received	From F.S.	Sent		SAR
£	d.			By Katherine	At	m.	16/9/16
Charges to collect				To			
Service Instructions F.S.				By			

Handed in at .... Office .... m. Received 10.16 p.m.

TO: SALMON

*Sender's Number	Day of Month	In reply to Number	A A A
BM 50	16th		

STOP FIRING on present target AAA The Guards hold the Triangle in T8D thence trench to T9D68 thence northwards AAA Barrage is as follows to protect their flanks to be barraged 4.9A Cafe to show when will be ATTACKED MORVAL AAA ROACH T10C28 to T10C00 AAA SALMON thence to T15B4585 AAA SEAL thence to T15A8580 AAA HAKE thence to T15A28 AAA Until dark occasionally burst in fire as follows AAA SEAL on Trees T15B48 to T9C72 AAA HAKE on Copse T15A78 to T15A28

FROM: FISH ADVANCE
PLACE & TIME: 4.10 pm

"A" Form. Army Form C. 2121
MESSAGES AND SIGNALS. No. of Message_____

Prefix____ Code____ in Office of Origin and Service Instructions.	Words	Charge	This message is on a/c of: _____ Service. (Signature of "Franking Officer.")	Recd. at____m Date____ From____ By
	Sent At____m To By			

TO { PRAWN.

Sender's Number.	Day of Month	In reply to Number	AAA
*JH29	16th		

The line allotted to us for to-night firing is as follows:— T.10.c.5.2½ to T.10.c.4.2½ aaa Rate of fire 4 Salvos at irregular intervals from hours until 5.30 a.m. aaa.

From OC 107 FA B
Place
Time 12.20 am

J.H. Cawley Lt

The above may be forwarded as now corrected.   (Z)

SECRET

Copy No. 6

Centre Divisional Artilleries, XIV Corps, Operation Order No. 5.

Reference. Trench Map 1/10,000. Sheet 57.c. 1/40,000.
Special Map issued with O.O. No. 3.

16th September, 1916.

1. The Fourth Army will continue the attack to-day at Zero (9-25 a.m.).

2. The objectives will be LESBOEUFS and GUEUDECOURT to enable the Cavalry to push through.
The XIV Corps will attack LESBOEUFS and the XV Corps GUEUDECOURT.

3. The Guards Division will carry out the attack of the XIV Corps in two bounds.

The first objective being the main German Blue line from about T.9.d.6.7. to T.3.a.2.9½.

The Second objective LESBOEUFS from its Southern extremity about T.10.b.5.7. to N.34.a.1.9. where touch will be obtained with XV Corps.

4. The assault of the 1st objective will be at Zero.
The assault from BLUE line will be at Zero + 35 (10-0 a.m.).

5. The Centre Divisional Artilleries will assist the Guards to the utmost of its power.
Two Brigades (three 18-pounder and one Howitzer Battery each) Left Group will be entirely at the disposal of the G.O.C.R.A., Guards Division, and orders for their employment are being issued herewith.

6. The remainder of the Centre Divisional Artilleries will be employed in forming barrages as follows:-

9-25 a.m. to 10-20 a.m.

LEFT GROUP.
1 Brigade (3-18-prs and 1 How. Battery) on the QUADRILATERAL and the trench T.14.d.8½.4½. to T.14.b.9.6.
1 Brigade (3 18-prs.) on the Western end of High Ground in MORVAL.

RIGHT GROUP.
2 Brigades on trench T.16.a.8.6. to T.10.c.1.6.

* NOTE. A report has been received at 1-0 a.m. to the effect that our Infantry are bombing down the trench T.14.d.8½.4. to T.14.b.9.6. from the North, and have reached T.14.d.9.7. They hope to occupy the whole trench by dawn. If this proves correct the barrage detailed for this trench will be placed on the Western end of the high ground in MORVAL instead. When definite information on this point is received, it will be passed to Groups by wire.

10-20 a.m. onwards.

LEFT GROUP.
2 Brigades on the Western end of the high ground in MORVAL.

RIGHT GROUP.
2 Brigades on the trench T.16.a.8.6. to T.10.c.1.6.

7. RATES OF FIRE.

9-25 a.m. to 10-15 a.m.   Intense.   3 rounds per gun per minute.
10-15 a.m. to 10-25 a.m. Medium.   2 rounds per gun per minute.
10-25 a.m. onwards.   Ordinary.   1 round per gun per minute.

8. Watches will be synchronised from this office at 8-0 a.m.

9. Acknowledge by wire.

[signature]
Major, R.A.

Brigade Major, Centre Divisional Artilleries, XIV Corps.

Issued at 2-30 a.m.

Copies to:-
    Right Group. (3).
    Left Group. (5).
    R.A., XIV Corps.
    6th Division "G" (4).
    Guards Div. Arty.
    56th Div. Arty.
    S.C.R.A., 6th Div.
    Liaison Officer Heavy Artillery.

No. B.M. 921/14.

No. 9 Squadron, Royal Flying Corps.
Right Group.
Left Group.

With a view to obtaining accurate registration for a barrage on the trench T.14.d.8½.4. to T.14.b.8½.5. and the QUADRILATERAL, an aeroplane will register one portion of those trenches for one gun of each battery of each Brigade.

The Aeroplane will go up about 9 or 10 a.m. to register the batteries.

Masts will be at the places shown on the Programme, and all batteries will be connected by telephone to the Mast of their own Group.

The Programme will be a long one for the aeroplane, so every endeavour must be made to get the registration done quickly.

Targets must be taken in the order of the attached Programme.

Sufficient copies of this Memorandum and the Programme are issued for all batteries and Brigade Headquarters to have one copy.

Major, R.A.

17/9/16. Brigade Major, Centre Divisional Artilleries, XIV Corps.

List of Targets to be registered by Aeroplane. 17/9/16.

LEFT GROUP.

Brigade.	Target No.	Map Reference of Target.	Approximate Map Reference of Batteries.
109th	1	T.14.b.8½.1½.	) S.30.c.4.4.
	2	T.14.b.8½.4.	)
106th	1	T.14.d.8½.5.	)
	2	T.14.d.8½.7.	) B.1.c.2.8.
	3	T.14.d.8½.9.	)
107th	1	T.14.b.8½.1.	)
	2	T.14.b.8½.3.	) T.25.d.8.1½.
	3	T.14.b.8½.5.	)
108th	1	T.14.d.8½.5.	)
	2	T.14.d.8½.7.	) S.25.a.4.6.
	3	T.14.d.8½.9.	)

MAST at S.30.c.4.4. for all batteries.

RIGHT GROUP

180th	1	T.15.c.1.½.	)
	2	T.14.d.9¾.1½.	) T.25.c.6.8. - T.25.d.2.0.
	3	T.14.d.9.3.	)
2nd	1	T.15.c.1.½.	)
	2	T.14.d.9¾.1½.	) T.25.d.0.5. - 1.1.
	3	T.14.d.9.3.	)

MAST at T.25.d.1½.½. for all batteries.

"C" Form (Duplicate).
MESSAGES AND SIGNALS.

Army Form C. 2123.
(In books of 50's in duplicate.)

SM EFPM

Service Instructions. FS

Office Stamp. SAR 17/9/16

TO SA

Sender's Number	Day of Month	In reply to Number	AAA
BM 69	17th		

STOP AAA All reported quiet left division front

FROM FISH
PLACE & TIME 5.25 pm.

Copy No. 3

Centre Divisional Artilleries, XIV Corps, Operation Order No. 6.

Reference. LONGUEVAL and COMBLES Sheets. 1/10,000
Sheet 57.c. S.W. 1/20,000 and Special Map attached.

17th September, 1916.

1. XIV Corps will renew the attack to-morrow.

2. 56th Division will advance to the line T.21.b.7.3. - Copse, at T.21.b.2.8.
   20th Division will capture the BLUE Line from their present left to T.3.a.2.9.

3. 6th Division will attack and capture the QUADRILATERAL and the German trench running thence Northwards to T.14.b.8.9. and will establish itself on the line, Copse at T.21.b.2.8. exclusive - Road at T.15.d.5.5. - Ravine T.15.Central to about T.15.a.7.9.

4. (a). The attack of the 6th Division will be carried out by the 16th Infantry Brigade on the right and 18th Infantry Brigade on the left.
   The dividing lines between Brigades throughout the attack will be the line of railway from T.20.b.0.7. to point 141.7 and thence along the ravine to T.15.Central (inclusive to both Brigades).

   (b). 16th Infantry Brigade will establish touch with the 56th Division at Copse T.21.b.2.8.; 18th Infantry Brigade with 20th Division at about T.15.a.7.9.

   (c). The QUADRILATERAL and trench running Northwards to T.14.b.8.9. will be consolidated when gained.

5. Zero hour will be 5-50 a.m.

6. Programme of Standing and Creeping Barrages (Tables A & B) and 4.5" Howitzer Bombardment (Table C) from Zero hour onwards are attached.
   50% of 18-prs. will be employed on the Creeping Barrage and 50% on the Stationary Barrage.

7. 71st Infantry Brigade will remain in Divisional Reserve in its present position, but will be prepared to move at a moment's notice.

8. Three Tanks will be to-night in the valley about T.26.a.0.0., and will move forward to the head of the Valley in T.20.d. at Zero hour.
   These Tanks will be employed if the attack is held up at any point in the QUADRILATERAL.
   G.O.C., 16th Infantry Brigade is empowered to issue direct orders to the Tanks, reporting action taken to Divisional Headquarters.

9. Watches will be synchronised from this office after 10-0 p.m. to-night.

10. Attacking troops will light flares at 7-0 a.m. on 18th instant, when contact aeroplans will be in the air.

11. The usual Artillery Liaison Officers will be supplied to Brigade and Battalion Headquarters taking part in the attack.

12. Two 6" Howitzer Batteries have been placed at the disposal of the G.O.C., 6th Division for this operation.

114th Siege Battery will bombard the Copse, Banks and Trench in T.15.a. and T.9.c. from Zero to + 16 mins. Not to fire West of N. and S. Line through T.15.a.3.8. after + 5 mins.

+ 16 mins onwards will fire on the Trench T.16.b.5.5. to T.10.c.2.5.

15th Siege Battery will bombard as follows:-

<u>1 Section.</u> Sunken Road T.15.c.1.4. to T.15.Central from Zero to + 16 mins. Not to fire West of T.15.c.4.7. after + 5 mins.

<u>1 Section.</u> On Cutting T.15.d.8.8. to T.15.b.9.1. from Zero till + 21 mins.

On completion of above tasks both Sections lift to Sunken Road T.16.a.8.6. to T.10.c.8.9.

Special attention will be paid to the cross-roads T.16.a.8.6.

<u>Rates of Fire.</u> INTENSE on first target. ORDINARY on Second target.

13. ACKNOWLEDGE.

[signature]

Major, R.A.

Brigade Major, Centre Divisional Artilleries,
XIV Corps.

Issued at 9-0 p.m.

Copies to:-

Left Group (5).
Right Group (3).
S.C.R.A., 6th Div.
XIV Corps, R.A.
114th Siege Battery, R.G.A.
15th Siege Battery, R.G.A.
6th Division "G" (4).
Guards Div. Arty.
56th Div. Arty.
XIV Corps N.A.

TABLE A

STANDING BARRAGE 18-pounders.

	RIGHT GROUP.	LEFT GROUP.

0 to +6 mins. QUADRILATERAL (all faces) T.14.b.8½.4. - T.14.b.8½.9.
and new trench T.15.c.2½.½.
to 5.2.

+6 to +16 mins. 1 Battery on Road   4 Batteries on the Valley
T.15.c.4½.6½. -   T.15.a.3.8. Eastwards for
T.15.d.4.2.   about 500 yards.
2 Batteries on   Batteries on Sunken Road
Road T.15.d.0.2. -   T.15.c.4½.6½. to
T.15.b.9.1.   T.15.d.4.2.

+16 to +21 mins. Move barrage Eastwards down Roads 100 yards a minute.

+21 to +45 mins. Barrage the Valley   Barrage the Valley
T.16.c.7.4. - T.13.a.1.3.   T.16.a.1.3. - T.10.c.0.1.

+45 mins onward. Trench T.13.b.5.5. -   Trench T.16.a.7.6. -
T.13.a.7.6.   T.10.c.2.5. & Sunken Road
                        T.16.a.8.7. - T.10.c.7.9.

RATES OF FIRE.

Zero to +30. INTENSE.
+30 onwards. ORDINARY.

CREEPING BARRAGE. 18-pounders.   TABLE "B".

	RIGHT GROUP.	LEFT GROUP.
0 to +3 mins.	T.20.b.9½.8. - T.14.d.5½.4.	T.14.d.5½.4. - T.14.b.5½.9.
+3 to +6 mins.	Lift by 50 yards a minute to T.15.c.3.0. - T.14.d.8½.4.	Lift by 50 yards a minute to T.14.d.8½.4. - T.14.b.8½.9.
+6 to +11½ mins.	Lift by 50 yards a minute to the line T.15.c.6.3. - T.15.c.4½.7.	Lift direct at +6 mins to T.15.c.4½.7. - T.15.a.2½.9.
+10 to +16 mins.	Open to Line T.15.d.5.2. - T.15.c.6.3. - T.15.c.4½.7.	
+16 to +45 mins.	Lift by 50 yards a minute till the line T.15.d.6.2½. - T.15.b.6.1. is reached and remain on this line.	Lift by 50 yards a minute till the line T.15.b.6.1. - T.15.b.3.9½. is reached and remain on this line.
+45 onwards.	Creep forward into the Valley T.16.c.7.4. - T.16.a.1.3. and remain on this line till further orders.	Creep forward into the Valley T.15.a.1.3. - T.10.c.0.1. and remain on this line till further orders.

RATES OF FIRE.

Zero to +30   INTENSE.
+30 onwards.   ORDINARY.

TABLE "C".

4.5" HOWITZER BATTERIES.

RIGHT GROUP.

1 Battery.

   0 to +6 mins.   Road. T.15.d.0.2. - T.15.b.9.1.

 +6 to +16 mins. Road T.15.d.2.3½. to T.15.b.9.1.

+16 to +45 mins. Cutting T.15.d.8.8. - T.15.b.9.1.

+45 onwards.   Trench T.16.b.5.5. - T.16.a.7.6.

1 Battery.

   0 to +6 mins.   Road T.15.c.3.5. to T.15.Central.

 +6 to +18 mins. Road T.15.c.6.7½. to T.15.Central to Cutting T.15.d.6.7½.

+18 onwards.   Trench T.16.b.5.5. to T.16.a.7.6.

LEFT GROUP.

1 Battery.

   0 to +6 mins.   Road T.15.c.3.5. to T.15.Central.

 +6 to +18 mins. Road T.15.c.6.7½. to T.15.Central to Cutting T.15.d.6.7½.

+18 onwards.   ~~Trench T.16.a.7.6. to T.10.c.2.5.~~ or Sunken Road T.16.a.8.7. - T.10.c.8.9.

2 Batteries.

   0 to +16 mins. Road T.15.a.3.8. to T.15.b.2.7.

+16 to +20 mins. T.15.a.8.8. to T.15.b.5.7.

+20 onwards.   Trench T.16.a.7.6. - T.10.c.2.5. and Sunken Road T.16.a.8.7. - T.10.c.8.9.

RATES OF FIRE.

Zero to +30   INTENSE.
+30 onwards. ORDINARY.

Service Instructions.	£ s. d.	
Handed in at...................	Office............m. Received............m.	
TO	BREAM SHRIMP SHARK	

Sender's Number	Day of Month	In reply to Number	AAA
M 55	17		

Following programme will be carried out today aaa Half hour fires will fire on SOS line & search almost up to Road in T.10.c. aaa 1 Am. to 1.10. Am HE ordinary rate 1.30.Am to 1.40.Am Shrapnel ordinary rate 1.55 to 2.5 Am medium rate 50% HE aaa

K H Cawley Lt.

FROM
PLACE & TIME

Service Instructions.		
Handed in at .... Office .... m. Received .... m.		
TO	Avion	

Sender's Number	Day of Month	In reply to Number	AAA
JH.54	19		

Following programme will be carried out in conjunction with 18 prs today aaa
Fire will fire on T15.a.5.9 aaa 1 gun to 1.10 am ordinary 1.30 am to 1.40 am ordinary 1.55 am to 2.5 ordinary

Signed G.H. Cawley Lt.

FROM PLACE & TIME

Handed in at .... Office .... m. Received .... m.

TO: All 18 pdr batteries

Sender's Number: N.69   Day of Month: 18   In reply to Number: A A A

1. XIV Corps will renew the attack today
2. Zero hour will be 5.30 a.m.
3. Watches will be synchronised from this office at 5 a.m.
4. Officer presently doing LIAISON OFFICER will remain at his post until after cessation of today's operations. When B/10 will find an officer & signallers
5. 104 F.A.B. will have teams ready to move to forward position by 6.30 a.m. but will not move without orders from H.Q.
6. 18 pdrs will fire standing barrages as follows:-
   Zero to + 6 min
   A/104   T.14.b.8½.1½ — T.14.b.8½.4   ⎫
   B/104   T.14.b.8½.4 — T.14.b.8½.6½   ⎬ TRENCH
   C/104   T.14.b.8½.6½ — T.14.b.8½.9   ⎭

FROM:
PLACE & TIME:

Service Instructions.			
Handed in at............	........Office.........m.	Received.........m.	
TO			
Sender's Number	Day of Month	In reply to Number	A A A

+6 Min to +16 Min

A/10y   T.15a.8.8 — T.15a.6.8.   ) VALLEY
B/10y   T.15a.6.8 — T.15a.4¾.8.) EAST
C/10y   T.15a.4¾.8 — T.15a.3.8   )

+16 Min to +21 Min

A/10y) Move barrage down road 8100*
B/10y) away on will, so firing to be
C/10y) South of pt. T.16.a.1.6½.

+21 Min to +45 Min

A/10y   T.16a.1.6½ — T.16a.⅜.8   ) VALLEY
B/10y   T.16a.⅜.8 — T.16a.4.9½   )
C/10y   T.16a.4.9½ — T.10.c.0.1.   )

FROM
PLACE & TIME

| Handed in at | Office | m. Received | m. |

TO

| *Sender's Number | Day of Month | In reply to Number | **AAA** |

+4·5 min onwards

A/10y T.16.a.7.6 – T.16.a.½.9
B/10y T.16.a.½.9 – T.10.c.4.2
C/10y T.10.c.4.2 – T.10.c.2.5
aaa

Rates of fire. aaa

Zero to +30 min   INTENSE.
+30 min onwards   ORDINARY.
aaa

FROM
PLACE & TIME   Salmon   J.H. Curley Lt.

*This line should be erased if not required.

| Handed in at | Office | m. Received | m. |

TO: D/How 107 F.A.B

Sender's Number	Day of Month	In reply to Number	AAA
A 70	18th		

(1) XIV Corps will renew the attack today.
(2) Zero hour will be 5.30 a.m.
(3) Watches will be synchronised from this office at 5 a.m.
(4) D/107 will fire as follows:—

Zero to +16 min.
T.15.a.8.7½ to T.15.b.2.4.

+16 min to +20 min
T.15.b.1½.7½ to T.15.b.6.4.

+20 min onwards
SUNKEN ROAD T.16.a.8.4 to T.10.c.8.9.

Rate of fire Zero to +30 m. INTENSE.
+30 m. onwards ORDINARY.

FROM
PLACE & TIME: S.A.

J.H. Canton/Lt

*This line should be erased if not required.
Wt. 432—M437 500,000 Pads. HWV 5.16 Forms C.2123.

| Handed in at | Office | m. Received | m. |

TO: Bdes Shrops & Nth

Sender's Number	Day of Month	In reply to Number	AAA
JH.44	18th		

Reference my JH.42
of even date aaa
Brigade amended SOS
is as follows aaa
T.15.b.5½.5 — T.15.b.3½.7½.
aaa Above will be acted on
until further orders aaa
Shrops will find ROCKET
GUARD tonight aaa

FROM
PLACE & TIME

J.H. Curtay Lieut

Wt. 432—M437 500,000 Pads. H W V 5 16 Forms C.2123.

| Handed in at | Office | m. Received | m. |

TO: PRAWN.

| Sender's Number | Day of Month | In reply to Number | AAA |
| G475 | 18th | | |

Reliable information has come to hand that the German battery are on the move and tomorrow night firing will be as follows aaa In addition to harassing fire objective at Mograh already given for fire intermittently on X Roads T56 07½ & 35 b 39 aaa Rate 20 Rds per hour until 5. Am aaa.

H. Curley Lieut

FROM
PLACE & TIME

* This line should be erased if not required.
Wt. 432—M437 500,000 Pads. H W V 5 16 Forms C. 2123.

| | | Office | m. Received | m. |

TO: BREAM

*Sender's Number	Day of Month	In reply to Number	AAA
JH76	18		

For ... Rpt Enemy are
... South half of MORVAL
Village. ... 5AM ... SOS ... the
line ...

FROM
PLACE & TIME

Handed in at................. Office........... m. Received .... m.

TO SHRIMP & Bream

*Sender's Number	Day of Month	In reply to Number	AAA
JH97	18th		

Tour night firing will be as follows — aaa

~~Nights~~ of MORVAL

Rate six rounds per gun per hour to 5 Am. aaa
S.O.S. lines remain the same aaa

BREAM from 11pm to 2 Am.
Shrimp " 2 Am to 5 Am.
aaa.

J H Cudlipp

FROM
PLACE & TIME

* This line should be erased if not required.

MESSA... ...**D SIGNALS.**

Army Form C. 2123.
(In books of 50's in duplicate.)
No. of Message ....

SM   ML AM 27

Service Instructions. FS

Office Stamp.
SAR
14/9/16

Handed in at .... Office .... m. Received .... m.

TO SALMON

Sender's Number	Day of Month	In reply to Number	AAA
BM 71	14th		

Reference BM 739 AAA In para 2
line 3 for 107 FAB
read 109 FAB

FROM
PLACE & TIME FISH ADVANCE
12.20 a.m.

B.M.759.

TABLE "A".

Reference attached Orders:-

1. Standing barrages will be formed as under:-

       106th F.A.B. on the Right.
       107th " " " on the Left.

Zero plus)
6.mins.) Dividing point T.14.b.85.15.

Plus 6 min) 107th F.A.B. on Valley T.15.a.3.8, Eastwards to T.15.a.82.80.
" 16 ")   One Batty. 106th F.A.B. T.15.a.82.80 to T.15.a.8.8.

Plus 21 min.)
plus 45 ") Dividing point T.16.a.10.65.

TABLE "B".

2. Creeping Barrage will be formed as under :-

       108th F.A.B. on the Right.
       107th " " " on the Left.

   Dividing points will be:-
Zero to
Plus 3 min.) T.14.b.55.15.

Plus 3 min) T.14.b.85.15.
plus 6 ")

Plus 6 min) T.15.a.35.30.
plus 16 ")

Plus 16 min) T.15.b.45.55.
plus 45 ")

Plus 45 min) T.16.a.05.70.
onwards.)

(4.5" Howitzer.)

3. Left Group.

TABLE "C"

| | "One Baty. D/106"
"Two Batys" D/108 | & | D/107. |
|---|---|---|---|
| Zero to) | T.15.a.3.8 to | | T.15.a.80.75 to |
| Plus 16.min.) | T.15.a.80.75. | | T.15.b.2.7. |
| Plus 16 min.) | T.15.a.8.8 to | | T.15.b.15.75 to |
| Plus 20 ") | T.15.b.15.75. | | T.15.b.5.7. |
| Plus 20 min.) | Trench T.16.a.7.6 | | Sunken road T.16.a.8.7 |
| onwards.) | to T.10.c.2.5. | | to T.10.c.8.9. |

4.   O.C.,108th F.A.B. will be Liaison Officer with 18th Infy.Bde.
    O.C.,107th F.A.B. is furnishing Lisison Officer with Right Battn.
    (14th D.L.I.) H.Q. at T.20.a.7.6.
    O.C.,109th F.A.B. will furnish Liaison Officer with Left Battn.
    (1st West Yorks) H.Q. at T.20.a.7.6.
    106th 107th & 109th F.A.Bdes will have their teams ready to move to
forward positions by 6-30.a.m. but will not move without orders from
this Office unless communication is broken.

5. ACKNOWLEDGE BY WIRE.
17/9/16.
Issued at 12.m.n.
                                 Major.R.A.
      Brigade Major, 24th Divisional Artillery.

SECRET. B.M.741.

106th F.A.B.
107th " " "
108th " " "
109th " " "
Staff Captain, R.A.
================

1. RELIEFS.

The 6th DIV. will be relieved to-night by the 5th DIV.

Relief to be completed by 5-30.a.m. on 19th inst.

95th I.B. will be relieved by the 16th I.B. (H.Q. at B.1.b.8.4.)

15th. I.B. will be relieved by the 18th I.B. in the Left Sector. (H.Q. at CHIMPANZEE Trench A.5.d.3.3.)

2. OPERATIONS.

The next operations will consist of an attack on LESBOEUFS and MORVAL, and the capture of a line E. of those villages, somewhat further east than the original RED line of the scheme for 15th inst.

A heavy bombardment will take place on 20th & 21st inst. until "Zero".

18/9/16.

Major.R.A.
Brigade Major, 24th Divisional Artillery.

"C" Form (Original).
MESSAGES AND SIGNALS.
Army Form C. 2123
(In books of 50's in duplicate.)

TO: SALMON

Day of Month: 18

AAA

Ammn. on Hand 905-a

FROM: SHARK

"C" Form (Duplicate)
MESSAGES AND SIGNALS.

Army Form C. 2123.
(In books of 50's in duplicate)
No. of Message ....

Charges to Pay.
£   s.   d.

Office Stamp.

Service Instructions.

Handed in at .... Office .... m. Received .... m.

TO	SALMON

Sender's Number	Day of Month	In reply to Number	AAA
	18		

Forward dump 600a
Gun position 500A/504x
Wire 400A

FROM: SHRIMP

PLACE & TIME:

"C" Form (Original).
MESSAGES AND SIGNALS.

Army Form C. 2123.
(In books of 50's in duplicate.)

No. of Message ....

Prefix ..... Code ..... Words	Received	Sent, or sent out	Office Stamp.
£ s. d.	From	At .... m.	
Charges to collect	By	To	
Service Instructions.		By	

Handed in at .... Office .... m. Received .... m.

TO: SALMON

*Sender's Number	Day of Month	In reply to Number	A A A
A3	15		

Ammⁿ on hand a WL
1330 A 480 AX Guns 530 A
230 AX forward Dump nil

FROM
PLACE & TIME: BREAM

"A". Form. Army Form C. 2121
MESSAGES AND SIGNALS No. of Message_____

Prefix___ Code___ m.	Words	Charge	This message is on a/c of:	Recd. at___ m.
Office of Origin and Service Instructions.	Sent At___ m. To___ By___		_____ Service. (Signature of "Franking Officer.")	Date___ From___ By___

TO	SALMON.			
Sender's Number.	Day of Month	In reply to Number		**A A A**
G.F./1/1853	18-9-16			

Ammunition in possession at Wagon Lines. aaa

Bream   1330 A   480 AX. aaa
Shrimp. 400 A   NIL AX. aaa
Shark   NIL A   NIL AX. aaa
Total 3 18-Pdr Btp 1730 A 480 AX aaa

How Bty have no ammunition at Wagon Line

From: SALMON Wagon Line
Place:
Time:

"C" Form (Duplicate). Army Form C. 2123.
MESSAGES AND SIGNALS. (In books of 50's in duplicate.)
No. of Message ....

| | Charges to Pay. £ s. d. | Office Stamp. |

Service Instructions.

Handed in at .... Office .... m. Received .... m.

TO

Sender's Number	Day of Month	In reply to Number	A A A
900 a	200 ax		shrimp
360 a	340 ax		Bream
	HEwl T5 1110		SHARK

FROM

PLACE & TIME

"C" Form (Duplicate).
MESSAGES AND SIGNALS.

Army Form C. 2123.
(In books of 50's in duplicate.)
No. of Message..................

2nd BFAM

Service Instructions.
F5

Handed in at.................. Office........... m. Received........... m.

TO   SALMON

Sender's Number	Day of Month	In reply to Number	A A A
BM73	18		

Instructions have now been received to keep at the guns 18pr 500 rds and 4.5 how 400 instead of previous figures

FROM   Fish AD
PLACE & TIME   1.45 am

"C" Form (Original).
MESSAGES AND SIGNALS.
Army Form C. 2123.
(In books of 50's in duplicate.)
No. of Message............

Prefix.......... Code.......... Words..........	Received	Sent, or sent out	Office Stamp.
£ s. d.	From..................	At.................m.	
Charges to collect	By..................	To..................	
Service Instructions.		By..................	

Handed in at.. Office..........m. Received..........m.

TO   ADJT SA

*Sender's Number	Day of Month	In reply to Number	A A A
M 8	28		

LS ~~1~~ of Seal has relieved me and

FROM   LSSA
PLACE & TIME   7.30 a.m.

*This line should be erased if not required.

"C" Form (Original).
MESSAGES AND SIGNALS.
Army Form C. 2123.
(In books of 50's in duplicate)
No. of Message...............

| Prefix | Code ADM-25 | Words 25 | Received From FS By McNaraca | Sent, or sent out At........m. To........ By | Office Stamp 8AR 18/9/16 |

Charges to collect
Service Instructions. FS

Handed in at............................Office............m. Received...........m.

TO: SALMON

Sender's Number	Day of Month	In reply to Number	A A A
BM 72	18th		

In table A standing barrage
plus 45 min onwards AAA
107 takes trench and 106
Sunken Road

FROM PLACE & TIME: FISH ADVANCE 1 a.m.

D t 16min A T.14.6.8½.7½ — T.14.6.8½.2½
B T.14.6.8½.4½ — T.14.6.8½.6½
C T.14.6.8½.2 — T.14.6.8½.9

t.0min t +16min A T.15.a.8.8 — T.15.a.6.4
B T.15.a.6.4.8 — T.15.a.4.4.8
C T.15.a.2.2.8 — T.15.a.9.3.8

+16 min t+21min move barrage down road 1 100 every minute. Battery will not fire South of point T.16.a.1.6½

t+21min t+46min A T.16.A.1.6½ — T.16.A.½.8
Barrage Valley   B 16.A.½.8 — T.16.A.½.9½
C T.16.A.½.9½ — T.10.c.0.1

Track
+45 mins onwards
A - T.16.a.7.6. - T.16.a.½.9
B T.16.a.½.9 - T.10.c.4.2
C T.10.c.4.2 - T.10.c.25

Rate of fire
Zero h + 30 Intense
+ 30 onwards Normal

AAA

106th F.A.B.
✓ 107th F.A.B.
108th F.A.B.
109th F.A.B.
24th D.A.C.
Staff Captain, R.A.

B.M.742.

Following message from Corps Commander to 6th Division, begins. Hearty congratulations on your most successful day.

18/9/16.

[signature]
Major.R.A.
Brigade Major, 24th Divisional Artillery.

106th F.A.B.
✓ 107th " " "
108th " " "
109th " " "

B.M.743.

XIVth Corps R.A. wire that during daylight 19th., Batteries are to have a rest from firing, and only fire when the tactical situation demands, but Registration and preparation of of observing stations and communications, etc. must be pushed on with.

18/9/16.

[signature]
Major.R.A.
Brigade Major, 24th Divisional Artillery.

"C" Form (Duplicate).
MESSAGES AND SIGNALS.

Army Form C. 2123.
(In books of 50's in duplicate.)
No. of Message...........

Sm KBAM

Charges to Pay. £ s. d.

Office Stamp.
SAR
18/9/16

Service Instructions. ES

Handed in at .... Office .... m. Received 10.25 am.

TO: SALMON

Sender's Number	Day of Month	In reply to Number	A A A
BM 75	19th		

Slow Rate

FROM
PLACE & TIME: FISH ADVANCE 10.5 am

SECRET 107/7

Centre Divisional Artilleries, XIV Corps, Operation Order No. 7.

Reference.   Tracing from 1/10,000 map attached. (issued only to Groups)

NB Programme postponed 24 hours.   M.   19th September, 1918.

1. The XIV Corps will resume the offensive on 21st September.

2. One composite Brigade (three 18-pr. and one 4.5" Howitzer batteries) 56th Divisional Artillery will come under the orders of Officer Commanding Right Group from 6-0 p.m. to-night to assist in the operations.

3. The Centre Divisional Artilleries will cover the attack of 5th Division on 21st, and assist in the preliminary bombardment by the Heavy Artillery on 20th and 21st instant prior to 'Zero hour'.

4. Zero hour will be notified later.

5. A tracing of the trenches and roads to be bombarded by the Heavy Artillery and 4.5" Howitzers is attached.

6. A steady bombardment of the hostile positions will be commenced at 7-0 a.m. on 20th September, and will be continued until 6-30 p.m. It will be recommenced at 6-30 a.m. on 21st September.
    The ground in front and in rear of the German trenches, including roads leading into MORVAL not specially detailed for treatment by 4.5" Howitzers, will be searched occasionally with 18-pounder Shrapnel and High Explosive Shell.

7. Night firing will be carried out nightly between the hours of 6-30 p.m. and 6-30 a.m.

8. There will be no intensive fire previous to Zero.

9. Trenches, roads, etc., to be bombarded during the steady bombardment are shown on the attached tracing.

    RED will be shelled very heavily.
    GREEN will be shelled heavily.
    YELLOW will be shelled.
    BROWN will be dealt with by 4.5" Howitzers.

    The small trenches West and South-West of MORVAL will also receive treatment from the Heavy Artillery.

10. Counter-battery work will be carried out during the bombardment by Heavy Guns and a proportion of Heavy Howitzers.

11. Zones will be allotted to Groups as soon as the Divisional and Infantry Brigade Zones are known.

12. The Right Group will detail two 4.5" Howitzer batteries to shoot on BROWN target "A", and one on the Southern half of BROWN target "C"

The Left Group will detail two 4.5" Howitzer batteries to shoot on BROWN target "B" and the Northern half of BROWN target "C".

On the night of 20th/21st September, from 6-30 p.m. to 12-30 a.m. the Right Group will be responsible for fire on the whole of BROWN target "C", and from 12-30 a.m. to 6-30 a.m. the Left Group will be responsible for this target.

At night one battery of each Group should be responsible for fire on targets "A" and "B" respectively.

13. Rates of Fire:-

	By day.	By night.
4.5" Howitzers.	15 rounds per Howr. per hour.	20 rounds per battery per hour when employed.
18-pounders.	As required.	200 rounds per battery per night.

14. Detailed orders for action of the Artillery from Zero hour onwards will be issued later.

15. ACKNOWLEDGE.

L. M. Savile.

Major, R. A.
Brigade Major, Centre Divisional Artilleries, XIV Corps.

Issued at 3-45 p.m.

Copies to:-

Right Group (4).
Left Group (5).
S.C.R.A., 6th Div.
XIV Corps R.A.
5th Division "G" (4).
Guards Divisional Arty.
56th Divisional Arty.
XIV Corps H.A.
Liaison Officer Heavy Arty.

"C" Form (Original). Army Form C. 2123.
MESSAGES AND SIGNALS.

Prefix SM Code 1A.P.M Words

TO SALMON

Sender's Number: BM/89/2   Day of Month: 19th

Night firing aaa Roads in T10C T10D T11C aaa A new German trench T10A60 to T10A 55 95 to be kept under occasional fire day & night to stop work aaa Normal Expenditure aaa HE only

FROM PLACE & TIME   F16H 9.15p

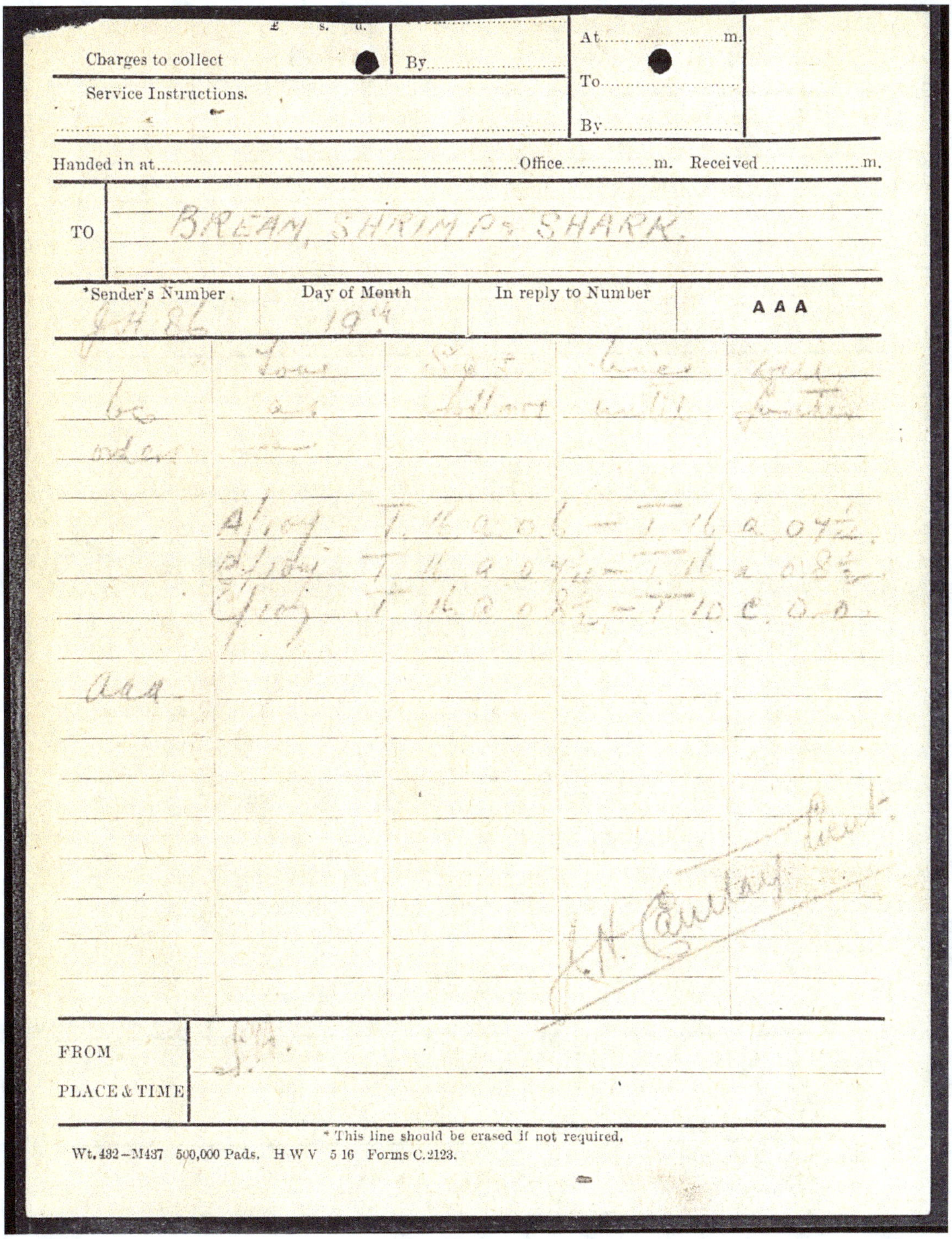

Charges to collect		By	At......m. To......	
Service Instructions.			By	

Handed in at................... Office........m. Received........m.

TO: BREAM, SHRIMP & SHARK.

*Sender's Number	Day of Month	In reply to Number	AAA
JH 86	19th		

[illegible handwritten message]

FROM
PLACE & TIME

Service Instructions.		£ s. d.	

Handed in at .... Office .... m. Received .... m.

TO BREAM, SHRIMP, & SHARK.

Sender's Number	Day of Month	In reply to Number	AAA
ft 92	14		

Tonight tows night horses for
Tonight girls be by followon
nully junker orders are
Roughly B/T. 10.1 T10d T 11g are.
A/10/ from 11-30 pm to 1.30 Am
B/10/ " 1.30 Am to 3.30 Am
C/10/ " 3.30 Am to 5.30 Am.
are
Rate 1/- Reg per tow.
aaa.

FROM SA.
PLACE & TIME 11.10 pm   H Cawley Lt

Service Instructions.

Handed in at .... Office .... m. Received .... m.

TO PRAWN

Sender's Number	Day of Month	In reply to Number	AAA

JR 93. , 17th

Joining two light and day
farming ae until Joining orders until
ae any follow.

New GERMAN Trench @
Firebolt T10a5.9 to

and Rate 8 Rds per hour all
except for SOS reshooting & like
place on Trench T9d.8.3 to
T16a.8.6 after 5 A.M. until
results of attack along it reported
bombing aa.

FROM
PLACE & TIME   S.M.   11.20 p.m.   J.A. Curtay Lt.

Service Instructions.

Handed in at .... Office .... m. Received .... m.

TO: O C SHARK.

Sender's Number: JH 114 Day of Month: 20th In reply to Number: AAA

Please instruct F.O.O. to cut wire at T.10.c.1.6 to T.10.c.0.6½ and not as to verbal instructions as our infantry reported at T.9.d.9.7½. any enemy may open fire as soon as food fires out in position also.

J H Cowley Lieut

FROM
PLACE & TIME: SH 2 pm

		Office	m. Received	m.
	atteurs.	J H Lyest		
			11D	

ber	Day of Month	In reply to Number	AAA
	20th		

S.O.S. lines are amended and now as follows:—

T.10.c.23 to T.10.c.16

night firing and will be the same as last night aaa from will fire on squares allotted (22) T.10c T.10d 11c Roads aaa Rate 8 Rds per battery per hour at odd intervals aaa

J W Curley Lt

FROM PLACE & TIME: S.A. 9.25/p.m

Wt. 432—M437 500,000 Pads. H W V 5/16 Forms/C.2123.

"C" Form (Duplicate).
MESSAGES AND SIGNALS.
Army Form C. 2123.
(In books of 50's in duplicate.)
No. of Message..................

SM 1A

Charges to Pay. £ s. d.

Office Stamp.

Service Instructions.
FS

Handed in at.................. Office............ m. Received............ m.

TO SALMON

Sender's Number	Day of Month	In reply to Number	AAA
BM 93/4	20		

SOS lines aaa T10c23 to T10c16 aaa night firing as last night

FROM
PLACE & TIME

E15H
9.15

B.M.91.

106th F.A.B.
✓ 107th " " "
108th " " "
109th " " "
==============

1. This morning's bombing attack did not succeed.

2. The Infantry report that they have dug a trench from

T.9.d.5.8 to T.9.d.9.0

but this requires confirmation.

Meanwhile S.O.S. barrage of 107th & 108th Brigades will be established 100 yards further East than given in this Office No.B.M.82 of 19th.

20/9/16.

Major.R.A.

Brigade Major, 24th Divisional Artillery.

SECRET.
Reference GUILLEMONT & COMBLES, Sheets 1/10,000 Map.

OPERATION ORDER No.1
by
Brigadier General H.C.SHEPPARD,
Commanding Left Centre Divisional Artillery, XlV.Corps.

21st Sept. 1916.

1. The 6th Division will on night 21st/22nd Sept. take over the front approximately from T.9.d.6.8 to T.3.d.4.1, and will become the "Left Centre Division", XlV.Corps.
Advanced Divisional H.Q. will be at A.3.c.1.6.

2. By 5-30.a.m. on 22nd Sept.

(a) The 16th Infantry Brigade will hold from T.9.d.6.8 to T.9.b.8.2 (incl)
H.Q. temporarily at BRIQUETERIE A.4.b., until Adv.H.Q. are arranged probably at QUARRY T.10.c.2.3.)

(b) The 17th Infantry Brigade will hold from T.9.b.6.2 (excl) to T.3.d.4.1.
(H.Q. temporarily at BRIQUETERIE A.4.b. until Adv.H.Q. are arranged probably at QUARRY T.19.c.2.3.)

3. Until 9.a.m. 22nd inst. the 6th Division front will be covered by the Guards Divisional Artillery; from that hour the 24th Divisional Artillery, reinforced by the 38th F.A.Brigade (6th Division) and the 92nd F.A.Brigade (20th Division) will be responsible.
H.Q. LEFT CENTRE D...., XlV.Corps, will be at Adv.6th Divisional H.Q. (A.3.c.1.6.)

4. The Artillery will be grouped as under:-

GROUP.	COMMANDER & HD.QRS.	UNITS.	
Right.	Lt.Col.E.R.BURNE. D.S.O. (T.26.a.1.7.)	106 F.A.B.) 109 F.A.B.)	Covering Right (16th) Inf.Bde.
107 F.A.B.	Lt.Col.D.R.COATES. (ARROW HEAD COPSE.	107 F.A.B.	
Left.	Lt.Col.E.C.W.D.WALTHALL. D.S.O. (T.25.a.70.95.)	108 F.A.B.) 38 F.A.B.) 92 F.A.B.)	Covering Left (18th) Inf.Bde.

Right and Left Group Commanders will each detail one Brigade to furnish Liaison and work in conjunction with the Infantry Brigade respectively whose front they cover.
Group Commanders will arrange for direct communication between the Liaison Officer and Group H.Q., and between the Liaison Officer and his Brigade H.Q.

5. Brigades will be registered on their new zones by 6.p.m. to-day, and all communications will be completed by the hour of taking over, (9.a.m. 22nd September.)

6. The Divisional Zone will be between a line T.9.d.6.8 - T.11.a.0.0 and the GINCHY - LESBOEUFS road (excl)
The Boundary between zones of Right and Left Groups will be a line T.9.d.6.8 - T.5.c.0.0.

P.T.O.

7. Reference para 4, until active operations begin the Liaison Officer provided by Groups may be a Subaltern Officer.
   They will report to Infantry Brigades respectively this afternoon and will be established at Infantry Brigade H.Q. by 8.a.m. 22nd September.

8. ACKNOWLEDGE BY WIRE.

B.Crozier

Issued at 3-15.p.m.
                                                     Major.R.A.

                  Brigade Major, 24th Divisional Artillery.
                     (Left Centre Divisional Artillery, XIV.Corps.)

Copies to

106 F.A.B.
107 " " "
108 " " "
109 " " "
 38 " " ")
 92 " " ") through 108 F.A.B.
GUARDS D.A.- 6th D.A.
6th DIVN.
16th INF.BDE.
18th " "
R.A.,XIV.CORPS.
OFFICE.

"A" Form.　　　　　　　　　　Army Form C. 2121.
MESSAGES AND SIGNALS. No. of Message

Prefix ... Code ... Words ... Charge ...
F.S.

TO Salmon

Sender's Number	Day of Month	In reply to Number	
BM 104	22		AAA

SOS lines from 9 AM AAA
T10 b 0085 to T9 B 5535
T9 B 7565 to T3 D 7530
AAA of which Salmon from
T10 A 0035 to T9 B 85

From / Place / Time — Fish　8 am

TO: BREAM + SHRIMP

Sender's Number	Day of Month	In reply to Number	AAA

Day firing from 6.0am
to 6.30pm will be as under —

(1) as per rept. firing JH 134 aaa
(2) at irregular intervals guns will
burst fire Roads as follows —
BREAM & SHRIMP

(a) Road running N.W. from T.4.b.4.3.
(b)   "   "   N.E.   " T.4.b.2.3.
(c)   "   "   East   " T.4.b.4.4.
(d)   "   "   South " T.4.b.4.4.
(e)   "   "   South " T.4.d.1.6½.
(f)   "   "   S.West " T.4.a.9.0. aaa

firing 3 shots each gun to be at intervals of
100x, lifting 100x and sweeping one degree
commencing with (a) at 6.30am (b) 6.30am
and so on aaa. Rate 4 rounds per gun per hour aaa

FROM
PLACE & TIME

		Office......m. Received......m.
TO	PRAWN	

Sender's Number	Day of Month	In reply to Number	AAA
RA54	22		

Reference my J.H. 133 aaa please apply Cross Roads only if possible in T.4.C.3½.4½ aaa. Right Jenny aaa harass the whole of LES BOEUFS VILLAGE from 6.30 pm to 6.30 am. aaa Rate of eight rounds per battery an hour aaa ammunition must not be wasted but enemy must be allowed no peace or opportunity to work day or night aaa.

Night Jenny as above daily until further orders aaa.

J.H. Curley Lieut

FROM PLACE & TIME	Telrock 6.30 pm	

*This line should be erased if not required.
Wt. 432—M437 500,000 Pads. HWV 5 16 Forms C.2123.

| Handed in at | Office | m. Received | m. |

TO: BREAM & SHRIMP

Sender's Number	Day of Month	In reply to Number	AAA
S.H.134	22nd		

Night firing from 6.30 pm
to 6.30 am daily until further
orders is as follows:—
BREAM 3 Guns will search Southern
half of VILLAGE of LES BOEUFS, T.H.C & D.B.
boundaries SUNKEN Roads running North
& South in T.H.C & D exclusive, and main
GUINCHY LESBOEUFS Road. aaa.
BREAM 1 Gun will search along main road
from Road junction T.H.C.d.9.2 to T.14.b.2.5
aaa SHRIMP will search area Northern portion
of Village of LES BOEUFS boundary main
GUINCHY LES BOEUFS Road Sunken roads
exclusive aaa Rate of fire four rounds per
gun per hour aaa Enemy must not be hurried
but enemy must be allowed no peace or opportunity
to work day or night aaa

FROM
PLACE & TIME: Salmon
6.20 pm

J.H. Curley

| Handed in at | Office | m. Received | m. |

TO: SHARK...

*Sender's Number	Day of Month	In reply to Number	AAA
FA 120	22		

Your SOS line is
now as follows until further
orders will be as follows:

T.10.a.00.35 to T.9.b.80.50.

aaa

FROM
PLACE & TIME: 1st A... 8.45 AM   J H Munday

*This line should be erased if not required.
Wt. 432—M437 500,000 Pads. H W V 5 16 Forms C.2123.

"C" Form (Duplicate).
MESSAGES AND SIGNALS.

Army Form C. 2123.
(In books of 50's in duplicate.)
No. of Message ....

	Charges to Pay. £ s. d.	Office Stamp.
Service Instructions.		

Handed in at.................................... Office.............m. Received...............m.

TO	PRAWN

Sender's Number	Day of Month	In reply to Number	A A A
M.139	22nd	firing	will
11m 6 6.30pm Day		150 EVFB	be
Shoot DES		8 Rds	per battery
Rate		a.a.	
per hour			

FROM PLACE & TIME: Salmon 10.25 pm J H Cawley

"C" Form (Duplicate).
MESSAGES AND SIGNALS.

Army Form C. 2123.
(In books of 50's in duplicate.)
No. of Message ....

S.M.   MHPM

Charges to Pay. £ s. d.

Office Stamp.
SPF
22/9/16

Service Instructions. FE

Handed in at .... Office .... m. Received .... m.

TO SALMON

Sender's Number	Day of Month	In reply to Number	A A A
BM 05	22nd		

During operations left group will form stationary barrage on division front and Rifle groups and Salmon the creeping barrage Salmon being on the left AAA Addressed Right, Left and Salmon.

FROM FBN

PLACE & TIME 12 30 pm

LEFT CENTRE DIVISIONAL ARTILLERY.

RIGHT GROUP.
LEFT GROUP.
107th F.A.B.

1. The steady bombardment by Heavy Artillery will start at 7.a.m. 24th inst. and will continue until 6-30.p.m., to be resumed at 6-30.a.m. 25th and continue until Zero.

2. O.C.,107th F.A.B. will detail his Howitzer Battery to bombard the Sunken Road T.11.a.2.3 to T.11.b.10.85, coloured purple in the tracing already issued to Group Commanders and O.C.,107th F.A.B.

   Rate of fire 15 rounds per Howitzer per hour.

3. During the bombardment Group Commanders and O.C.,107th F.A.B. will arrange to search with their 18-prs the ground in front and in rear of the German trenches in their respective zones, as well as all unseen ground and approaches.

   Expenditure 8 rounds per gun per hour. - 60% H.E.

   The 107th F.A.B. is allotted the zone between the road T.10.b.35.80 - - T.4.c.30.85 (incl) and the Sunken Road T.4.d.6.0 - - T.4.b.2.5 (excl)
   of
4. Short summary/programme will be submitted as usual.

5. ACKNOWLEDGE BY WIRE.

23/9/16.

Issued at 8.p.m.

Major.R.A.

Brigade Major, Left Centre Divisional Artillery.

Service Instructions.

Handed in at .... Office .... m. Received .... m.

TO O.C. BREAM + SHRIMP

Sender's Number: JH 140 Day of Month: 20 In reply to Number: AAA

Please cancel my no JH 134 of yesterdays date aaa Tonights firing will be as follows: aaa from 6.30 pm to 6.30 am.

SHRIMP will search area LES BOEUFS village boundaries. Road junct. T.4.c.8.8½ South East to junct: T.4.d.½.6. line East to SUNKEN Road T.4.d.5.6 North along SUNKEN Road to T.4.b.2½.w.½ + Road running South West to junction road T.4.c.8.8½ aaa no firing to be South of line T.4.d.½.6 to T.4.d.5.6 aaa SUNKEN Road exclusive aaa. Rate of fire 4 Rds per gun per hour aaa.

FROM
PLACE & TIME

SECRET.   Copy No. 6

LEFT CENTRE DIVISIONAL ARTILLERY.
XlV. Corps.
OPERATION ORDER No. 2.

Reference LONGUEVAL)   24th September. 1916.
          COMBLES) Sheets 1/10,000 Map.
and Sheet 1/20,000 attached (Groups & 107 F.A.B. only.)

1. The XlV. Corps will renew the attack on the 25th September, the objectives including the villages of MORVAL and LESBOEUFS.
    The attack will be carried out by the Guards Division on the left, the 6th Division in the centre, and the 5th Division on the right, the 56th Division on the extreme right forming a protective flank facing South.

2. At zero hour the 5th Division (on the right) and Guards Division (on the left) will advance to the attack of their first objective (GREEN Line). 6th Division does not advance.

    At zero plus 1 hour The Infantry (including 6th Division) advance to attack 2nd Objective (BROWN Line.)

    At zero plus 2 hours The Infantry (including 6th Division) will advance to the attack of the 3rd Objective (BLUE Line.)

    After consolidating the latter objective the 6th Division will push forward strong patrols to seize vantage points at MORVAL MILL and along the ridge running North through T.5.central.

    The objectives of the XlV. Corps and Divisional Boundaries are shown on attached map.

3.   Objectives of the 6th Division are:-

First Objective.   Line of road from road junction at T.10.c.8.9 to
(BROWN Line.)   T.10.a.7.6 to cross roads T.4.c.40.75 (excl)

Second Objective. T.11.a.1.0. along road to road junction T.10.b.6.5 -
(BLUE Line.)   T.4.d.6.0 to T.4.b.25.50.

    16th Inf. Bde. on the right, 18th Inf. Bde. on the left, dividing line T.9.b.6.2 - T.10.a.7.6 - T.4.d.6.0 - T.5.c.25.20 all inclusive to 16th I.B.

4.   A steady bombardment by Heavy Artillery will begin at 7.a.m. 24th September and be continued till 6-30.p.m., to resume at 3-30.a.m. on 25th inst.

    The tasks of the 6" Howitzers are too heavy to admit of any of them being placed under the G.R.A., but should a Battery be urgently required, it can be arranged for, through the Heavy Artillery Liaison Officer with Divnl. Artillery H.Q.

5.   Group Commanders will arrange to search occasionally with their 18-pr Shrapnel and H.E. the ground in front and rear of the German trenches which are being bombarded.

6.   Night firing will be carried out nightly by Divisional Artillery between 6-30.p.m. and 3-30.a.m.

7.   The Left Group will form the Stationary Barrage.
    The Right Group on the right and 107th F.A.B. on the left of a dividing line through T.10.a.0.8 and T.5.c.00.75 will form a creeping barrage.

                                                        P.T.O.

* 2 *

18-pr Barrages will be as under:—
(The coloured lines on map referred to below are intended to make the scheme clearer, but co-ordinates must be used in allotting tasks).

AT.	STATIONARY BARRAGE.	CREEPING BARRAGE.
Zero plus 5.mins.		Starts 200 yards beyond GREEN Line (6th Div. Front Line.)
Zero plus 1 hour.	Starts on BROWN Line.	Starts creeping forward 50 yards a minute.
Zero plus 1.hr.8.mins. (Infy assault BROWN Line.)	Lifts straight to YELLOW Line. (T.10.b.65.00 – T.4.c.75.85.)	Joins Stationary Barrage on BROWN LINE and creeps on to 150 yds. beyond BROWN Line.
Zero plus 2.hours.	"Extra Barrage" starts on road T.11.a.1.0 to T.4.d.65.00 (right portion of BLUE Line.	
Zero plus 2.hrs.2.mins.		Starts creeping forward 50 yards a minute.
Zero plus 2.hrs.4.mins.	Left portion (T.10.b.6.5 to left) lifts straight to BLUE line. Right portion (T.10.b.6.5 to T.10.b.65.00) remains on YELLOW Line.	
Zero plus 2.hrs.7.mins. (Infy.assault BLUE Line.)	Both portions and "Extra barrage" lift straight to line MORVAL MILL – T.5.central – cross roads T.5.b.00.65., with the exception that the Southern 100 yards of the "Extra barrage) (T.11.a.1.0 to T.11.a.05.20) remains till Zero plus 2.hrs.11.mins. when it lifts straight to line MORVAL MILL – T.5.central.	Reaches BLUE line and creeps on to 200 yards beyond BLUE Line where it remains till ordered to creep on to join Stationary Barrage on line MORVAL MILL etc.

8. RATES OF FIRE

From Zero plus 5.mins. to Zero plus 10.mins. ... ... INTENSE.
From Zero plus 10.mins. to Zero plus 1 hour. ... ... SLOW.
From Zero plus 1 hour to Zero plus 1.hour 15.mins. ... ... INTENSE.
From Zero plus 2 hours to Zero plus 2.hours 15.mins. ... ... INTENSE.
At other times. ... ... ORDINARY.

Group Commanders will lessen rate of fire after final Objective has been obtained if the situation so permits.

* 3 *

	For 18-prs.	For 4.5" Hows.
INTENSE will be	3 rds per gun per min.	2 rds per How per min.
ORDINARY " "	1 rd. " " " "	1 rd " " " "
SLOW " "	1 rd per Batty." "	1 rd per Batty." "

9. 4.5" Howitzer Programme will be issued later.

10. A smoke barrage will be placed as shown by the green grid lines on attached map.

11. O.C. Right and Left Groups will detail as Liaison Officers

    A Field Officer with Hd.Qrs. 16th & 18th Inf.Bdes. respectively, and a Subaltern Officer with Hd.Qrs. of each Battn. of the respective Brigades in front line.

    O.C.,107th F.A.B. will detail a Subaltern as Liaison Officer with Hd.Qrs. 71st Inf.Bde. (BRIQUETERIE from Zero).

    Liaison Officers will report at least 2 hours before Zero.

12. Zero hour will be notified later.

13. Watches will be synchronised from this Office at hours to be notified later.

14. ACKNOWLEDGE BY WIRE.

Issued at 9 a.m.

                                        Major. R.A.

    Brigade Major, Left Centre Divisional Artillery.

Copies to	No.
RIGHT GROUP.	1 - 2.
LEFT GROUP.	3 - 5.
107th F.A.B.	6.
RIGHT CENTRE D.A.	7.
LEFT D.A.	8.
6th DIV. "G".	9 - 12.
GUARDS DIV. "G".	13.
5th DIV. "G"	14.
R.A. XIVth Corps.	15.
Staff Captain. R.A.	16.
WAR DIARY.	17.
SPARE.	18 - 19 - 20.

SECRET ~~T. CENTRE D.A. XIVth Corps~~

Reference Operation Order No. 2.

4.5" Howitzer Programme.

1. Targets.

RIGHT GROUP.

Zero to Zero plus 1 hour.	Road T.10.c.75.90 to T.10.a.7.5
Zero plus 1 hour to Zero plus 1 hr 58 mins.	Sunken Road T.11.a.0.1 to T.10.b.4.7. and Strong point T.11.c.08.96.
Zero plus 1 hr 58 mins. Onwards.	Sunken Road T.11.a.8.7 to T.11.a.55.50 and New Trench T.11.b.35.80 to T.5.c.70.35.

107th F.A.B.

Zero to Zero plus 1 hour.	Work at T.10.b.3.3 and work at corner of fence T.10.b.6.9.
Zero plus 1 hour to Zero plus 1.hr.58.mins.	Work at corner of fence T.10.b.6.9 and Sunken road T.11.a.55.50 to T.11.a.1.2.
Zero plus 1 hr 58 mins Onwards.	MORVAL MILL and Sunken Road T.11.b.1.8 to T.11.a.8.7.

LEFT GROUP.

Zero to Zero plus 1 hour.	Sunken Road T.10.a.7.5 to T.4.c.4.7 (especially the Northern 100 yards.)
Zero plus 1 hour to Zero plus 1.hr.58.mins.	Road T.10.b.4.7 to T.4.c.75.85, [especially house T.10.b.4.9. (1 Battery for latter.) and cross roads T.4.d.0.6.] and Sunken road T.10.b.65.80 to T.4.b.5.2.
Zero plus 1 hr.58 mins. Onwards.	Search valley E. of a line T.5.c.1.0 to T.4.b.9.4 (especially new trench T.5.c.10.45 to T.5.a.1.3.)

2. After the final Objective is consolidated and the Infantry push out patrols, 4.5" Howitzers will not fire W. of a line T.11.b.5.9 – Cross roads T.5.c.00.65 unless specially ordered.

3. In allotting the above tasks arrangements must be made by Left Group Commander and between Right Group Commander and O.C., 107th F.A.B. for a redistribution of tasks to enable one Battery each to comply with any special call for assistance by G.O's.C. 18th and 16th Infantry Brigades respectively. The call will be made through the Liaison Officer attached to Infantry Brigade H.Qrs.

4. Rates of fire as in Operation Order No.2 para 8.
   Group Commanders will lessen rate of fire after the final Objective has been obtained if the situation so permits.

24th Sept.1916.

B. Crozier Major.R.A.
Brigade Major, Left Centre Divisional Artillery.

TO BREAM & SHRIMP

Sender's Number: JH 169 Day of Month: 21st AAA

During tonight's firing you will pay particular attention to SUNKEN ROAD running NORTH & SOUTH through T.14.d. central. aaa.

Brigade Commander wishes you to check all barrages allotted you for tomorrow's programme by 11 a.m. aaa.

Acknowledge by wire. aaa.

Every care must be taken not to make your barrages too apparent. aaa.

From: Lafuson
Time: 10 p.m.

J.H. Cawley Lieut.

| Handed in at | Office | m. Received | m. |

TO : PRAWN

Sender's Number	Day of Month	In reply to Number	AAA
JH166	24/9/16		

Programme for 4.5" How on 25/9/16 — 3 hrs to zero.

You will fire all the 75 in your possession into an area (to be notified later) in LES BOEUFS village.

Rate of fire as quickly as possible

FROM

PLACE & TIME

Handed in at..Office.................m. Received..................m.

TO Continued

| Sender's Number | Day of Month | In reply to Number | AAA |

Zero to + 1 hour.
Work at T 10 b.33 & work at corner of fence T 10 b 6.9

Zero to + 1 hour

Zero to + 1 hr 58 mins

Work at corner of fence T 10 b 69 & Sunken road T 11 a 55.50 to T 11 a 4.2

FROM

PLACE & TIME

TO	continued.		
Sender's Number	Day of Month	In reply to Number	**A A A**

Zero + 1 hr 58 mins onwards.
MORVAL MILL +
Sunken Road T 11 c 1.8
to T 11 a 8.7
2. After final objective is consolidated
+ the infantry push out patrols
4.5 How will not fire West of a line
T 11 b 5.9 to X roads T 5 b 00 65
unless specially ordered.

FROM	
PLACE & TIME	

TO: BREAM + SHRIMP

Sender's Number: JH 164
Day of Month: 24th

Operation orders No 3 by Lt. Col. O.R. Coates

1. XIV Corps will renew the attack on 25th Rpts. Objectives including the villages of MORVAL, and LES BOEUFS.

2. The 6th Div. part of which 107 F.A.B. is covering, will advance to the attack of 2nd objective as per Map which Adjutant will explain at Zero + 1hr 5hrs. 3rd Obj. Zero + 2 hrs

3. The H. Arty. will bombard the objectives at 7 AM on 24th Rpts. to 6.30 pm and resume again at 6.30 am 25th Rpts.

4. Day & Night firing will be continued as per operation orders JH 141 + 160.

5. 107 F.A.B. will fire the following creeping barrage. Boundary line on South T.10.a.0.8.6 + T.10.c.0.0.45.

FROM:
PLACE & TIME:

| Handed in at | Office | m. Received | m. |

TO: *Continued*

| Sender's Number | Day of Month | In reply to Number | AAA |

6 Contd. Zero plus two starts creeping forward from above line 50x a minute to
BLACK LINE.
BREAM. T.4.c.3½.7½. to T.4.c.5½.4.
SHRIMP. T.4.c.5½.4. to T.4.6.6½.1.

Remarks.
Joins stationary barrage on Blue
LINE and creeps on to 150x beyond BLACK LINE
and remains stationary.
Zero + 2hrs 2 mins. starts creeping forward
50x a minute to BLUE LINE.
BREAM. T.4.b.4.5. to T.4.d.4.9½.
SHRIMP. T.4.d.4.9½. to T.4.d.5.5.
Zero + 2 hrs 9 mins. From BLUE LINE creeps on to
200x beyond and remain there till ordered
to creep on to join stationary barrage on line
MORVAL MILL to shifted by orders.

FROM
PLACE & TIME

| Handed in at | Office | m. Received | m. |

TO Continued.

| Sender's Number | Day of Month | In reply to Number | **A A A** |

5 Cont. Northern boundary GUINCHY – LES BOEUFS
Road from our front line T.3.d.3½.1. to
~~T.9.b.~~ T.d.b.2 & 5. Barrage commencing
200ˣ from blue line. Left gun of BREAM.
will follow road. Right gun of SHRIMP
overlaps 30ˣ to 50ˣ with 2/109 F.A.B. who is
firing South of our line and whom mutual
overlap has been arranged.

6. PROGRAMME of CREEPING BARRAGE.

Zero plus 5 mins. BREAM. T.3.d.7½.3½ to T.9.b.8.9½.
SHRIMP. T.9.b.8.9½ to T.9.b.7½.7.

Remarks above starts 200ˣ from GREENLINE
T.3.d.3¾.1. to T.9.b.4.1.

FROM

PLACE & TIME

		Office m. Received m.
TO	Contain.	

Sender's Number	Day of Month	In reply to Number	AAA

1. Rates of fire.

From Zero plus 5 Min. to Zero plus 10 min — INTENSE.
" " 10 " to " 1 hr. — SLOW.
" " 1 hr. to " 1 hr 15 Min — INTENSE.
" " 2 hrs. to " 2 hrs 15 Min — INTENSE
at other times ordinary.

INTENSE will be 3 Rds per gun per minute.
ORDINARY " 1 Rd " " "
SLOW. " 1 Rd Battery " "

2. Zero time will be notified later.
3. Watches will be synchronised from this office at hours to be notified for later.

Acknowledge

FROM
PLACE & TIME   S.d.   M Cantlay Lieut

Wt. 492—M497 500,000 Pads. HWV 5/16 Forms C.2128.

TO: BREAM & SHRIMP

Sender's Number: JW160
Day of Month: 24
AAA

Operation order No 2

1. The Heavy Bombardment by Heavy Artillery will start at 7 A.M. 24th inst and will continue until 6.30 p.m. to be resumed at 6.30 a.m. 25th and continue until Zero, aaa.

2. During the bombardment fire will reach the ground in front and in rear of the German trenches as well as all known ground and approaches in the areas allotted for day and night firing aaa.
Rate of fire 18 Rounds per gun per hour aaa.

FROM: Johnson

TO	PRAWN		

Sender's Number	Day of Month	In reply to Number	AAA
M160	24th		

Operation order N° 1.

1. The steady bombardment by Heavy Artillery will start at 4 P.M. 24th Inst. and will continue until 6.30 p.m., to be resumed at 6.30 a.m. 25th and continue until Zero. aaa

2. D/How/109 will bombard the SUNKEN ROAD T.11.a.2.3 to T.11.b.1.8½ aaa Rate of fire 10 rounds per gun per hour aaa

FROM: Colaroy 4 p.m.

J H Caulvert Lieut

"A" Form.   Army Form C. 2121.
MESSAGES AND SIGNALS.   No. of Message_____

Prefix....Code....m.	Words	Charge	This message is on a/c of:	Recd. at........m.
Office of Origin and Service Instructions.				Date............
	Sent		..........Service.	From...........
	At........m.			
	To......			
	By		(Signature of "Franking Officer.")	By........

TO   PRAWN

Sender's Number.   Day of Month   In reply to Number   AAA
  JH.168   21

During tonight's firing you
will pay particular attention to
Large House at T.10.b.3½.9,
SUNKEN Road running North and
South through T.4.d. Central, also
new work at T.4.d.9.1. and
its vicinity. aaa.
The Bde Comdr. wishes
to check fuse use and
any targets you can see
allotted you for tomorrow by
11.a.m. aaa.

acknowledge by wire. aaa.

                                J H Cawley Lieut.

From   Telegram
Place   10 a.m.
Time

"A" Form.
MESSAGES AND SIGNALS.

Army Form C. 2121.

No. of Message _____

Prefix _____ Code _____ m. | Words | Charge
Office of Origin and Service Instructions.
_____ Sent
_____ At _____ m.
_____ To _____
_____ By _____

This message is on a/c of:
_____ Service.
(Signature of "Franking Officer.")

Recd. at _____ m.
Date _____
From _____
By _____

TO | PRAWN

Sender's Number. | Day of Month | In reply to Number
JA 168. | 24. | | A A A

during tonight's firing you
will pay particular attention to
large house at T.10.b.3&9
SUNKEN ROAD running North and South
through T.4.d. Central, also new work at
T.4.d.9.1. and its vicinity.

From _____
Place _____
Time _____

The above may be forwarded as now corrected. (Z)

Censor. Signature of Addresser or person authorised to telegraph in his name.
* This line should be erased if not required.

(4198) Wt. W14042—M 4. 300000 Pads. 12/15 Sir J. C. & S.

"A" Form.
MESSAGES AND SIGNALS.

Army Form C.2121 (in pads of 100).

TO ~~RE Group~~
~~Left Group~~
107 FA Bde.

Sender's Number: 127
Day of Month: 24

AAA

Special points for night firing in respective zones. BM 107 of 22nd

* All places bombarded by Heavy Artillery
New trenches.
Strong points.

* Especially area round T4c36 which was not shewn as a place to be bombarded on the coloured tracing issued to Bde Commanders.

From: 24 DA
Place:
Time: 7.45 pm

BM

"A" Form.
MESSAGES AND SIGNALS.

Army Form C.2121 (in pads of 100).

TO ~~MACKE~~ SALMON ~~...~~

Sender's Number.	Day of Month.	In reply to Number.	
* BM 128	24		A A A

Reference this office BM 126 the poison shell (4.5 how. "PS") are to be fired at LESBOEUFS CHURCH as rapidly as possible at zero - 3 hours ie 9.35. (No lachrymatory shell are to be used SK).

From FISH
Place
Time 11.30 pm

(Z) WLewin Lny RA

B.M.126.

~~RIGHT GROUP.~~
~~LEFT GROUP.~~
107th F.A.B.

At Zero minus 3 hours.

Some 600 or 700 rounds in all of poison shell are to be fired simultaneously by all 4.5 Howitzers into an area in LESBOEUFS of not more than 100 square yards. rate - as quickly as possible.

Instructions as to area selected and as to drawing the ammunition will be wired you later under the Office number of this letter.

24/9/16.

Major. R.A.

Brigade Major, (24th Divisional Artillery.)

Left Centre Divisional Artillery.

"C" Form (Duplicate).
MESSAGES AND SIGNALS.
Army Form C. 2123.
(In books of 50's in duplicate.)
No. of Message...................

		Charges to Pay.	Office Stamp.
8/1	KCPM	£ s. d.	
Service Instructions.	F8	Holland	CA 25/9/16

Handed in at.................... Office............ m. Received............ m.

TO: SALMON

Sender's Number	Day of Month	In reply to Number	AAA
BM/136/2	25th		

Night firing for your howitzers vicinity of T6B54 and T6C5065 aaa 25 rounds per howitzer aaa Reference BM 134 barrage will only be pulled back by order from this office in extreme emergency

FROM
PLACE & TIME: F15+1 10.20 pm.

"C" Form (Original).
Army Form C. 2123.
MESSAGES AND SIGNALS

| Prefix SM Code HRPM Words: | Received From FS By | Sent, or sent out At ... m. To ... By | Office Stamp 25/9/16 |

Charges to collect

Service Instructions. FS

Handed in at .... Office .... m. Received 9p m.

TO **SALMON**

| *Sender's Number | Day of Month | In reply to Number | AAA |
| BM 134 | 25th | | |

Night barrage for 18 prs T12B06 to T5B38 aaa Dividing the line between groups through T5C00 and T5D76 aaa SALMON HAKE northern third of right groups zone aaa Barrage fire at intervals, also search valleys, roads and approaches aaa Expenditure 50 rounds per gun during night aaa More if required aaa Should enemy counter attack in force barrage must be prepared to drop straight back to 300 yds beyond BLUE line, thus jumping over our infantry post aaa Acknowledge Addressed HAKE SALMON and ROACH

FROM FISH

PLACE & TIME 8.45 pm

TO PRAWN

Sender's Number: AH 185. Day of Month: 25th. AAA

Nyht firing aaa

You will fire on SUNKEN Road and its vicinity from T.6.6.5.4 – T.6.6.5.6½. aaa Rate of fire 25 Rds per gun per hour from receipt of this to 6.30 A.M. aaa. Please acknowledge by wire aaa.

J.H. Curtayne Lieut

From: Bala...
Place: 10.35...
Time:

				This message is on a/c of:		Recd. at .... m.
Office of Origin and Service Instructions.		Sent				Date ....
....		At .... m.			Service.	From ....
....		To		(Signature of "Franking Officer.")		By ....
		By				

TO — **BREAM & SHRIMP**

Sender's Number.	Day of Month	In reply to Number		AAA
A 183	25th			

Night barrage fire Brigade
will be as follows aaa.

SHRIMP ~~T5d.8~~ ~~T5d.4~~ ~~5~~
T5d.4.v. — T5d.3. & 3½.

BREAM ~~T5d~~ ~~T5d~~
T5d.3.3½ — T5d.2.5.

 on left fire occasional
bursts of fire on this
line and in addition to keep
Gonch villey pass & approaches
beyond this line. aaa
Rate of fire
50 Rounds per gun during
the night (re.) from 6.30 p.m. to
6.30 a.m. more if required aaa
This is for SOS Lines.

From				
Place				
Time				

The above may be forwarded as now corrected. (Z)

Censor. Signature of Addresser or person authorised to telegraph in his name.
* This line should be erased if not required.

(4198) Wt. W14042—M 4. 80,000 Pads. 12/15 Sir J. C. & S

for tonight aaa In case of
an attack you may be
required to drop our barrage
back as follows:—

SHRIMP T.5.c.3.2 — T.5.c.2.3½

BREAM T.5.c.2.3½ — T.5.c.2.5

aaa In will not drop back
to this line without orders
from this office aaa.

aaa. Please acknowledge by begint.

From   Belmy
Place   O.1. B.M
Time

"A" Form. Army Form C. 2121.
MESSAGES AND SIGNALS. No. of Message_____

TO PRAWN

Sender's Number: JH.170 Day of Month: 25 AAA

P.S. You will fire four Shell at LESBOEUFS Church as rapidly as possible at Zero - 3 hours. i.e. 9.35 A.M. 25th Septr. aaa

From Salmon
Place
Time 7 AM

"A" Form.   Army Form C. 2121.
MESSAGES AND SIGNALS.

TO PRAWN

Sender's Number: M209 Day of Month: 26 AAA

... road ... and ... right
... will be ... to follow
for tonight ...

Track junctions @
(1) T.12.a.5.7. (Scot)
(2) T.12.a.6.4. (Gen)
...

Rate of fire 20 rounds per
gun until 6.30 A.M.

The Colonel would like to
see Capt. FOSTER at Bn H.Q. @
9.30 A.M. tomorrow morning 27th instant

From Place: Salmon
Time: 10 p.m.

J.H. Curtis

"A" Form. Army Form C. 2121.
MESSAGES AND SIGNALS. No. of Message_____

Prefix_____ Code_____ m. | Words | Charge | This message is on a/c of: | Recd. at_____ m.
Office of Origin and Service Instructions. | | | | Date_____
_____ | Sent At_____ m. | | _____ Service. | From_____
_____ | To_____ By_____ | | (Signature of "Franking Officer.") | By_____

TO BREAM

Sender's Number. | Day of Month | In reply to Number | A A A
JH 207 | 21st | |

[illegible handwritten message]

T6 68 - 76 28
SUNKEN ROAD ...
... 100 yards ...
...
...

From _____
Place _____
Time _____

The above may be forwarded as now corrected. (Z)
Censor. Signature of Addressor or person authorised to telegraph in his name.
* This line should be erased if not required.

"A" Form.

Army Form C. 2121.

MESSAGES AND SIGNALS.

No. of Message

Prefix ... Code ... m. Office of Origin and Service Instructions.	Words	Charge	This message is on a/c of: ... Service. (Signature of "Franking Officer.")	Recd. at ... m. Date ... From ... By ...
	Sent At ... m. To ... By ...			

TO SHRIMP

Sender's Number.	Day of Month	In reply to Number	AAA

Our guns fire barrage and lift jumping with 1st a[illegible] as follows the SUNKEN ROAD @ T.6.c.6.0 – T.6.c.6.8 Two [illegible] for firing aaa Rate of fire 30 rounds per gun during the lift [illegible] Z 20 [illegible] 60% Shrapnel 50% H.E. to be used. Ends.

From Calonne

Place

Time 9.50 pm

The above may be forwarded as now corrected. (Z)

Censor. Signature of Addressor or person authorised to telegraph in his name. J. H. [illegible]

* This line should be erased if not required.

(4198) Wt. W14042—M 4. 300000 Pads. 12/15 Sir J. C. & S

	* Sent At ● m. To ● By	Service. ● (Signature of "Franking Officer.")	Date. From. By
TO	PRAWN.		

Sender's Number.	Day of Month	In reply to Number	
* AA95.	26		A A A

Enemy battery firing from N.76.C.52.43 on
20 Rds I believe you all step
_ _ by the _ _
this Target was also fire on
SUNKEN ROAD in T.6.C. and
rate of fire _ _ _
_ _ _.

From: _
Place: _
Time: _

TO: BREAM SHRIMP

Sender's Number: M.193 Day of Month: 26 AAA

Please search *[illegible handwritten message]*

"A" Form. Army Form C. 2121.

MESSAGES AND SIGNALS. No. of Message

Prefix .... Code .... m. Words 30 Charge

FS

TO Palmer

Sender's Number: BM 145 Day of Month: 26 In reply to Number

AAA

Ref BM 761 para 6
+ BM 144 aaa
Target for 18 p⁰ Sunken Rd
T6c60 to T6a68 aaa
Hows Track junctions
T12a52 & T12a64

From: FISH
Time: 9.35 pm

"A" Form.   Army Form C. 2121.

MESSAGES AND SIGNALS.

Prefix ...... Code ...... Words: 21

FS

TO: Salmon

Sender's Number: BM 116   Day of Month: 26   AAA

Ref BM 761 para 5 aaa Barrage comes into force at 10.15 pm aaa ack

From: FISH   9.45

SECRET.

LEFT CENTRE DIVISIONAL ARTILLERY.

BM/466

Arrangements for relief of 24th Divisional Artillery by 4th Divisional Artillery.

1. The 24th Divisional Artillery will be relieved in the line by the 4th Divisional Artillery, half on night 27th/28th and the remainder before noon on the 28th September.

2. **RIGHT GROUP.**

   Lt.Col.E.R.BURNE, D.S.O. and 106th & 109th F.A.Brigades will be relieved by Lt.Col.TILNEY and 32nd F.A.Brigade (plus 1 Battery 29th F.A.Brigade.)

   Lt.Col.D.R.COATES and the 107th F.A.Brigade will be relieved by Lt.Col.HEAD and the 29th F.A.Brigade (less 1 Battery.)

   LEFT GROUP.

   Lt.Col.E.C.W.D.WALTHALL, D.S.O., and the 108th F.A.Brigade will be relieved by Lt.Col.LLOYD, D.S.O. and the 14th F.A.Brigade.

3. Only half the guns or howitzers of each Brigade will be relieved at one time.
   Details to be arranged between Group Commanders

4. Guns will not be handed over.
   All ammunition dumps will be handed over.

5. The 24th D.A.C. will be relieved before noon on the 28th inst. under arrangements to be made between O's C.

6. Trench Mortar Batteries will also be relieved on the 28th inst. in reserve under arrangements to be made between D.T.M.'s.

7. Brigades will march on the 28th September probably to neighbourhood of MORLANCOURT, under orders to be issued later.
   The 24th Divisional Artillery will be clear of their wagon lines before 12 noon. On the 29th inst. the Divisional Artillery will march to TALMAS.

8. The G.O.C., 24th Divisional Artillery will hand over command of the "Left Centre" Divisional Artillery, XIVth Corps to G.O.C.,R.A. 4th Divisional Artillery at 8.a.m. on 28th September,

   Group Commanders of 24th Divisional Artillery will hand over Command by 12 noon on 28th September.

27/9/16.   Acknowledge   Brown   Major.R.A.
                            Brigade Major, Left Centre Divisional Artillery.

RIGHT GROUP. L.C.D.A.
107th F.A.B.
LEFT GROUP. L.C.D.A.
24th D.A.C.
24th D.T.M.O.
194 Coy.A.S.C.
Staff Captain.R.A.
6th Div."G"
24th Div."G"
24th Div."Q"

	m.	Words	Charge	This message is on a/c of:		Recd. at	m.
Office of Origin and Service Instructions.		Sent			Service.	Date	
		At	m.			From	
		To					
		By		(Signature of "Franking Officer.")		By	

TO   O C PRaw.

Sender's Number.	Day of Month	In reply to Number	AAA
JH. 10	24		

JH 11 Please cancel my number
JH 11 AAA and send following instead
will be as follows AAA

One section Track Junction
T.6.C.6.1.

One section Track Junction
T.6.C.5.4.

Release per JH.11   AAA

From: Saturn
Place:
Time:

The above may be forwarded as now corrected. (Z)

Censor.   Signature of Addressor or person authorised to telegraph in his name.
* This line should be erased if not required.

(4198) Wt. W14042—M 4. 300000 Pads. 12/15 Sir J. C. & S

"A" Form.
MESSAGES AND SIGNALS.
Army Form C. 2121.

| Prefix...Code...m. | Words | Charge | This message is on a/c of: | Recd. at......m. |
| | Sent At...m. To... By... | | ......Service (Signature of "Franking Officer.") | Date... From... By... |

TO SHRIMP

Sender's Number: GHJ
Day of Month: 27th
AAA

The following barrage will be required for a "CHINESE" ATTACK this afternoon.

ZERO 2.15 p.m.

You will fire a creeping barrage as follows commencing at above time on the line T5d.1.5½. to T6d.5½.4 It will advance at 50 yards a min until barrage reaches enemy's trenches in N35b when fire will stop. Rate of fire 2 rounds a gun per min please. See map attached & then BREAM map to be returned by orderly.

From
Place
Time 12·40 pm

Johnson

(Z)

TO BREAM

Sender's Number: JH6
Day of Month: 27th
AAA

The following barrage will be required for a CHINESE ATTACK this afternoon.

ZERO 2.15 pm
You will fire a creeping barrage as follows commencing at above hour.

T 5 d 1.5½ T 5 c 6 7
will advance 50x a minute until barrage reaches enemy trenches in N 35 b when fire will stop. Rate of fire 2 rounds a gun per min acknowledge

"A" Form.   Army Form C. 2121.

MESSAGES AND SIGNALS.

Prefix ... Code ... Words ... Charge ...
Office of Origin and Service Instructions: FS

Recd. at 7.58 a.m.
Date 27/9/16
From SA FS
By Payne

TO: Salmon

Sender's Number: BM 157
Day of Month: 27th
AAA

Brigade march to Bois des Tailles tomorrow HAKE 7.30 SALMON 8am ROACH 8.30am SEAL 9.0 DAC 9.30am aaa Billeting parties meet Staff Capt at Camp Commandant office 8am aaa Brigades to use track as far as possible detail of roads available not yet received aaa Sections not relieved by hour of start will follow under Brigade arrangements aaa address Brigades + wagon lines

From / Place / Time: Fish 7.30pm

"A" Form.
MESSAGES AND SIGNALS
Army Form C. 2121.

TO: ~~Right Front~~ ~~Left Front~~ 107 Bde.

Sender's Number	Day of Month	In reply to Number	AAA
BM 151	27		

Ref a standing and creeping barrage required today for a CHINESE attack orders for which will be sent by wire

Zero hour will be 2.15 p.m.

From: Left Centre BA
Place:
Time: 8.30 a.m.

Major RA

"A" Form. Army Form C. 2121.
MESSAGES AND SIGNALS. No. of Message_____

Prefix ___ Code ___ m. | Words | Charge | This message is on a/c of: | Recd. at 12.75
Office of Origin and Service Instructions. | | | | Date 27.9.16
_____ | Sent | | _____ Service. | From F5
F5 | At ____ m. | | | By _____
Priorili | To ____ | | (Signature of "Franking Officer.") |
 | By ____ | | |

TO { SA

Sender's Number | Day of Month | In reply to Number |
BM154/2 27TH | | | AAA

Ll Zero aaa Creeping Barrage T5D5&4 to T5C67 Start at 50 yds a minute aaa fire will STOP when barrage reaches trenches in N35B aaa Rate Intense two rds per minute

From Place: F15H
Time: 12 noon

The above may be forwarded as now corrected. (Z)

Censor. Signature of Addressor or person authorised to telegraph in his name.

* This line should be erased if not required.

O.C. 107 Bde. R.F.A

24th DIV. ARTY
March Table.

The 24th D.A. will march tomorrow to the area ORVILLE, AMPLIER, AUTHIEULE, BRETEL, HEM, moving via BEAUVAL – & leaving their present billets at following times to destinations as under:–

		Time of leaving
106th to	AUTHIEULE	2-30 p.m.
107th to	ORVILLE	2- pm
108th to	BRETEL	2-30 pm
109 to	AMPLIER	3- pm
D.A.C. to	HEM	2- pm

Billeting parties of Bdes & D.A.C. will meet Staff Captain as follows

106th	AUTHIEULE	– 12-30 pm
107th	ORVILLE	– 11 am
108th	BRETEL	– 1-15 pm
109th	AMPLIER	– 11-45 am
D.A.C.	HEM	– 2 pm

Billeting Certificates will be handed to Mayor of Villages before leaving.

REFILLING POINT

On the main BEAUVAL–DOULLENS Road (at the H in HAMENCOURT about 1 mile S of DOULLENS Citadelle (Ref Map: LENS 1/100,000) Guides to be at this point at 2 pm to conduct Supply Wagons to their units

29/9/16

R.H.M.
Captain
Staff Captain, 24 Div. ARTY.

24th DIVISIONAL ARTILLERY MARCH TABLE.

1. All times in this Order are ~~Greenwich Mean Time~~ Standard Time, Standard time being put back one hour – 3 – 2.a.m. on the night 30th September / 1st October.

2. 24th D.A. will march to-morrow as under from present billets to BLANGERMONT, BLANGERVAL, BOUBERS – SUR – CANCHE, LIGNY – SUR – CANCHE, VACQUERIE – LE – BOUCQ, route via OCCOCHES – BARLY – BONNIERES, the whole to be clear of BARLY by 11.a.m.

	FROM.	TO.	STARTING AT.
D.A.C.	HEM.	BOUBERS – SUR – CANCHE.	6–15.a.m.
108 F.A.B.	BRETEL.	"	7–30.a.m.
106 " " "	AUTHIEULE.	"	7–15.a.m.
107 " " "	AMPLIER.	LIGNY – SUR – CANCHE.	7–15.a.m.
109 " " "	AMPLIER.	"	7–45.a.m.

Destinations of 108th 106th & 109th Brigades are not yet allotted.

3. Billeting parties will meet the Staff Captain at VACQUERIE – LE – BOUCQ Church at 7–30.a.m.

4. Refilling Point will be FREVENT STATION at 11.a.m.

30/9/16.

(Sd) B.CROZIER. Major.R.A.

Brigade Major, 24th Divisional Artillery.

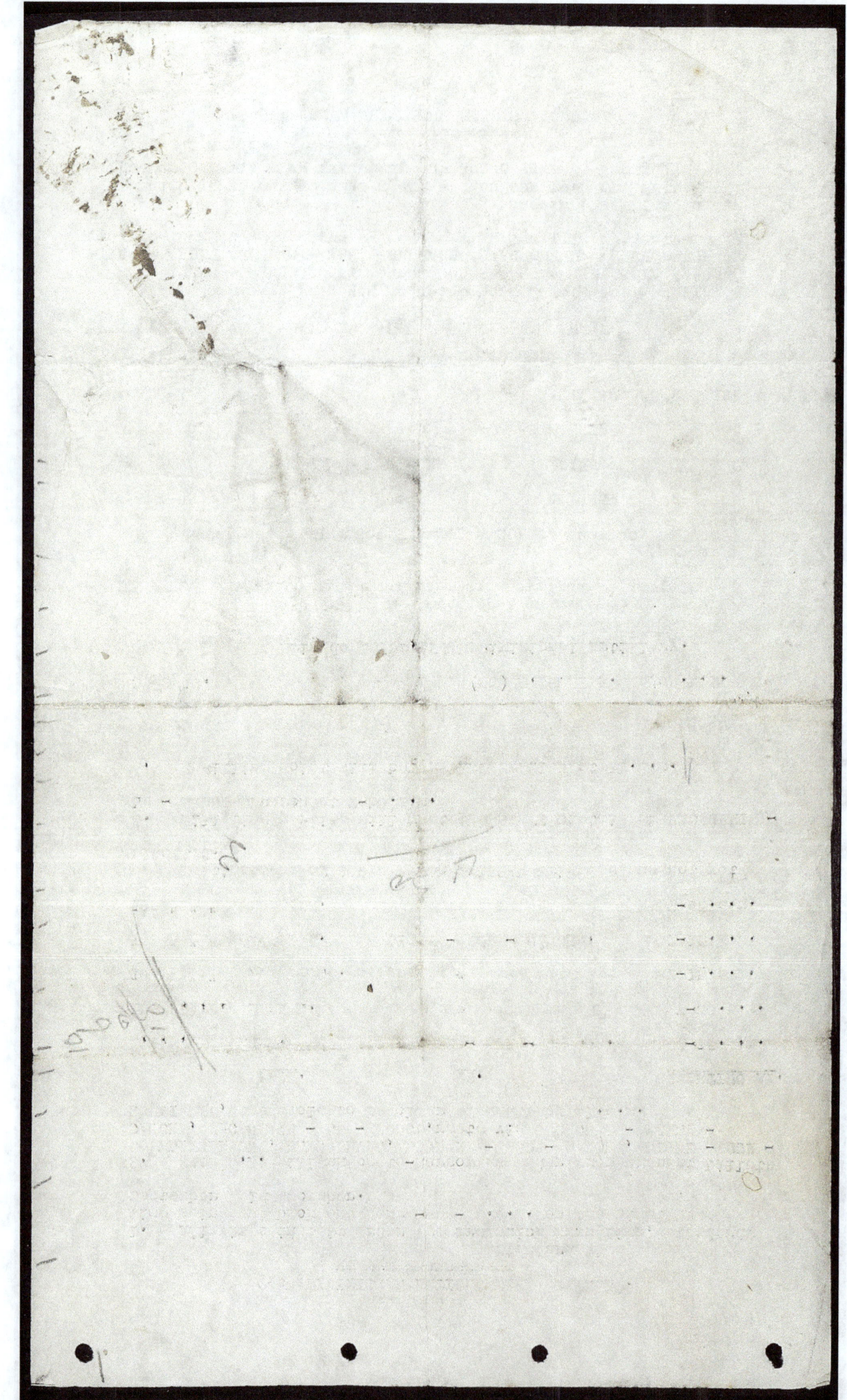

Army Form C. 2118.

WAR DIARY
or
INTELLIGENCE SUMMARY.
(Erase heading not required.)

107/F.A/S.A.C.

VOL 13
24
XXXV

Place	Date	Hour	Summary of Events and Information	Remarks and references to Appendices
	October			
	1st		107 F.A.B. marched to LIGNY-SUR-CANCHE, and billeted for night.	Map Ref. LENS 11. 1/100,000 Macdonwall
	2nd		107 F.A.B. marched to MAREST and billeted for night. A Battery en route shelled. 107 F.A.B.	ditto
	3rd		107 F.A.B. marched to Bivouac in trenches BOIS d'OLHAIN Q.15.C.N.W. one section per battery. 107 F.A.B. relieved 52nd Bde 9" F.A. on right, and 2 guns under Rt. Group attached 4 guns under 6" F.A. on right.	Map Ref. 36.b.SE. 1/10000
			A/107 relieved of 6v. B/107 " C/50. C/107 " C/6v. D/107 " D/6v.	BM 266 attached
	4th		107 F.A.B. relieved remaining batteries of 52 F.A.B. position just north as under: A/107. X.4.C.5.5. C/107. X.3.9.2.6. } all batteries reported. D/107. X.4.C.8.3.	Map Ref. 36.b.S.E. 1/10000
Bois de Bouvigny	5th		107 F.A.B. HQ Os moved up into 52nd Bde HQ Bn position at X.2.b.5.3. relief completed 12 noon.	

WAR DIARY
or
INTELLIGENCE SUMMARY.

Army Form C. 2118.

XXXVI

Place	Date	Hour	Summary of Events and Information	Remarks and references to Appendices
Bois de Bruny.	6th		Situation normal. Infantry called for Retaliation S.13 m of Givenchy.	Maps Ref. VIMY. 36.C.SW. Special attached.
	7th		" " " " " " " " " "	
			A minor Enterprise was carried out by the 4/3rd I.B. which was quite successful, one two and one dead hun being captured in the raid. 10th F.A.B. barraged as per Bard orders attached. A107. C114 checked registrations.	
	8th		Situation normal.	
		2.45pm	Army Regis fired.	
		3.45pm	Retaliation S.13 called for by infantry, all batteries fired.	
	9th	10.15am	Situation normal.	
		2pm	Retaliation S.C. called for by infantry all batteries fired.	
		3pm	27th Inf. Bgd. fired Zero line.	
	10th	10.15am	Hy + Shy fired on retaliation S.7c being called for by infantry.	
		11.15pm	" " " " " " " " " " " "	
		4.15pm	Hostile movement, guns, horses and trucks in Avion.	
	11th	11am	Situation normal. Army Shy. Bty opened.	
		12.00pm	3/1st Cab. Bde 9th W. S.9.a + 3.Z. worked out very effectively.	Maps Ref. VIMY 36. C.S.W.

Army Form C. 2118.

WAR DIARY
or
INTELLIGENCE SUMMARY.
(Erase heading not required.)

XXXVII

Instructions regarding War Diaries and Intelligence Summaries are contained in F. S. Regs., Part II. and the Staff Manual respectively. Title pages will be prepared in manuscript.

Place	Date	Hour	Summary of Events and Information	Remarks and references to Appendices
Basra	12th		Relieved from in Futuri Depôt. Lt Col Spiller to England on leave. Major	Staff R/ 36.C.S.W.3 Ed.76 Operation 01 attached
Benigny		9 a.m.	[illegible] on operation orders/reply Major D.S.O. assumes Supreme Command.	
		9 a.m.	Enemy reported the Rapids 54 a & c	
		10 am	Dupes	
		11 am	People on fire	36.C.S.W.3 Ed.76 Operation 08 attached
			Commenced preparations for operations orders N° 8 [illegible] to Tigris	
		11.30 am		
			[illegible] attacks positions at x9 b 84	
			[illegible]	
			[illegible]	
			[illegible]	Operation 1st attached
		10 pm	[illegible] enemy [illegible] position x h 00 c 10	
			[illegible] an operation order N°10 [illegible] for the	Operation N°10 attached
		5 pm	Chryshoad at Dupes a few [illegible]	
			[illegible]	

2353/ Wt. W2541/1454 700,000 5/15 D. D. & L. A.D.S.S./Forms/C. 2118.

Army Form C. 2118.

WAR DIARY
or
INTELLIGENCE SUMMARY.
(Erase heading not required.)

XXXVIII

Instructions regarding War Diaries and Intelligence Summaries are contained in F. S. Regs., Part II. and the Staff Manual respectively. Title pages will be prepared in manuscript.

Place	Date	Hour	Summary of Events and Information	Remarks and references to Appendices
Boesinghe	17th	11 am	Carrying out work as per operation order no. 10	Map Ref. 36 C Sw 3 Ed. 4. b.
		2 pm	Coy reported 5.8 fire from 10am Rifle	
		4 pm	Cut wire as per O.O. no. 10	
		3 pm	Army fired at Manuscript Side 5.3	
		4 pm	Cut wire as per operation order no. 10	
	18th	4/17 Bn	417 Bn arrived and forming preparations as per operation order no. 7	
		4 hrs		
		5 pm	Enemy very lively. Enfilading road heavily. Left flank of 7.15pm retained reply without returning	
			Co. Relay Land Lg shrapnel of H.V. 7a.13.pm Cd d.36.a.a	Operation order no. 11 attached
			Situation normal	
	19th		Situation normal operation order no. 11	
	20th		Situation normal.	
	21st		Situation normal.	
	22nd		Situation normal.	

Army Form C. 2118.

WAR DIARY
or
INTELLIGENCE SUMMARY.
(Erase heading not required.)

XXXIX

Instructions regarding War Diaries and Intelligence Summaries are contained in F. S. Regs., Part II. and the Staff Manual respectively. Title pages will be prepared in manuscript.

Place	Date	Hour	Summary of Events and Information	Remarks and references to Appendices
	23rd		Situation normal. 18 prs fired on J.3. Area at Infantry's request.	
	24th		Situation normal. Lt. Col Spiller returned from leave and took over Command Right Group.	
	25th		Major G.E. Popham D.S.O. L. Popham on leave. Major J.E.S. Brown assumed temporary Command in his absence.	
	26th		Situation Normal.	
	27th		Jorn Officers appt Lt. H.L. Webber, 2/Lt W.I. Beacon, 2/Lt J.M. Cooper 2/Lt A.O. Foster. Posted away to 40th D.A. Weather is hindering observation and work.	
	28th		Normal.	
	29th		Normal.	
	30th		Normal. Capt W.S.N. Cale on leave to England.	
	31st		Normal.	

[signature] R.F.A.
Lt. Col.,
Commanding 167th Brigade, R.F.A.

O.C. "GINGER" Secret.

Following received from CORKSCREW
"
1. At 9.20 a.m. to-morrow the 176th Tunnelling Coy are going to blow two small mines between NEWER CUT CRATER & MILDREN Crater.

2. 12th R.F. are going to vacate their front line & saps between THIEPET trench & RABINEAU trench at 9.15 a.m. & will re-occupy it immediately mines have been blown.

3. Mines are merely being exploded to blow in a HUN gallery.

4. Could you please arrange for Artillery to be standing by ready to retaliate opposite these craters in case the enemy annoy us with Trench Mortars. "

Please arrange for necessary retaliation if called for & warn your liaison officer with 12th R.F.

11 10/16

C. Mosworth Lt R.A.
Adjt. Left Group
R.F.A.

OPERATION ORDER NO.7.
BY
LIEUT. COLONEL D.W.L. SPILLER., COMMANDING 107/F.A/BRIGADE.

Copy No. 1.   S E C R E T.   11th October 1916.

1.   At 9.20 a.m to-morrow the 12th instant the 176 Tunnelling Company are going to blow two small mines between NEWER CUT CRATER and MILDREN CRATER both in S 6 d., N.E.Corner.

2.   12th RIF's are going to vacate their front line and saps between THIERET trench and RABINEAU trench at 9.15 a.m. and will occupy it immediately mines have been blown.

3.   You will please stand by ready to retaliate opposite these craters, in case the enemy annoy our infantry with trench mortars.

4.   Liason Officer must be warned to keep in touch with 12th R.F's, and to keep this Office informed of the situation.

Copy No. 1 War diary.
        2. A/107.
        3. C/107.
        4. D/107.

                                                    Lieut. R.F.A.
                                        Adjutant 107/F.A/Brigade.

OPERATION ORDER NO.9.
BY

MAJOR G.L. POPHAM D.S.O.,   COMMANDING 107/F.A/BRIGADE.

Copy No. 1.   S E C R E T.   14th October 1916.

S.O.S. BARRAGES.

Previous orders with regard to S.O.S. are cancelled and the following substituted.

A/107 North and South line between points S 3 c ¼.6 to S 9 a ¼.7.

C/107 North and South line between points S 9 a ¼.7 to S 9 a ¼.3 and along trench to S 9 c 0.8½.

Rate of fire will be 6 rounds gun fire followed by Section fire 10 secs., Subsequent procedure according to tactical situation.

NIGHT FIRING.

1.   A/107 along trench tramway running N.E. between points S 9 a 6.6 to where it cuts trench at S 4 c 2.7½.
2.   Along track from S 3 d 2½.6¼ to S 3 d 7¼.8¾.

1.   C/107 along trench tramway running east between points S 9 a 6.6 to point S 3 d 9½.0 to where it cuts road.
2.   Along track from S 3 d 7¼.8¾ to S 4 a 2½.8½.

Rate of fire 20 to 30 rounds per battery per night at irregular intervals.

In future all references will be:- Reference Map VIMY 36 c S.W.3 Edition 7 (redrawn) 'B.

Airplane photos No's 16 a 93, 16 a 48 will be circulated and all tracks will be noted and fired at occasionally, as part of Night Firing programme.

Copy No.1 War diary.
     2. A/107.
     3. C/107.
     4. D/107.
     5. Left Group.

                                                Lieut. R.F.A.
                                      Adjutant 107/F.A/Brigade.

OPERATION ORDER NO.10.
BY
MAJOR G.L.POPHAM D.S.O., COMMANDING 107/F.A/BRIGADE.

Copy No. 1. SECRET. 14th October 1916.

1. A/107 and C/107 will cut wire on the 16th and 17th instant.

2. C/107 will, with one gun take up a forward position, range about 2000 yards, from wire to be cut, and will cut as wide a gap as possible at S 9 a 1½.8½ (astride road)

3. A/107 will cut wire from present position, at the following points, S 9 a ½.5 - S 9 a 1½.7 - S 3 c 2.2. *2 p.m. to 4 p.m.*

4. C/107 will fire on 16th and 17th instant from 11.a.m to 1.p.m. & A/107 " " during the day, at hours other than those allotted to C/107.

5. Amount of ammunition to be expended will be notified later.

Copy No 1. War diary.
2. A/107.
3. C/107.
4. Left Group.

Lieut. R.F.A.
Adjutant 107/F.A/Brigade.

OPERATION ORDER No.11

BY

MAJOR G.L. POPHAM, D.S.O., COMMANDING 107 F.A.BRIGADE.

Copy No. 1.   SECRET.   19th October 1916.

1. GAS ALERT.

Previous instructions issued to Batteries while it is "GAS ALERT" are to be strictly observed.

2. S.O.S. SIGNAL.

The S.O.S. Signal consisting of three green rockets will be sent up from Battalion Headquarters at S.6.b.2.4. Bearings should be taken by all Batteries from guns to this point and steps be taken to mark the direction for the information of the Guard.

3. GUARD.

The Officer mounting Guard with each Battery will satisfy himself, that all members of the Guard are thoroughly acquainted with the S.O.S. Signal, i.e., three green rockets, and the direction it will be seen.

4.   B.C.s will please ensure that the instructions contained in foregoing are carried out.

Copy No.1 War Diary.
2 A/107.
3 C/107.
4 B/107.

Lieut., F.A.
Adjutant, 107 F.A. Brigade.

Operation No 8 by Lt Col H.W.R. Spiller Cmdg 107 F.A.B.

Artillery Programme.

For the morning of the 14th Inst. In Conjunction with 108 F.A.B. and 2' T.M.

Battery	Time From	Time To	Objective	Projectile	Rate of Fire	Remarks
"D" How /107.	4 A.M.	4.10 A.M.	One Gun on Trench Junct. S.9.c.10.69. " " " 89.c.12.83.	B.X.	2 Rds per gun per min.	One additional allotment of 408x is made from 6 rounds This operation.
"A" /107.	4 A.M.	4.40 A.M.	One gun on trench S9c1373 - S9c4660 " " " S9c1383 - S9c4510	60% A 40% A.X.	4 A.M. to 4.5 A.M. 3 Rds per gun per min	Areas up to 6.100m Recker sides of Comms trenches named are to be swept.
	4.45 A.M.	4.50 A.M.			4.5 a.m. to 4.40 a.m. 1 Rd per gun per min at irregular intervals.	
					4.45 a.m. to 4.50 a.m. 3 rds per gun per min.	

trenches will be synchronised at 10 p.m. to-night and an officer per Bttty will attend the phone at that hour.

Please acknowledge by wire.

13/16

J.H. Curshaw Capt
Adjt 107 F.A.B.

Secret. CN/11.

Artillery Programme
for the morning of the 14th inst.

Battery	TIME from — To	Objective	Projectile	Rate of Fire	Remarks
*D/107.	4 a.m — 4.10 a.m	{ one gun on Trench Junction S.q.c.10.69. " " " " S.q.c.12.83.	} Bx	2 rds per gun per minute	
*/107 (18Pdr) (A-C)	4 a.m — 4.40 a.m 4.45 a.m — to 4.50 a.m	{ one 18 Pdr gun on Trench S.q.c.13.73 — S.q.c.46.60 " " " " S.q.c.13.83 — S.q.a.42.10.	} 60% A. 40% Ax.	4-0 to 4-5 a.m 3 rds per gun per min 4-5 to 4-40 a.m 1 rd per gun per min at irregular intervals 4-45 – 4-50 a.m 3 rds per gun per min	Area it to 100× on either side of communication trenches are not to be swept.

* An additional allotment of 40 Bx is made to you to cover the function.

Watches to be synchronised at 10 p.m. tonight.

Acknowledge by wire.

Monro ??
Lt-Col. RFA
Comdg. 108 Bde R.F.A.

Copies all
Bdes 3.10.16

24th DIVISIONAL ARTILLERY.

Relief of 9th Divisional Artillery.   B.M.766.

1. Reference previous instructions for relief of 9th Divisional Artillery, the following amendments have been made in the LEFT GROUP.

The 107th Brigade will relieve the 52nd Brigade and the

108th Brigade will relieve the 50th Brigade.

The 107th. having one Battery detached - 4 guns under the 60th Divisional Artillery on the right and 2 guns under the Right Group.

2. The table issued on 1st inst. is cancelled and the following substituted.

Unit of 24th D.A.	Hands over to 9th D.A.	AT
106.	Corresponding Battery of 51st.	GAUCHIN LEGAL.
A/109(Rt X)	A/51.	" "
A/109(L.X.)	B/51.	" "
B/109(Rt.X)	C/51.	" "
A/107 & B/109(L.X.)	A/52.	GAUCHIN LEGAL.
C/107 & C/109(L.X.)	C/52.	" "
D/107.	D/52.	" "
C/108 & A/108(Rt.X)	A/50.	CAUCOURT.
B/108 & A/108(L.X.)	B/50.	GAUCHIN LEGAL.
D/108.	D/50.	CAUCOURT.
B/107 & C/109(Rt.X)	C/50.	GAUCHIN LEGAL.
D.A.C.	Corresponding Unit.	CAUCOURT.

Guides from 9th Divisional Artillery will meet Batteries, etc. in OLHAIN on arrival to direct the guns and ammunition wagons.

3. The Command of the Divisional Artillery in the line will pass to G.O.C.,R.A. 24th Division at 10.a.m. on the 5th October. Command of Brigades and Batteries on completion of relief as previously arranged.

2/10/16.

Major.R.A.
Brigade Major, 24th Divisional Artillery.

Copies to
106 F.A.B.   24th D.A.C.
107th " "   Staff Captain,R.A.,24th D.A.
108th " "   9th D.A.
109th " "

107" Bde RFA Army Form C. 2118.

40

05/14

WAR DIARY
or
INTELLIGENCE SUMMARY.

(Erase heading not required.)

Instructions regarding War Diaries and Intelligence Summaries are contained in F. S. Regs., Part II. and the Staff Manual respectively. Title pages will be prepared in manuscript.

Place	Date	Hour	Summary of Events and Information	Remarks and references to Appendices
		1.	Situation Normal. Our activity mainly night firing	
		2.	Situation Normal.	
		3.	Situation Normal.	
		4.	Quiet — night uneventful. 2/Lts Wilk & Evans to Gunnery Course at Army school	
		5.	Enemy Trench Mortars slightly more active. 2/Lt Wilkinson Shorland, Hobin and Poole to Ladder D.A.	
		6.	Normal — Enemy machine gun active from Souchez Valley. Col. & Spiller Commanding the Group. Major Popham RA Brig Dr	
		7.	Situation normal	
		8.	Normal.	
		9.	Our Artillery more active. A & C Btys registering by aeroplane.	
		10.	Normal.	
		11.	Normal	
		12.	Misty. Our heavies active on left.	
		13.	Normal. Major Popham goes to 24th D.A. School. Major Cowan takes command of his Brigade — HQrs move to this Battery.	
		14.	Normal.	
		15.	Normal	
		16.	A considerable amount of retaliation asked for	

2353 Wt. W2544/1454 700,000 5/15 D. D. & L. A.D.S.S./Forms/C. 2118.

WAR DIARY or INTELLIGENCE SUMMARY.

Army Form C. 2118.

Place	Date	Hour	Summary of Events and Information	Remarks and references to Appendices
	17.		Situation normal.	
	18.		Misty. 20.0 put up French Board at Ind Crata	
	19.		Enemy Trench Mortar activity has afterwards increased Capt Galloway & Capt Ryan to Gunnery Course at Larkhill	
	20.		Normal. Capt McCombie invalided to England Capt Galloway promotion major (London Gazette)	
	21.		Normal.	
	22.		Normal.	
	23.		Colonel Spillers returns from commanding the Group.	
	24.		Situation normal. Lt Cautley returns after sick leave in England.	
	25.		Situation normal	
	26.		Situation normal	
	27.		Situation normal	
	28.	9.50pm	2nd Canadian I.B. raided enemy trenches S15A 10.25 - S15C44. Right party entered & found none of the enemy. Left party found trenches heavily manned & came back. Mine was exploded. The	4

Army Form C. 2118.

WAR DIARY
or
INTELLIGENCE SUMMARY.

(Erase heading not required.)

Instructions regarding War Diaries and Intelligence Summaries are contained in F. S. Regs., Part II. and the Staff Manual respectively. Title pages will be prepared in manuscript.

42

Place	Date	Hour	Summary of Events and Information	Remarks and references to Appendices
	28/10		Brigade barraged to the North of the attack.	
	29		Situation normal. Misty.	
	30		Situation normal.	

L. Buller
LIEUT COL., R.F.A.
COMMANDING 107TH BRIGADE, R.F.A.

Army Form C. 2118.

Vol / 5 24

107 Bde R.F.A.
43

WAR DIARY
or
INTELLIGENCE SUMMARY.
(Erase heading not required.)

Instructions regarding War Diaries and Intelligence Summaries are contained in F. S. Regs., Part II. and the Staff Manual respectively. Title pages will be prepared in manuscript.

Place	Date	Hour	Summary of Events and Information	Remarks and references to Appendices
Vimy	1.		Situation normal	
	2.		Situation normal. 1st part of relief of 24 DA by 10th DA	Relief Order attached.
	3.		Relief completed by 10th DA. Relief of 40 DA by 24 DA begun	
	4.		Relief completed by 24 DA. Brigade covers front line in Magnigarh. H 31 B and D, N1A Brigade R.Q.Ts in Magnigarh	
Gossville d'Rouse	5.		Normal. 2/Lt G.R. Garnett-Clarke evacuated to England. Capt P.L. Vining attached from 40 DA to 13/1/07.	
	6.		Situation normal. 2/Lt. M.S.H. Harwell - Smelleton appointed Orderly Officer. 2/Lt M.N.P.S. Coghill posted to 8/1/07 (previously attached)	
	7.		Normal	
	8.		Normal.	
	9.		Normal.	
	10.		Normal. 2/Lt H.S. Martin joins the Brigade and is attached to 9/107.	

Army Form C. 2118.

WAR DIARY
or
INTELLIGENCE SUMMARY.

(Erase heading not required.)

167 Bde. R.F.A.

44.

Place	Date	Hour	Summary of Events and Information	Remarks and references to Appendices
FOSSE VII a MAROC	11		Enemy more active.	
	12.		Normal.	
	13		Normal.	
	14.		Enemy trench mortars active at night.	
	15.		Normal.	
	16.		Enemy action on Right Bts. front at night.	
	17		Normal. Bombardment by French mortar activity postponed. Major R L Galloway takes command of 1st Brigade, Colonel D. Spiller on sick list.	
	18.		Bombardment of N/A with H.A. 2/Lts J. Bassitt, A.M. Ramsay, N. McCaig attached to A, B and D Btys. respectively.	
	19.		Normal. Colonel D. Spiller return from hospital to command of Brigade. Counter attack blown by us on Right Bth front.	
	20		Normal	

Army Form C. 2118.

WAR DIARY
or
INTELLIGENCE SUMMARY.
(Erase heading not required.)

10⁴ F.A. Bde. 45.

Place	Date	Hour	Summary of Events and Information	Remarks and references to Appendices
FOSSE VII (MAROC)	21		Normal.	
	22		Enemy more active.	
	23		Enemy active along whole front. Two 2" Trench mortars blown up – 6 casualties.	
	24		Enemy less active.	
	25		Our Artillery action to prevent enemy fraternising	Operation Order No 5 attached
	26		Normal	
	27		Bombardment carried out with HA.	
	28		Normal.	
	29		Normal.	
	30		Normal.	
	31		Normal.	

B. Spiller Lt Col

OPERATION ORDER No. R.30
by
Brigadier General H.C. SHEPPARD, D.S.O.
Commanding 24th Divisional Artillery.
================

1. The 24th Div. Artillery will be relieved by the LAHORE Div. Artillery on the nights of the 2/3rd & 3/4th December 1916. The details of the relief being made between unit Commanders by mutual arrangements.

2. In the case of 6 gun batteries. 4 guns will be relieved the 1st night, 2 guns the second night.

   In the case of 4 gun batteries, 2 guns will be relieved each night.

   In the case of 4 guns with Lahore Heavy Arty. 2 guns will be relieved each night.

   In the case of 2 remaining guns of last mentioned Battery, 2 guns will be relieved the first night.

   In the case of H.T.M. Battery will be relieved the first night.

   In the case of Med.T.M. Batteries, half the number of mortars will be relieved each night.

3. All guns, howitzers and mortars will be taken out of action, with the exception of the Heavy Trench Mortars, which will be handed over in position with all stores.

4. All ammunition will be handed over, batteries making up as far as possible, to 400 rounds per gun, in the case of 18-prs; 240 rounds per Howitzer in the case of 4.5 Hows. in the gun positions.

5. 24th Div. Arty. will leave the Canadian Corps area with all vehicles empty of ammunition. The 24th D.A.C. will dump all the ammunition in the vehicles at their present wagon lines, handing it over to the Lahore D.A.C. on relief.

6. Those portions of units of 24th Div. Arty. relieved by Lahore Div. Arty. on the night 2/3rd Dec. will march to billets on the Northern edge of NOEUX LES MINES. The remaining parties of units following them there when relieved on the night 3/4th Dec.

7. Billeting parties will report to the Staff Captain, R.A. 24th Div. at Hd.Qrs. 24th Division at NOEUX LES MINES at 11.am on 2nd Dec.

8. The 24th Div. Arty. will relieve the 40th Div. Arty. in the LOOS AREA on the night of the 3/4th & 4/5th Dec. Those portions of units relieved on the 2/3rd, relieving similar portions of units of 40th D.A. on the night 3/4th Dec. The remaining portions of units completing the relief on the night 4/5th Dec.

9. The B.G.,R.A., 24th Div. will hand over command to Lahore D.A. at 10.am on the 4th. and will take command of the LOOS AREA R.A. at 10.am on the 5th.

30/11/16.

Major. R.A.
Brigade Major, 24th Divisional Artillery.

ADDENDUM TO O.O. No.R.30.

8. The 24th D.A.C. will be relieved on the 4th Dec. by the Lahore D.A.C. The 24th D.A.C. will move direct to HOUCHIN and HESDIGNEUL and will take over from the 40th D.A.C. the same day.

9. Receipts will be given for all ammunition taken over from 40th Div.Arty. and amounts of ammunition taken over will be telephoned to R.A.H.Q. by 11.am 5th Dec by Brigades and D.A.C.

10. All maps (other than those required for the move) papers concerning the area, registrations, O.P. log books, etc. will be handed over and taken over, to and from units of the Lahore and 40th Divisional Artilleries respectively.

11. Reports on the completion of relief each night will be sent to 24th D.A.H.Q. on completion.

30/11/16.

Major.R.A.
Brigade Major, 24th Divisional Artillery.

SECRET.   Copy No. 5

OPERATION ORDER NO.5
by
Lt.Col.WALTHALL, D.S.O.
Commanding 24th Divisional Artillery.
===============================

1   In conjunction with the 1st Corps Heavy Artillery, the 24th Div. Artillery will carry out a bombardment of the enemy's trenches in H.25.c and thereabouts, where much recent work by the enemy has been in progress.

2   The 1st Corps Heavy Artillery are bombarding the following points :—
    H.26.c.08.63 to H.25.c.15.60. (9.2" Hows)
    H.25.c.00.52. Trench Junctions.(6" Hows)
    H.26.a.14.00. (6" Hows)
    H.25.d.40.15 to H.25.c.S.3. (60-pdrs)
    Trenches and tramway.

3   The Centre Group, 24th Div. Artillery will co-operate with the following programme, one battery 4.5 How being detailed by Right Group Commander to act with the Centre Group, and being placed by Right Group Commander under the command of Centre Group Commander for the operation.

Time.	Group.	No.of guns.	Target.	Rate of fire.	Approximate No.of rounds
As soon after 11 o'clock as the 1st Corps Heavy Arty. will have completed their ranging on their targets.	CENTRE.	2 4.5 Hows.	New trench H.26.a.15.00 to H.26.c.12.45.	1 round per How. per 2 minutes.	240
		2 4.5 Hows.	Old trench H.25.a.15.00 to H.25.B.05.08.		
		2 4.5 Hows.	New trench H.25.c.15.60 to H.25.c.05.33.		
		2 4.5 Hows.	Old trench H.25.c.05.33 to H.25.d.35.30.		
		2 18-prs.	Comn.Trench H.26.a.15.00 to H.20.d.67.22. (Searching whole length).		100
		6 18-prs.	Comn. Trench in area H.26.c.a.d in area of bombardment.		100
		2 2" TMs.	Front line H.25.c.95.06 to H.25.d.30.40.	Bursts of fire.	50

- 2 -

4. The Centre Group Commander will get into touch with the 1st Corps Heavy Artillery from whom he will get time at which guns are to open fire.

5. Sketch of new trench herewith.

6. ACKNOWLEDGE.

25/12/16.

Copy No.1 to 24th DIVISION.
" " 2 " 1st CORPS.R.A.
" " 3 " 1st CORPS.H.A.
" " 4 " LEFT GROUP.
" " 5 " CENTRE GROUP.
" " 6 " RIGHT GROUP.
" " 7 " D.T.M.O.
" " 8 " FILE.

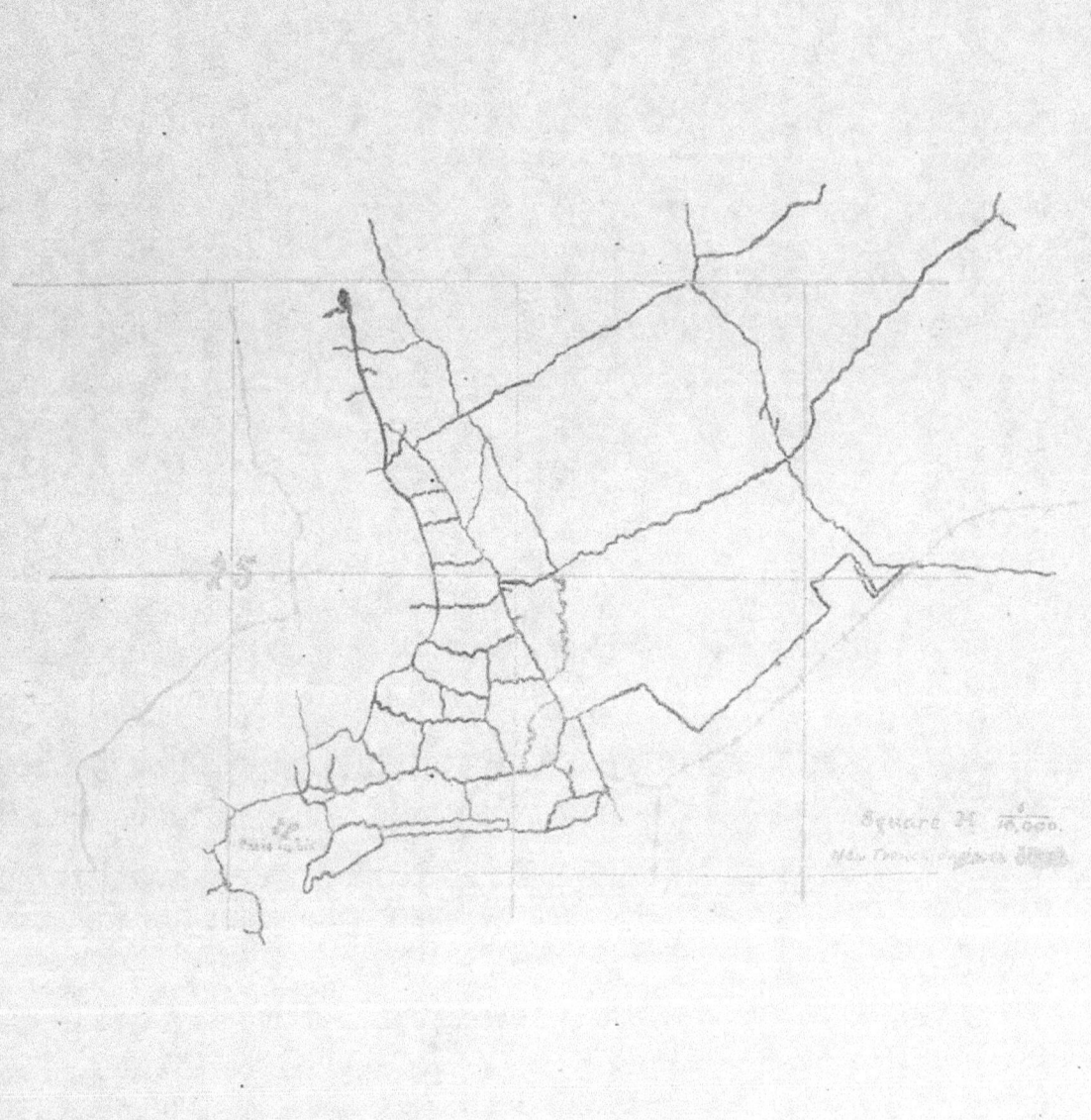

Army Form C. 2118.

N4/51 Vol 16

WAR DIARY
or
INTELLIGENCE SUMMARY.

(Erase heading not required.)

10/1F A/Brigade   46.

Instructions regarding War Diaries and Intelligence Summaries are contained in F. S. Regs., Part II. and the Staff Manual respectively. Title pages will be prepared in manuscript.

Place	Date	Hour	Summary of Events and Information	Remarks and references to Appendices
FOSSE VII and MAROC	1.	12/n	Normal.	
	2.		Normal.	
	3.		Trench mortar activity.	
	4.		Trench mortar activity.	
	5.		Enemy made a successful raid on trenches in N.6.B.	
	6.		Quieter. Lieut E.S. Connor posted to 106 Bde. RFA from A/107.	
	7.		Normal.	
	8.		Normal. Wire cutting in front of Pruits 14 Bis.	
	9.		Wire cutting continued.	
	10.		Normal. 2nd Lieut. C.A. Brown to hospital, sick.	
	11.		Normal.	
	12.		Our Artillery active.	
	13.		Continued activity.	

Army Form C. 2118.

WAR DIARY
or
INTELLIGENCE SUMMARY.
(Erase heading not required.)

107/FA/Brigade.   47/5

Place	Date	Hour	Summary of Events and Information	Remarks and references to Appendices
FOSSE VII and MARoc.	14.		A successful raid carried out by 1st R. Fusiliers at PUITS 14 BIS 4 prisoners taken (153rd Prussians) our casualties slight 50 men went over	10/45 pm
	15.		A Reinforcing Battery, C/94, is brought up during the night and taken up the reinforcing position 7 C/107 at G 26 D 7.5. 2nd Lieut Nixon, as assistant instructor to 2nd D.A. School.	
	16.		Normal. 2nd Lieut A.F. Townsend posted to Brigade and attached to B/107.	
	17.		Normal. 2nd Lieut. T.N. Robinson posted to Brigade and attached to C/107.	
	18.		Normal.	
	19.		C/94 goes out of action. Situation normal.	
	20.		D/107 assists in successful raid on Right front front. Lieut J.H. Carithy to Bars for 2 months as assistant gunnery instructor.	
	21.		Normal.	
	22.		Our Artillery active. Front line in H 31 central bombarded by 9.2" and 4.5" Howitzers	

Army Form C. 2118.

WAR DIARY
or
INTELLIGENCE SUMMARY.
(Erase heading not required.)

107/F.A/Brigade No. 48.

Place	Date	Hour	Summary of Events and Information	Remarks and references to Appendices
FOSSE VII and MAROC	23.		Wire cutting by B/107 at H 31 c 13.98.	
	24.		Normal. 2nd Lieut T.G. Jefferies to Royal Flying Corps.	
	25.		Heavy Artillery bombard front line in N.1.A.	
	26.		At 6/6.45 am a successful raid carried out by 8th Buffs and 12th R. Fusiliers. Supported by 107th Brigade R.F.A + C/108 + A/108 + B/106 + D/106 + Heavy Artillery. 18 prisoners taken (153rd Prussians) 200 men both front enemys casualties estimated at 60. Our casualties 2nd Lieut. Phillips + 4 O.R. killed 4 officers 30 O.R. wounded.	
	27		Normal.	
	28.		Normal.	
	29.		Normal.	
	30		Normal.	
	31		The 1st Corps H.A. bombarded neighbourhood of Hostile T.M. emplacements in H 25 D. 105 rounds 9.2.	

.... LIEUT COL., R.F.A.
COMMANDING 107TH BRIGADE, R.F.A.

SECRET.

ONE BATTERY 106. 6 18-prs.(LEFT GROUP).

Zero probably 9.p.m. 14/1/17.

"ALL CLEAR" about Zero + 35'.

CASE I and CASE II.

TIME.	OBJECTIVE.	RATE OF FIRE.
Zero to ALL CLEAR.	H.25.d.45.60 to H.25.b.60.20. Front line and searching 100 yds. back.	2 rounds per gun per minute.
At ALL CLEAR.	Enemy's support line behind above.	3 rounds gun fire.

AMMUNITION :- 420 AX. approximately.

Lieut. Colonel, R.F.A.
Commanding 107th F.A. Brigade.

SECRET.

ONE BATTERY RIGHT GROUP.

(4 4.5" Hows)

R.P/562.
12/1/17.

Zero probably 9.p.m. 14/1/17.
"ALL CLEAR" about Zero + 35'.

CASE I (~~~~~~~)

TIME.	TARGET.	
Zero to Zero + 10	Distributed along trench H.31.b.25.70 to) H.25.d.27.00)	B2.
+10 to ALL CLEAR	On trench junctions 1 H.31.b.75.20 (New trench)) 2 H.31.b.65.60 (New trench)) 3 H.32.a.40.90 (~~New trench~~)) 4 H.26.c.30.20)	B3.

CASE II (~~~~~~~)

Zero to Zero + 6	B2.
+6 to "ALL CLEAR"	B3.

Rate of fire 2 rounds per gun per minute.

AMMUNITION :-   280 BX.

Lieut.Colonel, R.F.A.
Commanding 107th F.A.Brigade.

SECRET.

R.P/563.
12/1/17.

LEFT GROUP (B/106) CO-OPERATION IN ENTERPRISE ON CENTRE GROUP FRONT

~~ZERO~~ ~~about~~ ~~9~~ ~~pm 14/1/17.~~
~~"ALL CLEAR"~~ ~~about ZERO +35'.~~

CASE I

Zero to Zero +10½	Along enemy's front line trench H.25.d.0.2. to H.25.d.29.40	B.1.
+10½ to +14	Along trench H.25.d.29.40 to H.25.d.36.10.	B.2.
+14 to "ALL CLEAR"	H.25.d.50.55 to H.25.d.65.20.	B.3.

At "ALL CLEAR" drop to B.2.   3 rounds gun fire.

RATE OF FIRE :- 2 rounds per gun per minute on B.1., B.2., B.3.

AMMUNITION :-   420 AX.

CASE II

Zero to Zero + 5½	B.1.
+ 5½ to + 9	B.2.
+ 9 to "ALL CLEAR"	B.3.

"ALL CLEAR" drop to B.2.   3 rounds gun fire.

RATE OF FIRE :- 2 rounds per gun per minute on B.1., B.2., B.3.

AMMUNITION :-   420 AX.

Lieut.Colonel, R.F.A.
Commanding 107th F.A.Brigade.

SECRET.

R.P/564.
12/1/17.

B/107.

MINOR ENTERPRISE ON CENTRE GROUP FRONT.

CASE I (With GAS).

Zero to Zero + 10½	(Along enemy's front line) H.31.b.00.92 to H.31.b.13.70.	B.1.
0 + 10½ to 0 + 14	H.31.b.28.92 to H.31.b.23.72.	B.2.
0 + 14 to "ALL CLEAR"	H.31.b.68.80 to H.31.b.30.52.	B.3.

At "ALL CLEAR" drop to B.2. 3 rounds gun fire.

CASE II (Without GAS).

Zero to Zero + 5½	B.1.
0 + 5½ to 9	B.2.
+ 9 to "ALL CLEAR"	B.3.

"ALL CLEAR" drop to B.2., 3 rounds gun fire.

RATE OF FIRE :- 2 rounds per gun per minute.

AMMUNITION :- 420 AX.

Lieut.Colonel, R.F.A.
Commanding 107th F.A.Brigade.

SECRET.

R.P/565.
12/1/17.

C/107.

MINOR ENTERPRISE ON CENTRE GROUP FRONT.

CASE I or II.

~~(ZERO & ALL CLEAR UNKNOWN)~~

Zero to "ALL CLEAR"   H.31.d.05.95 to H.31.b.15.45.   2 rds. per gun per minute.

(Front line and searching back 100 yards)

At "ALL CLEAR" enemy's support line
behind above.   3 rds. gun fire.

AMMUNITION :- 420 approximately.

ZERO probably 9.p.m. 14/1/17.

"ALL CLEAR" about Zero + 35'

Lieut.Colonel, R.F.A.
Commanding 107th F.A.Brigade.

SECRET.   D/107.   R.P/566.
                                                                 12/1/17.

MINOR ENTERPRISE ON CENTRE GROUP FRONT.

CASE I

0 to 0+10'   Distributed along trench
                         H.25.d.36.08 to H.25.d.34.27.   B.2.

0+10' to "ALL
CLEAR"   On trench junctions
                    (1) H.25.d.76.18   ) (new Trench Junction)
                    (2) H.25.d.82.30.   )
                    (3) H.25.d.66.34.   )   B.3.
                    (4) H.25.d.67.50.   )

CASE II

         Zero to Zero + 6   B.2.

         + 6 to "ALL CLEAR"   B.3.

         RATE OF FIRE :—   2 rounds per gun per minute.
         AMMUNITION :—   280 BX.

                                              Lieut.Colonel, R.F.A.
                                       Commanding 107th F.A.Brigade.

ARTILLERY ARRANGEMENTS.

TIME.	No: of GUNS.	NATURE OF GUNS.	TARGET.	Rds:per gun per minute.	A.X.	B.K.	P.	D.	M.	2"T.M.
0 to 0.10.	24	18 pdrs:	Creeping barrage. 0 to 0.1 on Saps in front of enemy's line. 0.1 to 0.5 on B.1. At 0.5 creep 50 yds: per minute forward without changing line. At 0.10 on B.3.	2	480	-	-	-	-	-
0.10 to ALL CLEAR.	24	18 pdrs:	On B.3.	3	1440	-	-	-	-	-
0 to ALL CLEAR.	8	18 pdrs:	On B.4.	2	420	-	-	-	-	-
0 to 0.5.	8	4.5 Hows:	On B.2.	2	-	80	-	-	-	-
0.5 to ALL CLEAR.	8	4.5 Hows:	On H points.	2	-	480	-	-	-	-
0 to ALL CLEAR.	4	4.5 Hows:	On flank barrage marked h.	2	-	330	-	-	-	-
0 to 0.5.	4	6" Hows:	On B.2.	1	-	-	20	-	-	-
0.5 to ALL CLEAR.	4	6" Hows:	On points K.	1	-	-	120	-	-	-
0 to ALL CLEAR.	3	60 pdrs:	On points S.	2	-	-	-	350	-	-
0 to ALL CLEAR.	2	9.2 Hows:	On Headquarters H.32.d.1.7.	½	-	-	-	-	53	-
0 to ALL CLEAR.	6	2" T.M.	On points marked T.	1	-	-	-	-	-	200
				TOTALS	2340	840	140	350	53	200

SECRET

MINOR ENTERPRISE ON CENTRE GROUP FRONT.

> 107th BRIGADE, R.F.A.
> No. R.P/601.
> Date 23/1/17.

Area to be raided — H.31.b.30.13 - H.31.d.20.62.

B.1.

    A/107   H.31.b.25.00 — H.31.d.16.86.

    B/107   H.31.d.16.86 — H.31.d.20.70.

    C/107   H.31.d.20.70 — H.31.d.17.45.

TIME.

    0 to 0+1   on saps in front of each Btys. zone, as above.

    0+1 to 0+5   on B.1.

RATE OF FIRE. THROUGHOUT.

    2 rounds per gun per minute.

    0+5 to 0+10   Creep forward 50 yards per minute without changing line.

B.3.

    A/107   H.31.b.6.4 — H.31.b.55.00.

    B/107   H.31.b.55.00 — H.31.d.48.63.

    C/107   H.31.d.48.63 — H.31.d.15148.

TIME.

    0+10 to all clear on B.3.

2/Lieut.R.F.A.
Adjutant, 107th F.A. Brigade

SECRET.

107th BRIGADE,
R.F.A.
R.P/601.
No.
Date 23/1/17.

MINOR ENTERPRISE ON CENTRE GROUP FRONT.

Area to be raided   H.31.b.13^{30} - H.31.d.20.62.

D/107.

   O to O+5   on B.2.

        H.31.b.33.38.
        H.31.b.35.24.
        H.31.b.36.15.
        H.31.b.37.05.

   O+5 to all clear.

        H.31.b.70.17.
        H.31.b.60.15.
        H.31.b.61.10.
        H.31.d.72.51.

Please acknowledge.

2/Lieut.R.F.A.
Adjutant,107th F.A.Brigade.

R.P./608.
25/1/17.

Officer Commanding,

"A","B","C" "D"/107 F.A.B.
"A" & "C" 108 F.A.B.
"B"/106 F.A.B.

	Rate of fire for 18-prs.	
18-prs.	Zero to Zero +10	3 rounds per gun per minute.
	+10 till all clear	2 rounds per gun per minute.

Applies only to 18-prs. 107 Bde. & B/106
{ DROP if sent, means drop on to enemy support line on front covered by you on front line barrage (B.1)

A watch is passed round herewith.

Time will be checked at 5.a.m. by telephone.

18-prs.   If H.E. runs short, continue with Shrapnel.

25/1/17.

Lieut.Colonel, R.F.A.
Commanding 107th F.A.Brigade.

All Batteries,

107th F.A.Bde.

107th BRIGADE,
R.F.A.
R.P.603.
23/1/16.

Barrage B.1 to be worked out carefully by B.C's and if visibility is good, officers of "A", "B" & "C" Btys. will report to O.C. Brigade at MANTRAP at 11.a.m. 24th instant to test the LEFT gun of each battery on B.1.

Above officers may be an officer on O.P. duty who may leave his O.P. if necessary, or Liaison Officer from a Battalion.

O.C. "A" Battery will run a temporary telephone line to B/106 before 11.a.m. to register this battery for O.C. B/106.

23/1/17.

2/Lieut.R.F.A.
Adjutant,107th F.A.Brigade.

Head Quarters,
24th D.A.

107th BRIGADE,
R.F.A.
No. R.P./55.5.
Date.................

I have got into touch with G.O.C., 1st Corps. H.A.

As a result I have shown where he recommends the 60 pdrs. His idea is a 60 pdr., to sweep with shrapnel the trench junctions damaged by the howitzers. He says 60 pdrs., are safer than 6 Howitzers for our infantry, with 'D'.

9.2 } 100 rounds 9.2 are allotted. There will only be time to fire at
100.} most 40 rounds with one gun. He says he can give me two 9.2 Hows.

60 pdr.} He tells me that the allotment of 60 pdr., ammunition is meant to
246. } be over and above what is required for counter battery work.

51 to } He suggests using 5 guns for this and two for counter battery
55.   } work.

May No. 3 Barrage be slightly altered as in sketch X attached, on account of new trench.

May Howitzers fire on points as in sketch Y attached.

The schedule of ammunition requires amending as the number of guns is changed. I have made the alterations in pencil.

10/1/1917.

Lieut. Colonel. R.F.A.
Commanding 107/F.A/Brigade.

Army Form C. 2118.

WAR DIARY
or
INTELLIGENCE SUMMARY.
(Erase heading not required.)

107/F.A./Brigade   WQ.   Vol 17

Instructions regarding War Diaries and Intelligence Summaries are contained in F. S. Regs., Part II. and the Staff Manual respectively. Title pages will be prepared in manuscript.

Place	Date	Hour	Summary of Events and Information	Remarks and references to Appendices
FOSSE W.	1. 2/7		Much enemy movement which seemed to show that a hostile relief had taken place.	
4 MAREE	2.		Again abnormal movement was observed. Our B/7 & A/7 dispersed two parties.	
	3.		Hostile T.M's rather active. P/107 cut one in H.B.F.	
	4.		No hostile movement observed. Hostile T.M's inactive. Banging guns heard on Right Batn front during the night.	
	5.		1st Corps W. A. 9.2" Hows did much damage at M6 & 74 to enemy trenches & wire. Enemy retaliated with T.M's and put some 4.2" onto LOOS but did very little damage. A quick burst of our artillery 18 pdrs. fire dispersed a strong enemy working party. 2½c. Mortars fired 60 to B/107. Shots from Z 24 TM Battery thus observed observation. Enemy artillery slightly more active. Effective retaliation given for hostile T.M's.	
	6.		Weather again showing signs for shortly T.M's. Normal.	
	7.		Normal.	
	8.		Hostile T.M's fairly active, but were effectively dealt with.	
	9.		At 4.30 am Left Coy of Left Batn. were rather heavily shelled with T.M's. Enemy's attitude looked like a raid. This apparently took place	
	10.		just on our Left. We were supporting an M6 F by B/107.	

Army Form C. 2118.

WAR DIARY
or
INTELLIGENCE SUMMARY.

(Erase heading not required.)

107/F.A./Brigade.

Place	Date	Hour	Summary of Events and Information	Remarks and references to Appendices
FOSSEUX & MAROC.	11.		Wire cutting by B/107 on M6.E. Raid by N. Staffords on our Right. We gave support. This was at 7.15 p.m. The rest of the 3rd Rifle Brigade in M6.E. was cancelled. During the day, enemy Artillery (astray Bargo) cut our wire in front of ENGLISH ALLEY. 2/Lt. Ramsey to 1st Army Artillery School AIRE.	
	12.		First night of relief by the 124 F.A.B.	
	13.		Relief completed by 6 p.m. when 124 F.A.B. H.Qrs. took over Command. Lt. Col. Spiller OC. 107 F.A.B. stayed until morning of 14th in the capacity of Pilot. Major E. Opham D.S.o. sick to Hospital. Brigade in rest. H.Qrs. C.T.D. at ANNEZIN A & B. at VAUDRICOURT.	
ANNEZIN & VAUDRICOURT.	14		Cleaning up for French G.O.C.'s inspection.	
	15		Inspection of Brigade by Gen. NIVELLE at HESDIGNEUL.	
	16		General cleaning up of Wagons, Billets etc. Half holiday. 2/Lt. Ca. Brown	
	17		Lt. Col. Spiller on leave to ENGLAND. ARTILLERY SCHOOL LARKHILL. Temporary command of Brigade taken over by Major J. a. B. Cowan. Lt. A. J. Townsend sick to Hospital.	

2353 W2 W2544/1454 700,000 5/15 D.D.&L.   A.D.S.S./Forms/C. 2118.

WAR DIARY
or
INTELLIGENCE SUMMARY.

(Erase heading not required.)

Army Form C. 2118.

107 Brig. RFA

51/

Place	Date	Hour	Summary of Events and Information	Remarks and references to Appendices
ANNEZIN & VAUDRICOURT	19		Section Training	
	20		do	
	21		do Half Holiday.	
	22		do	
	23		do Half Holiday.	
	24		do	
	25		Sunday.	
	26		Battery Training. Lt. N. Piers Clarke to T.M. School.	
	27		do	
	28		do Half Holiday.	

Wiran Anong Lieut Col., R.F.A.
Commanding 107th Brigade, R.F.A

Army Form C. 2118.

WAR DIARY
or
INTELLIGENCE SUMMARY.
(Erase heading not required.)

107 Bdg RFA   Vol 8   52

Place	Date	Hour	Summary of Events and Information	Remarks and references to Appendices
ANNEZIN & VAUDRICOURT	1/3/17	1	C. & D (How) calibrating at FONTAINE les HERMANS under Major J. de Brisay. Capt. P.K. Vining. Noted to "B" Bty in command. Capt. J.G. Dutton M.C. de "B", now Capt. P.K. Vining.	
		2	A & B calibrating at FONTAINE les HERMANS	
		3	Battery training	
		4	— do —	
		5	— do — Lt. McCorquodale posted to C/107. Lt. Stannard to D/107 & Rackney vice do.	
		6	Batteries moved from Rest at ANNEZIN & VAUDRICOURT to Wagon Lines at NOEUX les MINES. One section of each Bty relieved one section of 151 Can. Div. Arty. Relief completed at 8pm & 107 F.A.B. took over defence of the Line.	
SOUCHEZ		7	Normal. All Btys registering	
		8	Normal. Zenith registration	
		9	Normal. Some trench mortar behind enemy lines. Attempted hostile raid on left.	
		10	Zone 6 set alight by Neuries. Enemy arrested gun.	
		11	Enemy quiet. Hostile arty. very active, attempting a movement near at	
		12	No SOS action, some active, attempting heavy train to Bois de NOULETTE.	
		13	Low clouds & thick mist made observation almost impossible. Enemy arty	
		14	sup. various columns to rel. dump the evening. Loc no return fire used. Transport being behind enemy lines. This was engaged by our counter	
		15	with good results. Hostile artillery fairly active on front line. Rt. Gp Arty retaliated successfully.	
		16		

Army Form C. 2118.

WAR DIARY
or
INTELLIGENCE SUMMARY.
(Erase heading not required.)

107 Bde RFA No. 53

Instructions regarding War Diaries and Intelligence Summaries are contained in F.S. Regs., Part II and the Staff Manual respectively. Title pages will be prepared in manuscript.

Place	Date 3/1/17	Hour	Summary of Events and Information	Remarks and references to Appendices
SOUCHEZ	17		Rt. Gp Arty bombarded hostile trenches for two hours today, in conjunction with shares. We expect a large bombshare & did much damage to hostile defences. The Infantry OP report 50% direct hits on enemy trenches. Sent hostile TM activity. Effectively silenced by our Artillery. Otherwise normal. Zft seemed to work at 3rd Ger. defence.	
	18			
	19		Hostile artillery active, adding for much retaliation by Rt Gp Arty & shares. Enemy unusually silent. Much movement behind enemy lines. Enemy attempted a raid (?) but were unsuccessful. Hostile artillery again active but silenced effectively.	
	20		Normal.	
	21		Continued shoot at 5.8am. Enemy did not retaliate. Rest of day quiet.	
	22		Desultory hostile artillery fire throughout the day. Our artillery	
	23		fairly active.	
	24		Hostile TM activity which was effectively silenced.	
	25		Normal.	
	26		Enemy bombarded the left of the sector on the evening, our retaliation silenced the enemy.	
	27		Normal hostile activity. Our artillery very active at engaging the enemy set up some heavy fire on the Tyn out sector. Our retaliation was very heavy.	
	28		Enemy artillery very active, & Infantry report on "Intercomme" in all seen found & heavy.	

Army Form C. 2118.

WAR DIARY
or
INTELLIGENCE SUMMARY.

(Erase heading not required.)

107 Bde RFA   54

Place	Date	Hour	Summary of Events and Information	Remarks and references to Appendices
Somme	29		Enemy artillery again very active, calling for heavy & effective retaliation.	
	30.		Enemy artillery quiet.	
	31.		Enemy artillery very active, especially in back areas. 4.5" how has a successful shoot on hostile guns at N.33.a.22.22. This battery has been quiet since.	

W Evan Davis
Lieut Col, R.F.A.
Commanding 107th Brigade, R.F.A.

107th BRIGADE R. F. A.

24th DIVISION

APRIL 1917

WAR DIARY
or
INTELLIGENCE SUMMARY.
(Erase heading not required.)

107 Bde R.F.A. No 55.

Army Form C. 2118.

Place	Date	Hour	Summary of Events and Information	Remarks and references to Appendices
SOUCHEZ	1.		Trench bombardment carried out as per programme, enemy retaliated with guns of all calibre in fast areas.	
	2.		Our zone very active during the morning whilst hostile artillery heavily bombarded AIX NOULETTE. This day and night bombardments continued. At 10.30 p.m. enemy bombarded our trench in CARNEY SECTION heavily. S.O.S was sent up to which we replied; enemy did not come over.	
	3.		Bombardment continued on trenches and Communcty GIVENCHY heavily bombarded with all calibres available during the afternoon. Hostile retaliation practically nil.	
	4.		Hostile barrage on Eiver Batt. Front during early morning; this was efficiently dealt with. Day and night bombardments proceeding on the programme. Hostile bombardments during evening uneventful, dealt with	
	5.		8th Batt. Buffs carried out raid at 2.30 a.m. (SILENT) Our artillery only covered enemy's back of raiding party. Bombardment of VIMY carried out retaliation. Bombardments continued. Hostile artillery active during the day.	
	6.		Offensive bombardments continued. Enemy alert; nervous.	
	7.		Day & night bombardments continued. Hostile artillery heavily barraged SOUCHEZ VALLEY & ARRAS ROAD.	

Army Form C. 2118.

WAR DIARY
or
INTELLIGENCE SUMMARY.
(Erase heading not required.)

107 Bde R.F.A.   No. 56

Instructions regarding War Diaries and Intelligence Summaries are contained in F. S. Regs, Part II. and the Staff Manual respectively. Title pages will be prepared in manuscript.

Place	Date	Hour	Summary of Events and Information	Remarks and references to Appendices
SOUCHEZ	8.		Enemy attitude during night very nervous. He is very busy north. Very light & short-time barrages. Offensive bombardments continued.	
	9.		Canadians attacked VIMY. Our artillery cooperated in turn on sets of attack. Much movement of troops & transport. Engaged and some success. This	
	10.		continued throughout the day. Enemy attitude nervous & alert.	
	11.		Still much movement (reinforcements?) engaged by Field & Heavy Artillery. Attack on BOIS en HACHE by LEINSTERS & SUSSEX. Enemy opposition strong,	
	12.		but objectives gained. Examination of enemy trenches show our bombard seems to have been very effective.	
	13.		Enemy attitude nervous & alert. Several fires burning behind enemy lines during night.	
ANGRES.	14.		Enemy retired, closely followed by our infantry. Forward batteries moved up into No Mans Land & forward Bde HQr established.	
	15.		Batteries complete in forward position.	
	16.		Forward section moved up into LIEVIN.	
LIEVIN	17.		The Bde HQrs established in LIEVIN. One section per Bty, in action in LIEVIN.	
	18.		Batteries complete in action in LIEVIN which was shelled intermittently both day & night.	
	19.		Hostile shelling of LIEVIN continued. Situation in front unchanged.	
	20.		Enemy aeroplanes active & shelling continuous, also good observation afforded good shelter for our men.	
	21.		Enemy shelling continued, our artillery also very active. Fires seen & several explosions heard in LENS.	

2353 Wt W2544/1454 700,000 5/15 D. D. & L.   A.D.S.S./Forms/C. 2118.

Army Form C. 2118.

WAR DIARY
or
INTELLIGENCE SUMMARY.

(Erase heading not required.)

107 Bde RFA

No H57.

Place	Date	Hour	Summary of Events and Information	Remarks and references to Appendices
LIEVIN	22		Attack on Hill 65 unsuccessful. Our artillery very active. Enemy also very active. Our aeroplanes very active	
	23		Situation generally more quiet, tho' enemy still shelled LIEVIN & CITÉ de ROLLENCOURT at intervals. Enemy retired forward section of 231 Bde RFA relieved sections of 107 Bde RFA	
do	24		— do —	
do	25		Remaining — do —	
HESDIGNEUL			and O.C. 231 Bde RFA took over the line. HdQrs & Batteries of 107th Bde RFA moved to HESDIGNEUL DOURIN & NOUSHIN	
QUERNES	26		Hdqrs " Batteries 107 Bde RFA moved to QUERNES as a Bde	
VERQMIN	27		— do — as a Brigade moved to REST BILLETS at VERQMIN	
	28		Generally cleaning up. Half holiday.	
	29		Church parade service & general holiday.	
	30		Training as laid down by O.C. 107 Bde RFA	
	31		— Supplement —	
GOUCHEZ	1		Casualties 1 O.R. killed 3 wounded.	
	2		" 1 O.R. wounded	
	3		" 1 O.R. wounded	
	5		" 1 O.R. killed	
	7		" 1 O.R. wounded, since died.	
	9		" 3 O.R. wounded	

Army Form C. 2118.

WAR DIARY
or
INTELLIGENCE SUMMARY. No. 58.

107 Bde RFA

(Erase heading not required.)

Instructions regarding War Diaries and Intelligence Summaries are contained in F. S. Regs., Part II. and the Staff Manual respectively. Title pages will be prepared in manuscript.

Place	Date	Hour	Summary of Events and Information	Remarks and references to Appendices
STEENWERCK	10.		Casualties. 1 OR Killed 1 wounded.	
	11.		2 OR wounded	
ANQUIERES	16.		1 OR -do-	
LA VIH	18.		1 OR Killed 1 wounded	
	20.		1 OR wounded	
	24.		1 OR -do-	
	25.		1 Off. -do- un ca died.	
			1 Off. -do- (Lt. A.J. Tournend) + 2 OR wounded.	
SOMMER	1.		2/Lt A.B. Longman posted to A/107.	
	9.		2/Lt. JW. Morris returned from 1st Army Arty. School. (C/107)	
			Capt. JG Dutton MC to Infantry Course at Boulogne (B/107)	
			2/Lt. C. Thomas posted to A/107.	
ANDRES	13.		Lt. Col. Fuller sent to Hospital (A/107) since to ENGLAND	
	15.		2/Lt. JW. Tantrey struck off the strength. Invalided to ENGLAND	
	16.		2/Lt. H.L.B. Stroud returned from 2nd Bde. School (D/107)	
LIGNY VERCOIN	18.		Capt. H.B. Stewart posted to D/107.	
	29.			

W. Earl Evans
Lt Col RFA

Sd..... LIEUT COL. R.F.A.
COMMANDING 107TH BRIGADE, R.F.A.

Army Form C. 2118.

WAR DIARY
or
INTELLIGENCE SUMMARY.
(Erase heading not required.)

107. Bde RFA   No. 59   Vol 20

Place	Date 5/17	Hour	Summary of Events and Information	Remarks and references to Appendices
VERCHIN	1		Brigade at Rest. Training as laid down by O.C. 107. F.A.B.	
	2		Training contd. Half holiday. Lieut. E. Nixon B/107 awarded M.C.	
	3		do - Lieut G.T. Meagre posted to B/107 from D.A.C.	
	4		do -	
	5		do - Half-holiday. Brigade Sports. Bde wheelwright Gunn R. actg B/107.	
	6		Parade Service 9.30 am at VERCHIN	
	7		Training contd	
	8		do - Col Styles returned to Bde. having been to 8 FA	
	9		Bde moved to QUERRIES	
	10		- do - HAZEBROUCK	
	11		- do - HARDIFORT.	
HARDIFORT	12		General cleaning up harness etc. Half-holiday	
	13		Parade Service 9.30 am at HARDIFORT.	
	14		Training contd under Battery arrangements.	
	15		Brigade & Battery Commrs viewing new positions at YPRES	
	16		Brigade plus 1 Sect. A/106 moved to Wagon Lines at 4.9 a.m.	
YPRES	17		One section of each Bty + sect. of A/106 in action at YPRES. Situation	
	18		very quiet. Whole Brigade in action in relief of 189 A.F.A.B. The O.C. 107 F.A.B. took over from the O.C. 189 A.F.A.B. on completion of relief at 2.5 am. The night was quiet on the Bde. front.	
	19		Hostile Artillery inactive.	
	20		Except for desultory shelling of Ypres Situation unchanged.	

WAR DIARY or INTELLIGENCE SUMMARY

Army Form C. 2118.

107 Brigade R.F.A.   No. 60.

Place	Date	Hour	Summary of Events and Information	Remarks and references to Appendices
Ypres	21		Wire cutting carried out by 18 Pdr Batteries with success. B/107 (How) shelled a Hostile 4.9 gun to cease firing. Hostile Artillery active on back areas. A/107 position heavily shelled with 5.9 H.E. and 4.2 Hrasbyting gun. 2 guns out of action. Captain Washington R.G.A. in post to A/107 Bdy and supporting left and supporting A/107 Bdy.	
	22		Wire cutting continued. Right Btn lightly shelled during morning. B/190 Btn is shooting forward B/107 Stokes Captain Newman to command Hostile Artillery very active on Right Btn front.	
	23		At 7.45 P.M. S.O.S. signals from centre and right coys Right Btn (8th R.S.R.) The hostile attack was broken up by our artillery and rifle fire. Casualties 3 other ranks wounded.	
	24		Enemy very quiet throughout the day on front line. Hostile Artillery shelled B/107 and D/107 Battery positions putting 1 gun of each Battery out of action. Wire cutting was returned by 18 Pdr Batteries Gunner 3.o.R. wounded. Wire cutting carried out successfully opposite left Btn front. B/107 and D/107 heavily shelled during afternoon, 2 gns of D/107 put out of action. Casualties. 1 Officer killed (Captain W.N. Shewart) 2 Officers wounded (at duty)(Major J.o.R. Cowan, 2/Lieut K.S. Witt.) 5 other ranks wounded.	
	25			
	26		Our Artillery very active on right gone. Antitank Artillery quiet. Wire cutting continued by 18 Pdr Batteries. Heavy hostile shelling during the night on our Right Btn. Enemy made gas attack on division on our right	
	27			

Army Form C. 2118.

WAR DIARY
or
INTELLIGENCE SUMMARY.

(Erase heading not required.)

107th Brigade R.F.A.   No. 61.

Place	Date	Hour	Summary of Events and Information	Remarks and references to Appendices
Ypres	28		Wire cutting continued by 18pdrs. Hostile Artillery quiet on front trenches but active on back areas. A/107 Battery position being heavily shelled, two guns knocked out of action. 1 Section B/107 relieved by 1 Section C/189 A.F.A.B. 2/Lieut. J.C. Follitt joins Brigade.	
	29		2/Lieut. A.G.C. Booth joins Brigade is attached to C/107 Bde. 2/Lieut. Bay Jones gunnery on Brigade front. Shelter found for Gunners of A/107 achieved to two sections C/189 A.F.A.B. Remaining two Gunners of A/107 relieved by two sections C/189 A.F.A.B.	
	30		A/107 with 4 guns in their new position near BLAUWE POORT FARM.	
	31		B Batteries 147 Bde relieved 1 section A Batteries 107 F.A.B. Which proceeded to new position near BLAUWE POORT FARM.	
	31		One half gun pits of 107 F.A.B. by 149 F.A.B. Batteries consolidated in new positions	

B. Mullan Col
Cmg 107 Bde
R.F.A.

2/6/17

WAR DIARY
or
INTELLIGENCE SUMMARY

Army Form C. 2118.

104 Bde R.F.A.

Place	Date 1917	Hour	Summary of Events and Information	Remarks and references to Appendices
YPRES	June 1		Registration from new Bty position could not be carried out as concealment was impossible to maintain. Casualties 2 ORs killed 3 OR wounded	
	2		Registration carried out and wire cutting begun. Hostile artillery very active on back areas. Casualties 1 OR killed 2 OR wounded	
	3		Wire cutting continued. Hostile arty very active. Casualties 1 OR wounded	
	4		– do –	
	5		– do –	
	6		– do – Casualties 6 OR wounded	
	7		Zero day. Zero hour 3.10 and all objectives gained. Casualties nil. Hostile artillery not so active on batt area, being concentrated on our attack. Casualties 1 OR killed 2 OR wounded. Night very quiet.	
	8		Very quiet day	
	9		BLAUWE POORT VALLEY heavily shelled. Capt W.E. Lewis D/104 wounded & 1 OR	
	10		do. also RAILWAY DUGOUTS.	
	11		do.	
	12		do	Maj. W.W. Cave M.C. Wounded
	13		do	2nd Div attack
	14		do	
	15		SPOIL BANK 6 ORs killed 11 ORs wounded. Enemy commenced Drive strafe, varying in intensity. Bee Hedge transferred to LANKHOF FARM.	

Army Form C. 2118.

WAR DIARY
or
INTELLIGENCE SUMMARY.
(Erase heading not required.)

107 BDE RFA. Page 63.

Place	Date July	Hour	Summary of Events and Information	Remarks and references to Appendices
YPRES	16		Area strafe continued. 2 ORs wounded.	
	17		- do -	
			2nd Lt Col Daly Spiller P.S.O.	
	18		2nd Lt Stuar CMG Temp in command. Area strafe continued, situation normal	
	19		- do - 4 ORs wounded	
	20		- do - 2 ORs wounded	
	21		Day more quiet. Area strafe not so frequent as morning except for 1 hr during afternoon. Capt LH3 Govan MC C/107 wounded. One OR killed & 4 ORs wounded.	
	22		Area strafes more frequent. Col WK Smee CMG C/7 to 106 Bde RFA. Major J.W.S Cowan Temp in command.	
	23		Intense area strafe to all day. 1 OR killed. 9 ORs wounded.	
	24		- do - 2 ORs wounded.	
	25		- do -	
			LANKHOF FARM received particular attention 5 ORs wounded	
	26		Area strafes continued	
	27		do LANKHOF FARM again received attention. 2 OR killed 3 ORs wounded	
	28		Fairly quiet day. 1 ORs wounded.	
	29		Area strafes more concentrated & intense. BEDFORD HOUSE heavily shelled.	

Army Form C. 2118.

WAR DIARY
or
INTELLIGENCE SUMMARY.
(Erase heading not required.)

104 Bde RFA (page 64)

Place	Date	Hour	Summary of Events and Information	Remarks and references to Appendices
YPRES	May 1917 30		Lt. Col. R.W.K. Spiller D.S.O. resumed command. Day fairly quiet.	
			Promotions appointments etc	
			2Lt. Jas Brens M.C. to be Major	
			2Lt. J.G. Dutton M.C. to be acting Major	
			2Lt. R.E. Coulcher to be a/Major	
			2Lt. A.B. Ferguson to be Lieut. (Hon. Eng. 2nd May 19)	
			2Lt. W.G. Evans to be a/2Lt. "officer without so employed (Hon Eng.	
			June 11th, ante dated to Feb. 7th 1917.)	
			R&n. ret its to be 2/e. 31 June 17	

Spiller
Lieut. Col. RFA
Commdg. 104 F.A.B.

Army Form C. 2118.

WAR DIARY
or
INTELLIGENCE SUMMARY.
(Erase heading not required.)

107 Bde RFA   Page 65.   No 2

Instructions regarding War Diaries and Intelligence Summaries are contained in F. S. Regs., Part II. and the Staff Manual respectively. Title pages will be prepared in manuscript.

Place	Date	Hour	Summary of Events and Information	Remarks and references to Appendices
YPRES	1		Fairly quiet day	
	2		One Bty in action	
	3		One section per Battery relieved by one section per Battery of 103 FA Bde. Sections relieved on the move to staging Area at PRADELLES. Remaining sections relieved by 103 FA Bde, who took over command.	
	4			
PRADELLES	5		Remaining sections concentrated at PRADELLES	
RECQUINGHEM	6		Brigade moved to Rest Billets at RECQUINGHEM	
	7		Overhauling guns, cleaning vehicles & harness. Half holiday	
	8		Divine Service Parade	
	9		Training as per order of O.C. Brigade	
	10		-do-	
	11		-do-	
	12		-do-	Half holiday
PRADELLES	13		Brigade moved to PRADELLES	
DICKEBUSCH	14		Brigade concentrated in Wagon Lines near DICKEBUSCH. Ammunition carrying commenced.	
	15		Brigade in W.L. Ammunition carrying continued	
	16		-do- -do-	
YPRES	17		Forward section moved into action	
	18		Remaining sections moved into action	
	19		107 Bde took command at 10 am. No. 2 KANKHOF FARM. Balloon registering	
	20		Tuesday registration continued. Night bombardment commenced which continued very often	
	21		Day & Night bombardment continued	
	22			
	23		50th RFA Bde came into action. Took over command of 50th RFA Bde. 107 FA Bde with 50 RFA Bde. under Lt. Col. Rpsdale BSO RFA. L. Group. Bombardments continued	

WAR DIARY
or
INTELLIGENCE SUMMARY.

(Erase heading not required.)

104 Bde RFA   PAGE 66

Army Form C. 2118.

Place	Date July 17	Hour	Summary of Events and Information	Remarks and references to Appendices
YPRES	24		Enemy bombarded Group Area during early morning with GAS SHELLS, & shells of all calibre. Day & night front bombardment continued.	
	25		First day of Intense Counter Battery work, followed by night bombardment.	
	26		Day & night trench bombardment continued. Practice barrage for "J" day in the afternoon covered a raid of the 30th Division.	
	27		Day and night trench bombardment continued.	
	28		Second Intense Counter Battery day, followed by usual night bombardment.	
	29		Usual day and night bombardment continued.	
	30		Third Intense Counter Battery day, followed by usual night bombardment.	
	31	4.50	New fired night Barrage Gas Programme.	
			Fifth Army attacked at 3.50 am. Very hard fighting reported in parts of the front. Hostile artillery put up a very strong barrage with guns of all calibres. Majority of objectives gained. 2nd Lt. L. Nixon M.C. B/104 wounded.	

B.Miller
Lt. Col. RFA
Cmdg 104 Bde RFA

Army Form C. 2118.

WAR DIARY
or
INTELLIGENCE SUMMARY.
(Erase heading not required.)

107 Bde RFA   PAGE 67   VI 23

Place	Date 1917 AUG	Hour	Summary of Events and Information	Remarks and references to Appendices
YPRES	1		Group (107 Bde RFA with 52 Army F.A Bde) settled down to Harassing fire on Enemy approaches and tracks by night and day. Hostile artillery about Normal	
	2		Harassing fire continued. Enemy artillery Normal on Group front	
	3		- do - - do -	
	4		- do - - do -	
	5		- do - Fresh Bty Possibly registering	
			- do - more active	
	6		From new positions Enemy artillery firing from a more Southerly direction, tho it is still active from GHELUVELT	
	7		Normal on Group front	
	8		- do - Our average dominates still. E.a. not active at night bombing back areas	
	9		A quiet day	
	10		107 Pde HQ relieved of command of Group by 52nd A.F.A. Bde 1/42	
	11 to 27th		HQ in rest in Wagon Lines	
	28		Took over command of Group from HQ 52nd Army F.A. Bde.	
	29		Group continue Harassing fire by day + night on enemy back areas	
	30		Hostile Artillery quiet, which could now appear to be normal	
	31		Normal	

W. Van Straubenzee RFA
Adj for Lt. Col. Comdg 107 FA Bde

Army Form C. 2118.

WAR DIARY
or
INTELLIGENCE SUMMARY

(Erase heading not required.)

Vol 24

107 Bde RFA

Sept 1917

Army Form C. 2118.

WAR DIARY
or
INTELLIGENCE SUMMARY.
(Erase heading not required.)

107 Bde R.F.A. Page 66.

Place	Date Sept/17	Hour	Summary of Events and Information	Remarks and references to Appendices
YPRES.	1.		A quiet day. Enemy shells sent over very much about our front line during the night. Shelling of enemy approaches by night continued. The situation is now about normal.	
	2.		Slightly above normal amount of good visibility probably caused aeroplane registrations carried out during day. Firing on enemy approaches continued at night.	
	3.		Working parties carried out on enemy centres of movement, viz. Crow and Bunker roads, ALASKA HOUSES and KENT FARM. Enemy L.T.M. in action today. They were engaged by our How. Bty. with success.	
	4.		Normal day. do.	
	5.			
	6.			
	7.		Hostile Artillery slightly more active during the day, principally on forward areas. Enemy aircraft active at night.	
	8.		Hostile Artillery quieter again – normal. Normal retaliation.	
	9.		do.	
	10.			
	11.		A quiet day. Forward sections relieved by forward sections of 39th Div. Arty.	
	12.		Relief complete by battery of 39th Div. Arty. Forward Group at 2.30pm. Brigade concentrated in Wagon Lines at OUDEZEELE.	

Army Form C. 2118.

WAR DIARY
or
INTELLIGENCE SUMMARY.

(Erase heading not required.)

107 Bde RFA. Page 69.

Place	Date	Hour	Summary of Events and Information	Remarks and references to Appendices
PRADELLES	13		Brigade marched to Cat Billets at PRADELLES.	
	14		Brigade concentrated at PRADELLES.	
	15		Brigade marched to EECKE.	
	16		Brigade entrained for BAUPAUME.	
BAUPAUME	17		Entrainment completed and Brigade concentrated at BAUPAUME in evening.	
	18		Battery Parades as per programme laid down by Brigade Commander.	
	19	9.35	-do-	
PERONNE	26		Brigade marched to WagonLines and concentrated at PERONNE.	
	27		Forward sections moved into action in relief of 160 Bde RFA 31 IDA.	
	28		Forward sections registering and calibrating.	
	29		Relief completed and command taken over HQ 160 Bde to HQ 107 Bde RFA at 10 am. Group consists of 16) RFA plus 2 Bty 166 RFA formerly known as CENTRE GROUP.	
	30		Registrations and calibrations continued.	

Bpuller
Lt. Col R.F.A.
Comdg 107 Bde RFA.

Confidential

WD 25

War Diary
for October 1917
of 107 Bee R.F.A.

Army Form C. 2118.

WAR DIARY
or
INTELLIGENCE SUMMARY.

(Erase heading not required.)

107 Bde R.F.A.   Page 20

Instructions regarding War Diaries and Intelligence Summaries are contained in F. S. Regs., Part II. and the Staff Manual respectively. Title pages will be prepared in manuscript.

Place	Date	Hour	Summary of Events and Information	Remarks and references to Appendices
HERVILLY	Oct 17 1st		Repolishen	
	2nd		Repolishen	
	3rd		Repolishen	
	4th		Repolishen completed	
	5th	12 noon	Conducted shoot in BUISSON GAULAINE FARM trench system. Wire establishes weak.	
	6th		Normal day. Wish on in May Faichen enhanced.	
	7th		Normal day	
	8th		Normal day	
	9th		Normal day	
	10th	2.30 pm	Conducted shoot in FARM TRENCH, PEG LANE, New trench C.14 c.6.4 to C.14 d.1.9. & many C.14 a.d.2.	
	11th		Enemy retaliation mild. Took over front of 293 A.F.A. Bde. in addition of Bangue to Wigan train, & became LEFT GROUP. Consisting of B/107 F.A.G. C/RHA, C/106 & on which D/106. C/107 occupies position vacated by D/293.	
	12th		Moor of C/107 completed.	
	13th		C/RHA left Group ourselves & to Ypres train. C/107 ammunition supply taken might from ammunition	
	14th		Repolishen of C/107	
	15th		Repolishen of C/107 completed	2020 per battery per night
	16th		Normal day	
	17th		Normal day	
	18th		Normal day	
	19th		Normal day	

Army Form C. 2118.

WAR DIARY
or
INTELLIGENCE SUMMARY.
(Erase heading not required.)

107 Bde R.F.A.   Page 71

Place	Date	Hour	Summary of Events and Information	Remarks and references to Appendices
HERVILLY	20th		Normal day	
	21st		Normal day	
	22nd		Normal day	
	23rd		Normal day	
	24th		Normal day	
	25th		Normal day. C/107 1 O.R. killed. 3 O.R. wounded	
	26th	Morn	1st North Staffs passed New Trench between Tran Lane & the RAILWAY CUTTING. Re-park, and 8 Germans & their M.G. prisoners were taken. The 460 Regt was discovered having a dinner dist.	
	27th		Normal day	
	28th		Normal day	
	29th		Normal day	
	30th	3pm	On certified about at BELLICOURT by B/107 with incendiary shell. Three guns were carried. Enemy	
	31st		retaliated on VILLERET with H.E. & 77mm	
			Normal day	

B. Butler
Lieut Col R.A.
Commanding 107 A.F.B.

Vol 26
24 Dn

War Diary.
107th Bde R.F.A.
From Nov 1st To Nov 30th.
1917

Secret.

Army Form C. 2118.

WAR DIARY
or
INTELLIGENCE SUMMARY.
(Erase heading not required.)

Page 72

Instructions regarding War Diaries and Intelligence Summaries are contained in F. S. Regs., Part II. and the Staff Manual respectively. Title pages will be prepared in manuscript.

Place	Date Nov	Hour	Summary of Events and Information	Remarks and references to Appendices
HERVILLY	1st		Normal Day	
	2nd	3.30pm	Hurricane bombardment of new trenches S. of Ruby Wood. One our bn A/1/6 came in trenches at TEMPLEUX.	
	3rd		9.0am under orders of Right Group, except for S.O.S. when they were under left Group. C/106 left left Group. B/106 came under left Group.	
	4th		Same order in J/A/1/106 came under right Group. 2 from B/106 came under right J left Group for S.O.S. only.	
	5th		Their section of A/1/106 came under left Group.	
	6th		Normal Day	
	7th		Normal Day	
	8th	3-3.30pm	Artillery concentration on WIND TRENCH A25b6034-42m, & Rd.s & Dug.s A25b34 25-66.78	
	9th		Normal Day	
	10th	1am	7th Norths made a raid said on Enemy trenches between A25d139 A25d13M. Raid successful one enemy killed, one prisoner, one casualty m.s. Artillery slow to form barrage, his were all regimen.	
	11th		Normal Day	
	12th		Normal Day	
	13th		Normal Day	
	14th		Normal Day	
	15th		Normal Day	
	16th		Normal Day	
	17th		Normal Day	
	18th	10am	4th Norths. no prior warning raid in trig. but did not succeed in entering the enemy trenches. Artillery stood to from 1am till 3.30am. he was not expected to raid. Our casualties 10 B slightly wounded. C/107 wired one far forward to own wire. Capt. A/107 took up position immediately behind C/107. Capt. Pope wound at G16.15-18 & wounded 4 signallers. A/106 took forward one gun and at G14 26 25-35.70	

Army Form C. 2118.

WAR DIARY
or
INTELLIGENCE SUMMARY.
(Erase heading not required.)

Page 73

Place	Date	Hour	Summary of Events and Information	Remarks and references to Appendices
HERVILLY	19.4		In early morning A/106, B/107, C/107 moved into position about RONSSOY & came under orders of 55' D.A. formed a sub group under Major W.S.N Nails M.E. of 75/107. D/107 moved into a position near LEMPIRE & came under orders of VII CORPS counter battery Group. One Section D/106 came into action in HARGICOURT from RLY Group & remained in gun battery with D/107 & the remaining section of D/106 already attached to B/107. B/106 stamped in RLY Camp Heavy tractor teams moved batteries of H/A Group. C/106 down under orders of Left Group. All 9 units were successful in engaging with a large operation carried by the Division on our left. 8th Queens who captured our Group's entire front line (Railway Gully at 6.6c. Several enemy batteries who were successful left of line (G3). 6th Survey Regt at 82002. An enemy war force after operation 43 of Artillery. Raid C. The 2nd Hants Regt with a totally of R.E. mines enemy line N of RUBY WOOD. TRENCH. 2 Germans were bayoneted & their intelligence an officer was killed. A considerable amount of equipment & ammunition was blown up by M.R.E. An enquiry was with the 25th Essex to 2nd line included with 50 dumping of pigeons & two packets of pigeons were in places in front MPSQA &c. When on advancing from bush in front, were killed. How & pistol for 5 advancing him. When an advance was ordered, the enemy opened a demolition of mines.	
	20	6.20am	A/106 B/107 returning from 55D.A. B/106 moving from hostels of B/107 & the other hand mining stores of	
			Rly Camp.	
	21		A/107 but the 55° D.A. moved into action at VILLERS GUISLAN	
	22		Normal day	
	23		B/106 & D/107 each sent a few parties of men early parties.	
	24		A/106 out into to G136 B/107 out into G140	
	25		A/106 out into to G134 D/107 out into G140	
	27		A/106 out into G134 D/107 out into G144 D/106 Gunnery Section out into G156	
	28		F/106 withdrawn was early from	
	29		D/107 withdrawn from early fire.	

Army Form C. 2118.

WAR DIARY
or
INTELLIGENCE SUMMARY.

(Erase heading not required.) Page 74

Instructions regarding War Diaries and Intelligence Summaries are contained in F.S. Regs., Part II. and the Staff Manual respectively. Title pages will be prepared in manuscript.

Place	Date	Hour	Summary of Events and Information	Remarks and references to Appendices
HERVILLY.	Nov 30	6.15am	The enemy attacked and broke through to MISC Div front northwards. The 51st infantry retired in disorder upon through the form J A/107 in VILLERS GUISLAIN. The battery continues firing for fifteen minutes after the last infantryman had passed. After which time the enemy charged the position. Capt. Cann. R.S. who was commanding the battery gave the order to retire. The nearest Infantry being a No 7 midnight position. An from This was carried out when the enemy were within 500 yards of the battery, very successfully. Casualties were about 200 wounded & OR unaccounted for all our guns at present remain in the hands of the enemy. The battery was in action from 3.30am to 6.15am. 2 Lieut F.E.H. FRANKLYN R.F.A. joined 107 Bde from D.A.C. in Nov 25th & was posted to A/107 2 Lieut E. ATKINS R.F.A. was posted from 8/107 to 15th D.A.M Nov 10th	

Bpiller
Lieut Col R.F.A.
Comdg 107 Brigade R.F.A.

WAR DIARY
or
INTELLIGENCE SUMMARY

Army Form C. 2118.

107 Bty RFA

Pages 75

Vol 27

Place	Date	Hour	Summary of Events and Information	Remarks and references to Appendices
HERVILLY	Dec 1st		Owing to Enemy Interference on 55th Div front, situation is somewhat obscured. Neutral night firing programmes were carried out as also an organisation with Div T.M. Bys. Neutral bombardment was carried out at dawn. During the day no Hostile Btys were engaged by Group H/3 Hows, and Hostile Btys dispersed some enemy assembly parties.	
	2		Neutral night firing until dawn. Our Arty reinforced by RHA slow normal. A quiet day.	
	3		Night firing and neutral morning strafe in conjunction with the Enemy artillery active & T.B. Bngd. on line by Group Hows. Enemy working parties was dispersed by these. Enemy average in active on front of 55th Div.	
	4		Night firing. Dawn bombardment maintained. Night sore bombard & registration. Batteries very active. Neutral aircraft activity	
	5		Night firing and neutral bombardment on organisation. Fire can ncured off Hostile Battery in action at 18'10am. Enemy reported over 300 Rds. was active no aircraft anything. During the day firing stopped & specials. A quiet day. At about 11pm 3rd US raided enemy trenches. No Prisoners taken, & no Hun seen.	
	6		Night firing a neutral engaged (normal)	
	7		Normal.	
	8		Normal. Bys reinforced by 4 Bys 6" Hows.	
	9		Batteries strafed enemy approaches during the night and carried out a bombardment during the early morning. Enemy replied. Signals in conjunction with French Btys (Section Rennecourt) employed enemy T.M. Emplacements) and T.M. Infantry trenches are a salient next out accounted for prisoner.	
	10		Normal.	
	11		Infantry raided enemy trenches supported by Group Artillery. No Hun recovered. Night firing was carried out on enemy approaches. Day as	
	12		usual	

Army Form C. 2118.

WAR DIARY
or
INTELLIGENCE SUMMARY.

(Erase heading not required.)

107 Bde. R.F.A.   Page 46

Instructions regarding War Diaries and Intelligence Summaries are contained in F. S. Regs., Part II. and the Staff Manual respectively. Title pages will be prepared in manuscript.

Place	Date 1919 Dec.	Hour	Summary of Events and Information	Remarks and references to Appendices
HERINLY	13		Normal	
	14		do	
	15		Hostile Artillery and aircraft very active. Movements and working parties were engaged by Group 18pdrs with success	
	16		Normal	
	17		Normal	
	18		Normal	
	19		Group HQ went into Reserve and were relieved by O.C. & HQ Staff 106 Bde. RFA.	
	20		In Reserve	
	21		do	
	22		do	
	23		do	
	24		do	
	25		do	
	26		do	
	27		do	
	28		do	
	29		Relieved O.C. & HQ Staff 106 Bde. RFA & took over command of Centre Group	
	30		O.C. & HQ Staff assumed command of Right Group 2nd Div. comprising A/107, B/107, C/107. A quiet day	
	31		Day quiet. Some registration carried out. Harrass night firing	

N Gallwey
Major R.F.A.
Comdg 107 Bde RFA

Army Form C. 2118.

WAR DIARY
or
INTELLIGENCE SUMMARY.

(Erase heading not required.)

107 Bde R.F.A. Page 77.

Place	Date	Hour	Summary of Events and Information	Remarks and references to Appendices
HERVILLY	1918 Sept	1.	New that fighting was firm by Battino. The day was generally quiet, and very foggy. There was much about actively on both sides. The AA gun fire was assisted only. 5 out of 15 R.A. opened out times.	
		2.	Visibility was very poor throughout the day and Group batteries were only engaged on "repress" for enemy troops. Canadian Not.	
		3.	Visibility was better and movement was seen and observed. Generally quiet. Nothing to report.	
		4.	The movement was seen and engaged with success. An enemy AA section in BELLICOURT was engaged and made to change position by Group 18pdrs, at who later engaged in harassment by 4.5" How and started.	
		5.	Batteries engaged in gripping enemy parties all day, and BELLICOURT was observed during the evening. Nothing to report.	
		6.	— do —	
		7.	— do —	
		8.	Hostile artillery more active. Our shares caused no close concentrations during the afternoon, and Group 4.5" engaged BELLICOURT during the evening with concentrated fire by way of reprisal. Hostile AA Section on BELLICOURT was engaged and silenced, failing lights prevented further observation. Enemy tracks, which joinson CPN to Rendhomise town should hamby during the evening & continuing made form in the hope of catching a transport convoy relief.	
		9.		
		10.		
		11.	Reprisals for enemy shows were carried out by Group batteries, nothing to report.	

WAR DIARY or INTELLIGENCE SUMMARY

Army Form C. 2118.

104 Bde T.M.B. Page 48.

Place	Date	Hour	Summary of Events and Information	Remarks and references to Appendices
HERVILLY	1918 Jan. 12		BELLICOURT was shelled as a reprisal for hostile shooting and enemy dump area was again shelled in view of an enemy (unreadable) relief.	
	13		A quiet day.	
	14		Trench Mors engaged at daybreak good success, & MALAKOFF was shelled in the evening by way of reprisals.	
	15		A quiet day.	
	16		Registration shooting carried out and movement in gaps.	
	17		Enemy trenches were raided by Brigade on our right and an intensification was obtained without loss. Prisoners confirmed relay engaged on our front.	
	18		Reprisals were again taken against BELLICOURT for enemy shoots.	
	19		A quiet day.	
	20		do –	
	21		Enemy trenches were raided at dawn. The raiding party was covered by the Group Arty and two prisoners were taken. Barrage put up by the enemy was very slight. The day was quiet. A party of Huns was found returning wound some bombs in No Mans Land. The party was engaged with several hits observed, no further groaning was heard. The state of the ground & enemy machine gun fire prevented an examination being obtainable.	
	22		Our Stokes were very busy on C/3 work. Hostile Bty dropped at 9.10 & 5.00 was operated each Shrapnel throughout the night.	
	23		Hostile party seen trying to fly a towel was engaged by 4.5 How. Tri Enid defended a pit & disappeared, as also did the party. C/107 and 1 Section K1 Coy/106 leave ends the Group in a reduction of armament.	

Army Form C. 2118.

WAR DIARY
or
INTELLIGENCE SUMMARY.

(Erase heading not required.)

107 Bde R.F.A. Page 19

Instructions regarding War Diaries and Intelligence Summaries are contained in F. S. Regs., Part II. and the Staff Manual respectively. Title pages will be prepared in manuscript.

Place	Date 1918 Jan	Hour	Summary of Events and Information	Remarks and references to Appendices
HERVILLY	24		A quiet day	
	25		do	
	26		do	
	27		do	
	28		do	
	29		do	804 Enemy bombing during night
	30		do	do
	31		do	do
			Extensive defensive construction has been in progress during the month and is still going on. Dumps + such as wagon lines have been fortified against hostile bombing attacks. Two anti-tank gun positions are under construction, in addition already fortified positions. Intermittent hostile shell fire is at present a chief feature. No counter fire has been done, except that all movement seen is immediately engaged. Reprisals for enemy shoots are intense and concentrated.	

W. Evan Evans
Lt. Col. Comdg 107 Bde R.F.A.

Army Form C. 2118.

WAR DIARY
or
INTELLIGENCE SUMMARY.
(Erase heading not required.)

107th Bde R.F.A.   Page 83

Instructions regarding War Diaries and Intelligence Summaries are contained in F. S. Regs., Part II. and the Staff Manual respectively. Title pages will be prepared in manuscript.

Place	Date	Hour	Summary of Events and Information	Remarks and references to Appendices
			The following officers joined the Bde:— 2/Lt E. Gilson " R. Bolton " G.W. Godwin " M. Featherby " E.J. Gottlieb " E. Spurring Casualties. Officers 2/Lt D.W. Sheehy (D/7) wounded. O.R. 2 (wounded).	

E. Wheler Farm 107 F.A. RFA.
Lt Col Comdg. 107 1/9/18.
107 Bde RFA.

SECRET.

CODE WORDS FOR MINOR ENTERPRISE.

WIND.

GIRL................Wind favourable for 4" Stokes Guns.
GAMP................Wind unfavourable for 4" Stokes Guns.
GLOVE...............Stop 4" Stokes.

RAIDING PARTY.

MUSTARD.............Raiding party have left our trenches.
SALT................Raiding party are advancing.
PEPPER..............Raiding party have entered enemy's trenches.
IRON................Raiding party still in enemy's trenches.
TIN.................Raiding party are withdrawing.
COAL................Raiding party back in our trenches.
STEEL...............Raiding party have failed to enter enemy's trenches.

ZERO.

TAKE................Raid postponed, new Zero at........
TOM.................Raid cancelled.

CASUALTIES, ENEMIES.

....PRUNE...........Prisoners so far.
....PIT.............Total prisoners.
....POOL............Wounded prisoners.
....PUMP............Unwounded prisoners.
....PAN.............Estimated killed and wounded.

OUR CASUALTIES AS FAR AS AT PRESENT ASCERTAINED.

....B NAB...........Killed.
....NICE............Wounded.
....DICE............Missing.

ARTILLERY.

ALEC................18 pdrs. on or behind objective falling short.
ATTIC...............Continue barrage.
APPLE...............Increase counter-battery.
AWAY................Continue counter-battery.
APE.................Stop barrage.
AUNT................Barrage behind objective falling short.

24/1/17.

2/Lieut. ....
Adjutant, 17th F.A.Brigade.

Army Form C. 2118.

WAR DIARY
or
INTELLIGENCE SUMMARY.
(Erase heading not required.)

107^K B^{de} R.F.A.   Page 80.

Vol 29

Place	Date	Hour	Summary of Events and Information	Remarks and references to Appendices
HERVILLY	Feb 1918 1		Slight enemy T.M. activity.	
	2		Indistinct activity.	
	3		During the evening 107th Bde shelled tracks leading to enemy front & relief being effected. TEMPLEUX received considerable attention from hostile artillery.	
	4		At 10.30 pm the enemy put down a heavy barrage on the trench system of our Centre battalion & back area. S.O.S. rockets were sent up & all batteries replied. Activity of hostile artillery noticed to be gradually increasing.	
	5		HARGICOURT Tidy heavily shelled. Fired offensive concentration at 6.25 am "SMASH" BELLICOURT.	
	6		Normal movement & activity.	
	7		Quiet day	
	8		Normal activity.	
	9		Enemy artillery active	
	10		All batteries fired on selected targets during the night.	

Army Form C. 2118.

WAR DIARY
or
INTELLIGENCE SUMMARY.
(Erase heading not required.)

107 A Bde R.F.A. Page 81

Place	Date	Hour	Summary of Events and Information	Remarks and references to Appendices
	11		At 4.55 p.m the enemy put down a barrage on our Centre & left Battalion fronts. He fired red & green lights from A 23d. A sentry mistook these for S.O.S. & sent up a rocket accordingly. The batteries fired in response. Hostile artillery activity on our night. Enemy activity increasing. Normal day.	
	12		"	
	13			
	14			
	15			
	16			
	17		A number of red balloons floated over our lines & fell in the Cav. Corps area towing Papers in English & French.	
	18		Hostile artillery activity BENJAMIN & VILLERET shelled	
	19		activity below normal.	
	20		At 3.30 p.m. an offensive concentration was fired on RUBY WOOD. Our batteries participated.	
	21		The enemy activity was quite light firing on suspected relief. Enemy bombarded our front line system from 4 to 6.30 a.m.	
	22		Normal activity	

WAR DIARY
or
INTELLIGENCE SUMMARY.
(Erase heading not required.)

Army Form C. 2118.

107th Bde R.F.A.   Page 82.

Place	Date	Hour	Summary of Events and Information	Remarks and references to Appendices
	2.3		Mounted officers seen at CABARET FARM; thought to be artillery staff.	
	2.4		Enemy shelled L.15b & around A. Interpretation.	
	2.5		Increased activity. A' battery position again shelled.	
	2.6		Normal.	
	2.7		At 12.35 a.m. enemy party about 30 strong attempted to raid our lines, but fired S.O.S. which failed to reach our lines.	
	2.8		Observed artillery activity; vicinity of CARPESA COPSE heavily shelled. Fourth on the whole quiet, but enemy's activity steadily increased. Batteries did considerable work on secondary position during the month.	

Supplement

Major D.Spiller D.S.O. took command of the Bde Arty as CRA from 1st to 15.5. Major N.R.L. Galloway D.S.O. assuming to Bde.

Captn W.E. Evans Adjt to Hospital & subsequently England (9.3rd Feb. approximately). Lt C.A. Bacon took over duties as A/Adjt & 2nd i/c W.D Shedy. Hon. of Intelligence officer.

During the month the following officers left the Bde:—

Lt C.O. Hudson (England to Amplete machine studies)
Lt J.H. Marks
2/Lt A.E.J. Clarke   (N R.H.A)

Army Form C. 2118.

WAR DIARY
or
INTELLIGENCE SUMMARY.

(Erase heading not required.)

107^A Bde R.F.A.   Page 84

Instructions regarding War Diaries and Intelligence Summaries are contained in F.S. Regs., Part II. and the Staff Manual respectively. Title pages will be prepared in manuscript.

Place	Date	Hour	Summary of Events and Information	Remarks and references to Appendices
HERVILLY	March 1918			
	1		Slight shelling activity on our right & left.	
	2			
	3			
	4		Relieved by 930 Bde 66th Div.	
	5		Marched to MENCHY LAGACHE	
	6			
	7		Spent in inspecting, cleaning & overhauling equipment. D A football tournament	
	8		Commenced. Concerts given by batteries.	
	9			
	10		Bde H'qrs show under patronage of Divl Commander & C.R.A.	
	11		Advance parties went forward to view new position	
	12			
	13		Marched to new position opposite BELLENGLISE with H.Q. at VERMAND & wagon lines	
			at COURAINCOURT. The Bde Commander forecast commanded a group of 8 Batteries	
			including a 60 pdr. group consisting of A B 108 R.G.A., D/278 & A B/RCHA under Lt. Col. ELKINGTON	
	14		Registration	
	15			
	16		Aerial activity.	
	17		Considerable aerial activity on both sides.	

Army Form C. 2118.

WAR DIARY
or
INTELLIGENCE SUMMARY. (Erase heading not required.)

107 Bde RFA   Page 85

Place	Date	Hour	Summary of Events and Information	Remarks and references to Appendices
VERMAND	Aug 18		Normal activity.	
	19		A Bty withdrew to a new position in rear of D. Bty new position.	
	20		A Bty moved to position again.	
	21		Enemy opened a heavy bombardment at 4.30 am during a thick mist which did not clear until nearly midday. He used a large quantity of gas shells as well as some smoke shells. The enemy attacked at 10.30 am & advancing rapidly forced B & C batteries in MAISSEMY to leave their guns, though many broke back blocks & dial sights. The barrage on the approaches to MAISSEMY was especially heavy. The OC of B battery (Major H.S.N. Crowe M.C.) was missed. 18AR captured at the battery position & during stampeding them from the position flank. A number of men of C battery took up a position with the Infantry in a trench in rear of their battery position & caused heavy Lewis gun & rifle casualties. 'A' battery lost two forward guns and it suffered when it was in charge of 2 Hrs of D battery were destroyed by shell fire. Batteries have withdrawn to new positions in the afternoon.	
	22		10 Q took over the early morning to new POEUILLY. The Bde commander took over the Infce of 15BA of QUIVINCOURT. This afternoon & seemed them as well relieved by 63 Sterling Horse Arty later. The Boche.	Lt ELKINS Bde as Staff Commander.

WAR DIARY or INTELLIGENCE SUMMARY

Army Form C. 2118.

107th R.G.R.F.A. Page 86.

Place	Date	Hour	Summary of Events and Information	Remarks and references to Appendices
BOUVINCOURT	22		The infantry held the green line short battery took up position south of VRAIGNES	
	23		The Bde. was withdrawn across the SOMME & went into action E of MORCHAIN	
	24		The enemy crossed the SOMME & Canal de SOMME at 9 am & captured BERTHENCOURT & continued to advance in spite of a counter attack. The batteries fell back to position around HYENCOURT but could not stop the enemy advance. The enemy pushed on & the brigade retired changing position three times during the day. Bde HQ for the night was at MARICOURT with the batteries in action around CHILLY & HALLU.	
	25		CHAULNES having been secured by the enemy the bde fell back to positions in the valley of BEAUFORT. The Bde retired to positions near CAIX.	
	26		The Bde. suddenly came into action E of BEAUCOURT, but on the fog, in our right flank with the whole Bde. in unknown beyond the river AVRE	
	27		Position was taken up E of ROUVREL.	
	28		The enemy attacked MOREUIL. French infantry came up & were covered by the Bde. a new of the positions advance of the enemy. The Bde. withdrew to the Bois de SENECAT	
	29			
	30			
	31		The Bde. assembled in the position taken up by it on the previous day. B.G.C. Lieut Col. Argyle Galloway D.S.O. both wounded. Lt Col [?] assumed command of Bde.	

WAR DIARY or INTELLIGENCE SUMMARY

101st Bde RFA Page 87

Summary of Events and Information

Supplement

Casualties.

Offr: Major W.S.N. Carple MC missing.
2/Lt E Saffield
" A.G. Storey (Sigs) } wounded 21/3/18
" W T Walsh
" 2nd Lt H Roberts RE.

O.R.	Killed	Wounded	Missing	Gassed
	8	4	12	3	21/3/18
	1	5	—	—	22/3/18
	2	6	—	—	24/3/18

2/Lt M Freathy } evacuated sick 7/3/18
F.G.H Frankleyn } 8/3/18

Major Carple MC rejoined HQ Bde 11/3/18 ?
2/Lt A.P. Beazley O/C Signals was with the Bde for training duty for the — 2/2/18

E Vaughan Beem Capt RFA
M OC 101 PABB
24/4/18

Army Form C. 2118.

24th Div.

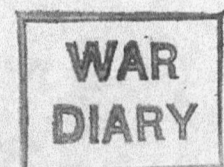

Headquarters,

107th BRIGADE, R.F.A.

A P R I L

1 9 1 8

Box 2197

Army Form C. 2118.

WAR DIARY
or
INTELLIGENCE SUMMARY.

(Erase heading not required.)

104th Bde RFA   Page 88.

Place	Date	Hour	Summary of Events and Information	Remarks and references to Appendices
	1918 April 1		Brigade in action about 1 kilometre S of HAILLES awaiting orders to move. Enemy activity still considerable.	
	2		GENTELLES area reconnoitred in view of moving orders to move.	
	3		A great deal of firing carried out by the brigade. Forward M.Q. established about a mile S. of HAILLES.	
	4		Heavy attack by the enemy from MOREUIL Southwards. No great advance achieved. During bombardment our batteries (C & D) were heavily shelled, moving eventually into sheltered positions. The horses of both batteries, the Bde wireless personnel	
	5		CASTEL was H.Q. for the Chateau behind in the afternoon the batteries were withdrawn across the River. The Bde remainder in action in reserve positions with D battery at the PARACLET.	
	6		Armed moment of firing done by Bde.	
	7		Bde marched in reserve for two A battery crossing the river.	
	8		Bde. went from front line to St FUSCIEN at 7 a.m. marched to REVELLES.	
	9		Marched to ANDAINVILLE.	

Army Form C. 2118.

WAR DIARY
or
INTELLIGENCE SUMMARY.

107 Bde RFA Page 94

Place	Date	Hour	Summary of Events and Information	Remarks and references to Appendices
	April 10		Rested at AMBAINVILLE	
	11		Moved to SOREL	
	12		Rested at SOREL. Bde engaged in refitting & marking up horses etc.	
	13		Bde Commander took over duties of CRA & Major J Henry DSO assumed command of the Bde.	
	14			
	15			
	16			
	17		Moved to YAUCOURT	
	18		BEALCOURT	
	19		GAUCHIN VERLOINGT	
	20		Rested at GAUCHIN	
	21		Moved to BERLENCOURT	
	22		teaching something	
	23			
	24			
	25		DA Racemeeting	
	26		DA Jumping Competition	
	27			

Army Form C. 2118.

WAR DIARY
or
INTELLIGENCE SUMMARY.

(Erase heading not required.)

107 Bde RFA   Page 1

Place	Date	Hour	Summary of Events and Information	Remarks and references to Appendices
	28		2/A shoot Parade. D/A - Staff Officer a shoot. B/C Shelter DSO personnel command at A Bty.	
	29		Refitting & training.	
	30		Training.	

Supplement.

During the month the following casualties were sustained:—

(1) Major J R Gibson MC killed 4/4/18.
    " G Galloch " wounded " (died of wounds 5/4/18)
    Lt K S Willis with me wounded
    2/Lt G W Gordon "
    " E Fleming DCM "

The following men tp Bde:—

Capt R A G Ingram MC in Command 5/7 8/4/18
Lieut L B Green MC   13/4/18
2/Lt A Macdonald   8/4/18
" J A Gunnell   12/4/18
2/M & GS cogbill

OR K W M
  8
  2
  6 17   9
     33 — 3

14/3/18
5/4/18
18/4/18

Bomb. O'Hara
2/PAB

27/4/18 Same to 107 DC 2/5/18
Not/h OC 107 2/5/18

24
107th Bde: R.F.A.
Vol: 5

Army Form C. 2118.

WAR DIARY
or
INTELLIGENCE SUMMARY.
(Erase heading not required.)

104th Bde RFA   Page 91

Place	Date	Hour	Summary of Events and Information	Remarks and references to Appendices
LIEVIN	May 1918 1		Training at BERLENCOURT.	
	2		Bde Commander with advance parties from Bde HQ & Batteries went forward to arrange relief of 10th Bde CFA in action in LIEVIN with Wagon lines at ABLAIN ST NAZAIRE. Section of batteries moved into the line. Lorries were sent for the men.	
	3		Relief of 10th Bde CFA completed by 2 p.m.	
	4		Registration. Harassing fire carried out at night.	
	5		Normal. Night harassing fire.	
	6			
	7		Reports received that enemy likely to attack on the following night. Harassing fire increased.	
	8		One S/Battery went to Infantry Bde & began Gallery both new Bdes. Slow harassing fire open mirrored.	
	9		Normal.	
	10		Usual harassing & sniping. Enemy quiet.	
	11			
	12		Counter shot a action harassing fire at night. B/7 forward section was shelled during the morning no casualties. S.A. unusually active.	
	15		Occasional machine gun firing on to suspected points.	

Army Form C. 2118.

WAR DIARY
or
INTELLIGENCE SUMMARY.

(Erase heading not required.)

104th Bde R.F.A.   Page 92

Instructions regarding War Diaries and Intelligence Summaries are contained in F. S. Regs., Part II. and the Staff Manual respectively. Title pages will be prepared in manuscript.

Place	Date	Hour	Summary of Events and Information	Remarks and references to Appendices
	16		H.Q moved to a hostile area ceded to the batteries. Enemy artillery more active at night. Enemy artillery quiet during the day. Short harassing bombardments of our trenches at night.	
	17			
	18			
	19		Promise operations. Enemy activity normal.	
	20			
	21			
	22			
	23		A/7 forward section shelled with gas & gun-kit. Decreased harassing fire at night by our artillery.	
	24		Section assisted in raid by Royal West Kents during their barrage at 10.34 p.m. This attempt was unsuccessful. 3 prisoners being captured and being unwounded.	
	25		Decreased sniping of movement which was very pronounced during the day. Offensive bombardments undertaken in retaliation for enemy shelling which was exceptionally slow & accurate.	
	26		Hostile artillery quiet during day. Bombarded AKIEVIN at night. Left gun shell undenis A/7 D/7 forward sections & e/7 D/7 main positions. Enemy to front all & goo arrangements. No serious guessed casualties occurred. Annoyed.	
	27			
	28		Enemy active during both days & night. Chemical bombardment of hostile batteries carried out by the cross? Bde at night.	

Army Form C. 2118.

WAR DIARY
or
INTELLIGENCE SUMMARY.

(Erase heading not required.)

107th Bde R.F.A. Page 93.

Instructions regarding War Diaries and Intelligence Summaries are contained in F. S. Regs., Part II. and the Staff Manual respectively. Title pages will be prepared in manuscript.

Place	Date	Hour	Summary of Events and Information	Remarks and references to Appendices
	29		Proceeded harassing fire by night.	
	30		} horse.	
	31		}	
			Supplement	
			(a) Casualties during the month. 2 O.Rs. wounded.	
			(b) 2/Lt A.M. O'KELL joined the Bde 24/5/18.	
			2/Lt B GUNWELL was attached D.A. Gas Officer 12/5/18.	
			(c) The following received decorations	
			...Lt Col D W L SPILLER DSO — bar	
			Major J G DUTTON M.C. — bar	
			Major D.G. TWYCROSS M.C. — bar	
			Lt C B S FULLER — M.C.	
			One Gunner was awarded the D.C.M. and several M.Ms & bars were won by O.Rs	

E.Noel Burn
Capt R.F.A.
Adjt
107 Bde
3/6/18.

WR 33

Confidential

War Diary.

of

107th Bde Royal Field Artillery

From:— 1st June, 1918.

To:— 30th June 1918

Army Form C. 2118.

WAR DIARY
or
INTELLIGENCE SUMMARY.

(Erase heading not required.)

107th Bde R.F.A.   Page 9/4.

Place	Date	Hour	Summary of Events and Information	Remarks and references to Appendices
LIEVIN	Sept 1918			
	1		Usual day fire & night harassing.	
	2		All batteries cooperated in repelling raid by N. Staffs. I.M.G continued by Infantry.	
	3		Normal. Enemy shelled LIEVIN during the afternoon.	
	4		Usual day and night firing. Much individual movement.	
	5		Much sniping done. Enemy artillery more active.	
	6		Normal.	
	7		Considerable sniping of enemy movement. Effective shoots. Bright firing doubled. Enemy artillery more active. LIEVIN bombarded with gas shells during the night.	
	8		Night firing trebled.	
	9		Day normal. Night firing increased.	
	10		Much sniping. Instructional & registration shoots. Enemy artillery more active especially at night.	
	11		Normal.	
	12		Much sniping. Small concentrated shots on centres of activity. Movement above normal.	

Army Form C. 2118.

WAR DIARY
or
INTELLIGENCE SUMMARY.
(Erase heading not required.)

104th Bde R.F.A. Page 95.

Instructions regarding War Diaries and Intelligence Summaries are contained in F. S. Regs., Part II. and the Staff Manual respectively. Title pages will be prepared in manuscript.

Place	Date	Hour	Summary of Events and Information	Remarks and references to Appendices
	Oct 13		Much movement observed. Night harassing fire checked owing to suspected relief.	
	14		Much sniping. G.S. trench engaged with success by C/7 casualties being observed.	
	15		Considerable sniping & movement, which was also sniped. Night firing increased	
	16		Normal	
	17		Sunset offensive shoot carried out	
	18		Much movement. Successful sniping.	
	19		Normal day. Assisted raid by N. Staffs.	
	20		Relatively short carried out to fire on enemy trenches.	
	21		Much movement.	
	22		Normal. Wagon lines inspected by G.O.C. Corps R.A.	
	23		Much sniping.	
	24		Offensive shoot on enemy trenches opposite MASON'S HOUSE.	
	25		Normal. CITÉ ST LIEVIN road shelled by enemy during the day.	
	26		Normal	
	27		Enemy artillery more active, whole area being subjected to desultory shelling	

WAR DIARY
or
INTELLIGENCE SUMMARY.

Army Form C. 2118.

10th Bde R.F.A. Page 96.

Place	Date	Hour	Summary of Events and Information	Remarks and references to Appendices
	June 28		Small counter offensive started in NABOB ALLEY. Enemy active on intermediate areas. C/7 moved to a new position near CALONNE. C/7 found section withdrawn to main position.	
	29		Offensive shorts & registration. Enemy quiet during the day but shelled the whole area with gas shells for 2 hrs during the night.	
	30		During the month work was done by all batteries on alternate & rear positions. Several "Silent days" were observed & squadrons practised in visual.	

Supplement.

Lt. SPILLER on leave 2nd – 16th. Major GALLOWAY D.S.O. A/7 Battery command of the Bde. during the remainder of the month. Col. SPILLER was accidentally 72 I.B. H.Q.

Changes in Officers:
2 Lt. R. BOLTON posted to 24th Div T.M.S. 30/6/18.
Lt. R. LISTER (signal officer) evacuated sick 15/6/18.

Casualties: Officers nil
OR a few slightly gassed. (2 in hospital)
Bde only slightly affected by FLANDERS GRIPPE.

E. Warren Bonn
A/C.R.A
Maj A/C OC 151 2/7/18.

WR 34

CONFIDENTIAL

WAR DIARY

of

107th. BRIGADE, R.F.A.

From 1st JULY, 1918.   To 31st JULY, 1918.

Army Form C. 2118.

WAR DIARY
or
INTELLIGENCE SUMMARY.
(Erase heading not required.)

107 Bgde R.F.A.   Page 97   July 1918

Place	Date	Hour	Summary of Events and Information	Remarks and references to Appendices
LIEVIN	July 1.		Day firing normal. Increased harassing at night. Enemy artillery active at night, battery and subjected to gas shell. Enemy much less active.	
	2		Normal day and night fire. Hostile Artillery harassed LIEVIN & CALONNE at intervals during night. Increased movement.	
	3		Usual sniping and offensive shoots.	
	4		Much sniping of movement. Usual harassing fire, counter offensive shoot on GTE ST. AUGUSTE 11 pm. Hostile Artillery more active.	
	5		Normal. Organised shoot in conjunction with Stokes on T.M's at night.	
	6		Normal.	
	7		Harassing fire carried on after day break. Counter offensive shoot 'SMASH GONDE')	
	8		Normal. B/92 section moved back to main position	
	9		Our fire normal. Hostile Artillery more active, a few gas on LIEVIN at night. A.A. fire very heavy against all our planes.	
	10		Normal	
	11		Much sniping. Gas shoot on enemy batteries carried in, and support given to raid by Centre group.	
	12		Special harassing at night in conjunction with gas projection. Much movement seen & sniped. Special hands at W/r. attended by C.R/A for training young officers in open warfare A (Lt-Col) SPILLER D.S.O.	

Army Form C. 2118.

WAR DIARY
or
INTELLIGENCE SUMMARY.

(Erase heading not required.)

107 Bgde, R.F.A.   Page 98.

Place	Date	Hour	Summary of Events and Information	Remarks and references to Appendices
LIEVIN	JULY 13.		Desultory harassing fire at night after previous night's gas.	
	14		Increased night fire for hostile T.M. activity. Special shots seen on enemy trenches. E.A's active. Many E.O.B's spotted. D/107 arrived from LIEVIN to CALONNE.	
	15		Both artilleries more active. Special shots on suspected dumps. Much movement.	
	16.		Normal. E.A's & E.O.B's more in evidence.	
	17.		Day normal. Assisted special shoot on enemy wires at night in addition to increased harassing.	
	18.		Suspected enemy relief harassed at dusk and increased night fire in this account. Training of subalterns in open warfare at W.L. by Lt. Col. Spiller D.S.O.	
	19.		Increased harassing of movement. E.A active at night.	
	20.		Hostile artillery more active.	
	21.		Increased enfying offensive shoots, usual night fire. Enemy artillery more active. E.A down over LENS.	
	22.		Normal. Our guns associated 20" Div. raid at night.	
	23.		Movement above normal. Gas projection at night.	
	24.		Day normal. Associated raid by 9" E. SURREY at night. 1 M.G. captured. E.A. active. One of our O.B's brought down.	
	25.		Increased harassing at night for suspected relief. "Smash CONDÉ" fired in afternoon. Hostile artillery more normal.	

WAR DIARY
INTELLIGENCE SUMMARY

Army Form C. 2118.

167 Bde, R.F.A.   Page 99

Place	Date	Hour	Summary of Events and Information	Remarks and references to Appendices
LIEVIN	26.		Normal.	
	27.		Start of wire cutting, registration programme to enable emplmn. of attack. Night normal. Special shoots cont. Increased harassing at night for increased movement.	
	28.		Above programme cont. Hostile T.M.'s active, increased night fire by our guns. H.Q. 107 Bgde. moved to Fosse II de Bethune.	
	29.		Normal.	
	30.		Normal day. Coordinated raid by T.E. Surreys at night. 1 prisoner captured.	
	31.		During month riving guns of 81st C.F.A. and later 52nd R.F.A. coordinated night fire. Work on alternate and rear positions continued. Several "Silent days" in which usual was practised, observed.	

Supplement

(a). Casualties during month. 10 O.R. killed. 3 wounded. A few slight gas cases.

(b). 2-Lt S.H.J. Cox R.E. joined as Signal Officer 18/7/18
    2-Lt H.J. FOREMAN R.F.A. joined Brigade 31/7/18

(c). Following on leave in France.
    Capt. C.A. BROWN   Paris   28/7/18
    Lt. C.B.S. FULLER   Trouville 30/7/18
    Lt. M.S.H. MAXWELL   do
    Following on courses of instruction.
    Maj. W.C. FAIRER.   Gymnastics. 1st Army Art. School,
    Lt. A.G. EVERITT.   attached C Bty A.A.

W B Sheehy 2/Lt B[?], 167 Bgde, R.F.A
of Capt 167 Bgde, R.F.A.

WR 35

CONFIDENTIAL.

WAR DIARY

OF

107th Brigade, Royal Field Artillery.

From:- 1st August 1918.   To:- 30th August 1918.

Army Form C. 2118.

WAR DIARY
or
INTELLIGENCE SUMMARY.

107th Bde RFA

(Erase heading not required.) Page 100

Place	Date	Hour	Summary of Events and Information	Remarks and references to Appendices
LIEVIN	Aug/18 1		Offensive shoots by Hows in work, TMs etc. Usual night firing assisted by roving guns of 52nd Bde.	
	2		Offensive shoots by Hows.	
	3		Increased sniping of movement.	
	4		Normal	
	5		Usual day & night firing. Hows assisted in Retaliatory shoot "Smash CITE ST AUGUSTE".	
	6		Enemy artillery very active on CITE St PIERRE. Increased enemy movement & artillery activity.	
	7		Normal.	
	8		Considerable sniping of movement. Night harrassing fire shelled to rouse enemy suspicions.	
	9		Normal sniping. Assisted raid by 20th Divn. Hostile artillery more active. Some gas shelling & harassing of roads. Divisional Horse show. The Brigade won the majority of the prizes including 1st & 2nd in Sub-section Turnouts.	
	10		Many enemy balloons up; otherwise normal.	

Army Form C. 2118.

WAR DIARY
or
INTELLIGENCE SUMMARY.

(Erase heading not required.)

107th Bde R.F.A.   Page 101.

Instructions regarding War Diaries and Intelligence Summaries are contained in F. S. Regs., Part II. and the Staff Manual respectively. Title pages will be prepared in manuscript.

Place	Date	Hour	Summary of Events and Information	Remarks and references to Appendices
LIEVIN	Aug/18 11		Enemy artillery active on forward areas. Short hurricane bombardments carried out on our trenches during the afternoon; otherwise normal.	
	12		Usual sniping. Hostile artillery active on our trenches. E.A. active during the morning.	
	13		Our fire normal. Enemy shelled ST PIERRE & forward areas.	
	14		Hostile artillery still active. LIEVIN & our trench system shelled.	
	15		Considerable sniping. Registration effected. Enemy quiet.	
	16		Enemy shelled DOUBLE CRASSIER & our trenches. Enemy bombing machines active at night. D/7 withdrew with 2 hours to W.L. D/52 took over their forward section.	
	17		Much enemy movement & increased firing by us. Hostile artillery inactive.	
	18		Increased sniping. Parties of the enemy seen in marching order. Hows assisted in gas shelling of roads. E.A. active bombing at night.	
	19		Continued enemy movement. Hostile artillery active on MAROC & CALONNE. 52nd Bde withdrawn & forward section taken over by D/7.	
	20		Much sniping & movement & transport. E.A. active our forward areas. ST PIERRE & forward trenches shelled.	

Army Form C. 2118.

WAR DIARY
or
INTELLIGENCE SUMMARY.
(Erase heading not required.)

107th Bde RFA.   Page 102.

Place	Date	Hour	Summary of Events and Information	Remarks and references to Appendices
LIEVIN	Aug/18 21		Assisted raid by 17th 1.B. Burst of fire on our trenches during the day. E.A. active at night.	
	22		North artillery shelled CITE de la PLAINE. Covered raid by 61st I.B. at night.	
	23		Normal.	
	24		ST PIERRE, LIEVIN & CALONNE shelled. Enemy night bombing machines active.	
	25		Coys Horse Show. One fast prize won by Bde. Slight harassing of enemy tracks by enemy at night.	
	26		Increased sniping of movement. Enemy harassed roads at night.	
	27		D/7 returned to action & B/7 withdrew to Mobile reserve at Wagon lines. Both artilleries very active. Enemy shelled villages & tracks in back areas.	
	28		Much sniping of movement. D/7 fired "SMASH ST AUGUSTE". Enemy artillery still very active both to front & back areas.	
	29		Normal day. MAROC & BULLY GRENAY shelled at night.	
	30		Normal day. Supported raid by N. Staffs. MAROC shelled during the night.	
	31		Normal.	

WAR DIARY
INTELLIGENCE SUMMARY

Army Form C. 2118.

Place: 107th Bde R.F.A. Page 103

Supplement

Lt Col D.W.L. SPILLER DSO took over duties of C.R.A. on 12th. Major R.L. GALLOWAY DSO A/7 assuming command of the Bde.

The following have joined the Bde.
- Lt R. C. Bush 17/8/18.
- 2Lt H. J. Foreman 29/9/18.

The following officers left the Bde.
- Lt A. B. Longmuir 17/8/18 to 52nd R.F.A.
- Lt A. G. Emmett 22/8/18 to A.A.
- Capt A. Cooper 24/8/18 to Australia.

Casualties Nil.

C. Andrew Bower Capt. R.F.A.
A/c O.C. 107 R.F.A.B.

Army Form C. 2118.

WAR DIARY or INTELLIGENCE SUMMARY.

(Erase heading not required.)

109R Bde R.F.A. Page 104.

Place	Date	Hour	Summary of Events and Information	Remarks and references to Appendices
LIEVIN	Sept 1/8		Usual Sniping; increased night firing. Hostile artillery except for H.V. guns inactive	
	2		Considerable sniping of movement on CANADA Road.	
	3		Fixed protective barrage in front of our posts which were raided by enemy.	
	4		Hostile artillery active against our forward trenches & posts.	
	5		Checked a hostile raid by protective barrage in the early morning. Enemy shelled forward area between LOOS & RIAUMONT.	
	6		Hostile artillery less active	
	7		Exceptional movement about O.31.d. Hostile artillery shelled CAMERON CASTLE & area round FOSSE 11 with gas shell. Hostile aircraft active. Bde HQ moved M15a.	
	8		Destructive shoot carried out by our Heavies on AUGUST CITY Road. Precautionary barrage called for by Infty in front of our posts.	
	9		Destructive shoot on LOISON. B/7 returned to action from W.L.	
	10		Successfully checked enemy raid on our posts in early morning. Supported raid by Left Battalion Bde. Successful shoot in cooperation with Heavies on SLAG & SLASH. Retaliated to shelling of our posts. C/7 withdrew to W.L. for training.	

Army Form C. 2118.

WAR DIARY
or
INTELLIGENCE SUMMARY.

(Erase heading not required.)

107th Bde R.F.A.   Page 105.

Place	Date	Hour	Summary of Events and Information	Remarks and references to Appendices
	Sept/18			
	11		Normal. Wire cutting started along Divisional front.	
	12		Exceptional movement of trains observed & work on MERICOURT LINE & in O.13.d.	
	13		Enemy active. Retaliated three times at request of Infantry.	
	14		Harid sniping, harassing & wire cutting.	
	15		E.A. very active.	
	16		Normal	
	17		Fired a distracting demonstration on N.2.d during raid by 17th I.B.	
	18		Wire cutting completed apposite Rt Battalion.	
	19		Wire cutting commenced on Left Battalion front. Hostile artillery active.	
	20		Normal	
	21		Wire reported sufficiently cut on Left Battalion front. Considerable sniping.	
	22		Fired on SMASH CONDE. Raids reported repulsed on left front.	
	23		Wire cutting commenced on support lines. Points at which enemy reported massing to said kept under fire throughout the night.	
	24		Considerable retaliatory fire to hostile shelling. A/7 withdrew to W.L. for turning & C/7 took over their position.	

Army Form C. 2118.

WAR DIARY
or
INTELLIGENCE SUMMARY.
(Erase heading not required.)

107th Bde. R.F.A.   Page 106.

Place	Date	Hour	Summary of Events and Information	Remarks and references to Appendices
	Sept/18 25.		Considerable sniping during the day. Small parties observed in full marching order. "Silent" night observed along whole corps front.	
	26		Several daylight raids attempted by enemy successfully repulsed by our fire. Arrested 8th R.W. Kents in successful raid. W.Q.W.R. shelled a few casualties to horses. H.Q. Wagon lines temporarily moved.	
	27		Wire cutting very satisfactory. Hostile raid repulsed at dawn. 5.30 a.m. demonstration along Corps front. Weak retaliation by hostile artillery.	
	28		Engaged enemy T.M. which was firing on Left Battalion front. Scrapped in front of our posts.	
	29th		Normal. 58th London Regt. came into the line.	
	30		Slight enemy movement. Artillery unusually quiet.	

Army Form C. 2118.

WAR DIARY
or
INTELLIGENCE SUMMARY.

107th Bde R.F.A.   Page 107

Place	Date	Hour	Summary of Events and Information	Remarks and references to Appendices

	Sept/18		Supplement:
			
			From 1st to 9th Col SPILLER ma A/C R.A. & Major GALLOWAY commanded the Bde.
			
			The following left the Bde:
			
			  Lt E.V. Stephenson to R.A.H.Q. 1.9.18.
			  2/Lt J.C. Follett DCM to Hospital 6.9.18
			  2/Lt E.H. Abery to Hospital 6.9.18
			  Major R.L. Galloway DSO " " 7.9.18
			  2/Lt W.D. Sheely " " 7.9.18 } gassed
			  2/Lt S.H. Cox (Sig) " " 7.9.18
			  Lt M.S.H. Maxwell Gumbleton " " 9.9.18
			  Lt R.C. Bush to JHAFA 18.9.18
			
			The following joined the Bde:
			
			  Lt J.S. Roffey 2.9.18
			  2/Lt E.H. Abery 6.9.18
			  Lt B. Turner (Sig) 8.9.18
			  2/Lt J. Clouston MM 15.9.18
			  " " Lt Ireland 16.9.18
			  Lt W.S. Clark 20.9.18
			  2/Lt W. Roten 21.9.18
			
			                O.R's
			         Casualties.
			        Died of wounds 2.
			        Wounded 2
			        Wounded (gassed) 3.
			
			E.V.S. o/a RA
			Major o/c 107 RFA
			Lt Col R.C. 107 art/18	

Army Form C. 2118.

Vol 37

WAR DIARY
or
INTELLIGENCE SUMMARY.

(Erase heading not required.)

October 1918. 107th Bde de M.G.A. Page 168.

Place	Date	Hour	Summary of Events and Information	Remarks and references to Appendices
LIEVIN.	1st		Usual sniping and harassing fire.	
	2nd		Enemy started to withdraw blowing up NINGLE'S TOWER and FOSSE 6. All Batteries were to forward positions. Intense Barrages put down on various points in conjunction with H.A.	
	3rd		Blue line reached by 173 Inf. Bde. SALLAUMINES taken. Roads through LENS put under construction.	
	4th		Organised sweeps on M.G. emplacements and snipers.	
	5th		Explosions in COURRIERES, DOURGES, CARVIN.	
	6th		LOISON bombarded in conjunction with H.A.	
	7th		A/H withdrawn to W.L. for training.	
	8th			
	9th		Harassing fire continued. Explosions in HARNES.	
	10th		An attempt to take LOISON under creeping barrage. A/H comes back into action.	
	11th		The whole of the 48th A.F.A.B. joined the Brigade Group. LOISON taken.	
	12th		CARVIN ROAD BRIDGE across HAUTE DEULE CANAL blown up.	
	13th		HARNES-ANNAY Switch evacuated by enemy. B/M withdraws to W.L.	
	14th		A/H & C/H withdraws to W.L. H.Q. & B.A. relieved by 56th Div. x 48th A.F.A.B.	
	15th		Brigade marched to ECURIE.	
	16th		Brigade marched to WANCOURT. Brigade (Staff) to CAMBRAI.	

WAR DIARY
or
INTELLIGENCE SUMMARY.

Army Form C. 2118.

HQrs 107th Brigade R.F.A.   October 1918.   P.age 109.

Place	Date	Hour	Summary of Events and Information	Remarks and references to Appendices
CAMBRAI AREA	17th		Reconnaissance of new positions and found near ST AUBERT Wolves goes to Bn. Major Turgeross to 107th Bde.	
	18th		Guns taken to positions N.E. of ST AUBERT. W.L. established at RIEUX. Men withdrawn to W.L.	
	19th		Batteries come into action. HQ established at ST AUBERT.	
	20th		Battle of the SELLE RIVER, Btys. West move to AVESNES.	
	21st		Batteries move to West bank of LA SELLE RIVER.	
	22nd		Batteries move to positions just North of AMOINNE FARM. M. W. of SAULZOIR	
	23rd		Battery Wagon Lines moved to banks of LA SELLE.	
	24th		Attack on ECAILLON RIVER and ridges beyond. Enemy fell on to VENDEGIES. Fell evening.	
	25th		Batteries move to positions in front of VENDEGIES. H.Q. to VENDEGIES.	
	26th		Minor operations. Bde. put down Smoke Barrage on high ground beyond River RHONELLE.	
	27th		Questions and Artillery very active on both sides.	
	28th		Harassing fire carried out. Targets of opportunity successfully engaged.	
	29th		Harassing fire continued. Back areas of hostile shelled with Blue Cross & Yellow Cross.	

WAR DIARY
or
INTELLIGENCE SUMMARY.

Army Form C. 2118.

October 1918. 107th Brigade R.F.A. Page 110.

Place	Date	Hour	Summary of Events and Information	Remarks and references to Appendices
CAMBRAI AREA.	30th		Harassing fire continued. Infantry (61st Div) pushed out patrols to reconnoitre enemy lines. Sparnochi hotel shelled at areas on our Bde front. Several zone calls were successfully answered by our Artillery.	
	31st		Usual harassing fire carried on at Hotel Artillery Quicker Dow wood. Joined up the following to the Brigade. 27/10/18. Captain H. Thorne. from T.M.S. to C/107. 28/10/18. Lieut. M.S.H. Maxwell-Gumbleton from Hospital to B/107. 28/10/18. 2/Lieut. Robbins from T.M.S. to A/107. 26/10/18. Captain A.A. Emmett from T.M.S. to A/107.	Q.O.R.s Gassed 28/10/18. I.O.R. Killed 29/10/18. I.O.R. Wounded 27/10/18.

Major R.F.A.
A/Odg 107th Bde RFA.

Army Form C. 2118.

WR 38

WAR DIARY
or
INTELLIGENCE SUMMARY.

(Erase heading not required.)

Summary of Events and Information

November 1918   Page 111.

Place	Date	Hour	Summary of Events and Information	Remarks
VENDEGIES	1st		107th Brigade R.F.A. 61st Division supported by 26th Div Arty attacked with objectives which included the high ground across the River RHONELLE and the villages of MARECHES and PRESSEAU. One section each from B/107 and C/107 were ordered to cross the river, in close support of the attacking infantry in case a hostile counter attack should develop with tanks. The final objectives of the day were not gained. The enemy counter attacked strongly supported by tanks two of which were knocked out one by each section. By the evening the 107 Brigade was in close support of the infantry both C/107 across River RHONELLE and the other Batteries round ARTRES.	
ARTRES.	2nd		At 05.15 hours the attack was renewed and all final objectives of the previous day taken. All Batteries crossed the river RHONELLE. H.Q. moved to ARTRES.	
SEPMERIES.	3rd to 4th		All Batteries in position round MARESCHES. H.Q. at SEPMERIES. 24th Div Infantry came into line and carried out successful attack EAST of MARESCHES. Lt.Col Spiller D.S.O. proceeded on leave. Major R.P. Torpious took Command of Brigade.	
JENLAIN.	5th		107th Brigade in reserve under C.R.A. moved to JENLAIN.	
LA BOIS CRETTE	6th		107th Brigade relieved 106th Brigade as Advance Guard Artillery, Batteries in action W. of ST WAAST. HQ moved to LA BOIS CRETTE.	

Army Form C. 2118.

WAR DIARY
or
INTELLIGENCE SUMMARY.

(Erase heading not required.)

107th Brigade RFA   November 1918   Page 112.

Place	Date	Hour	Summary of Events and Information	Remarks and references to Appendices
BAVAY.	7th		107th Brigade fired a barrage on ST WAAST, 17th I.B. attacked and captured town. 72nd I.B. went through 17th I.B. and cleared BAVAY. Batteries took up positions E. of BAVAY. HQ moved to BAVAY.	
	8th		Advance continued by 72nd I.B. Batteries took up positions in LA LONGUEVILLE with forward sections at BERLIERE. HQ moved to LA LONGUEVILLE.	
FEIGNIES	9th		72nd I.B. continued the advance with MONS-MAUBEUGE ROAD as objective this was reached by 1100 hours. Batteries took up positions West of MONS-MAUBEUGE ROAD. HQ moved to FEIGNIES.	
	10th		Advance stopped on account of difficulties of supply. 2nd Sir Infantry relieve 2nd Div. Infantry. Advanced HQ established on MONS-MAUBEUGE Road.	
FEIGNIES	11th		Armistice signed hostilities ceased at 1100 hours. Advanced HQ withdrawn to FEIGNIES.	
	12th		Batteries in same positions. All defensive measures taken.	
	13th		Normal day.	
	14th		Normal day.	
	15th		Church Parade held XVII Corps Senior Chaplain officiated.	
	16th		Normal day.	
BRY.	17th		Brigade marched to BRY.	
ESCAUDAIN	18th		Brigade marched to ESCAUDAIN.	
LEWARDE	19th		Brigade marched to LEWARDE.	

Army Form C. 2118.

WAR DIARY
or
INTELLIGENCE SUMMARY.
(Erase heading not required.)

November 1918. 102nd Brigade RFA. Summary of Events and Information. Page 113.

Place	Date	Hour	Summary of Events and Information	Remarks and references to Appendices
LEWARDE.	20th		Normal day.	
	21st		Normal day.	
	22nd		Normal day.	
	23rd		Lieut. Col. Spiller D.S.O. returned from Leave.	
	24th		Normal day.	
	25th		Normal day.	
	26th		Normal day.	
LANDAS.	27th		Brigade marched to LANDAS. A/102 at LE QUENNE.	
	28th		Normal day.	
	29th		Billeting Parties went forward to new area near TOURNAI.	
	30th		Normal day.	

Supplement :-

The following officers left the Brigade.
Captain C.A. Brown.   1.11.18. (wounded).
2/Lieut. W. Robson.   1.11.18. (wounded).
Lieut.   J. Bassett. 3.11.18. (wounded).

The following officers joined the Brigade.

2 Lieut. W. Robson. 20.11.18. from Hospital.

Q. Spiller
Lieut Colonel RFA
Cmdg 102nd Brigade RFA

Army Form C. 2118.

WAR DIARY
or
INTELLIGENCE SUMMARY.
(Erase heading not required.)

107th Brigade R.F.A.   December 1918.   Page 114.

Place	Date	Hour	Summary of Events and Information	Remarks and references to Appendices
LANDAS.	1.		Normal Day.	
	2.			
	3.		Brigade Paper chase.	
	4.			
	5.			
	6.			
	7.		Normal Day.	
	8.			
	9.			
	10.			
	11.			
	12.			
	13.			
	14.			
	15.			
	16.		Billeting Parties go forward to Final Area. Brigade marches to Final Area. H.Q and B/7 to VAULX. D/7 & C/7 CALONNE. A/7 CHERCQ. Col D.W.L.SPILLER D.S.O. 9CRA.	
TOURNAI.	17.			
	18.			
	19.			
	20.			
	21.		Normal Day	
	22.			
	23.			
	24.			
	25.			
	26.			
	27.			
	28.			
	29.			
	30.			
	31.			

Supplement.

Officers left Brigade.
27/12/18. Capt & Adjt A.A. Emmett to T.M.

Officers joined Brigade
?/12/18. Lieut H. Bibbey. from England
29/12/18. Major R.L. Galloway. D.S.O. from Cyprus.

T. Thornhill Lieut
Lt/Col R/A
10/7 BdeR.F.A
Commanding 107 Bde R.F.A.

Army Form C. 2118.

WAR DIARY
or
INTELLIGENCE SUMMARY.
(Erase heading not required.)

24 16/3

107th Brigade R.F.A.   JANUARY 1919.   Page 1115.   YB 40

Place	Date	Hour	Summary of Events and Information	Remarks and references to Appendices
VAULX LEZ TOURNAI	1,2,3,4,5,6,7,8,9,10,11,12,13,14,15,16,17,18,19,20		NORMAL DAY.	
	21		12th Div Regt Meetg. Lt Col D.W.L. SPILLER D.S.O. won VICTORY CUP. 1½ mile Steeple chase open to officers 1st Army.	
	22,23,24,25,26,27,28,29,30,31		Normal Day.	

Supplement.

Officers left Brigade. Lieut Capt C.B.S. FULLER M.C. (Demobilised) 12/1/19.

Officers joined Brigade. Lieut. G.M. HASLAM. to B/107 on Appointment. 11/1/19.

4/1/19.

T. Chandler Lieut R.F.A.
A.O.C. 107 Brigade R.F.A.

Army Form C. 2118.

107 Bde R.H.A

WAR DIARY
or
INTELLIGENCE SUMMARY.

(Erase heading not required.)

February 1919.   107 Brigade. R.H.A.

Place	Date	Hour	Summary of Events and Information	Remarks and references to Appendices
VAULX-LEZ-TOURNAI	1.		Normal day.	
	2.		Normal day.	
	3.		Authority is given to reduce Brigade to Cadre 73.	
	4.		Normal day.	
	5.		Lieut. and A.H. RAMSAY is granted one months leave to CANADA and struck off strength of Bride.	
	6.		Normal day.	
	7.		Lieutenant. J.C. DICKINSON demobilised	
	8.		Normal day.	
	9.		Normal day.	
	10.		Normal day.	
	11.		Normal day.	
	12.		Normal day.	
	13.		Demobilisation continues at a rapid rate every day.	
	14.		Normal day.	
	15.		Normal day.	
	16.		Normal day.	
	17.		Lieut and G. Upson demobilised	
	18.		Demobilisation stopped for all except Z.32. men.	
	19.		Normal day.	
	20.		Major J. LUDLAM. M.C. demobilised.	
	21.			
	22.			
	23.			
	24.			
	25.			
	26.			
	27.			
	28.		Normal day.	

N Lumbata
Captain R.A.
for Lieut. Col. d.g.
107 Bde. R.H.A.

6/3/19.

WAR DIARY
or
INTELLIGENCE SUMMARY.

(Erase heading not required.)

Army Form C. 2118.

104 Bde R.F.A. March 1919. Page 114.

Place	Date	Hour	Summary of Events and Information	Remarks and references to Appendices
VAULX-LEZ-TOURNAI.	1		Normal Day.	
	2		Normal Day.	
	3		Normal Day.	
	4		Normal Day.	
	5		Normal Day.	
	6		Normal Day.	
	7		Normal Day.	
	8		Normal Day.	
	9		2/Lieut W.S. Rodney A/104 Demobilised	
	10		Lieut-Col D.W.L. Skiller D.S.O., H.Q. 104 Bde R.F.A posted to 108 Bde R.F.A.	
	11		Normal Day.	
	12		Normal Day.	
	13		Normal Day.	
	14		Normal Day.	
	15		Normal Day.	
	16		Normal Day.	
	17		Capt M.S.H. Maxwell Singleton posted to 108 Bde., R.F.A. 2/Lieut J. Evanston D.S.O., M.M., B/104 posted to 1" Div. Arty.	
	18		Capt A.A. Emmett M.C. from B/104 to A/104 on appointment to A/104. Normal Day.	
	19		2/Lieut B. Sumner B/104 Demobilised.	
	20		Normal Day.	
	21		Major R.S. Yeldoway D.S.O. A/104 Posted to 38" Bde R.F.A.	
	22		Capt S.B. Greenway M.O. H.Q. Demobilised	
	23		Major W.C. Arsenies assumes Command of Brigade.	
	24			

Army Form C. 2118.

WAR DIARY
or
INTELLIGENCE SUMMARY.
(Erase heading not required.)

March 1919 (Contd.) 10⁴ Bde., R.F.A. Page 118.

Place	Date	Hour	Summary of Events and Information	Remarks and references to Appendices
VAULX-LEZ-TOURNAI.	25		2/Lieut J.H. Mowby A/104 D demobilised. Lieut Bd'y S. Roffey M.C. C/104 Demobilised. Lieut Bd'y St. Quintin, Horsemaster, H.Q. Demobilised. Capt M.S.H. Maxwell Rimington returned to Brigade.	
	26		Normal Day.	
	27		Normal Day.	
	28		Normal Day.	
	29		Normal Day.	
	30		Normal Day.	
	31		Normal Day.	

A. Macdonald 2/Lt. R.F.A.
for Capt. Adjt. 104 Bde R.F.A.

www.ingramcontent.com/pod-product-compliance
Lightning Source LLC
Chambersburg PA
CBHW080812010526
44111CB00015B/2545